Mary's World

Mary's World

Love, War, and Family Ties in Nineteenth-century Charleston

Richard N. Côté

Mount Pleasant, S. C.

Publishers Cataloging-in-Publication Data
(Provided by Quality Books)

Côté, Richard N.
Mary's world: love, war, and family ties in nineteenth-century Charleston / Richard N. Côté. – 1st ed.
p. cm.
Includes bibliographical references and index.
LCCN: 00-103324
ISBN: 1-929175-19-1 (hc)
ISBN: 1-029175-04-3 (pb)

1. Pringle, Mary Motte Alston. 2. Charleston (S. C.)–History–Civil War, 1861-1865. 3. Women–3. Charleston–South Carolina–Biography. Charleston (S.C.)–Biography. I. Title.

F279.C453C67 2000 973.7'092
QBI00-481

This book is printed on archival-quality paper which meets the guidelines for performance and durability of the Committee on Production Guidelines for Book Longevity for the Council on Library Resources.

Corinthian Books
P.O. Box 1898
Mt. Pleasant SC 29465-1898
(843) 881-6080
http://www.corinthianbooks.com

To Peter Manigault,
without whose vision, knowledge, guidance, and unflagging support this book would not have been possible.

CONTENTS

To understand today,
You have to search yesterday.

—Pearl S. Buck

Preface

This book was written with a single goal: to help the reader to learn how Mary Pringle and her family and slaves thought and lived. It had its genesis in a collection of approximately 1,500 letters and twenty-five manuscript record volumes which had accumulated in the Miles Brewton House over the last two centuries.

In 1989 I was commissioned to read, arrange, and prepare a manuscript guide to what came to be known as the Alston-Pringle-Frost Collection. While arranging and describing the collection, I located another large group of Pringle manuscripts: the Edward J. Pringle Family Collection at the Bancroft Library, University of California-Berkeley. It took three trips to Berkeley to exhaust those papers.

In Charleston, the South Carolina Historical Society's Mitchell-Pringle Papers provided additional letters. The Middleton Place Foundation provided twenty more. In 1991 papers of John Julius Pringle were located in Birmingham, Alabama, where family members kindly made them available for copying and study. In 1995 descendants in Mobile, Alabama, shared another cache of Pringle letters and photographs.

Mary's nephew, Jacob Motte Alston (1821-1909), lived with the family from 1823 to 1837, and recorded many of his remembrances in a candid, outspoken manuscript entitled, "Random Recollections of an Inconspicuous Life." It is chiefly from these sources, and from family lore compiled or published by Mary Pringle Fenhagen, Susan Pringle Frost, and Mary Pringle Frost that I have drawn this study.

Between 1988 and 1994, grants from the Post-Courier Foundation enabled me to survey, arrange and describe the collection, photocopy over 9,000 pages of Pringle papers, and consult the thirty-six manuscript collections and 160 secondary sources which shed light on Mary's family and her world.

There have been excellent studies of Southern planter families which, like Theodore Rosengarten's classic, *Tombee: Portrait of a Cotton Planter,* explore the intricate details of plantation life through careful examination of plantation journals. For the Pringle family, no such journals survived.

Then again, there are fine publications of carefully edited family letters, such those of the Rev. Dr. Charles Colcock Jones, edited by Robert Manson Myers and published as *The Children of Pride*. However, the bulk of the Pringle correspondence, its considerable redundancy, and the large gaps in its coverage, made this approach unworkable.

Mary and her family are worthy of study for two reasons. First, they were extremely conventional, thus making them good representatives of the class of which they were a part. Second, they left behind a large enough body of personal records to make a serious study possible. Their papers present us with an intensely personal—and often raw—reflection of Southern social attitudes for the period from 1840 through 1880. *Mary's World* chronicles their activities and convictions. We learn, for example, that Mary Pringle, a planter's wife, had amazingly strong anti-slavery sentiments.

Mary Pringle's willpower was the glue that held the family together. She was also its chief correspondent. Of the Pringle family letters which survive, about three hundred were penned by Mary and less than two dozen by her husband, William. As a well-educated, clear-thinking member of an intellectually monolithic social class, Mary did not waste a moment fretting about the political correctness of what she wrote. On paper she expressed herself freely on every subject which interested her. Unlike her contemporary, Mary Boykin Chesnut of Columbia, Mary Pringle wrote only for her family and not for posterity or publication. For that reason, her letters provide a large, clear window into the hearts and minds of the high-born antebellum rice planters.

I found the letters and lives of the Pringles so powerful and graphic that I wanted to share them with a wide audience. I wrote this book so that it could be read and understood by readers with no extensive knowledge of South Carolina history, the planter class, or rice cultivation. Everything important is in the text. Endnotes have been used only for source citations and those comments which, while necessary for the specialist, would distract the general reader.

I wrote this book so that readers can learn about the hopes, fears, elations, trials, tragedies, and dreams of a family who represented the planter elite. However, the Pringle manuscript material is so voluminous, variegated, and rich as to preclude anyone from wrapping up the Pringles and their experiences in a neat package. Instead, *Mary's World* was written to provide the door through which readers and scholars alike may pass to meet them.

The Pringles' own words begged for the lion's share of the available space. Yet I realized that if I did not give their thoughts a context in which to be understood, their meaning might be lost. Consequently, I have tried to strike a balance between quoting, summarizing, and interpreting their writings.

The first three chapters provide the reader with a context in which to understand the family's history, their physical and social culture, and the agricultural system which produced their wealth. Chapters four through nine present the story of the young Pringle family growing up in the Miles Brewton House and follow them through the gruesome chaos of the Civil War.

By the end of the war the second generation had come into its own and its members had scattered. Although the grand old house on King Street was still the archive of the family's past, it was no longer the center of its activities. Sons Robert and Charles were dead. Another, Brewton, was in an asylum for the insane in Columbia. A daughter, Mary Frances, was in retirement with her husband, Yale professor Donald G. Mitchell, in West Haven, Connecticut. Their son Julius and his wife, Maria, were flitting back and forth between Paris, London, New York, Newport, Natchez and his Louisiana cotton and sugar plantations and shooting preserves. When she wasn't in Charleston preparing for the birth of her children, daughter Rebecca was most often with her husband, Frank Frost, on the North Santee, while sons Edward and James were plying the legal trade and establishing their families in San Francisco.

Each of the children who followed a separate path away from Charleston has his or her own chapter. A separate chapter was allotted to the family members who remained at the Miles Brewton House: William, Mary, their unmarried daughter, Susan, and son, Alston, who moved back into the Miles Brewton House after his wife died. A brief epilogue describes the restoration of the Milews Brewton House to its Alston-era glory.

It is my hope that the readers of this book will find themselves developing the same bonds of concern and affection with the Pringle and Stewart families that I did while researching and writing about them during these past twelve years.

Richard N. Côté
Mt. Pleasant, S.C.
October 2, 2000

Introduction

In the middle of the nineteenth century, life seemed good for Mary and William Bull Pringle's family in Charleston. They enjoyed all the advantages of South Carolina 's legendary antebellum rice planters. Mary and William's parents belonged to the highest social stratum of American society. The family had cordial personal relationships with presidents Washington, Jefferson, Madison, Monroe, and Van Buren, and close ties to their neighbor, Henry Middleton, an American ambassador to Russia.

Mary, her husband, and their large flock of children lived in great luxury in the Miles Brewton House. By 1860 their stunning Palladian mansion at 27 King Street was filled with costly china, crystal, and silverware; beautiful furniture; handsome oil portraits; and was staffed by thirty-two household slaves.

The Pringles wore the latest fashions and rode in an elegant coach driven by liveried servants and drawn by high-stepping thoroughbred horses. They traveled for pleasure to the spas of the Eastern seaboard and sent their children on grand tours of Europe. Their wealth flowed from four prosperous plantations where almost three hundred black field hands produced more than a million pounds of rice for them each year, as well as other crops. In terms of slave ownership, agricultural production, and affluence, the William Bull Pringle family ranked in the top one-half of one percent of South Carolina plantation society.

The profitable cultivation of rice was established in South Carolina by 1730 and it soon became a major export crop. Between the time of the American Revolution and the Civil War, a tightly interwoven group of 500 to 600 white planting families brought Southern rice production to its zenith. In 1860 South Carolina produced 63.6 percent of the nation's rice. Georgetown District's 1859 rice crop of 55,805,385 pounds constituted 46.9 per cent of the state's total. That enormous amount was grown by only eighty-eight planter families, a number of whom, like the Pringles, owned one hundred or more slaves and produced annual crops in the million-pound range.

Mary Pringle took full advantage of the opportunities available to her. She grew into a strong, focused, intelligent, complex woman who devoted her entire life to God, her family, and the Southern way of life. Her character was shaped both by ancestry and free will. Her achievements were limited only by the restrictions placed in her era upon those of her sex. Mary did everything expected of her. She spared no effort to ensure that every task was performed impeccably and with style and grace.

As a nineteenth-century woman, a wealthy rice planter's wife, the mother of thirteen children, and the mistress of three dozen household slaves, Mary shouldered burdens and faced challenges unknown today. From the outside, Mary's world may have appeared idyllic. Viewed from Mary's perspective, it was far more problematic.

Unknown to most was the fact that the Pringles, like many other antebellum rice planters, were deeply in debt from living far beyond their means. That wasn't the worst of their problems. Sealed off in the self-imposed economic and intellectual cocoon that South Carolina had evolved into by the 1850s, the Pringles had little warning that that an approaching war would soon rip apart their family, free their slaves, destroy their ability to make a living, and render their social class extinct.

Mary was an eloquent eyewitness to history during the glory years of the Old South, the bloody mayhem that was the Civil War, and the wrenching social and political catastrophe euphemistically named Reconstruction. In hundreds of letters to friends and family and in her intimate personal journals, she boldly recorded her views on everything from marriage and icebergs to God, slavery, and military strategy.

Her writings letters address all of the Pringle family's fears and joys, prides and prejudices, challenges and rewards, achievements and failures. Untainted by any need to display political correctness, they offer a priceless view into the mind of an affluent white Southern woman in the nineteenth century. Mary's writings are an enormously valuable historical record, but they offer much more than a chronicle of local events. Indeed, readers may well find that their role as a mirror of Mary's heart and soul is their greatest gift.

The book starts with a description of Mary and William's ancestors, whose examples she revered and whose maxims, morals, and household recipes Mary learned at her mother's knee. The story progresses through her marriage in 1822 to William Bull Pringle, and the "large and amiable" family they reared in the Miles Brewton House, where she and her thirteen children were born.

Mary and her family may have actually heard the shot which ignited the Civil War, as the cannon from which it was fired could have been seen from the balcony of their house. The Union navy blockaded Charleston harbor soon after the start of the war. Mary's anguished wartime letters describe the family's evacuation of their slaves and other personal property from Charleston and their plantations. Later, she records their plight as refugees near Society Hill, a hundred miles inland.

Their personal losses were heavy. Of their eight sons who volunteered to defend their home, family, and the Southern way of life, three of Mary's "brave Christian heroes" were lost. In 1865. the vanquished but unbowed Confederate family suffered the ultimate indignity when the commanders of the Union Army occupying Charleston chose their ancient family homestead on King Street as their headquarters.

The last section of the book describes the aged, demoralized Pringle survivors as they sought to regain possession of their house and plantation lands. It chronicles in detail the dedication of Mary's son-in-law Frank Frost as he spent a decade of eighteen-hour days in a valiant but futile effort to restart rice planting on the Santee River. Finally, it follows the paths of Mary 's children who left the Holy City to seek new opportunities in New Haven, France, and California.

Her letters describe her chafed relationship with Southern plantation society, which rigidly defined her role as a woman, wife, and mother. At home, she had to deal with an aloof and emotionally distant husband, whose free spending led them to the brink of financial disaster long before the Civil War dealt their fortunes a death blow.

In the religious sphere, Mary found herself at odds with the Protestant Episcopal church, whose ministers preached redemption but sanctioned slavery, which Mary herself found morally indefensible but nevertheless necessary. Perhaps the most visceral of Mary 's writings are the tortured pages which record her personal relationship with God, especially the anguish she felt over His apparent abandonment of her, her family, and the Confederate cause.

Mary's world was a maze of other challenges. The health of her family was under constant threat from malaria, yellow fever, and typhoid fever. Every pregnancy and illness was fraught with danger. Often, the greatest threat lay hidden in medical treatments such as blisters and bleeding, as well as patent medicines now known to cause convulsions, blindness, and permanent brain damage. It was nothing short of a miracle that twelve of her thirteen children lived to adulthood.

For every white Pringle family member, the family owned

about twenty-five slaves. Virtually nothing is known about the field hands as individuals. However, because the house servants were part of the Pringles' everyday lives, we get at least a glimpse of them. Though hampered by a serious shortage of records, *Mary's World* also describes the lives of Cretia and Scipio Stewart, African American slaves born on Col. William Alston's Fairfield plantation on the Waccamaw River. Cretia was Mary Pringle's personal maid, and Mary developed a deep affection for her. In 1856 Mary presented Cretia with a family Bible, filled with the transcribed birth, marriage, and death records for all of Cretia and Scipio's children. This Bible is one of the most important slave family records in South Carolina history.

In 1865, the jubilation of the freed slaves over their emancipation quickly dimmed as they learned that the first freedom they received was the freedom to starve. Mary 's letters describe how the freedmens' anger turned to arson on the one remaining Pringle rice plantation on the Santee River. In Charleston, the freed slaves who found employment with the bitter, ruined Pringle family found that working conditions had not improved and attitudes had worsened. Thus the stage was set for the century of Southern poverty and racial strife which followed.

In both their prewar affluence and postwar poverty, the Pringle family's experiences mirrored those of the South Carolina planter elite. How they and their slaves lived before the Civil War, desperately clung to life in the eye of the maelstrom, and coped with the crushing aftermath is the story of this book.

Mary's Family

When a person mentioned in the text is identified only by a given name, that person is one of the fifteen Pringle family members. The four exceptions are Frank, Francis L. Frost, who married Rebecca Pringle; Jacob, who is Jacob Motte Alston, a nephew who lived with the Pringle family in the Miles Brewton House from 1823 to 1837; Cretia, Lucretia Stewart, Mary's African-American maid; and Scipio, Scipio Stewart, Cretia's husband.

MARY: Mary Motte Alston was born in the Miles Brewton House in 1803. She married William Bull Pringle in the drawing room of the Miles Brewton House in 1822. Her thirteen children were all born in the adjacent withdrawing room. From 1862 to 1866 the family lived as refugees on rented plantations in Darlington District, South Carolina. Mary died in the Miles Brewton House in 1884.

WILLIAM: William Bull Pringle was born at his father's home on Tradd Street in Charleston in 1800. He moved into the Miles Brewton House after marrying Mary and planted rice in Georgetown District, South Carolina. He died at the Miles Brewton House in 1881.

ALSTON: William Alston Pringle was born in 1822. He graduated from South Carolina College and was admitted to the bar in 1843. He married Emma Clara Pringle Smith and they had thirteen children. He served as Charleston City Recorder (municipal judge) from 1857 until his death. He served briefly as a lieutenant in the 16th Regiment, S. C. Militia, during the Civil War. When his wife died in 1886, he moved into the Miles Brewton House with his unmarried sister, Susan. He died there in 1895.

JULIUS: John Julius Pringle was born in 1824. Offered a law education at The Temple in London, he instead served as a U.S. Navy midshipman, and graduated from the U.S. Naval Academy in 1846. He was wounded during the Mexican War. In 1849 he married Maria Duncan, daughter of a wealthy cotton planter of Natchez, Mississippi, with strong ties to the North. Julius may have served briefly in Confederate uniform but his allegiance was equivocal. He spent the postwar period enjoying his villa in Biarritz, France, and his hunting preserve in Louisiana. He died in France in 1901.

EDWARD: Edward Jenkins Pringle was born in 1826. He attended South Carolina College in 1841 and transferred to Harvard, where he graduated with honors in 1845. He was admitted to the bar in 1847 and embarked upon a two-year grand tour of Europe soon thereafter. Upon his return, he wrote a defense of slavery entitled *Slavery in the Southern States*. Finding insufficient legal work in Charleston, he emigrated to San Francisco in 1853, where he practiced law. He did not serve in the Civil War. In 1868 he married Cornelia Letitia Johnson, who bore him seven children. He died in Oakland, California, in 1899, shortly after being named a commissioner of the California Supreme Court.

MOTTE: Jacob Motte Alston Pringle was born in 1827. There is no record that he attended college. In 1850 he married Gabriella Ravenel. After apprenticing as a factor's clerk, he formed a short-lived partnership with Hermann Thiermann as factors and commission merchants. During the Civil War, Motte held the rank of major and served as assistant quartermaster for the Department of South Carolina and Georgia. He died in Charleston in 1886.

SUSAN: Susan Pringle was born in 1829. She attended private schools in Charleston and spent two years at the Pelham Priory in upstate New York. She never married. Prior to the war, Susan lived the life of a Southern socialite. After the war she made a trip to California to scout the possibility of emigration for the family. She devoted the rest of her life to caring for her aging parents and elder brother Alston. She died at the Miles Brewton House in 1917.

MARY FRANCES: Mary Frances Pringle was born in 1831 attended private schools in Charleston. In 1852 she met Yale professor Donald G. Mitchell. They were married at the Miles Brewton House in 1853. A passionate Confederate, Mary suffered the scorn of her New Haven neighbors during the war. She lived out her life in seclusion with her retired husband and died at their country estate near New Haven in 1901.

WILLIAM, JR.: William Bull Pringle, Jr. was born in 1833 and graduated from South Carolina College in 1852. He was employed as a civil engineer for several years by the Blue Ridge Railroad. In 1857 he took over operation of his father's rice mill at Richfield plantation. He fell ill shortly thereafter, and died in bed at the Miles Brewton House in 1859.

BREWTON: Miles Brewton Pringle was born in 1835 and graduated from South Carolina College in 1856. He took a position as a clerk in a Charleston counting house and later opened a hardware store. In 1862 he enlisted in Company K, 4th (Rutledge's) Regiment, South Carolina Cavalry. He was wounded at the battle of Pocotaligo, S.C., in 1862, and dodged bullets as a mounted courier between Battery Wagner and Battery Gregg on Morris Island. His mental health deteriorated rapidly after the war. In 1866 he was taken to live at the South Carolina Lunatic Asylum, where he remained until the summer of 1874. He died at the Miles Brewton House later that year.

ROBERT: Robert Pringle was born in 1837 and graduated from South Carolina College in the 1850s. For several years he clerked for his uncle's firm, Coffin & Pringle, factors, on Adger's North Wharf. In 1861 he obtained a lieutenant's commission in Company B, 15th (Lucas's) Battalion, S.C. Volunteers, a heavy artillery unit. In 1863 he was mortally wounded by a shell from a federal ironclad. His funeral was held in the south parlour of the Miles Brewton House.

REBECCA: Rebecca Motte Pringle was born in 1839 and received home schooling. She enjoyed the spas of the North and made trips to Europe in 1856 and 1857. She married Dr. Francis L. ("Frank") Frost in 1866. After the war, Frank took over the operation of Richfield plantation, which he ran until 1871. None of their six children married. Rebecca died in 1905. The three Frost daughters, Susan, Mary and Rebecca, purchased the Miles Brewton House from the other heirs in 1919 and lived there until Susan, the last, died in 1960.

ELIZABETH: Elizabeth Pringle, a twin of Rebecca, was also born in 1839. She died in the Miles Brewton House in 1844 at the age of four.

CHARLES: Charles Alston Pringle was born in 1841. He entered Harvard in 1857 and studied there until his father withdrew him and sent him and his younger brother, James, to study in Europe. Both boys slipped back through the Union blockade when the war erupted. Charles obtained a commission as a lieutenant. While stationed at Camp Evans on John's Island, he contracted typhoid fever. He died in the Miles Brewton House in 1862.

JAMES: James Reid Pringle was born in 1842. He left for France with Charles in 1859. After their return to Charleston, James obtained an appointment as a lieutenant and was stationed at Battery Gregg, a half-mile north of Battery Wagner on Morris Island. In 1866 he emigrated to San Francisco where he worked with his brother Edward. In 1868 he married Coralie Butterworth. He became gravely ill and was put aboard a steamer for Charleston, accompanied by his pregnant wife and parents-in-law. He died in a New York City hotel in 1871.

FRANK: Francis LeJau Frost was born in Charleston in 1837. He graduated from South Carolina College in 1859 and obtained a medical degree from the Medical College of South Carolina in 1861. During the war he served as a surgeon. After his marriage to Rebecca Pringle in 1866, he attempted to reachieve profitable rice planting at Camp Main, a Frost plantation adjacent to Richfield, his father-in-law's plantation, which he also managed. His efforts failed. He died in 1912.

JACOB: Jacob Motte Alston (1821-1909) was the son of Mary's brother, Thomas Pinckney Alston (1795-1861) and his first wife, Jane Ladson Smith. His mother died in 1823 when he was two years old. That year, Jacob went to live with William and Mary Pringle in the Miles Brewton House. He spent a happy childhood there until 1837, when he left for college.

CRETIA: Lucretia Stewart, the daughter of Lucy, was born on Fairfield Plantation, Waccamaw, in 1807. She married Scipio, another Fairfield slave, in 1825, and they had twelve children. Cretia was Mary Pringle's personal servant and a skilled cook. She remained with the Pringles after emancipation. Cretia died in 1879. Her children and grandchildren worked for the Pringles and Frosts well into the twentieth century.

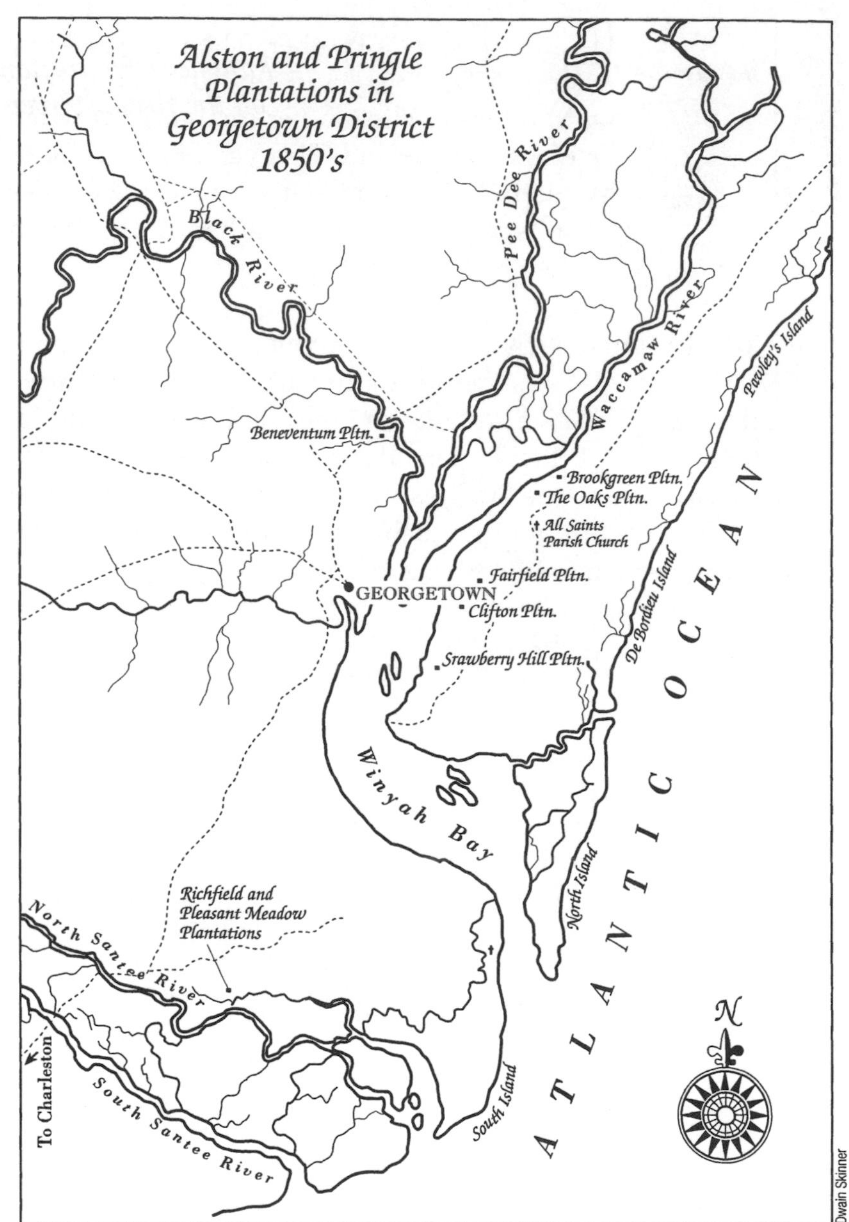
Alston and Pringle
Plantations in
Georgetown District
1850's
Black River
Pee Dee River
Waccamaw River
Pawley's Island
Beneventum Pltn.
Brookgreen Pltn.
The Oaks Pltn.
All Saints
Parish Church
Fairfield Pltn.
GEORGETOWN
Clifton Pltn.
Srawberry Hill Pltn.
De Bordieu Island
ATLANTIC OCEAN
Winyah Bay
North Island
Richfield and
Pleasant Meadow
Plantations
North Santee River
South Santee River
To Charleston
South Island
N
Dwain Skinner

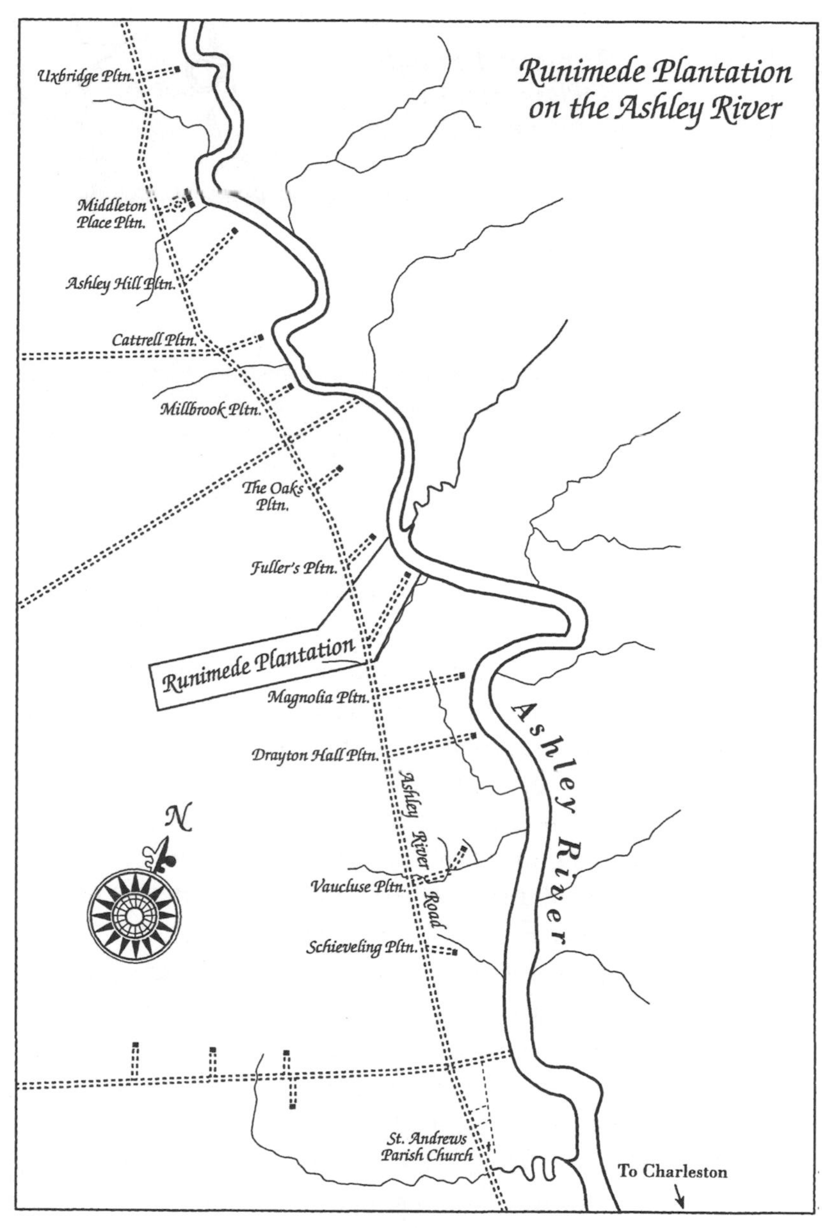
Runimede Plantation on the Ashley River
Uxbridge Pltn.
Middleton Place Pltn.
Ashley Hill Pltn.
Cattrell Pltn.
Millbrook Pltn.
The Oaks Pltn.
Fuller's Pltn.
Runimede Plantation
Magnolia Pltn.
Drayton Hall Pltn.
Ashley River Road
Ashley River
N
Vaucluse Pltn.
Schieveling Pltn.
St. Andrews Parish Church
To Charleston

CHAPTER ONE

Mary's Charleston

The people of Charleston live rapidly, not willingly letting go untasted any of the pleasures of life." —Johann David Schoepf

Mary Motte Alston was born into a household accustomed to affluence and achievement. The youngest daughter of Col. William Alston and his wife, Mary Brewton Motte, she drew her first breath of life June 17, 1803, in the withdrawing room of the elegant Miles Brewton House in Charleston, South Carolina.

In 1803 Charleston was a city of striking contrasts. The wealthy rice-planting families such as her own were experiencing a period of unparalleled prosperity, but their enormous crops came at the expense of grueling, back-breaking labor by slaves. The city's public pride was reflected in her stately public buildings, but Charleston's sky was filled with the melancholy shapes of vultures, who fed upon the offal from the slaughter pens on the outskirts and garbage from the city markets. Its streets were lined with beautiful residences and lush gardens, yet every family which could afford to do so fled these homes each summer for seaside and pineland resorts, Northern spas, or Europe. Those left behind, black and white alike, sweated out the summer's oppressive heat and humidity and prayed that the annual yellow fever and malaria epidemics would pass them by.

By the time of Mary's birth, Charleston had recovered from the damage and looting suffered at the hands of the British during the Revolutionary War. As Johann David Schoepf observed, "The people of Charleston live rapidly, not willingly letting go untasted any of the pleasures of life. . . . Luxury in Carolina has made the greatest advance, and their manner of life, dress, equipages, furniture, everything, denotes a higher degree of taste and love of show, and less frugality than in the northern provinces."[1]

Mary's family tree was filled with Revolutionary heroes, heroines, public figures from the top echelons of government and the first ranks of the South Carolina social structure. The first of them was Mary's great-great-great-uncle, Miles Brewton. He emigrated from Barbados to Charles Towne with his parents in 1684, when he was nine years old and the colony was fourteen years old. When he came of age, he took up the goldsmith's trade and also shouldered the duties of public service. He was married three times and fathered at least six children before his death in 1745.[2]

His son, Robert Brewton, was born in 1698. Among his six children were Miles, the future merchant; Frances, who married Charles Pinckney; and Rebecca, the future heroine, who married Jacob Motte, Jr. By 1722 Robert was also practicing the goldsmith's trade. He succeeded his father as Powder Receiver, serving until his death in 1759.[3]

Miles Brewton, a third-generation South Carolinian, was born in Charleston in 1731. As a young man he went to work in one of Charleston's counting houses. When he sat for the London artist Sir Joshua Reynolds in 1756, he was a young man of twenty-five, already active in transatlantic trade.

By the time of his death it was said that "to habits of the strictest order and regularity, he added a character of honesty and integrity unsullied by the slightest taint of wrong."[4] While this standard of saintliness would have been hard to sustain for a lifetime in the mercantile business, it is clear that Brewton was admired and respected by his contemporaries.

Miles Brewton,
Charleston merchant and patriot.

So talented and industrious was he that after being in the counting house for only a few years, Brewton was already acknowledged as a natural leader among Charleston's colonial merchants. In 1759 at the age of twenty-eight, he married Mary Izard, daughter of Joseph Izard, a substantial rice planter of French Protestant (Huguenot) descent. Although he married the daughter of a major planter and had his own investments in rice plantations, Brewton chose to remain a merchant and became one of South Carolina's largest slave dealers.

Along with Miles Brewton, Henry Laurens (later president of the Continental Congress) topped the list of the colony's most active slave traders. Not only was there no stigma attached to the slave merchant before the Revolution, but "the person who faintly suggested that slave dealing was reprehensible was looked upon as a weak-minded sentimentalist."[5] After the Revolution, the social status of slave dealers started to fall in direct proportion to the growing awareness that slaves were, in fact, human beings worthy of respect.

Miles Brewton invested his wealth in "ships, land, and conspicuous consumption." He owned interests in eight transatlantic vessels, purchased a number of plantations, and acquired by marriage Mt. Joseph, the Izard plantation on the Congaree River.[6] In 1771 Peter Manigault, a London-educated rice planter who already owned nearly 6,000 acres of plantation land, fine furniture, "pictures done in oil" and a substantial library, wrote his London agent, "I stand in need of some plate and furniture of which I enclose you a list. . . . I suppose you will think either my wife or myself very extravagant. I should almost think so myself if I had not seen Brewton's."[7]

Miles Brewton was thirty-four years old and six years married in 1765 when work was begun on his house on King Street. Everything about it was to be done on a grand and lavish scale, inside and out. Its inspiration came from the Italian villas built by Renaissance architect Andrea Palladio.

Brewton's splendid townhouse is one of the most sensuous residences in America, but his was not the only large, elegant house in Charleston. Many were larger and some as elaborate. However, as historian George Rogers observed, "these homes lacked something in taste; they were less refined than their earlier neighbors. One need only compare Patrick O'Donnell's house on King with its neighbor to the north, the Miles Brewton House."[8]

The Brewton house measures 54' x 65'. Its foundation is of brick. The primary (structural) wood is native tidewater cypress, which is perfectly suited for building in humid subtropical climates, as it is impervious to termites and rot. The floors

The Miles Brewton House at 27 King Street in the 1920s.

are of heart pine, which withstands abrasion better than cypress. A classical, two-story portico extends across the face of the house and on the drawing-room floor, providing a balcony with an expansive view of Charleston. The floor of this balcony was originally covered with lead, but that was stripped off and melted down for Confederate bullets during the war. [9]

Both the decorative and functional aspects of the woodwork design are extraordinary, as exemplified by the single- and double-panel wooden "inside" shutters in the house, which fold into ingeniously designed receptacles in the wall. The brick wall which separates the house from its neighbor to the south was part of the original construction plan. The house sits behind a stately brick and iron fence which provided the residents privacy and safety. The lock on the massive gate still functions with Brewton-era efficiency and Miles Brewton's original key is still in use.

In 1822 Denmark Vesey, a free black who lived in Charleston, was apprehended, convicted, and hanged as the ringleader of a planned slave insurrection. Some time shortly thereafter the house's handsome iron fence, gate, and walls were topped with the most menacing piece of residential defensive ironwork ever seen in Charleston. Known as a *cheval-de-frise,* it consists of a central shaft onto which sharpened, eight-inch long iron spikes are attached in a radial pattern. Additional spikes, twisted to inflict maximum bodily damage, top the otherwise graceful original gate pediment. The foreboding fence remains a monument to the insecurity of Charleston's antebellum white population.[10]

Although the building has remained basically unchanged since 1769, each generation of owners subsequent to Brewton put their mark on the house. During the 1820s and 1830s Col. William Alston added a considerable amount of neoclassical ornamentation. William Bull Pringle conceived the two-story, two-bay additions added onto the rear of the house in the late 1830s, which provided dressing rooms on the second floor. He also added the handsome Gothic Revival façade to the street side of the coach house.[11]

The cheval-de-frise topping the Miles Brewton House fence.

Once in his new house, Brewton entertained often and on a grand scale. In 1773 he had as his dinner guest the Boston lawyer and patriot, Josiah Quincy, Jr., who marveled at the opulent display:

> Dined with considerable company at Miles Brewton, Esqr's, a gentleman of very large fortune: a most superb house said to have cost him 8000£ sterling. The grandest hall I ever beheld, azure blue satin window curtains, rich blue paper with gilt, mashee borders, most elegant pictures, excessive grand and costly looking glasses etc. . . . A most elegant table, three courses, nick-nacks, jellies, preserves, sweetmeats, etc. After dinner, two sorts of nuts, almonds, raisins, three sorts of olives, apples, oranges, etc. By odds the richest wines I ever tasted. . . . At Mr. Brewton's side board was very magnificent plate: a very large exquisitely wrought goblet, most excellent workmanship and singularly beautiful. A very fine bird kept familiarly playing over the room, under our chairs and the table, picking up crumbs, etc., and perching on the window, side board and chairs: vary pretty.[12]

Although an astute and successful businessman, Brewton

The north parlor, used as the dining room.

placed his principles and the welfare of his countrymen above the interests of his purse and became one of the colony's foremost early patriots, albeit a conservative one. At considerable cost to himself, Brewton supported the South Carolina Non-Importation Association, which had been formed to protest the Townshend Duties. The Association members agreed to suspend imports of slaves and most other goods from Great Britain, and signers were to boycott trade with anyone not subscribing to the Association.[13]

In the conflict with the Crown, Miles Brewton esteemed both his American countrymen and his British king. He fervently hoped that bloodshed might be avoided. Despite his close ties to the Mother Country, when it came time to stand and be counted, he stood with the patriots, not the Tories.

In 1775 he was elected to the Provincial Congress and also served on the Council of Safety.[14] He made his final act of deference to the crown when Lord William Campbell, the last royal governor, arrived in Charleston. Campbell was married to the former Sarah Izard, a sister of Mrs. Arthur Middleton, and the Brewtons offered the Campbells the hospitality of their home on King Street until their official residence was ready.[15] Campbell's presence proved to be superfluous, for the royal government had already been superseded by the South Carolina Provincial Congress, and the Campbells soon returned home.

In July of the same year, the Continental Congress sent out an urgent appeal for gunpowder. Miles Brewton and William Henry Drayton were commissioned to go to Savannah to request 5,000 pounds of powder which had been seized from a British ship. They were successful. The powder was shipped north and it enabled the defense of Boston to continue.

Miles Brewton did not live long enough to see the fruits of his patriotism. In the summer of 1775 he and his wife packed their trunks. On August 24, the Brewtons and their three children took ship for Philadelphia, where he evidently planned to leave them with relatives while he returned to his business and patriotic duties in Charleston. They never arrived. The entire family was lost at sea. His two sisters, Rebecca Brewton Motte and Frances Brewton Pinckney, inherited his house and the rest of his considerable estate.[16]

Miles Brewton's sister, Rebecca, was cut from the same cloth as her brother. Even in a family tree full of men and women of intelligence, patriotism, and strong moral fiber, Rebecca Brewton Motte was extraordinary. Born in Charleston in 1738, she married Jacob Motte, Jr., twenty years later. The combination of the two inheritances made Jacob a wealthy planter in St. Paul's Parish.

Their marriage produced three children who lived to adulthood: Elizabeth, who married Major Thomas Pinckney of the 1st South Carolina Continental Regiment; Frances, who married first John Middleton, and, after both he and her sister Elizabeth died, Maj. (later Maj. Gen.) Thomas Pinckney; and Mary, who married Col. William Alston and brought forth the family we consider here.[17]

After inheriting her brother's house, Rebecca Motte, her husband, and her children moved in sometime near the onset of the Revolution. Rebecca's first contribution to the war effort came when she offered her plantation field hands for building fortifications to defend Charleston.[18]

Sir Henry Clinton's redcoats landed on Johns Island south of Charleston on February 11, 1780. Governor John Rutledge left the city the next day to avoid capture. The British began bombarding the city with two hundred cannon on February 13. The city held out for two months before surrendering.

The British commanders—men of impeccable taste, it seems—chose Miles Brewton's house for their headquarters.[19] The occupiers included Sir Henry himself, who departed Charleston on June 8, 1780, for New York[20]; Lt. Col. Nisbit Balfour, commanding officer of the troops in Charleston; and Lt. Col. Lord Rawdon, supreme commander of British troops in South Carolina.[21]

Rebecca Motte's husband, Jacob, died in 1780, leaving her, her three daughters, and the rest of the civilian population prisoners on parole at the mercy of the occupying troops. "Mrs. Motte refused to give up her home—but she always sat at the head of her table in the large drawing-room and commanded the respect, at least, of his lordship and followers," wrote Jacob Motte Alston.[22] The British officers "showed her great courtesy and always referred to themselves as 'her guests.'"[23] Rebecca was remembered for her "quiet courtesy and unalterable dignity of bearing towards them."[24]

During the occupation, Rebecca's chief concern was for the safety of her three daughters: the newly married Elizabeth Pinckney, Frances, and eleven-year-old Mary, who was said to have been chased in Charleston by a drunken British soldier.[25]

Mrs. St. Julien Ravenel wrote that Rebecca "kept her three pretty daughters tight locked in the garret, guarded by a faithful 'mauma,' who would smuggle them dainties and dessert in her apron."[26] This suggests a grueling experience. Although the third-floor garret had two good-sized rooms and seven-foot ceilings, it was hellishly hot in the summer, unheated in winter, was lit and ventilated only by two small dormer windows and was without bathing or toilet facilities, save for chamber pots. In later years, generations of Alston and Pringle children used the garret as their playroom, wrote with chalk on the bare wooden walls, and carved their names into the rafters.

The earliest recorded version of this garret story makes the most sense. An 1877 biographical sketch of Rebecca Motte stated:

> This was the only room in the house where the British officers, on installing themselves, allowed its occupants to retain for their own use; and here, Mrs. Motte, her daughters, and Mrs. Brewton (a widowed relative of the family) locked themselves in during the first hours of confusion and disorder, whilst the soldiers, with clanking swords and boisterous talk, were pervading every other part of the premises.
>
> After a while, someone knocked on the door; but the ladies dared not open it. At first they would make no answer even, but the knock was repeated again and again, with the half-whispered assurance that it was a friend who asked admittance. At length a black finger was thrust through the keyhole, to convince them there was no reason to doubt this assertion and they opened the door to find outside a faithful negro servant, who, when she got fairly in, sank on the floor, exclaiming, "Oh, missis, such a time, such a time as I had to git to you. . . ."
>
> Throughout the summer and autumn of 1780, Mrs. Motte continued to occupy with her family a small part of her own house in Charleston. . . . Under these trying circumstances her calm dignity of demeanor exacted unfailing respect from her unbidden guests. Every day she presided at the long dinner-table, which was laid in the big drawing-room and always crowded with officers. The three pretty daughters never appeared on these occasions. Meal-time was the signal for them to steal noiselessly and dutifully up the narrowest, darkest, and most crooked little staircase into the garret, where Mamma locked them up safe from the eyes of the British lion. Not for worlds would the good lady have suffered a daughter of hers to run the risk of possible flirtation with the enemies of her people.[27]

The five women endured their self-imposed isolation during some of the time from the fall of Charleston in May 1780 until the spring of 1781, when Rebecca obtained permission to leave Charleston for her Congaree plantation. Before she left,

Lord Rawdon "thanked her with scrupulous politeness for her 'hospitality', but 'regretted that he had not been permitted to make the acquaintance of her family'" – i.e., her three daughters.[28]

Lord Rawdon was a hated man, for he had ordered the execution of a South Carolina patriot, Col. Isaac Hayne, for treason.[29] During the occupation of Charleston, former officers such as Hayne had been given the opportunity to return to their homes on parole if they agreed to fight no longer. Hayne had accepted and returned to his family plantation in St. Paul's Parish. When the tide of the war turned against them, the British revoked all paroles and ordered Hayne and others back to Charleston to take up arms and fight for the British. Hayne, feeling that the terms of his parole had been broken, refused and gathered up a militia company in St. Paul's parish. He was captured by the British and imprisoned as a common criminal in the provost beneath the Exchange Building, a handsome structure which still stands on Charleston's waterfront.

In the late spring of 1781, after Rebecca Motte, her three daughters, and the widow Brewton had moved to her Mt. Joseph plantation on the Congaree River, the British Army was still using the Miles Brewton House as its headquarters. Subsequently, the British took possession of her plantation house for a barracks and erected earthworks around it, permitting the Motte family to remain inside until May 8, 1781.[30] On that day, Gen. Francis Marion, the legendary "Swamp Fox," and Lt. Col. Harry "Light Horse" Lee of Virginia surrounded the plantation, then called Fort Motte by the enemy. Rebecca and her flock were sent by the British to her nearby overseer's house.

Fort Motte remained under siege for four days. Colonel Lee felt that the only way to dislodge the British was to burn the house. General Marion hesitated to do this, in deference to Mrs. Motte, but it is said that Rebecca herself "immediately and cheerfully consented, assuring him that the loss of her property was nothing compared with the advancement of their cause" and ordered the house to be set on fire.[31] This was done with three chemically-tipped, East Indian fire arrows furnished by Rebecca. They had been "given to her brother, Miles Brewton, by a sea captain in the East India trade, and ignited upon contact with any hard substance." Cool-headed Rebecca, it seems, had the presence of mind to take the quiver of these arrows with her when she evacuated her home for the overseer's cottage.

The arrows were launched from a musket fired by one of Marion's men. The first two arrows hit the dry, cypress-shingled roof but failed to ignite. The third had the desired effect and the roof started to burn.[32] The soldiers inside—165 men under the command of a hapless lieutenant named McPherson—surrendered to avoid being shot off the roof by Marion's cannon, burned alive, or blown up by explosion of the gunpowder stored inside.[33] The fire was then extinguished by the labor of both sides, and the main body of the house was saved. Remembering the civility shown to her by the British in Charleston, Mrs. Motte then invited both the American and British officers to dine with her.

Her extraordinary grace under pressure became a part of the family tradition.

CHAPTER TWO

King Billy's Daughter

I beg that you will employ yourself as you ought, gaining some information every moment. . . . Reflect that the opportunity may not possibly be retrieved, and that "the mind untaught is a work wasted," where fiends and tempests howl.
— Mary Brewton Alston to her fifteen-year-old daughter, Mary, 1818

Mary Pringle's Alston ancestors were no less influential on her development than the Brewtons and the Mottes. She was descended from a long line of Alstons and Allstons whose combined talents helped turn Georgetown District into one of the most productive and profitable agricultural areas in the world. By the mid-nineteenth century, the Allstons and Alstons and the families with whom they intermarried owned over half of the arable land between Winyah Bay and what is now the Horry County line.

The immigrant founder of what later became the Allston / Alston rice dynasty was John Allston, who was born in England in 1666 and came to America between 1685 and 1694. He had six children. One was William Allston who married a Huguenot, Esther Labrosse de Marboeuf, in 1721. William and Esther moved to All Saints Parish, Waccamaw, in 1730 and purchased The Oaks, a 1,000-acre plantation, from Percival Pawley. It proved to be a purchase "that would keep his descendants in possession of the land for the next 138 years."[1]

William and Esther Allston's thirteen children included Jo-

Col. Alston's rice mill at Fairfield Plantation.

seph Allston, who married Charlotte Rothmahler. In 1744, Joseph inherited The Oaks, its house and a marsh island of 129 acres. These he took control of when he came of age in 1756. By the time of the Revolution twenty years later, he had become a wealthy man. In 1773 Josiah Quincy, Jr., visited The Oaks and wrote:

> Spent the night with Mr. Joseph Allston, a gentleman of immense income all of his own acquisition. He is a person between thirty-nine and forty, and a very few years ago begun the world with only five negroes—has now five plantations with an hundred slaves on each. He told me his neat [net] income was but about five or six thousand pounds sterling a year, [but] he is reputed much richer. His plantation, negroes, gardens, etc. are in the best order of any I have seen! He has propagated the Lisbon and Wine-Island grapes with great success. I was entertained with more true hospitality and benevolence by this family than any I had met with.[2]

Joseph and Charlotte had six children, including another William Allston, who would one day be known as "King Billy" for his great wealth and power.[3] William was born in 1756 at The Oaks, where he spent much of his childhood. He apparently did not obtain the English education which so many of his class enjoyed. Nevertheless, as an adult he acquired a large personal library containing the latest works of fiction, humor, the arts, sciences, politics, government, history, natural history, and travel, many of which were inherited by his son, Charles C. P. Alston.[4]

When the Revolutionary War began, William Alston was twenty, and he quickly joined the fight. He served as a junior officer in the state militia under the Swamp Fox, Gen. Francis Marion, and received a commission as captain of the Waccamaw Company, a part of Col. Hugh Horry's regiment, in 1781.[5] After the Revolution, William continued in the militia, ultimately rising to the rank of colonel, a title by which he was known until his death.

In 1777, at the age of twenty-one, William wed Mary Ashe, daughter of Brigadier General John Ashe of North Carolina, a man who had opposed the Stamp Act and served ably in the Revolution. One of their five children, Joseph Alston, married Theodosia, the only daughter of Vice President Aaron Burr, in 1801 and served as governor of South Carolina from 1812 to 1814.[6]

Theodosia was a particularly remarkable figure in the Alston family circle. She was the beautiful only daughter of U.S. Vice President Aaron Burr, and was thought by many to be the best-educated American woman of her time. A true prodigy, she read Horace and Homer in the original Greek by the age of ten and spoke fluent French, Spanish, and German.[7] In both appearance and sophistication, she was an ornament to the lives of both her father and her husband, each of whom loved her intensely.

When the Carolina rice planter married the cosmopolitan New Yorker in 1801, tongues wagged that the alliance was

The "Nag's Head" portrait alleged to be of Theodosia Burr Alston

chiefly political. To their friends, however, it soon became clear that Joseph and his Northern bride were deeply in love. Theodosia moved to South Carolina in the spring of that year and was welcomed into Low-country society.

William Alston bought Hagley plantation from Anthony Pawley in 1801 and gave it to Joseph as a wedding present.[8] While on the Waccamaw during the winter, Theodosia and Joseph resided at Hagley and The Oaks, which he had inherited from his grandfather, Joseph Allston.[9] They spent their summers both at his grandfather's summer home, "The Castle" at Debordieu Beach, and their quiet, country cottage near Greenville, within view of the Blue Ridge Mountains.[10]

Their first and only child, Aaron Burr Alston, was born in 1802, and it is likely that the Miles Brewton House was the place of his birth. The vice president came to see his grandson in Charleston from May 4 through early June, and most certainly stayed with his parents-in-law, Colonel and Mrs. Alston.[11] As a token of his respect, Burr gave the colonel a small bust of Napoleon Bonaparte.[12] The sculpture still resides in the house on King Street.

Theodosia was often noted as being a frail woman. A letter to her physician, Dr. William Eustis in Boston, dated October 3, 1808, revealed the reason. Since the birth of her son, Theodosia had suffered from a prolapsed uterus, combined with gruesome recurring uterine infections which left her not only infertile but in constant agony.[13]

In 1804 her father had his famous pistol duel with Alexander Hamilton, in which Hamilton was killed. As a result, Burr was ostracized. In the next years, Burr made two trips into the West, where he purchased large amounts of land in the Louisiana Territory. He was accused of planning to establish a separate republic in the Southwest and was indicted for treason in 1807 but was acquitted after a six-month trial.

Burr went to Europe in 1808 to try to enlist European help for his schemes, then quietly returned to the United States in July 1812 to resume his law practice in New York. His grandson, Aaron, died of malarial fever on June 30, 1812, in the north chamber of William Alston's summer home on Debordieu Beach.[14] His death took a heavy toll on Theodosia, and although she desperately wanted to visit her father, she was not well enough for the trip until the winter of 1812.

Joseph Alston had been elected governor of South Carolina in November 1812, and Jacob recalled that when his uncle was in office, "large dinner parties were given at the old King Street house. He was not an ambitious man," Jacob wrote, "but Aaron Burr instilled into him some of that of which he, himself, was overstocked."[15]

By the winter 1812, Theodosia had recovered enough of her health to plan a sea trip to visit her father. With her only child dead and her husband tied to his desk, Theodosia boarded a skiff at The Oaks plantation which took her to Georgetown. On December 30, 1812, she, her personal maid, and Dr. Timothy Green, a long-time family friend, departed on the pilot boat *Patriot,* for the six-day trip to New York.

As her passage was being attempted during wartime, she carried with her a safe-conduct request from Governor Alston to the commander of the British fleet which was patrolling the coast. A violent storm arose on Saturday afternoon and evening, January 2, 1813, which caused severe damage to several of the British warships.[16] Theodosia's ship was never seen again. Over the next eighty years, a series of intriguing shipwreck and pirate stories surfaced to explain her mysterious disappearance, but how Theodosia spent her final hours of life may never be known.

Joseph Alston survived his wife by less than three years. Haunted by his tragic personal losses as well as financial reverses, he died in the Miles Brewton House on September 10, 1816.[17] He was buried at The Oaks.

About 1783 William returned to cultivating rice on the Waccamaw and did so with such extraordinary success that Washington Irving called him "that greatest of all Southern planters."[18] Upon his father's death in 1784 William inherited Clifton plantation, which was located on the east bank of the Waccamaw and served as his country seat for more than twenty years. By 1786 he owned 26,590 acres which were worth over £1 million in South Carolina currency (about £142,857 sterling).[19]

With the proliferation of Allstons in Georgetown District, duplicate names soon became unavoidable—especially with the Allston penchant to reuse the same given names. To differ-

William Alston's new name recorded on the door of his wine garret.

Col. William Alston

entiate himself from his first cousin, William Allston of Brookgreen, William Allston of Clifton dropped the second "l" in his name, and his descendants spelled their name "Alston."[20] The change had been made by 1792, when he chalked his name on the door of one of the wine rooms in his garret.

Colonel Alston also inherited Fairfield, his father's vast, highly efficient agricultural machine on the Waccamaw River and commissioned Jonathan Lucas, Sr., to build him a rice mill there about 1787.[21] Clifton burned on December 6, 1806, and Alston moved his family to Fairfield that same day. He added two wings to the existing four-room house and used Fairfield as his country seat until he died.

William's wife, Mary Ashe Alston, died in Philadelphia in 1789.[22] In 1791, when he was thirty-five, Colonel Alston married twenty-three-year-old Mary Brewton Motte (known as "Hesse"), the youngest daughter of Rebecca and Jacob Motte, Jr. The wedding took place two months before the nation's first president, George Washington, visited them at Clifton—quite a heavy responsibility for a new bride. Washington, whose passion for agriculture knew few bounds, was deeply impressed by the perfection of Colonel Alston's rice plantations.

On Friday, April 29, 1791, Alston entertained President Washington "in a style which the president pronounced to be truly Virginian." Washington declared that "he had seen nothing in all his travels so justly entitled to be styled a fairy land, as the rice fields of Waccamaw in the genial month of May."[23]

When asked by her grandson how she dressed to meet the president, Mary Alston told Jacob that she wore a band on her forehead which was emblazoned, "Hail to the Chief."[24] President Washington was so pleased by his warm reception at Clifton that upon his return to Mount Vernon, he sent Colonel Alston an imported mare and a young jackass.

Like many wealthy planters, William Alston was a conspicuous consumer, and Charleston provided the perfect setting for him. Everything around him was designed to engage the intellect and indulge the senses. His formal English garden blazed with a diverse array of flowers. He also had a country retreat near Greenville, perhaps the same as that owned by his father, Joseph.[25]

Alston bestowed every conceivable luxury on his new bride. Less than two months after the wedding, he acquired the Miles Brewton House for her by buying out the interests of her mother and aunt, Frances Pinckney. He paid £7,000 sterling for the house and its enormous, 149' x 473' double lot.[26] He gladly footed the bill for her splendid wardrobe, including the stunning dress she wore when Edward Savage painted her life-size, full-length portrait in 1792.[27] About 1818 he commissioned another portrait by Samuel F. B. Morse. Jacob wrote, "During the Civil War it was impossible to remove the large frames of these portraits so they were taken out and carefully rolled and sent to me in Columbia for safe keeping, with valuable silver, old

Mary Brewton Motte Alston

wines, etc., etc. I will here add that altho' I lost so heavily by the burning of the city, I saved all that was committed to my care."[28]

Jacob described Colonel Alston as looking "somewhat austere, tall and straight, with his hair combed back from the forehead behind the ear. I do not remember ever having heard him utter an oath, and swearing was not uncommon in those days, or to have seen him in a passion—but his word was law, and his orders carried out to the letter. He had accumulated a very large fortune and took his *own* advice in all things."[29]

His family was attired in the most fashionable clothes that London and Charleston could supply. Although Alston was no dandy, he was stylish, dressed impeccably, and sported colorful Madras handkerchiefs.[30]

Hesse Alston was known for her compassion. After breakfast, she often fixed buttered bread and large mugs of tea and coffee and had them sent to needy downtown neighbors. Others she would visit privately, bringing clothing and other necessities. "To visit the sick and the afflicted in their distress, and to keep herself unspotted from the world, was her religion," wrote her nephew, Jacob Motte Alston. "It was only after her death that the family knew of her well-kept secret, by the poor who came to her door to pay a last tribute to her open handed charity."[31]

Mary Motte Alston, the youngest daughter of William Alston and Mary Brewton Motte, was born in the Miles Brewton House on June 17, 1803, when her father was forty-seven and her mother, thirty-four. She was named after her mother and also inherited her nickname, Hesse.

Young Mary spent most of her childhood on Fairfield Plantation or at the Miles Brewton House. The large flock of Alston brothers, sisters, and cousins summered at Debordieu Beach staying at "The Castle," their beach house. The pretentious name was a spoof of its unassuming, ramshackle appearance. Its well-designed underground frame anchored it against the hurricanes which often swept the coast. Built about 1800, The Castle sur-

"The Castle" on Debordieu Beach

vived the great hurricanes of 1822 and 1893. It was destroyed by fire in 1905.[32]

A conservative man, Colonel Alston nevertheless had his passions. He spent considerable time and money on his chief love: raising blooded horses. His horses and carriages were known throughout the Lowcountry for their grandeur. His large dark green and red coach was marked with the Alston arms and the motto, "Immotus," on the door.[33] His uniformed coachman and jockey, Thomas Turner, drove the carriage, which was drawn by four blooded bay horses, flanked by two out-riders on matching horses.

"The days of powdered hair, and knee breeches and stockings and large shoe buckles had passed," wrote Jacob. Colonel

The arms of Col. William Alston of Clifton Plantation

Alston's servants wore "dark green broadcloth coats and vests trimmed in silver braid and red facings with trousers of green plush. . . . On Sundays my grandmother [Mary Brewton Motte Alston] always rode to church in her carriage, but in the afternoon she always walked, in order that the servants might attend if so inclined, when she and I would always be seen together in the old family pew of St. Michael's.[34] My grandfather at this period never left the house, save now and then to walk as far as the large stable on the premises, and look at the horses, and talk to me about them."[35]

Colonel Alston was one of the founders of the Santee Jockey Club, which was established in 1791 and held races at the St. Stephens Course in Pineville. In Charleston he was a member and steward of the South Carolina Jockey Club, and when the club moved to the Washington Race Course in 1792, Alston was one of the original shareholders.[36]

No social event took place on the Santee or in Charleston without at least a brace of Alstons—if not the whole flock—present, and Race Week in Charleston was no exception. The racing season started in Charleston in the early spring and continued on into the summer in Virginia, where it was cooler. Alston's passion for thoroughbreds caused him to travel extensively in search of superior breeding stock. In 1802 Thomas Pinckney wrote of him, "His plan is to go immediately from here to Virginia, to be in the neighborhood of Race-horses and Democrats, two species of animals, you know, [of which] he is very fond."[37]

Colonel Alston maintained his own stud farm, and his papers include a plan for a private one-mile race course. In 1799

Alston paid $4,000 for Gallatin, one of his best racers, and "always considered him one of his cheapest horses." The descendants of another horse, Nancy Air, were valued at over $50,000. In 1802 he bought a black groom named Thomas Jackson from Col. John Tayloe, a well-known horse breeder of Mt. Airy, Virginia.[38]

Alston kept meticulous records of his breeding program from 1779 to 1808.[39] Betsy Baker, a winning mount and personal favorite of his, was stabled at home. John B. Irving wrote, "I remember meeting Betsy Baker at the corner of Friend and Tradd streets, on her return to Col. Alston's stables in King Street, after having beaten Rosetta in 1791—a great crowd following her."[40]

For whatever reason, Colonel Alston decided to retire from the turf in 1805. In 1807 he sold his entire stud, after having run some of the best horses that ever started in South Carolina.[41] His well-worn horse measuring stick survives as a testament to his passion for thoroughbreds.

As did all men of his rank in society, William Alston shouldered the burden of local office, and kept the company of presidents, statesmen, generals, and princes. In 1819 the Alstons had the honor and pleasure of entertaining President James Monroe, his wife, family, the Secretary of War, and several aides. The presidential party spent the night at Prospect Hill plantation and left the following day. Monroe was ferried across the Cooper River on "Colonel Alston's elegant New York barge which was rowed and steered by a competent number of responsible masters of vessels who had volunteered their services and over which proudly waved the Star Spangled Banner."[42]

In national politics, Alston "was prevailed upon to lend the weight of his name and influence to the party of which Mr. Jefferson was the head."[43] Alston and Thomas Jefferson met at Warm Springs, Virginia, in 1818 and soon became friends and political allies. Warm Springs was one of several favorite watering holes for planters who, like Jefferson and Alston, took deep pleasure in horse racing. There the patrician rice planter and the former president discussed many things, including their mutual interest in fine wines. On August 15, 1818, Jefferson jotted down his recommendations about the better French and Italian wines for his South Carolina friend. Later, reflecting that his personal recommendation alone might not be sufficient to enable the colonel to make gustatory decisions of this magnitude, Jefferson sent Alston several dozen bottles of his favorite wines to sample.[44]

Lowcountry planters of the eighteenth and early nineteenth centuries consumed great quantities of Madeira, a robust white wine fortified with brandy to boost its alcoholic content. Colonel Alston and his sons, Charles and Thomas, imported their Madeira by the pipe (126 gallons) directly from the island where it was made. The popularity of Madeira is attested to by the fact that several Lowcountry plantation homes, including True Blue and Rose Hill on the Waccamaw and Smithfield on the Combahee, had specialized wine garrets. The Carolinians found that twenty or thirty years in their fiery attics would only improve their Madeira, and 100- and 150-year-old bottles have been found to be perfectly drinkable.[45]

The louvered main wine room in the garret had a capacity of 1,200 bottles of Madeira.

The colonel stored and aged his Madeira in a spacious, specially built, louvered wine room in the garret of 27 King Street, where he chalked off the inventory changes on the walls and door.[46] One inscription noted, "39 dozn botles of Madeira Wine Drawn off." The 468 bottles were consumed in 1792 during a grand (and probably tipsy) tricentennial celebration of Christopher Columbus's authorization to sail to the New World. Alston's unfortified, heat-sensitive varietal wines were kept in the plantation room, a relatively cool, ground-floor room with a dirt floor where meat, fruit, and vegetables were stored.

Each Saturday night the Alstons had a formal family dinner which all the children were expected to attend. Jacob recalled that dinners were given in the yellow, or South, parlor, where "the table extended across the room, and the beautiful damask, china, glass, and silver were conspicuous."[47] His grandmother sent him to bring the appropriate wines and decant them, Jacob wrote. "After having the decanters filled she would always taste, to be certain I had not made a mistake, and I would always follow her example, and so I learned, at a very early age, to discriminate between the various kinds of wine, their ages, etc.... The old servants have told me what a gay old time was sometimes witnessed at the King Street house. The doors were frequently locked and no one was allowed to leave the table till the 'sun came peeping in at morn.'"[48]

In eighteenth- and early nineteenth-century South Carolina, public schools were virtually nonexistent. The planters, who lived on their widely dispersed plantations for at least six months each year, coped with the dearth of educators by employing private tutors, may of whom were imported from New England. Their use was regulated more by the scarcity of qualified educators than their high cost.

Colonel Alston's children had the finest education available. In their youth, his sons attended private school in Charleston. Later, his sons by his first wife attended the College of New Jersey (later Princeton University), while those of his second wife attended Yale College. Mary and her sisters were educated at home and received specialized instruction in languages and dancing from private teachers in Charleston.

From 1805 to 1810 the Alston sons had John Pierpont as their tutor. Pierpont had graduated from Yale College in 1804 with his classmate, John C. Calhoun, and taught for a brief time in Bethlehem, Connecticut. In a journal he kept during his Southern stay, Pierpont wrote, "On the 21st [November, 1805] I visited Mr. Allston's with Mr. Rutledge but found him sick. I agreed to call the next day. I did so on the 2nd, heard his proposal and after comparing the disadvantages probably attending either situation I waited on Mr. A. on the 23rd and closed with him on his own terms of 600$ per ann[um] free of all expense besides my clothing."[49]

Pierpont's $600 salary was handsome. The average annual salary of other tutors in the South was $350 to $500 at that time.[50] In comparison, an overseer on a rice plantation commanded $500 to $1,000 per year, about the same as the purchase price of a prime field hand. In addition, Pierpont's salary was virtually all bankable, as Colonel Alston also provided him with room and board.

Pierpont stayed with the Alstons in the Miles Brewton House for the few remaining weeks before they left on the annual fall migration to the Waccamaw. On December 13, 1805, he paid six dollars and boarded the northbound stage coach for Georgetown, sixty miles away. He described the journey as follows:

> There were in the stage 12 passengers—5 of whom were females, these with all their baggage together with the driver, very nearly filled the stage, for I found but little room either to move or lie at ease, and I believe that even my seat was envied by some of our fellow passengers. We all dined about 32 miles from Charleston, on a wild goose etc. The place of wine was supplied with Porter of not the most superior quality, and the whole was afforded us for the moderate price of 1.50 cents each! We arrived at the Sampit ferry after crossing 2 others about 9 in the evening, but our ferryman would not suffer greatly a comparison with Charon[51], for as it regards light, I am sure they are equally deprived of it, he having

> none but a burnt stick, and as to politeness Charon must certainly be considered as the more accomplished Frenchman. However we were ferried across without waiting like the unburied of the ancients for the space of 100 years and like them wandering on the banks of the Styx.
>
> I put up at old Mr. Graham's an old gentleman who by intemperance seems to have been hurried so near the grave that he is obliged to have a servant to feed him. . . . Here I starved on a supper and breakfast at the rate of 1.30 cents pr. day and in the afternoon was carried over the Waccamaw river to the plantation of Col. Alston who had arrived the day previous, with his family.[52]

A "natural rebel," Pierpont brought to the Alstons a keen intellect whose "mind laid fierce hold upon whatever interested him." These subjects included antimasonry, imprisonment for debt, temperance, phrenology, mediumship, and spiritualism—the last two of which the Pringles also became interested in.[53]

Pierpont enjoyed two traditional plantation sports: shooting deer and alligators.[54] He also liked some of the foods he found in the South, particularly the oysters, nuts and peaches. He was particularly fascinated by the sweetness and size of Colonel Alston's strawberries, the circumferences of which he carefully recorded in his journal. Yet in the end, no Southern delicacy could compare to anything from New England, and he wrote a friend in Connecticut, "I would exchange all the fruit in Carolina . . . for the Apples there."[55]

When Pierpont joined the Alston family, Mary was only two years old. She remembered and respected Pierpont throughout her life, and the Alston family kept in touch with him for many years after he returned to the North. For four years he instructed the Alston boys in English, Greek, Latin, and mathematics, giving them their daily lessons as they moved from Charleston to Clifton to Fairfield to Midway on the seashore. The daughters had to make do with the table scraps from Pierpont's intellectual plate, for Pierpont didn't feel that women should be educated past a certain point. "Had I my choice," he wrote, "I would prefer a sister to be a decent dancer rather than eminent with the pencil."[56]

His letters show that he was a sad, homesick, and disillusioned young man the whole time he lived with the Alstons. In 1806 he wrote to Samuel Hitchcock, a friend at Yale, that he had no friends, and that "the companions whose company I most enjoy are my books and the letters of my Northern friends."[57] In 1807 he again wrote to Hitchcock:

> If you in the space of 7 or 8 days feel so sensibly the loss of Bethlehem society, what are you to suppose I have felt for 19 or so long months at such an "infinite remove?" You will return occasionally—I perhaps never. Society is with me, quite out of the question. I have none. I wish for now that is within my reach. I philosophically try to do without & am become in that respect quite a stoic. Here in Charleston a city containing I suppose 25,000 inhab. I am as lonesome again as I was in B. where but here & there a house row upon my sight. The company that with the family is such as I do not wish to mingle with. I stir but little abroad am much by myself—sometimes studying—sometimes whittling. Money here vanishes like an early cloud or a morning dew, 26 dolls. for a coat—8 for a hat—15 for a pair of boots 15 for 3 or 4 shirts make it in the aggregate a great hole in my wages.[58]

Pierpont often wrote of the intellectual isolation of plantation life, and his strong Federalist views clashed strongly with Colonel Alston's close alliance with Thomas Jefferson. Although George Washington deemed the Alston rice plantations "a fairyland," John Pierpont was not as impressed. "The beauty of your fields, especially meadows, have nothing here to equal it," he wrote his Connecticut friend, Hitchcock. "Nothing here compares with what in Con[necticu]t surrounds the eye of every peasant."[59]

With the exception of some food items and the Alstons themselves, Pierpont found little to like about the South and its people, and his letters were often filled with disdain, contempt and outright hostility. In 1806 he wrote, "those who have changed their New England characters for those of Carolina have not, on their return, been considered by the N[ew] Englanders as having gained by the exchange. I have determined as much as in me lies, to keep my N[ew] England habits if I can't exchange them for those that are evidently better."[60]

He also held a low opinion of the character of Carolina women. "I have nothing to do with them," he wrote, "and as little as possible to say to them. I won't tread on them that are below me—and farther, if any one goes to tread upon me I'll kick—I'll show 'em Yankee play. That they may depend on."[61]

For a man who spent almost every day of four years in intimate contact with the family, Pierpont chose to remain totally aloof, embodying the old New England philosophy that "good fences make good neighbors." His extensive personal journal entries rarely mentioned the Alstons. Even when confronted by a family disaster he remained dispassionate and emotionally detached. Early in 1807, he wrote to a Yale friend, "Since my last, Mr. Alston's house was burnt, no lives lost, loss of property, exclusive of inconveniences, estimated at 30,000 dollars. No snow yet in Carolina, rather cool."[62] Though his feet were in South Carolina, his mind and heart had never left New England. In 1807, he wrote, "I'd give all my old shoes, Hitchcock, could I for 24 hours be in Bethlehem. I mean in real substantial presence, for mentally I'm there half of my time."[63]

The daily confrontation with the harsh realities of slavery strongly shaped Pierpont's life and sparked an Abolitionist fire which burned fiercely in his later years. The month after he arrived, Pierpont recorded his impressions of how the Alstons and their slaves celebrated the Christmas of 1805 at Clifton:

> Throughout the state of South Carolina, Christmas is a holiday, together with 2 of the succeeding days, for all literary seminaries, but more especially for the negroes. On these days the chains of slavery with which the blacks are loaded and in which they toil unceasingly for their masters, are loosed. A smile is seen on every countenance, and the miseries of the year seem amply recompensed by this season of hilarity and festivity. No restraint is imposed upon their in-

> clinations, no lash calls their attention from the enjoyment of all those delights which the most unconstrained freedom profers. Children visit their parents; husbands, their wives; brothers & sisters each other, who live at a distance, and partake in the pleasures of social connexions of which they are deprived during the remaining part of the year.
>
> On the morning of Christmas, Col. Alston gave orders that as many beeves might be butchered as to supply all with meat, which as a general thing is not allow'd them. No less than 21 bullocks fell sacrifices to the festivity. On my first waking, the song of serenading violin and drum saluted my ears, and for some time continued to prove that no mind is below feeling the powerful effects of music. Merry Christmas met me at every corner, and sounded in my ears even in retirement. During almost the whole of the second and 3 afternoons, the portico was crowded with these dancers, who by their countenances reminded me of the ancient nymphs, satyrs, and fauns, and the fiddlers & dancers brought Pan and Timotheus freshly to mind.[64]

In the summer of 1810, Pierpont ended his Southern sojourn and returned to Litchfield, Connecticut, with the three youngest Alston boys in tow: Thomas Pinckney, Charles Cotesworth and Jacob Motte. There he prepared them for admission to Yale College, where they were all enrolled.

For all his remoteness and distaste for the South, Pierpont paradoxically developed what would be a lifelong affection for the Alston family. So great was his esteem that he named his eldest child for William Alston.[65] Responding in 1852 to a request from Mary, Pierpont went through his papers and found the original poem he had composed after hearing, in 1818, that Mary's brother Motte Alston had died after falling from a horse.[66] In a postscript to the poem, he wrote, "That your children, my dear lady, may ever cherish for you as grateful and as filial an affection as do your mother's children for her; and that your memory, when you are gone, may be as secure to them, as is hers to them and to myself, is the sincere wish, and fervent prayer, of your first teacher, Jno. Pierpont."[67]

Guided by the direction and example of her mother and her forebears, Mary Motte Alston matured into a strong, highly principled and resilient woman. During her childhood, Mary was close to her grandmother, Rebecca Motte, as well as her mother, Mary Brewton Alston. In 1818 Mary Alston wrote her fifteen-year-old daughter:

> You surely, my dear Hess, are jesting when you tell me about your idling your time which is so very precious. Pray have your sober senses about you and employ your time as you ought to do. I have written to Mrs. Kershaw to give you $15 which I beg you not to spend foolishly and get four bonnets at once as you did last summer, but get useful things. I wish you had mentioned your brother Tom – whether he is in town or sailed to the Northward – if you received E's letter, and if you have sent the things she wrote for.
>
> No doubt, my dear, but that you are very anxious to be with me, as much as I am to have you here and should your cousin Hannah come to North Island.[68] I will write to my cousin to allow you to come with them, but not else. In the meantime I beg that you will employ yourself as you ought, gaining some information every moment. Swayed by the elasticity of youth, you appear to be guided only by the impulse of the moment and in a great degree regardless of that attention to your improvement which should be the important principle of action, and so lead, if duly encouraged inevitably would lead, to the conviction of the propriety and necessity of constant and diligent application to the studies with which you are at present engaged. Reflect that the opportunity may not possibly be retrieved, and 'that the mind untaught is a work wasted', where fiends and tempests howl. 'As Phoebus to the world is science to the soul.'[69]

Whatever her early shortcomings may have been, Mary grew into a critical and voracious reader. One of her journals, dated the same year as her mother's letter, contains 120 pages of meticulous commentaries on thirty-one biographies she had read.[70]

In another journal of the same year, she recorded a young woman's selection of quotations on marriage, parenting, and Christian life. The sayings she chose about love and marriage all reflect the expectation of reciprocal consideration and wishes for the other's happiness.

Some of the quotations she recorded in her early journals had a strong Calvinistic ring to them. "If a man wishes to be really happy, he needs not to enlarge his estate, but to contract his desires." (Plato) Others reflected her father's philosophy: "A man should live according to his own values rather than listen to the world." They were not idle jottings, for they reappear frequently in the letters she later wrote to her children, and many of these concepts worked their way deeply into her psyche. In 1818 she recorded the advice of Pythagoras: "Always review the day before going to sleep. Be troubled at the ill you have done and rejoice for the good." In 1859 she repeated the same advice to James and Charles, at school in Europe. King Billy's daughter was nothing if not thorough.

The destiny of upper-class Lowcountry women was one of flirtation, wedding, and motherhood. The expectation was not only that a young woman must marry, but that a vocation was out of the question, for "the marriage and its progeny be her life's absolute and only center." For men, youth was most often characterized as a time when "all seems possible and his destiny awaits him if he will but set his feet upon the path."[71]

Mary had met her destiny by the time she was twenty years old.

CHAPTER THREE

Judge Pringle's Son

A rice plantation is, in fact, a huge hydraulic machine, maintained by constant warring against the rivers. – *Edward King*

The immense crystal chandelier in the drawing room of the Miles Brewton House sparkled like a thousand diamonds for the wedding of Mary Motte Alston and William Bull Pringle on March 5, 1822. The nineteen-year-old bride was "lovely in appearance" and wore a veil of rare old Mechlin lace[1] which was later worn by her daughter, Mary Frances, and two generations of granddaughters.[2] As befitted a couple from high society, the Rt. Rev. Nathaniel Bowen, bishop of the Diocese of South Carolina – rather than an ordinary parish priest – performed the marriage ceremony.[3]

The twenty-one-year-old groom married well; the bride somewhat less well. Both were the promising youngest children of wealthy and distinguished parents, but Mary's family substantially outranked William's in terms of ancestry, wealth and high-level political connections. Although their fathers-in-law were of the same social class, the Pringles had no equivalent to a Rebecca Motte or a Miles Brewton to point to. Neither did the Pringles have the political connections of the Alstons, with their bevy of current and former governors, senators and representatives. Nor did the Pringles have the kind of wealth that the Alstons did, for when it came to money, King Billy's pockets were four times as deep as Judge Pringle's. Colonel Alston was worth over one million dollars when he died; Judge Pringle's assets were about $250,000. Too, Mary was much better-read than her husband and towered over him intellectually. In short, William Bull Pringle married up; his bride did not. Given the limited courtship options available to women in nineteenth-century America, it was not an unusual pairing.

The sturdy line of Pringles of which William Bull Pringle was the product had its roots in frugal Scotland.[4] Robert Pringle, the son of Robert Pringle and grandson of Thomas Pringle, a merchant burgess of Edinburgh and laird of Symington, Parish Stow, County Edinburgh, was born in 1702. He immigrated to Charleston by 1725 and soon became a prosperous factor and Indian trader.

In 1734 he married Jane Allen, who died in 1746. After a disastrous Charleston fire in 1740, which cost him his house and store on Tradd Street, Robert Pringle built a three-story brick single house which still stands on half of his Tradd Street garden lot.

By the 1750s Robert, by then one of the eminent merchants of the city, was turning from trade to politics and planting. In 1774 he built a splendid single house at 70 Tradd Street, which remained in the family until 1886.[5] Robert Pringle died quietly in his Tradd Street home in 1776. He was survived by three children: John Julius; Robert, who did not marry; and Elizabeth Mayrant Pringle, who married William Freeman.[6]

John Julius Pringle chose the law as his profession. In 1772 he read law in the office of Chief Justice John Rutledge. In 1773 Julius departed for London, where he, along with nine other South Carolinians, had been accepted by the Middle Temple.[7] There he was a fellow of Lincoln's Inn. The rights of the American colonists were a heated topic of discussion at the time he was studying for the bar. Julius put his pen to use for his country and wrote a lengthy article on the subject for a London newspaper.

Although Julius completed all his necessary studies, he

would not swear allegiance to the Crown, and was thereby denied admission to the British bar. He lived in France from 1778 to 1779, where he served as secretary to his fellow South Carolinian, Ralph Izard, who had been appointed commissioner to the court by the Continental Congress. After surviving a bout with illness and a circuitous trip back home, Julius Pringle was admitted to the South Carolina bar in 1781.[8] He excelled in private practice despite a speech impediment: stammering.

In the twenty-five years after the Revolution he held a succession of important posts. George Washington nominated him for the post of federal district attorney and Julius served from 1789 to 1792. In 1792 he was elected Attorney General of South Carolina and served for sixteen years. In 1805 Thomas Jefferson offered him the position of Attorney General of the United States. Although flattered, Judge Pringle declined the appointment. Several factors affected his decision. Charles Fraser, a close friend of the family, noted that Judge Pringle's mother was old and in declining health, and he did not want to leave her.[9] In addition, his prolonged absence from Charleston would have hurt his lucrative private practice, which is said to have earned him between $18,000 and $23,000 per year, an income which compared favorably to that of a rich planter. Finally, accepting the position would have kept him from exercising proper control over his rice plantations. For the rest of his life, Julius concerned himself with local matters and abstained from national politics.

Judge John Julius Pringle

In 1776 he inherited his father's brick house at 70 Tradd Street in Charleston, which became his city residence.[10] In 1795 he purchased Runimede, a 370-acre manor on the Ashley River which he made his country seat. He also acquired rice plantations on the Black and PeeDee Rivers.

In 1784 he married Susannah Reid. Of their ten children, the youngest son was William Bull Pringle, who was born in 1800.[11] When Judge Pringle died in his 89th year in 1843,[12] the courts of Charleston all adjourned the next day in respect. During a long legal career he earned a reputation for tenacity and success and enjoyed one of the most lucrative private practices in the city's history.

In his education, William lagged considerably behind his father, his older brother Robert, a Harvard man, and his cousins. This son of Charleston's wealthiest lawyer evidently did not attend college.[13] His lack of formal education was attested to by the lack of allusion to classical literary themes in his writing, the lack of references to contemporary literature, and his horrid handwriting. Compared to his wife's even, precise and open—though idiosyncratic—hand, William's handwriting was a coarse, jagged scrawl which in later life appeared to be aggravated by palsy. He lacked his wife's conciseness and clear sense of organization. In addition, his sentences were often worded awkwardly.

However, it is clear that William supported education as strongly as his wife. He held a succession of local offices which showed deep concern for education. He served as one of the Commissioners of Free Schools, who were appointed by the legislature every three years and had complete responsibility for the schools. They chose the location, hired and dismissed teachers, admitted pupils, and decided which texts to use.[14] The few schools actually established and run under this system were, of course, open only to white students.

In 1829, at the age of twenty-eight, he accepted the position as a trustee of the College of Charleston and served for ten years.[15] In 1836 he was a shareholding member of the Charleston Library Society.[16]

In 1821 William was elected a third-degree Freemason.[17] This "chivalric brotherhood" had been founded in England a hundred years earlier. Its teachings, which stressed morality, charity, and obedience to the law of the land, found enthusiastic adherents among the Southern aristocracy.

William was a handsome and imposing man who stood six feet tall.[18] A Middleton relative wrote that "Mr. Pringle was as remarkable for his height as Mrs. Pringle was for her diminutiveness; erect, graceful and dignified, he was a true type of the high-bred Southern gentleman, not only in appearance but in manner and spirit."[19]

For William, the potential benefits of the match were great. The youngest of six sons, he stood to move out of his father's house and into the Alston mansion on King Street. The wealthy have always conserved their assets by marrying their own kind. Since the control of Mary's property would devolve upon him as soon as they were married, he stood to acquire not only a home, but the plantations, slaves and other personal property she would bring as dowry or later inherit. His father gave him a wedding present of $20,000 in cash and bank stocks, so William was in no way a poor man himself.

William Bull Pringle, about 1855.

The providential alliance did have its drawbacks, for moving in with Colonel and Mrs. Alston was decidedly a mixed blessing. The marriage gave William direct access to Colonel Alston's considerable planting expertise and financial acumen, but the colonel rarely sought the advice of others and may not have felt it necessary to dispense it, either.

Sharing a roof with his parents-in-law also imposed limitations on the degree to which William could be his own man and master of his own household. Further, it meant that he and his new wife lived out their early years of marriage under the constant scrutiny of her parents and amid the never-ending flocks of brothers, sisters, other relatives, and friends—not an easy task for any newlyweds. Their bridal chamber was the withdrawing room of the Miles Brewton House, a custom which her daughters continued as they married.[20] By that time, the other Alston children had married and left the house, save for Mary's sister Elizabeth, who married Col. Arthur P. Hayne later that year. Her brother Charles Alston, who lived at Fairfield, also married later that year, to Emma C. Pringle.

On her wedding day, Mary penned a hopeful prayer for a Christian marriage. "I humbly implore God's blessing on the important transaction that is to take place this day. I am about entering into a relation the most important, sacred and solemn," she wrote. "Ratify and confirm in Heaven, O my God, what is about being done, by Thy gracious sanction on earth. May the lives of my husband and myself be honorable, happy and prosperous. May our love and harmony render our relations and our lives a true emblem of the union subsisting between Christ and the church. May our mutual love never expire; and may it be consecrated and dignified by Christian confidence and esteem." She recorded a similar prayer on behalf of her new husband.[21] From her mother, Mary received a handsomely bound Bible and *Book of Common Prayer,* underscoring the importance to the family of the place of church in marriage.

Mary received a letter from her brother Charles Alston full of mixed feelings about her marriage :

> I feel no small degree of sadness when I reflect on the change which your absence will cause at Fairfield. No one will feel this loss more severely than myself. . . . I cannot however but rejoice at your happiness which you are so deserving of. I feel this delightful assurance from the character of him to whom you are united, who has every good feeling which can make domestic life a happiness. Tho' severed from

> us I still consider you with the same ardent affection which always existed in my breast, tho' your society added not a little to our family enjoyments, yet it is with far more delight I view your prospect of happiness. . . . It gives me pleasure to be the first to address you by your new title. I suppose also some novelty and gratification to you to receive per mail a letter to Mrs. William B. Pringle.[22]

As the son of a large rice planter and the son-in-law of a great one, William Bull Pringle had ample opportunity to learn the details of planting. There were no schools for planters, nor were there any textbooks. Everything needed to plant, grow, and harvest the rice crop had to be learned on the job from experienced planters.

South Carolina's booming antebellum rice culture had its origin in the late 1670s or 1680s. Intentions of experimenting with rice as a staple crop are found in correspondence between the Lords Proprietors as early as 1677.

The productive portion of the Santee delta, containing approximately 16,000 fertile acres, extended from within a mile of the mouths of the North and South Santee Rivers to the point where the two branches join. The outlines of the rice fields were set by the rivers and streams themselves. Each field was engineered so that it could be flooded independently of any other.

Check banks, seven or eight feet wide at the base and three feet high, separated one field from another. The banks were built with great precision and maintained with unending care. They were repaired as necessary, and the ditches and drains cleared and cleaned with hoes. The ditching work was particularly odious, for it often required slaves to work chest-deep in cold water and mud during the early spring.

The widely successful method of using the rise and fall of South Carolina's tidal rivers to flood and drain the rice fields was pioneered around Georgetown in 1758, but wasn't popularized until about 1786 by Gideon DuPont, Jr. Unlike the reservoir method, the tidal flow method used the power of the tides to push fresh river water into the rice fields at high tide, and drain the fields at low tide. The greater availability of river water over reserve water significantly reduced the uncertainty of the water supply, but restricted the areas where rice could be grown.

Tidal flow rice fields had to be located at points along the river where they were low enough to be flooded at high tide, yet high enough to be drained at low tide. At a minimum, this required a tidal rise and fall of at least three feet. Salt water will stunt or kill rice, so the fields had to be located above the river's "salt point" — the point where the river's flow kept out any salt water from the sea.

For these reasons, rivers such as the Santee and Waccamaw, which flowed swiftly and carried large volumes of fresh water seaward, gave sustenance to tidal flow plantations which stretched close to the sea. Slower, lazier rivers, like the Cooper, which had neither the speed nor volume of the former two, forced would-be rice planters much farther upstream.

The weather was of constant concern to the planter. Too

Trunk gate in a rice field at White Oak Plantation, North Santee River.

little rain early in the season and the crop might be stunted; too much rain or rain at the wrong time could delay the harvest or cause the unthreshed grain to mold and decay. Freshets could flood the fields and strong winds could damage or break the stalks, permitting the heads to fall into the water and rot. Hurricanes, which often visit the South Carolina coast between June and November, could wreak havoc on carefully tended dikes, ditches, and expensive plantation equipment.

In addition to the elements, the planter faced a variety of natural enemies. Burrowing animals such as alligators, snakes, crayfish, moles, and rats made holes in the banks which then often turned into leaks and then breaks. Field hands equipped with terrier dogs were used to control the rats. The hands had a quota of so many rats per day to kill and had to turn in the rat tails as proof of their work. Among many of the Santee field hands, these rats, properly cooked, were considered a delicacy.[23]

Rice worms could eat the rice stalk down to the ground if not stopped by flooding the field. Grubs could get to the crop if the field was left too dry, maggots would eat the tender roots if the field was not properly drained, and the rice weevil was always ready to dine on the finished product.

A multitude of birds flocked to the rice fields, contributing more to the planter's woes than to his gain. Blackbirds and crows attacked the rice at every stage of its growth, and although they also ate insects, their fondness for the best grain generally outweighed their help. Ducks, which loved to glean the scattered grain in the Santee rice fields in winter sometimes also shoveled out newly-planted rice. Unlike the crows, the ducks at least provided the planters with many a tasty meal.

It was the innocent-looking little bobolink—known locally as the rice bird or the May bird (from the time of its arrival)—which caused the planter and his hands the most trouble. On their migration from South America each spring, rice birds arrived in "in flocks so dense as to cast a shadow on the green and golden fields just bending with the long ears of grain," wrote Jacob. Shotguns and bullwhips, made of the inner bark of the hickory tree, were used to scare off and kill the birds.[24] In September, when the birds started south again, the process had to be repeated.

During the winter, the fields were plowed and then dragged with a harrow to break up the clumps of earth. Maintaining a perfectly level field was critical, as failure to do so meant that the rice in one section would be at a different state of growth than in another, requiring different treatment—which, in a flooded field, is impossible.

The planter either prepared his own seed rice each year or bought it from others. The best grades of seed were not mill-threshed, but were hand-flailed and winnowed and contained less than three percent red rice.

A four-inch trenching hoe was used to lay off seed trenches, twelve or thirteen inches apart. Early in April, the seed rice was sowed at the rate of two and a half to three bushels per acre. The seed rice was pressed into balls of wet clay and then dried. When sewn, this made it unnecessary to cover the grain, since when the field was flooded, the seed would not float to the surface.[25] The first flow, or flooding of the rice field, took place immediately after the seed was sown. This sprout flow was kept on the field for three to fourteen days until the rice "pipped," or germinated; the water also served to kill weeds. After germination, the field was drained and hoed for weeds. The field was then kept dry until the planter could see the young, needle-state rice plants along each row and across the entire field.

Some planters used a "point flow" until the rice was three to four inches high and strong enough that the rice birds couldn't pull it up. This flow was followed by one or two hoeings. Next came the "long water," or "stretch flow," of three to four weeks duration. The field was flooded until the heads of the rice plants were completely covered; then the water was drawn down to six to twelve inches. This flow floated off the dead grasses killed by the previous hoeings and also killed insects.

The "harvest flow" generally began in late summer when

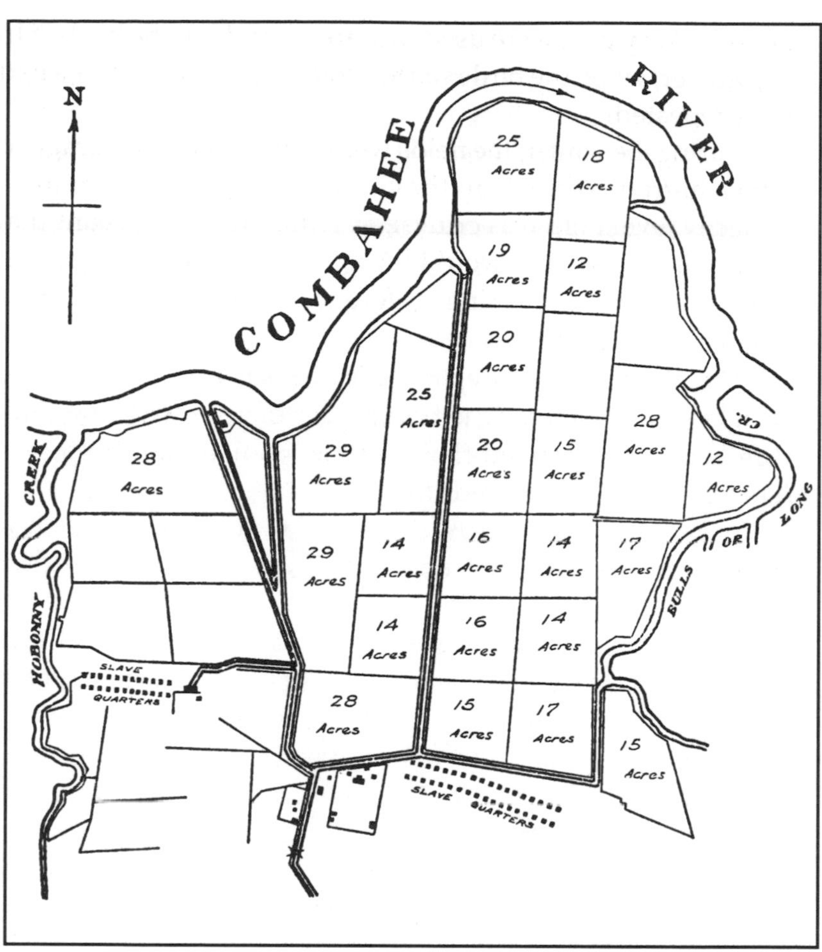

A typical South Carolina rice field

the plants were about fifteen inches high and had developed joints. The flow supported the maturing stalks and was kept on until shortly before harvest.

Throughout the year, the field hands worked by the task system. "For every kind of work there was a set task, and so, according to ability, there will be full task, half- and quarter-task hands," wrote Jacob Motte Alston. "When two tasks were accomplished in one day by any hand, he was not expected to work the next, and these tasks were *never* increased."[26]

The harvest season began around the end of August and

generally lasted five to seven weeks. During the harvest everyone worked at a frenzied pace. "From early morn, till late at night," Jacob wrote, "when torch lights were burned in the barn-yard to enable the hands to see how to put the newly cut sheaves into racks, the work went on." Sundays only were excepted.[27] Two or three days before the rice was to be harvested, the water was drained from the field. Then the field hands cut the stalks with sickles, known in the Lowcountry as rice hooks, and the grain was laid on the stubble to dry for a day or two. After this brief drying, the rice stalks were tied in sheaves and stacked in the field or the barnyard, in "ricks about seven feet wide, twenty feet long & built as high as a man can pile, from a stool two feet high."[28] Ben Horry, a former slave who worked at Brookgreen plantation on the Waccamaw, recalled that for the rice harvest, his task was one half acre a day, and that it was an "awful job."[29]

The rice was transported from the fields to the threshing area on mule-drawn carts and on flat-bottomed barges called rice flats, each drawing less than three feet of water. Rice was initially milled (hulled and polished) by hand, using wooden mortars and pestles. By the 1850s, steam-powered threshing mills were not uncommon. After milling, the rice was packed into plantation-made barrels constructed of pine and banded with birch and white oak hoops. Each barrel had a capacity of 600 pounds of rice.[30]

All of the Alston-Pringle holdings were extremely productive. They were located in the tidal rivers of Georgetown District, a two-day ride north of Charleston, an area ideal for the production of rice. By 1800 that region was known as a land where the planters "all made fortunes planting and growing rice . . . if they worked hard and malaria did not cut their lives short too soon."[31] For the slaves who produced the crop, rice planting meant grueling labor in steaming heat amid swarming horseflies and mosquitoes in one of the deadliest, most disease-ridden places on earth this side of the Black Hole of Calcutta.

At the center of the planter's universe was his plantation,

and his life revolved around it. But even when he was on his plantation, the planter was generally not the direct supervisor of his slaves. The chain of command ran from the planter to the overseer, to the slave drivers and then to the field hands. Most of the day-to-day supervision of the slaves was in the hands of white overseers. The slaves and their drivers were often better-informed about the state of the rice fields than the owners or overseers, who of necessity left to the drivers many of the details of planting.

The successful operation of a large rice plantation called not only for men and women with strong backs but also for skilled specialists. A slave was valued according to age, skill, and future productive capacity. All else being equal, a young slave was more valuable than an old one, a skilled one, such as a blacksmith or a cooper, was more valuable than a children's nurse, and a healthy slave was more valuable than a disabled one.

With the Pringles, as with most other informed planters, the slaves were generally not mistreated, because, if for no other reason, an unhappy slave was an unproductive slave. William Bull Pringle acquired most of his philosophies about the management and treatment of slaves from his father and father-in-law. When Colonel Alston died in 1839, Robert Y. Hayne, his son-in-law, wrote his obituary and described Alston's philosophy of plantation management:

> It was the opinion of Col. Alston that in the management of slaves the true interests of the planter were in exact accordance with the dictates of enlightened humanity. It was therefore a rule with him through life to treat his slaves with the utmost liberality and kindness, while he never relaxed the reins of a wholesome discipline. His rule was to provide them with dwellings of the best description, to clothe them in the very best manner and to allow them supplies of every kind on the most liberal scale. The consequence was that his numerous plantations were models of neatness and order, and his slaves always exhibited an appearance of health and comfort which spoke well for their treatment. They were devot-

> edly attached to their master, whose service they would not have exchanged for any other upon earth.[32]
>
> Col. Alston, however, was not one of those speculative philanthropists who sacrificed essential good to visionary theories. His system was based on a calculation of practical results. It was not his slaves only who were made prosperous and happy. If they were among the best treated in the state, his crops were also abundant, and his rice of the first quality brought to the Charleston market.[33]

The "enlightened humanity" of the Lowcountry planter, of course, embraced the institution of chattel slavery as literally blessed by God, and any white man who seriously suggested the possibility of the races being endowed with equal rights or abilities would have been considered dangerous or insane. The "utmost liberality and kindness" with which the colonel treated his slaves was measured on a scale set by the planter, not the slave, and it is unlikely that any Alston slave ever enjoyed more than the smallest taste of the freedom or plenty which was the birthright of every white Alston family member.

On Colonel Alston's plantations, his wife, Mary, distributed cloth, blankets and shoes to the slaves, listened to and resolved their complaints, and insured that the sick received proper care. Jacob noted that "my grandfather has nothing to do with all these matters; all is left to one who looks closely into the wants of each individual—her duties are never ending—day by day she learns all that is going on and her presence is everywhere. Kindness and gentleness was a part of her nature and evidenced in her every act—but idleness was to her the 'root of all evil.'"[34] Mary Pringle took on the job of tending to the needs of the slaves when she became mistress of the house.

Despite occasional fears of slave uprisings, rice planters generally felt quite secure on their plantations. "No home on earth was as safe as that on a plantation where the negroes outnumbered the whites from ten to twenty times," wrote Jacob in the

1890s. "The doors generally were unlocked at night. Of course petty thefts occurred but murder, arson and all the long list of terrible crimes were unknown. . . . The master of a large plantation would leave wife and children and all he held dear on earth in the hands of his negroes, and absent himself for weeks and months with less apprehension than he now would in a city whose municipal regulations were presumed to be of the very best."[35]

Now, in 1822, Mary and William Pringle began the task of learning how to maintain the enormous family business they would soon inherit.

CHAPTER FOUR

Children of the Pluff Mud

Our grandparents spent their youth and maturity in a period of prosperity. . . . In this period also there was danger; a temptation to yield to idleness and luxury. Since there were many servants there was a temptation to exalt oneself.

—Mary Pringle Frost, 1939

William was planting his own land by January 4, 1823, for on that date he purchased forty-one slaves from his uncle, Robert Y. Hayne.[1] He undoubtedly also spent much of his time helping both his elderly father and father-in-law with the operation and management of their plantations.

The house on King Street was the family's pride and joy, but it was their plantations which produced the food to feed them and their slaves, and the wealth to support their lifestyle. As long as King Billy was still alive, the Alstons and Pringles generally spent their winters enjoying the charms of country life at Fairfield.[2] To travel around the city and between the plantations, the family could choose between two fine coaches—Colonel Alston's handsome and roomy barouche, emblazoned with Alston arms, or a smaller, but still elegant, model.[3]

Runimede, Judge Pringle's 1,457-acre plantation, was located about eight miles or a two-hour horse ride from the Miles Brewton House. It was also about three miles south of Middleton Place, where the Pringle children often went to play with their cousins. Although others spelled it Runnymede or Runny Mede, the Pringles invariably spelled it "Runimede."

Runimede, the seat of John Julius Pringle, Esq., on the Ashley River

The handsome two-story house was stocked with elegant furniture, silver, and china and was surrounded by a manicured lawn, a fine garden, and expensive ornamental trees.

Runimede was the sanatorium where sick family members went to mend their health. William so loved the place that the family called it "Papa's Panacea." He and his sons kept dogs and horses there and hunted frequently; Mary and her daughters had four Shetland ponies and pony carts there.

By 1840 William was actively working Beneventum, Judge Pringle's rice plantation. Construction of Beneventum's magnificent Georgian plantation house was begun about 1750, when the front rooms of the first and second floors are believed to have been built. The rest of the house dates from about 1800.[4] The front entrance was remodeled in the Greek Revival style in the second quarter of the nineteenth century. The house was large enough to accommodate the whole family during the winter with sufficient space left over for guests. In November 1841 Motte wrote to Julius, "Papa has had erected a thrashing mill at Beneventum and has greatly improved the house. He has made the garrets into good sleeping rooms."[5]

Writing from Beneventum in February 1842, William described the property to Julius: "It is in bad order and I shall

Benevetum on the Black River, Georgetown District

with difficulty get only about 160 acres planted this year. But the next I shall plant the whole and I hope it will prove more productive than Youngville. It is about 32 hours ride from this [place] which enables me conveniently to see after it from this place, it being my habit to ride down once a week, passing one night there."[6]

In a letter to Arthur M. Manigault dated February 14, 1848, his mother wrote that "all of Mr. H[enry] Deas' property at Santee was purchased by Mr. W. Bull Pringle for $160,000."[7] William referred to his 1848 purchase as "Richfield" and used it as a residential plantation. He added the adjacent property, Pleasant Meadow, to it in 1854, after which the combined lands were known as Richfield. Both were located on the north bank of the North Santee River, six miles inland from the Atlantic Ocean. They lay between Milldam and Pine Grove plantations in the most productive part of the Santee delta, far enough upstream to be protected from salt water incursions driven by storms. They also received fresh water from nearby Pleasant Meadow Creek and Kinloch Creek.

The agricultural output of the Pringle plantations was pro-

digious. By the summer of 1850 Runimede consisted of 400 acres of improved land and 1,060 acres of unimproved land with a total land value of $10,000, with $800 worth of farming implements and machinery. Unlike the plantations on the Santee and Black River, which produced rice as a cash crop, Runimede grew only a small amount of rice. Instead, it produced a variety of foods for the polished mahogany tables of the Pringle family and pine plank tables of their slaves. It was stocked with four horses, three mules, forty milk cows and seventy other cattle, seventy sheep, and forty swine, valued together at $1,000. Its slaves raised 900 bushels of corn, 80,000 pounds of rice, 300 pounds of wool, 150 bushels of peas and beans, 800 bushels of sweet potatoes and 200 pounds of butter.[8]

After the Civil War and the loss of their property, many Lowcountry planter families waxed nostalgic about "life on the old plantation," but the letters of the Pringle women clearly indicate that they much preferred the comforts of the Miles Brewton House and the diversions of the city to the isolation of the rice plantations.

Jane Lynch, who had married John Julius Izard Pringle of Greenfield plantation on the Black River, described the "everlasting routine of plantation life": "Boxes of stores to be opened, and tidily put away (N.B. that last I confess to not doing) negro breeches that must be cut out, and coat sleeves that 'won't come out' (6 yds. to the contrary notwithstanding)—Cows that will not find their calves . . . and lavish their milky and maternal treasures on the wrong ones—oxen that run away in the swamp and are never to be coaxed back—invisible stomach aches and visionary pains in the side etc etc etc etc etc etc."[9]

The Pringle family migrated to one of their plantations after schools in the city closed the last week of November. The few weeks preceding the move were always busy. All the household linens, cooking utensils, and clothing had to be carefully packed into trunks and crates for the two-day trip by steamer and carriage. A skeleton crew of four servants was left to guard and maintain the Miles Brewton House during the winter.

For the men and their sons, the mild winters on the plantation meant hiking through the rice fields, hunting in the forests, shooting snipe and waterfowl, crabbing in the rich, odorous pluff mud of the tidal marshes, fishing in the creeks, and living out their fantasies of being English country gentlemen.

For women, plantation life often meant drudgery, isolation and boredom. Being stranded on the Santee, Waccamaw, or the Black River for five or six months meant being cut off from the social intercourse, public worship, genteel refinements and innocent pastimes to which women were supposed to confine themselves. When Mary Frances was eleven, she expressed this sense of isolation in writing about winter at Beneventum, "I do not like the country as well as town, as I find it too dull, particularly, situated as we are, so far from all our little friends."[10]

When in Charleston, the women spent much of their time shopping and making social calls. "Ladies visited from 12-2 o'clock, and in the afternoon," wrote Mary Frances Frost. "Visiting and receiving visitors was considered a duty. Infants were sent to visit their relatives and friends. Young people visited their elders."[11] The Pringles and the Middletons were on especially close terms. The women of the two families visited each other one evening every two weeks, and often gathered for dancing in the north parlor.[12] Many women found the rounds of town visiting boring, but they had few options available.

What entertainment they found in the country also came from visiting each other. This was done either by carriage or by boats rowed by slaves which transported the families among the plantations that lined the tidal rivers like pearls on a necklace. Entertaining at the evening dinner table was the chief form of social life. Planter families had plenty of time to enjoy themselves, as the slaves did all the heavy work and the overseers took care of most of the on-site management.

For amusement, the Pringle children tended their own gardens, rolled hoops, joggled on the joggling board, skipped rope,

The joggling board, a popular nineteenth-century entertainment.

played Prisoner's Base, King George and his army, and rehearsed scenes from their history lessons.[13] Jacob noted that while his more disciplined cousins would spend the afternoons in study, he "amused himself in the afternoons and would go on South Bay in the summer and swim around the vessels and leave the Latin and Greek for a more convenient season."[14]

The Pringle children were often sent to visit their relatives for weeks at a time. This separation—and time on their hands—encouraged letter writing. By the time the children were in their teens it was common for the older daughters to go to their Aunt Smith's plantations, Combahee and Smithfield, while Alston was at King Street with one or two younger boys, and the older ones were with William as he managed the Santee rice plantations.

In 1840 Mary wrote to Julius that William had "left Edward and Motte at Fairfield where they will remain until the first week in January. They are to spend a few days at Bannockburn.[15] They complain, a great deal, of the want of game, but I hope they will now be more successful. . . . Your sisters left me at noon today, to accompany the Mrs. Smiths to Combahee, where they will remain about a month. . . . Your sisters anticipated much pleasure, in being allowed to ride horse back."[16]

The boys looked forward to the end of school and to the move to the country. They learned to ride and hunt at an early age. Jacob wrote that his father gave him a "long-backed flea-bitten mare, of the 'marsh-tack' breed; three boys could easily be accommodated a time and have room to spare.[17] You can well imagine how fearfully the days rolled by, and how the return to school loomed in the near future as a purgatory with new appliances of torture artistically arranged."[18]

Mary wrote in 1845, "My thoughts are all for the quiet of Runimede, where we think of going toward the end of next week. The little boys are exceedingly anxious to get there, as their school breaks up on the 28th. Edward has possession of his pointer 'Czar' which now monopolizes his time and attention. He and Willy spent Saturday at Runimede to try dog Czar, which somewhat disappointed his master, altho' he pointed at a partridge, which was fairly shot and brought to town as a trophy."[19]

Even for the boys, the pleasures of country life wore thin at times. Motte, then fourteen, wrote to Julius in 1841, "The time passes heavily on our hands up here as there are no birds or fish. Bob Wilkin[20] is dead, papa has sent the new pony to Combahee with the girls, the Brown's back is still sore, and Sorrel horse which Grandpapa bought and lent to papa canters like a cow. My only amusement is flying a kite I have made."[21]

Towards the end of May, the wealthy Lowcountry families moved off their plantations and back into the city, frequently traveling to the seashore, to the North, or to Europe. For the Pringles, the preferred Northern watering holes included Newport, Rhode Island; Sharon, Connecticut; and Saratoga, New York. Southern planters also visited nearby resorts such as Glenn Springs in the South Carolina Upcountry and Flat Rock in the mountains of North Carolina.

Since early in the colonial period, Lowcountry planters knew that the summer and fall were the "sickly season," but could only speculate as to why. It is no surprise to learn that this period coincides exactly with the chief breeding season of the Anopheles mosquito, the carrier of malaria, and the Aëdes mosquito, which spreads yellow fever. The carefully regulated supply of standing water in the rice fields were perfect hatcheries for mosquitoes. They hatched in early spring and bred throughout the long summer until killed by the first heavy frost. It was this cycle which induced the annual migration to and from the country plantations each December and May.

Jacob Motte Alston wrote that in the mid-nineteenth century, "the first question asked of one who had visited Georgetown in the sickly months of August and September, was 'who was dead?'"[22] Such was life for the planter in Georgetown District, which in the heydays of rice "stood third in the class of unhealthfulness in the world—West Africa, Calcutta [and] Georgetown, S.C."[23] The fear of disease on the plantation in the summer was so great that one planter near the Waccamaw remarked, "I would as soon stand fifty feet from the best Kentucky rifleman and be shot at by the hour, as to spend a night on my plantation in the summer."[24]

William Bull Pringle wrote in 1841, "I will leave town on the second of November, an early frost having released us from our summer's imprisonment."[25] He wasn't always as careful, however, and on October 30, 1855, Edward accused his parents of being "obstinate as always" for returning to Charleston from Connecticut "before the back of the summer was broken."[26]

If the planter, his family and slaves could survive the usual run of childhood diseases along with the swamp fevers, the medical practices of the nineteenth century were the next health threats they had to face. Purging, bleeding and the use of blisters and leeches were among the common medical practices employed by Lowcountry doctors.

In the first half of the nineteenth century, a man aspiring to become a physician had only to apprentice himself to another physician for two years before he could obtain his license. Not a few patients found that their afflictions were aggravated and their life spans abbreviated by the well-intentioned but misinformed treatments by their physicians.

Others were considered lifesavers. When Sue was suffering from the summer heat and had an eye inflammation, Mary sent for Dr. Eli Geddings, a Charleston physician reputed to be "no less the master in the knowledge of drugs than he was in handling the surgeon's knife."[27] She reported, "He has already relieved her of many painful feelings. The eye is well and the stomach being strengthened, her animal spirits are becoming tranquil and cheerful."[28]

When Mary's mother married, she neatly copied into a journal all the family reciepts that a young wife would need in her new home.[29] Mary Pringle inherited the reciept book in 1838. It contained detailed instructions for preventing miscarriages, warding off fits in children, and healing sores, as well as others for curing hams, beef and beef tongues, killing rats and preventing cattle from destroying corn. The Pringles used a combination of patent medicines and traditional home remedies to treat their ills. The side effects of their ingredients were mostly unknown, and the cures were often quite literally worse than the diseases.

Their medicine cabinet was stocked with concoctions which included Francis' pills, Shallenberger's pills, bromide (potassium bromide, used as a sedative), and Seidlitz, a combination of powders which, when added to water, effervesced and acted as a laxative. Calomel, a powerful purgative and laxative, was a staple in the Pringle family's medicine chest. Calomel pills contained mercuric oxide, a tasteless white powder, and were used to treat a wide variety of illnesses. In an 1853 letter, Mary wrote to one of her daughters, "With much faith I struggled bravely on with Homeopathy in the treatment of Charlie's illness, but his fever last night was so hot and head so much affected that I threw Maria's innocent preparations out of the window and thrust an honest Calomel pill down his throat. This morning he is breathing the fresh air of the garden in full enjoyment of his 'phiffer.'"[30]

The family elixir to stop a fever consisted of four grains of camphor, an irritant and stimulant derived from the wood of the camphor tree, and laudanum, a mixture of opium in alcohol, all dissolved in tea. Their recipe to deal with infant bowel complaints when teething consisted of calomel, hippo (the "wine of Hippocrates," a wine highly flavored with spices), rhubarb and finely-ground chalk.[31] The resulting salve was rubbed onto the child's gums.

In December 1845 Mary wrote to Susan, "Will you appreciate this epistle in proportion to the trouble it gives me to write it. My poor fingers are in a deplorable state of inefficiency from chilblains,[32] which I attempted to cure by an application of caustic [caustic soda, a corrosive chemical], which did not much relieve the pain and added greatly to the disfiguration. My fingers and toes are now as black as ebony, and are sadly painful, then a great pin tore open the top of my middle finger. Thus disabled, I congratulate myself on Mary's well filled sheet having deprived me of all news."[33] A decade later, Mary Mitchell wrote to her mother, suggesting the use of alum and water or chloroform as treatment for chilblains. "I am told both afford relief," she wrote.[34]

While infant mortality rates were high in her time and children frequently died before their tenth birthday, all Mary's children were born alive and twelve of thirteen lived to adulthood.

Mary spent almost half of her reproductive life pregnant. She bore her first child three days short of nine months after her wedding. Mary was both fertile and lucky. She delivered thirteen healthy children (including twins) — a delivery about every twenty months. She evidently had no miscarriages, for the Pringle women freely discussed the miscarriages of their friends and relatives, but none was mentioned for Mary. Despite the rigors of pregnancy and childbirth in nineteenth- century Charleston, Mary's two married daughters also enjoyed excellent reproductive health, Mary Frances Mitchell had her first child 366 days after her marriage and bore twelve healthy children. Her sister, Rebecca Frost, gave birth 384 days after the wedding and bore six.

The pregnancy and birthing patterns of the white Pringle women and their black female house servants were nearly identical. Lucretia ("Cretia") Stewart, Mary's personal maid and head of the servant staff, was four years younger than Mary. She married Scipio, a cooper at Fairfield plantation, in 1825 when she was seventeen and a half. She bore her first child at the age of nineteen. Her reproductive life spanned twenty years, as Mary's did, during which she had ten pregnancies and bore eleven children, nine of whom survived into adulthood.

One challenge that both Mary and Cretia faced was that their pregnancies could not be planned. Their bodies hardly had time to recuperate and renew themselves before becoming pregnant again. (Under optimum conditions, a minimum interval of twenty-four months is now suggested between deliveries.) Other threats to their health were the risk of sepsis during childbirth, which resulted in the deadly childbed fever, and primitive surgical techniques. Difficult births often consigned both mother and child to the grave.

Mary also had to endure her pregnancies with two added burdens of the time: the heavy, high-necked, voluminous clothing of the Victorian period and Charleston's hot, humid and generally oppressive summers, where ninety-degree temperatures and ninety-percent humidity are the norm. Cretia and the female servants, with their more limited wardrobes, may actually have suffered less in this regard.

Mary had many advantages over working-class women and slaves in childbirth. She had a clean and comfortable place to give birth, for her maternity ward was the airy, spacious withdrawing room of the Miles Brewton House. Surrounded as she was by female relatives and close friends, she could to turn to and consult any of them. She also had access to the finest medical men of Charleston to assist her—as best they knew how.

Four to six weeks before the expected delivery of each child, Mary would begin her prenatal confinement at the Miles Brewton House. After each birth, she would remain in postpartum confinement, spending most of her time in bed or lying on a couch. With a yard full of servants, she also had a full range of helpers, from wet-nurses to cooks to cleaning maids to seamstresses, to assist her with her children. All of her advantages aside, being mother to thirteen children made large demands on her Mary's and energy.

Both Mary and William came from families with large staffs of liveried servants, some of whom had little to do except serve as proof other their owners' wealth and social status. Mary grew up in the midst of a large, busy and well-organized home. With her mother and elder sisters to guide her, she learned the household and plantation routines well. After her marriage and as her parents aged, she had to make the transition from child to parent and from student to teacher and caregiver.

Mary's allegiance was to the domestic sphere. She accepted her designated roles as wife and mother and lived out the expectations which she as a young woman recorded in her copybook: "The sensations of parental fondness are, I suppose, the most delightful of any our nature is capable of, except the conjugal, and these mutually adjust each other and complete complete domestic happiness."[35] She fully believed that children were gifts from God and that "Lo, children are an heritage of the Lord."[36]

Besides her own flock, Mary had an extra baby to rear: Jacob Motte Alston. He was the son of her uncle, Thomas Pinckney Alston, and his first wife, Jane Ladson Smith. Jacob was born in 1821 and came to live in the Alston home when his mother died in 1823. Mary reared Jacob as one of her own, and he lived with them until he was sixteen and left for college in 1837.

William and Mary did not pick out names for their children before they were born. After the birth of a baby in 1841, William wrote his son, Julius, "We have not decided upon the name of the youngster. I feel disposed to call him James after our worthy and lamented friend and relative,[37] whilst your Mama is inclined to call it after your Uncle Charles. By the time he is to be christened we will come to an agreement."[38] Mary's choice prevailed, and the boy was baptized Charles Alston Pringle. Two two years later, his younger brother was christened James.

Management of a large family and its staff of twenty or more servants required discipline, organization and good record-keeping. Mary was especially diligent in the latter. In one of her surviving household journals she recorded each item of clothing and pair of shoes issued to the household servants for their summer and winter allowances, their food and firewood rations and inventories of the cooking implements in the kitchen.[39] In another volume, she made detailed inventories of her bed linens, table linens, china, glassware, silver and listed the tasks each servant was expected to perform.[40]

Our grandparents," wrote a Pringle descendant, "lived in the home of their parents—in a beautiful house and garden, with servants, well-dressed and trained; plantations whose country life gave much enjoyment; relatives and friends of many generations."[41] That house, which Mary Pringle affectionately called, "our ancient family homestead," is the architectural treasure known as the Miles Brewton House, now a National Historic Landmark.

> In [King] Street. . . there stands a house a little back, upon whose face sorrow has struck many blows, but made no deep wounds yet; no scorch from the fires of war is visible, and the rending of the earthquake does not show too plainly; but there hangs about the house a gravity that comes from seeing and suffering much, and a sweetness from having sheltered many generations of smiles and tears.
>
> —Owen Wister
> *Lady Baltimore*, 1906

The original site plan for the Miles Brewton House included outbuildings containing a twin-bay coach house, stalls, a kitchen, a privy and living quarters for the servants. There were six double-tie stalls, adequate for the cows, the matched teams of coach horses, several riding horses for family use, and those of overnight visitors. Two tack rooms and a harness room were required for housing and maintaining the harnesses, and the harness room may also have served as residence for the coachman and his family.

The kitchen complex included a large cistern for storing water and a spacious baking oven. The entire back yard, extending all the way to Legaré Street, was at one time a formal garden in the English style. Jacob Motte Alston noted that in antebellum times, an English gardener "kept all in perfect order, and supplied all the vegetables of the season."[42] The broad walks were lined with sea shells, and mockingbirds and cardinals nested throughout. The snowdrops in the garden in the 1930s were believed to be the same brought by Miles Brewton

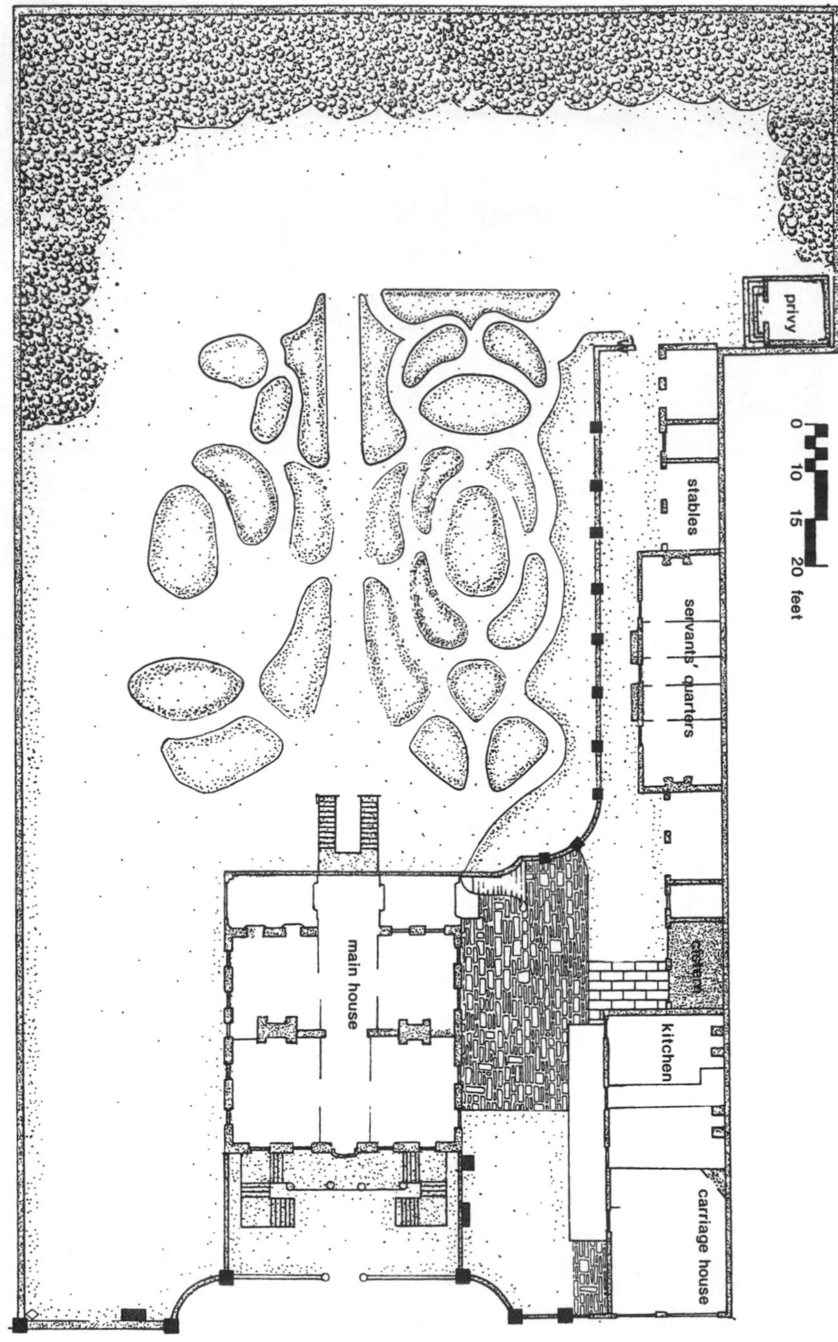

The present Miles Brewton House lot, 27 King Street

The kitchen and ovens which served the family and staff.

from England, and the garden was the beneficiary of seeds and cuttings from Edward Pringle in California, Julius Pringle in France, and friends and relatives throughout the Lowcountry. In spring and early summer the garden was a riot of colors and fragrances from Bermuda lilies, jonquils, sweet olives, lilacs, Cape Jessamine, oleander, English violets, pinks, carnations and a variety of roses. The garden also produced fruits and vegetables for the family, including oranges, pears, figs, peaches, grapes, pomegranates, bananas, French artichokes and corn.[43]

To the rear of the garden is one of the two original outhouses. Other buildings in the yard included coops and pens for the children's guinea pigs, rabbits, squirrels, cranes and other birds and animals.[44]

From King Street, visitors ascend two flights of stone steps and enter the house through the massive front door, made of cypress stained and grained to look like mahogany. Above the door is a Palladian fanlight. Inside is a stately entrance hall illuminated by two chandeliers and floored with Purbeck stone imported from England. The hall is embellished with floor-to-ceiling woodwork, as are all the front rooms of the house. The back rooms have wood paneling from floor to chair rail and wooden cornices.

The ground floor, or *rez de chauseè*, consists of four rooms. Entering at street level through the front door, the first room to the left was the plantation office, where Miles Brewton, William Alston, and William Bull Pringle kept the voluminous records required by large-scale farming. Down the hall to the rear of the office was the sewing room.

The room on the right side of the hall at the front of the house was called the plantation room or storeroom. It featured wrought iron meathooks to hang game, hams and sides of beef. The room was also used to store the fruits, vegetables and preserved foods shipped from the plantations or brought in from the garden, as well as the family's unfortified wines.

Upstairs, the first room to the left is the south, or yellow parlor, named for the color of the damask covering of the furniture and the curtains.[45] It was used to receive visitors and for formal occasions such the family's funerals. The ceiling decorations are made of paper maché cast in England.[46] Motte Pringle recalled, "I cannot well forget them for it was in this room, that as a school-boy I always slept—a little bed was put there for me and removed in the morning, and I can see the snowy doves[47] now as they coursed around the ceiling as I lay awake."[48]

The south, or yellow, parlor, used for receiving guests and for funerals during the Civil War.

Graffiti portrait labeled "Sir H. Clinton" etched into the marble mantel of the south parlor.

The center panel of the marble mantel in this room contains a diverse collection of Revolutionary War graffiti, including a profile caricature of Sir Henry Clinton, two square-rigged warships and three other vessels. The signatures of two generations of Alstons and Pringles are also scratched into the marble, along with several unidentified names which may have belonged to British or federal military personnel who occupied the house during the wars. The mantel in the north parlor suffered a similar fate.

The north parlor was chiefly used as the family dining room. A notable feature to the right of the fireplace is a gyb door—a door made to look not like a door. It prevents destroying the symmetry of the paneling around the mantelpiece, and leads to the adjoining breakfast room or warming room, where food brought from the outdoor kitchen and was kept warm over coals until serving. Indeed city ordinance then required that kitchens be located in a separate outbuilding to minimize the threat of fire.

Across from this room is one which probably served principally as a library for some of the more than 5,000 books owned by the family. It featured two book closets, one of which still contains its original shelving.

At the end of the first floor hallway is an imposing stairway which leads to the second floor, where, in Charleston, is usually located the grandest room in the house. The stairwell extends past the rest of the rear wall of the house, providing a formal entrance hall to two bedrooms and the drawing room. Above the stairwell landing is a deeply coved ceiling featuring a paper maché bas-relief of Apollo with his lyre. Paper maché fillets covered with gold leaf also decorated the coved ceiling. Similar fillets in white, as was Apollo himself, were used to outline the wainscotting and other features of the stairwell.

On both sides of the upstairs hallway are the bedrooms, which William Bull Pringle equipped with their dressing rooms. An 1834 inventory made by Mary Pringle showed that the house contained two feather beds, two hair mattresses, one "mattress of wood," one mattress of Spanish moss and two "straw beds;" many pillows and bolsters, linen and cotton sheets, blankets, quilts, and chintz counterpanes (bedspreads). Most of their newer French blankets were trimmed with either red or black borders.

At the end of the hall, through a classical entrance complete with columns and pilasters, is the most ornate room of this elaborate house: the drawing room or ballroom. The rare, coved ceiling set off a mural "which was painted to represent the sky, with fleecy clouds interspersed."[49] The centerpiece of the room

The drawing room or ballroom of the Miles Brewton House

The crystal chandelier, c. 1790.

is the breathtaking crystal chandelier, believed to be of English origin. Under the five-foot sweep of this "work of science and art" which dates from about 1790, generations of brides stood for their weddings. The room contains a set of eight Brewton-era armchairs and a gold-leaf mirror from the palace of Louis Philippe, described by one poet as "blind with age."[50] Destined to remain virtually untouched for seven generations, this room was at the end of the twentieth century considered by many architectural historians to be the finest remaining example of Georgian-era wood carving in America.

A withdrawing room or card room, entered from the drawing room, was similarly elaborate. In addition to its obvious social uses, it also served as a bridal suite and the maternity ward where all thirteen of Mary's children were born, along with those of her daughter, Rebecca (Pringle) Frost.

A corkscrew staircase off the upper hall leads to a garret. It contained two rooms where the three Motte daughters were said to have been hidden during the British occupation, as well as two wine closets where Colonel Alston stored his Madeira and brandy.

Two elaborate mechanical servant call systems were used in the house. When a family member pulled a tasseled cord on the side of the mantel or pushed a brass lever on the wall, a bell rang in the courtyard, informing the appropriate servant which room needed attention. The bell cords show clearly in an 1868 photograph of the drawing room. The bell levers may still be seen in the north and south parlors. The system was used by the Frost sisters well into the twentieth century.

This photograph of Susan Pringle Frost in the drawing room shows the black tasseled servant call pulls still in use in the 1920s.

Silver inventories made in the 1830s show that the Alston and Pringle families set a handsome table. The records list eight candlesticks with shades and snuffers; four silver waiters, coffee, tea and chocolate pots; salt sellers; four knife cases with two dozen knives; assorted tableware, two rice spoons; a sugar dish with tongs, a silver strainer, two decanter stands, a silver ink stand, ladles, sauce pans and dishes; a cake basket and butter boats. In 1858 all Mary's inherited silver was still intact. It was evacuated to Columbia in Alston Pringle's care sometime late in 1862. The Pringles were lucky. Their silver survived the burning of Columbia which followed Sherman's occupation in 1865. With hard times knocking at the door in 1870, Mary allowed William to sell most of her silver and accepted an assortment of Pringle family heirlooms in compensation.[51]

The family had a set of ordinary white china for everyday use, but for special occasions they had twelve place settings of white French china acquired in 1838 and twenty-four place settings of blue India china purchased in 1836 and 1840. Along with these were dozens of accessory pieces, including tureens, serving dishes, rice dishes, dessert, fruit and nut plates, fruit baskets, custard cups and sauce boats. Their inventory of glassware was also ample, and they had every possible type of glass dishes, bottles, decanters, goblets, wine glasses and tumblers.

A portion of the old white china was taken to Runimede in 1843, and a large collection of "red India china" (Chinese export) was kept at Beneventum until that plantation was sold. Beneventum's china and other household goods were sold at auction in 1863, but William had a friend buy back the red and white set for $75 and a green and white set for $50.

One of Mary's journals records her large inventory of damask table cloths, doilies and tea towels. Some of the table linens were marked "1797" in blue thread; the rest were comparatively new, and dated from 1832 through 1835.[52]

Art played a prominent role in the lives of South Carolina's wealthy antebellum planter families. As art historian David Shields wrote, "Charleston as early as the 1710s had become devoted to forms of competitive social display. The arts became the vehicles of that competition."[53] Social status was measured by the British standard and was derived from a combination of occupation, wealth and family ties. Portraits provided a visible link to those ties, and decorative paintings by the best artists demonstrated the sophistication, taste and affluence of the owner.

For the Pringles, their large wall portraits were tangible signs of the love that these closely-knit family members held for each other and for their ancestors, and their miniatures and daguerreotypes were touchstones of affection for the loved ones who lived away from the family circle at King Street.

Through extensive travel at home and abroad, the Pringles pursued their education and learned to appreciate the finest art that Europe and America had to offer. Then, when it came time to have the likeness of a family member painted, the Pringles had not only the financial resources but also the refined tastes to select the finest artists of their day.

The Brewtons, Alstons, and Pringles chose fine portrait and scenic paintings for their home. The earliest of the family's ancestral portraits was a pastel made before 1729 of Mrs. Robert

Brewton (neé Mary Loughton Griffith) by Henrietta Deering Johnston, America's first woman artist.[54]

Miles Brewton chose the London artist, Sir Joshua Reynolds, to paint his portrait in 1756. Reynolds, an English painter in the Grand Manner, was the foremost portraitist of his day, and his clientele was drawn from the cream of British society. He executed a straightforward, broadlit bust portrait of the young gentleman, then aged twenty-five, dressed in a pink silk doublet.[55] Jacob Motte Alston noted, "You notice a scar on his forehead but this wound was given as he now hangs, defenselessly on the paneled wall—a British officer having thrust the portrait with his sword."[56]

About the same time, Brewton's wife (neé Mary Izard), his younger sister, Rebecca Motte and her husband, Jacob Motte, Jr., were having their portraits painted by Jeremiah Theus, a Swiss limner who was working in Charleston by the early 1740s.[57] Jacob Motte Alston declared that the Theus portrait now hanging in the Miles Brewton House was not a portrait of Rebecca Motte. In an 1886 letter he stated, "No portrait was ever left of her. Those which are seen in such books as 'The Women of the Revolution', etc., etc., are not genuine. There hung in Col. Tom Pinckney's fine residence on Broad St., Charleston a portrait [the Miles Brewton House Theus] from which these engravings of Mrs. Motte were taken. The portrait was evidently of some member of the family—but it was *not* of Rebecca Motte. She, as I have said, was small and delicate while the portrait in question is most masculine."[58]

An imposing 92" x 56" oil painting of Mary Brewton (Motte) Alston, William Alston's attractive young second wife, is perhaps the most impressive of all the family portraits still in existence. It was painted by Edward Savage in 1792.[59]

In the 1820s Mary Pringle's brother, John Ashe Alston, was an extensive patron of portraitist Samuel F. B. Morse, a favorite of the Georgetown planters. Between 1818 and 1820, Morse painted the two regal portraits of Col. and Mrs. William Alston which commanded the attention of visitors to the Miles Brewton House.[60] These portraits were copied several times.

The portrait of Colonel Alston now hanging in the Gibbes Museum of Art in Charleston was painted by Thomas Sully from the Morse portrait; that of his wife was done from the Morse and also from an 1839 Charles Fraser miniature. Mary sat for Sully in 1842 and 1845. A typical, romantic Sully portrait of Mary descended outside the house through several generations of her heirs until 1994, when it was repurchased and brought home to the Miles Brewton House.

Mary Pringle.
Oil portrait by Thomas Sully, 1845.

The character study of William Bull Pringle which hangs in the drawing room of the house was painted in the 1850s by George Whiting Flagg. It and other portraits show a serious man with sandy brown hair and brown eyes.

Family members often commissioned miniatures when they were about to leave home or embark upon a perilous voyage—be it at sea or at the end of a long life. When the Pringles needed small copies of their portraits, they usually turned to their family friend, the popular Charleston miniaturist, Charles Fraser. Fraser's warm bonds to the Pringle family were established when he studied law in the offices of Judge John Julius Pringle, from 1798 to 1801 and again from 1804 to 1807. In 1800, at the age of eighteen, he executed a watercolor sketch of Runimede, Judge Pringle's newly acquired country estate on the Ashley River.[61] In 1818 he gave up law as a profession and spent the rest of his life as a working artist.

Between 1820 and his death in 1860, he noted making four miniature copies for the William Bull Pringles. In 1839, at the peak of his career, he painted miniatures of Colonel and Mrs.

Copy miniature painting of Robert Pringle, c.1865.

Alston based upon the Morse originals.[62] About 1840 Fraser painted his mentor, Judge Pringle, then about ninety years old.[63] Fraser painted at least nineteen works for the Pringle family and their relatives.

In an interesting artistic twist, John B. Irving, Jr., painted his wall portrait of John Julius Pringle not from another full-sized work but from one of the three Charles Fraser miniatures. Late in 1865, the family commissioned Henry B. Bounetheau, a Charleston native, to make miniatures of those who had died during the war: Robert and Charles Pringle, and little Hesse Mitchell.

However, after 1845 inexpensive photographic reproductions generally replaced expensive handmade paintings as the primary medium for family portraits. In 1850 or 1852, the Pringles had a surprisingly relaxed group photograph made in Newport. About 1855, William Bull Pringle's image was captured on a full-plate ambrotype.

During the Civil War, James Reid Pringle was photographed by Charleston photographer George Cook. James was portrayed in a carte-de-visite sized photograph of him in his Confederate army field uniform. Throughout the 1860s the Pringles went to Cook to have many inexpensive ferrotypes ("tintypes") made. In 1868 the Miles Brewton House's interior and exterior were the subject of several professional photographs. The 1868 exterior view was used for the dust jacket of this book.

❧

The Pringles and friends at Newport, 1850 or 1852. Back row, standing, l-r: Thomas Appleton, Grace Norton. Edward J. Pringle, Mary Frances Mitchell (Mrs. Donald), Professor Charles Eliot Norton. Front row, seated. l-r: Mary Pringle, Susan Alston, Susan Pringle.

The servant staff at the Miles Brewton House had responsibility to clean and dust the house, make and tend the fires which heated the rooms, empty the chamber pots, and polish the silver. Seamstresses made and mended the clothing and linens, and other servants washed the clothes, made baskets, minded the children and cooked and served the food. In the 1840s Mary listed the duties of four of the servants. The small amount of work assigned to each seems to indicate that it was tradition and not necessity which prompted the Pringles to keep such a large number of servants in the yard:

Yellow: to keep the drawing room, lamps and silver;
Cornelius: the street steps, cellar steps and private stair case;

Ishmael: the South parlour, the North parlour, dish covers and plates; and
Thomas: back parlour, knives, glasses and coal scoops.[64]

Outside the Miles Brewton House, other slaves cared for the lawns, flowers, vegetables, and fruit trees and swept the sidewalk every day. Hercules was the family coachman. As such, he only handled the reins. God forbid, the planters thought, that a coachman should smell of horses as he drove his master and mistress around the city! Caring for the horses and the family's two cows was work for his assistants, the hostelers.

Thomas Turner, who lived until the 1850s, was Colonel Alston's prized jockey. Mary Chisholm, a former Alston and Pringle servant, recalled that Turner "must have been part Indian, for he wore his hair in two long plaits."[65] One night when Turner had been gambling—a practice not allowed for slaves—he was arrested and taken to the guardhouse. Colonel Alston was so distraught that he couldn't sleep all that night. "Nothing was too good for him," wrote Jacob Motte Alston, who bailed out Turner at first light the next morning. "I expect he received from his Master a handsome money present for his uncomfortable night in the 'guardhouse.'"[66] In a highly unusual act, Colonel Alston manumitted Turner and left him an annuity of $600 per year after he sold his stud. Every morning for as long as he lived, Mary Pringle would send Turner his breakfast and her son, Alston, would send him his dinner.[67]

Throughout her life, Mary collected recipes for everything a nineteenth-century family would need, from practical instructions for making turtle soup to remedies for menstrual problems. Using only the most basic cooking implements but employing recipes and sophisticated cooking skills handed down through the generations, the cooks of the Miles Brewton House turned out enough food to feed between twenty and forty people every day. The Dutch oven was used every Sunday to make gingerbread for the children. Rolled thin and cut in squares, the children called it, "Aunt Hess's ginger bread."[68] Mary did not bake it herself, for cooking and baking was work for servants. Cretia Stewart, Mary's personal maid, was trained to make this special treat.

Most of the food served on the Pringle table and everything eaten by their servants and field hands was raised on their plantations. The plantation was a virtually self-sufficient community, and the rice planters raised not only their cash crop, but enough staples to feed their families and more than three hundred slaves.

When the planters were supervising the work on their plantations, they would arise at four or five o'clock in the morning and often had to ride on horseback for several hours before reaching the fields being worked that day. During the harvest season the work day ran late into the night, and the hard work demanded substantial meals to replenish the workers' energy.

With the sea and fresh water only three miles apart in some areas of Georgetown District, seafood was plentiful. Family letters and receipes tell us that the fresh water ponds and rivers yielded diamond-backed terrapin, sea trout, catfish, bass, and bream; the marsh and sea provided clams, stone crabs, oysters, shrimp, mullet, cavalli, black fish, mackerel, sheepshead, sea bass, whiting, and sea turtles. These went into a variety of dishes, including stewed oysters, oyster soup, terrapin soup, clam soup, shrimp pareé, shrimp pie, and fish Newburg.

Domestic fowl were also plentiful, including chickens, turkeys, guinea hens, and geese. Many varieties of wild fowl were attracted to the rice fields and the nearby marshes, including ducks, geese, wild turkey, partridge, doves, curlew, snipe, rail, and woodcock. Rice birds (bobolinks) were considered a delicacy. Jacob wrote that even the famed New York restaurateur, Giovanni Delmonico, "with all his art, could not produce a more delicate dish for breakfast than one of rice birds, in September. Nothing is more delicious than these birds. Two or three dozen simply cooked in a frying pan—no lard—no butter—seasoned only with a little salt. Their own fat makes a dishful of yellow gravy, which with some Carolina 'small-rice'. . . affords a repast which would inspire one to write love-verses."[69] The small birds were eaten "in one bite, bones and all."

Animals also had to be fed. Cattle ate rice straw in the winter and were turned out to forage in the scrub pinelands near the salt marshes in the summer. The hogs were fed coarse rice flour. Two cows quartered at the Miles Brewton House produced milk and cream for the household, while the plantation cows produced cream for butter (well salted, to retard spoilage). Venison came from the deer who lived in the forests surrounding the rice fields.

In nineteenth-century Lowcountry kitchens, the ability to prepare rice properly was a skill which would make or break a cooking reputation. Rice was eaten two or three times a day, in main dishes or as a side dish at almost every meal. Jacob claimed that few people outside the rice growing region of South Carolina knew how to properly cook rice. "The old negro women on the rice fields cook this grain to perfection. Uncover, as you walk along the banks of the fields, one of their little three legged iron pots, with its wooden cover and try, if only from curiosity, the rice which they have prepared for their mid-day meal. Boiled till done—the water 'dreened' off and set on the ashes to 'soak.' Around the pot there is a brown rice-cake, in the center of which are the snow-white grains each thoroughly done, and each separate. Unless one has eaten rice cooked in this way," he wrote, "he knows nothing about it."[70] Another rice planter seconded Jacob's sentiment: "Every old Negro woman on the Combahee can cook better rice that the best chef in a fashionable New York hotel."[71]

The Pringles grew corn, which they used for meal, grits, and flour; Irish potatoes (also used for potato flour), barley, and purchased wheat flour. Their baked goods included wheat, corn and potato breads, brown bread, ginger bread, muffins, yeast biscuits, waffles, and macaroni.

From the plantations and the garden of the Miles Brewton House came a variety of fruits and nuts, including apples, chinquepins (edible dwarf chestnuts), oranges, lemons, melons, muskmelons, blackberries, watermelons, peaches, pomegranates, and pumpkins, from which they made jams, jellies, preserves, marmalade, tarts, and pies.

The plantations were the source for most of their starches, which included Irish, sweet, and Spanish potatoes and yams, from which came their sweet potato pone, pudding, and soup; and vegetables, such as cabbage, cauliflower, corn, tomatoes, Sewee beans, beets, guinea squash (eggplant), onions, peas, pickles, red and green peppers, sugar cane, and turnips.

For special occasions they enjoyed cakes, cupcakes, custard, and fancy desserts like coconut pie, sunshine cake, Huguenot tortes, and Charlotte Russe. Cretia, an excellent cook, mastered the complicated recipe for this light, elegant, sherry-flavored dessert.

Their favorite beverages included tea, coffee, and hot chocolate along with whiskey, ale, a wide selection of French and Italian wines, brandy and a great deal of Madeira and planter's punch. South Carolina planter's punch recipes have a common theme: heavy use of tropical fruits, liquor and carbonation. The recipe for Charleston Light Dragoon Punch, for example, combines grenadine, curacao and raspberry syrups, green tea, red and white cherries, pineapple, oranges, lemons, whiskey, rum, and carbonated water. If followed properly, the recipe takes four days to prepare and serves a militia company or 300-360 close friends.

CHAPTER FIVE

A Family of Substance

Our grandparents spent their youth and maturity in a period of prosperity. They lived in a time of well-established business and well-ordered homes. Young men were sent to college in this country and abroad; young women were taught in private schools, and boarding schools, and by tutors. They were required to value industry and culture. In this period also there was danger: a temptation to yield to idleness and luxury. Since there were many servants there was a temptation to exalt oneself.

—Mary Pringle Frost, 1939

By 1837, the "ancient family homestead" on King Street was bursting at the seams with nine children, whose playful laughs and shrieks filled the house and gardens. The family was growing, but it also was to lose two of its venerable members.

After an extraordinarily full life, Colonel Alston's health began to decline in the late 1830s. No longer able to make the annual migration to Fairfield, he and his wife retired to their home on King Street. Jacob Motte Alston, then a young bachelor, stayed in town with them during the winters until he left for college in 1837. "I would go to school in the day," Jacob wrote, "but in the long winter evenings I would draw up a little chair at the feet of my dear grandmother while she would knit, and tell me of her early life, and what would I not give to have noted down all I heard from her dear lips."[1]

In 1838 Mary Brewton Alston contracted quinsy, an advanced stage of untreated tonsillitis, and died. On her deathbed she gave her daughter, Mary, then thirty-five, her copy of *The Imitation of Christ* by Thomas á Kempis.

Like so many widowers who had been long and happily married, Col. William Alston lived less than a year after losing "the beloved and excellent partner of his bosom." In 1839, at the age of eighty-two, Colonel Alston died in the house he had relished and embellished for forty-eight years. Jacob wrote that "his remains were brought on a pilot boat from the city, and as it became known along the river, a vast concourse of negroes hurried to The Oaks, and it was with great difficulty I could push my way through the dense mass of people who belonged to him and his sons, and only then to see the last spade full of earth thrown on one whom I had lived with from childhood and whom I had learned to love, honor and respect."[2]

The 1839 inventory of Colonel Alston's holdings revealed that he was one of the largest slaveowners in the state.[3] He left an estate which included 702 slaves valued at $351,000 on his Georgetown District rice plantations, twenty-one slaves valued at $8,600 in Charleston at the Miles Brewton House,and other personal property, cash, and securities totalling $573,232. Like most planters, Colonel Alston had significant investments in real estate. His home on King Street and plantations were worth well over a half-million dollars and his total net worth exceeded one million dollars.

Following the tradition of generations of South Carolina planters, Colonel Alston bequeathed residences, furniture, stocks, and cash to his daughters. His son Charles inherited Fairfield, which was producing 900,000 pounds of rice a year in 1850.[4] At various times Charles also owned interests in Midway, Weehawka, Strawberry Hill, Rose Hill and Bellefield plantations on the east bank of the Waccamaw and several buildings and lots in Browntown, Georgetown District. Most of the plantations went to his sons. Mary inherited the Miles Brewton House and its lot, extending the entire width of the city block between King and Legaré Streets, along with its furniture. She also inherited 200 shares in the Bank of the United States, valued at $23,333.33; fifteen shares in the Bank of Charleston and a one-sixth share of her father's cash in the bank. She and her sister, Rebecca Hayne, each received a half-interest in Strawberry Hill plantation.[5]

A few years later, in 1843, Judge Pringle died at the age of eighty-seven. Susannah Reid Pringle, his partner for forty-seven years, had died in 1831 at the age of sixty-three.[6] In his 1831 will and an undated codicil, Judge Pringle left Beneventum plantation and his house on Tradd Street to his three surviving sons, Edward, William, and Robert. Edward, his wife and two children died in 1838 aboard the steamer *Pulaski,* and his share passed to his surviving brothers. "In consideration of my love and affection for my son William Bull Pringle and his wife my amiable daughter in law Mary Pringle and their large family of pleasing and promising children," Judge Pringle devised his "plantation or villa called Runimede on Ashley River." He left his other plantations and 392 slaves to Robert, Emma, and William.

Inheriting two fortunes was one thing, but the high-living William Bull Pringle family of the 1840s found that maintaining and preserving them was quite another. The elegant and refined lifestyle they embraced reflected the Southern planter's dream, but when "the Joneses" were super-rich families like the Middletons and the Manigaults, keeping up was expensive.

When William Bull Pringle acquired his plantations they were in robust, working condition. It was the glory years of rice in Georgetown District. His challenge was not to clear new fields, but to continue the profitable operation of existing ones. To do so, he had to exercise good judgment in managing his extensive holdings. With his crops between 1850 and 1860 averaging one million pounds of rice each—among the largest in Georgetown District—the evidence suggests that William was a capable planter of at least average, if not above-average, ability.

During the 1850s, barrels of polished rice brought between 2.9 and 4.3 cents per pound, and the average selling price in 1859 was 3.2 cents.[7] If William Bull Pringle got this price for his

1859 crop of 1,015,000 pounds of rice, he would have grossed $32,480 for the year—a handsome sum, since his plantations were nearly self-sufficient. It is certain that he made a great deal of money, certainly well over his cost of production.

A substantial part of William's capital was invested in stocks. In 1836 he owned a 74.5 percent share in a diversified portfolio containing $15,700 worth of insurance stocks; an 1838 listing showed a 66.6 percent interest in $22,002 worth of Northern and Southern bank stocks. His financial portfolio, along with his position as one of the state's largest planters, helped gain him directorships on the boards of the Bank of Charleston, the State Bank of South Carolina[8] and the South Carolina Railroad. These powerful positions were competitive, not hereditary, and demanded high-level financial skills in addition to substantial investments of capital.

Yet by 1850 the family was slipping deeper into debt. Given their substantial income, the facts clearly indicate that they weren't earning too little—they were spending too much.

The Pringles shopped in the best stores of Charleston and New York, spent lavishly on Christmas presents, and enhanced their residence on King Street and their country estates at Beneventum and Runimede. They paid frequent visits to the country's most fashionable spas and helped form the nucleus of Newport's lively Southern Colony. "Only they very rich," wrote George Rogers, "could move so slowly and elegantly."[9]

With the hope of increasing his future income, William bought and leased more plantation land. Yet by the end of the 1840s, William and Mary's penchant for high living had produced financial strains. One clue that the family was in distress was that they could not afford to send Alston to Harvard or Motte to any university. Another appears in an 1846 letter from Mary to Susan Pringle, then still attending the Pelham Priory. Mary mentioned that William decided on short notice that they would attend a ball given in Charleston. "Our old gentleman promptly determined to go to Mrs. deS[aussure] this evening," Mary wrote. "But alas! I fear it will be with bare hands, for verily, the wedding gloves are too soiled now."[10] In better days, Mary would certainly have had an extra pair of gloves.

Late in 1840, just after he returned from Norfolk, where he had delivered Julius to start his career as a naval midshipman, William noted that he had been passing a "solitary, dreary time" at Beneventum, and continued, "For altho' I have been at all times fond of a country life with the family circle around me, yet there is no situation which can be one of choice to me when removed from that society."[11] He knew that such sacrifices were necessary in the life of any conscientious planter, but this aspect of planting did nothing to endear the planter's lifestyle to him.

At that time, in addition to Beneventum, William also planted at Rabbit Island,[12] which he rented from Mary's cousin, John Alston. In 1841 he wrote that his Youngville plantation was "too small for my force" and rented it to her brother Charles Alston. That year he also leased about 200 acres of uncleared land in Georgetown District.

Like Colonel Alston, William had important social and political connections and an active community life. In the 1830s he served as one of the senior managers of a "Fancy and Masquerade Ball." The gentlemen were required to remain masked until 11 P.M. To keep out the riffraff, the ball invitation stipulated that "Each gentleman previous to his admission to the Ball Room will be required to unmask to two of the managers, who shall not disclose the name of the party."[13]

In 1841 he was appointed one of the twelve commissioners of the Charleston Orphan House and remained active on that board for ten more years. Unlike some public offices, the commissioners of the Orphan House were directly involved in its daily operation. They met every Thursday afternoon to handle the institution's financial affairs, evaluate children prior to admission and discharge, and inspect homes and decide to which masters the children were to be indentured. After placement, the commissioners investigated the treatment of the children, and were also responsible for conducting religious services at the Orphan House.[14]

In February 1844 former president Martin Van Buren wrote to William, seeking to have his friend, James S. Wadsworth, a New York attorney and Democratic politician, introduced to Pringle's relative, Joel R. Poinsett, who had served in Van Buren's cabinet.

William served for many years as a vestryman for St. Michael's in the city and for St. Andrew's, located on the Ashley River Road between Charleston and Runimede. In 1861 he also was a member of the Society for the Relief of the Widows and Orphans of the Clergy of the Protestant Episcopal Church, to which he contributed ten dollars annually.[15]

An economic depression at the beginning in the 1840s may have curtailed some spending by planters. In 1842 William wrote that "I think Charleston will be more popular than it has been for some summers past—the great pressure for money keeping many at home who are in the habit of traveling."[16] But it did not stop the Pringles from spending money on art.

William Bull Pringle, late 1850s.

In adition to commissioning a number of miniature portraits and portrait copies by Charles Fraser, William Bull Pringle lavished money on an expensive portrait of his wife by one of high society's most fashionable painters: Thomas Sully. An American portraitist, Sully was born in England and was brought to Charleston in 1792. He was trained by his brothers as a miniaturist and was a friend of Charles Fraser, a specialist in miniatures. Sully ultimately settled in Philadelphia and painted about 2,000 portraits, all in a rich, romantic style.

Mary Pringle in the 1850s.

On the way back from New York in 1845, Mary and Mary Frances stopped in Philadelphia to see Sully. He portrayed Mary as a graceful, feminine woman with auburn hair and soft, brown eyes. A ferrotype photograph from the 1850s shows that she had pierced ears and wore drop earrings and stylish dresses.

During the summer of 1845 several members of the family visited White Sulphur Springs, Virginia, and Newport, Rhode Island. At Newport, Mary indulged in extensive holiday shopping, as evidenced by a letter she received from her niece, Sarah Middleton: "We received your very pretty and acceptable presents in due time, and thank you a thousand times for them. Helen is heard to repeat whenever she plumes herself in her new coat, 'how could Aunt Hess spend so much on us when she has so many of her own to provide for.'"[17]

Throughout the 1840s Mary was occupied with the responsibilities of running a large family. In the fall of 1845 she wrote to her daughter Susan:

> Notwithstanding my strong determination of writing to you regularly, I find it the most difficult matter possible to be punctual. Numberless claims on my time and attention are obtruded upon me at all hours, so that I seldom enjoy the privilege of being allowed to attend to one thing at a time, which I regret most when I am writing to you, because at such a time, I like to feel that I am communicating with you, and to be entirely absorbed by this pleasing idea. But

> alas! the vision vanishes when Charley calls upon me to teach him his lesson, then James rushes, with book in hand, and says, 'I'll say my lesson too'. Even before this hard task is over, a seamstress or a waiting-man comes up for orders or directions, or a neighbor sends a kind message, or a beggar makes a demand on my charity or a friend or visitor calls, and thus the *entire morning* is consumed, and half a page only written of my unfortunate letter.[18]

Mary did much of her writing in the evening. She wrote to Susan, "Now that all the little ones have gone to bed, I will devote a few quiet moments to you, more to satisfy your desire than to amuse you, for there is little variety in our everyday life. Was it not for your absence, I should feel as if I had been lingering here the whole summer."[19]

Correspondence was a major ingredient of the social glue which held the Pringle family so closely together. Part of the birthright of each Pringle child was the assurance that, whenever they left home for more than two or three days, Mary would write to them. Mary required reciprocity and wrote to her daughters, "You must write very frequently to us . . . and if you wish to hear often from me, as I give you fair notice that I will write only in answer to your letters."[20]

Her dutiful children were usually glad to do so. From San Francisco, Edward wrote his parents by every bi-weekly steamer, and while at Harvard, Charles wrote his family every week. This flow of mail from her loved ones was a source of joy to Mary, who commented to Mary Frances in 1853, "I have received your letters, so regularly, my dear daughter, that gratitude for them had become a part of my Sabbath's devotion."[21]

The women of the family were the chief letter-writers, but starting as early as age eight, both sons and daughters were expected to become regular correspondents with their far-flung relatives. By the age of nine, William Bull Pringle, Jr., was already producing coherent letters. In March 1842, in a large, disciplined hand, he wrote to Julius, "I think that I am now able to write a letter to you, which I have been long anxious to do, so will not wait until I improve more, as I am sure it will give you pleasure to receive a letter from me, however badly it may be written." In his two-page letter, the nine-year-old described his pastimes, his entry into Mr. Cotes's school and the visit of the former president, Mr. Van Buren.[22]

By their early teens, Mary's children were expected to write full-fledged, adult letters. Mistakes, though rare, were immediately corrected in a firm and loving manner. In 1860 Mary wrote to Charles, "James [then age seventeen] is . . . afflicting me more by his continual complaints of my rebukes for his careless writing. I will meekly endure the pain of having made him unhappy by my reproaches, so long as I see the beautiful effects of my corrections in his letters, which are now really admirable. You must not let my criticisms constrain your style, my dear sons, but let them only make you careful to avoid carelessness."[23]

In 1845 Mary wrote to Susan at Pelham Priory, "I am impatient to tell you how entirely satisfied your Papa and I were with [your last letter], notwithstanding its many little interlineations, which were accounted for by the hurry in which you wrote, its grammar and orthography were correct and its sentiment, ah, here it was that your father and mother exclaimed, 'our child will fulfill our hopes, and in God's own good time, we will be compensated for the present pain of separation.'"[24]

In style, the Pringle family letters were warm, intimate, newsy, well-organized, literate, articulate, and somewhat formal. Mary advised her children to avoid familiarity in their letter-writing, noting that it would "mislead you into a negligent and slovenly habit of writing," which would make it appear that they couldn't write a proper letter or that they held the person to whom they were writing in contempt.

The letters between Mary and her daughters and between the daughters themselves spoke chiefly of friends and family and seldom of business, planting, politics, or government. They were filled with social gossip, domestic issues, and health concerns: who was visiting whom or planning trips, who was courting whom, who had married whom, who was ill, and who was recovering. A comment made by Mary Frances, then living in New Haven, to her sister was typical: "Please Beck write a long letter, full of gossip and all about the different children and babies."[25]

The letters between Mary and her sons were entirely different in tone and content, for her sons treated their mother as their intellectual equal. They asked for and generally heeded her advice, In addition to family news, they discussed with her (as with their father) all their important career, financial, and personal questions. The daughters usually wrote to William only in care of both parents, and then talked solely about family matters.

Mary's generation still occasionally used British spellings, such as colour and parlour, but actual spelling mistakes were rare, even among the young children. Mary wrote with a neat, orderly, and open hand, and passed on her meticulous orthography to all her children. Each line looked as if it had been written with the aid of a ruler. Her husband's untutored hand was a different case altogether. Rough, jagged and almost palsied, it is nearly as hard to read as the Gothic-looking, German Fraktur script of the late nineteenth century. Susan and Mary

Married on the 31st of May 1853, by the Revd. P. T. Keith, Donald G. Mitchell to Mary F. Pringle —

Mary's handwriting in the 1850s.

Richfield 29th Decr '61
Mrs D. G. Mitchell
My dear dear daughter
Let me entreat you let me ap=
peal to that strength of mind
by which you have been endow=

William's handwriting in 1861.

Frances wrote with a hand which was nearly identical to their mother's, and all her boys wrote with a similar—if bolder—script. Rebecca wrote in an open, feminine hand, but fell into the habit of starting sentences with lower-case letters.

Donald G. Mitchell greatly admired his mother-in-law's handwriting. In 1880 he wrote to his daughter, Hesse, "your grandmother's hand is a beautiful one and you can do no better than to make make it your model."[26] Although Mary set the standard for the fineness of her hand and was responsible for shaping the literary style of the family, she was also the most idiosyncratic writer of them all. She capitalized nouns at random, used commas every time she inked her pen, and generally preferred terminal dashes to periods. She recognized that these were her own peculiarities of expression and, mercifully, did not pass them on to her children.

One trait which she did pass on was her ability to paint evocative word pictures. An example may be found in an 1853 letter she wrote to Mary Mitchell, then in Europe with her husband. "I have passed a moment to think how easily you could imagine our domestic circle, so little has it changed, except in numbers. The old clock has just struck eight—the gas light bums brightly in the back piazza. Charles and James are already in bed. Rebecca preparing for hers. Brewton and Robert at their studies. Your Papa stretched upon the sofa, in a comfortable nap—and I seize upon the quiet moment to fill a sheet to you."[27]

Mary devoted much of her energy to the careful, detailed, and methodical instruction of her children. She inculcated them with the Christian and social values they would need when they assumed their roles in upper-class plantation society. They included the importance of being responsible and loving members of a close-knit family. Kinship, family ties and duties were an integral part of Mary's world. Each family member was expected to work together for the common good and demonstrate genuine affection for each other. Her grandson, Stephen Duncan Pringle, said of her, "Grandma kept all the family together as a box keeps the spokes of a wheel."[28] The result was a large, extended family of members totally devoted to each other and who demonstrated their affection at every opportunity.

While Mary guided the children through their lessons each day, William footed the bill for tutors, private instructors and college educations. He also presented her with the Rev. William Barrow's *Essays on Education* for inspiration and instruction.[29]

Mary wanted her children educated in the classic sense. The college-educated planter class felt that a knowledge of the Greek and Roman classics was an "essential ingredient of a liberal education. . . . A classical education, as defined by its champions, lifted a person above sordid desires and purely material motives and filled him with an appreciation of the highest values life could offer."[30]

The social conventions of the early nineteenth century determined how the Pringle children were reared. Their sons were educated to lead, earn, and provide. They were expected to gain a university education, choose socially acceptable careers, marry, and become self-sufficient heads of families.

The daughters had to be content to master the "womanly arts" and wait for a good husband to come along, or resign themselves—as did Susan Pringle—to the inferior status of spinsterhood. At Mary's knee they were instructed in the domestic arts: sewing, knitting, embroidery, the efficient organization of the household, and the proper management of servants. From their tutors, they learned dancing, painting, music, French, and Italian: subjects which would add to their social polish and make them suitable ornaments of their husbands' lives.

Her correspondence with her sons reflected the prevailing attitudes that women were supposed to be such ornaments. After recounting the news of the engagement of William Smith to Miss Eliza Huger, Mary commented to Julius about the bride-to-be: "She is, I think, quite a lovely girl, accomplished, with very good manners, without great beauty, but one of the sweetest faces (owing to a very pretty mouth and perfectly beautiful teeth,) that I have almost ever seen – her temper, they say, is charming. The families on both sides, are much pleased at the engagement."[31]

The social graces she wished her sons to master included ballroom dancing, of which she approved—to an extent. When her boys were studying in Europe, she wrote to them,

> I am glad to hear of you taking dancing lessons, not that I am ambitious of seeing you caper in a ball-room (which is, I think, one of the most ridiculous situations in which a man can place himself) but rather that I should see you move with grace and ease as well when you walk in a dance, the elements of which, I think, consists in graceful ease and dignity, accurate attention to the time of the music and a knowledge and proper degree of attention to the figure of dancing. . . . I shall feel proud and happy not only of hearing that you are men of brilliant parts and great accomplishments—but some little pride, also, in having you remarked as elegant and polished gentlemen. True an empty head with a fine coat is a very contemptible thing, but a nice coat does not in the least detract, and need not interfere with, a well-stocked head. Neatness and attention to dress gives as

> little trouble and consumes as little time as would be required to arrange an awkward, or a shabby suit of clothes.[32]

Although she felt that dancing played a proper role in the life of her sons, she warned them against dallying with the "idle pleasures of a card table" or the "degrading pleasures of a wine party."

In the winter, when the Santee planters were living on their plantations, the educational options for white children consisted of home schooling by their parents, having a tutor, or attending one of several widely scattered country schools. In the first half of the nineteenth century, the Santee region generally had between one and three public schools in operation. A resident wrote, "The schools before 1860 were so moved about, especially in the upper part of the Parish, for convenience of pupils, that it is almost impossible to keep track of [their] location."[33] The Seashore School, near McClellanville, was the largest of the group, with thirty pupils in 1861.

The public "free schools" in the parishes and in Charleston provided primary education for the children of the smaller planters and their overseers. Families who could afford to do so were expected to pay for the schooling of their children, but these schools did not attract the sons and daughters of the planter elite, who were schooled at home and as they came of age, enrolled in private schools, colleges, and universities. In the late 1830s Charleston had five free schools educating 558 students on the peninsula, but the Pringle children were not among them.[34]

After the Pringle boys reached their eighth year, the job of providing them with a good primary education fell to Christopher Cotes. He was a dyspeptic, one-eyed Englishman who ran a highly-celebrated private school on Wentworth Street in Charleston from about 1820 to 1850. There they studied Greek, Latin, rhetoric, mathematics, history and geography. In 1842, William Pringle, then nine years old, wrote to his elder brother, Julius, "I am now a scholar of Mr. Cotes's. Mama still teaches

Brewton [age seven]. Robert [age five] has not yet made a beginning with books."[35]

Cotes "seems at an early day to have gained the confidence of the community, and the boys who were placed under his charge were principally the sons of well-to-do parents; so that it was generally considered that Mr. Cotes only received as scholars those whose families were socially and financially prominent."[36] Although Cotes had not received a university education, he was felt to be "perfectly competent as a teacher of the classics and mathematics, in consequence of his thorough training in an English school." His background suited the fathers of his pupils, many of whom had also been educated in England, where the school system was perceived as being "in every respect the best."[37] In 1842 Mary wrote, "His school has now increased to nearly a hundred scholars. He still employs both of the Lesesnes and another usher."[38]

Unlike some of his marginally trained contemporaries, Christopher Cotes was no small-town, backwater schoolteacher. The academic achievement of his graduates demonstrates that he operated a world-class preparatory school. The admiration for Cotes and his work was not limited to the gentry who paid him one hundred dollars per year to educate their sons. His scholars distinguished themselves not only at South Carolina's colleges but at Princeton, Harvard, Yale, and Oxford, where administrators also held Cotes in high esteem.

The Pringle, Alston, and Hayne boys in the city were driven to school in what was perhaps Charleston's first school bus: a mule-drawn covered wagon with seats at the side, which William Alston had built for this purpose. Jacob Motte Alston noted that the "Haynes and the Pringles had very ambitious parents who made their sons study all the afternoons and recite their lessons to their fathers, who were very jealous of their sons' standing at school."[39]

The Pringle boys were among the finest products of the Cotes school. In August 1842 William Bull Pringle accompanied his son Edward to Cambridge to take Harvard's entrance examinations. If he passed the tests, a boy could enter either the freshman or sophomore class. From Cambridge, William wrote back to the anxious family that Edward had passed the sophomore exams "with *great credit* to himself and his Instructor [Cotes], whose name was inquired." The examiner went on to say that Edward was "the best-instructed boy he had ever seen prepared out[-side] of New England."[40] This was the highest praise a Yankee was capable of paying a non-Yankee. Three years later, Edward graduated third in his class at Harvard.

Of the nine Pringle boys, eight attended college. Only Motte appears to have gone directly into business. Alston attended South Carolina College in Columbia and graduated in 1841, after extensive cramming all summer. Julius, another Cotes scholar, was offered admission to The Temple, but entered the U.S. Navy instead. Robert was studying at South Carolina College in 1853; William, Jr., graduated with high merit in 1852 and Brewton in 1856. Charles attended Harvard for one year before leaving to study in France and Germany, where he was joined by his younger brother in 1859. James studied in Paris and lived with his Uncle Robert in 1859, then went to Dijon and Germany with Charles before the war interrupted their studies.

Cotes and the Pringle family were on intimate terms, and he was often their dinner guest at King Street. "Old Christy," as he was called by some of his charges, was also a frequent guest on the Alston plantations on the Waccamaw and the Santee.[41] Cotes named William Bull Pringle a co-executor of his will and trustee of his estate. In 1850 his health failed, and he was forced to give up his teaching and return to England. He died in 1855. As a token of his esteem, he bequeathed William Bull Pringle a mourning ring.[42]

In addition to Mary's instruction, the Pringle children received part of their early education from a tutor in one of the south basement rooms. A cousin, Miss Kate Ravenel, recalled that she rose each school day at six o'clock, walked to the King Street house to join her fellow scholars, and received instruction until eight o'clock.[43]

Of all the private instructors Mary hired to educate her daughters, the names of six have survived: five from Charleston and one from Pelham, New York. In 1845 and 1846 Susan spent a year at the Pelham Priory, the Rev. Robert Bolton's exclusive school for young Southern women. In Charleston, a Mr. Raslam was a tutor for Susan and Mary Frances. Their mother said of him, "You must both now feel the advantage of Mr. Raslam's having exacted the duty of writing letters daily from you the last summer, altho' you did so bitterly complain of him for it. In time you will acknowledge his judicious instruction in many other respects, I trust."[44]

William Searle,[45] an old Englishman who succeeded Christopher Cotes,[46] taught Mary Frances as a general tutor and language instructor in 1846. Mary wrote to Susan of him, "[Mary Frances] has, at last, recommenced her studies, under Mr. Searles, who, I must tell you, is exceedingly ambitious of Mary's being as advanced, under his tuition, as you are at the Priory. He has begged to be allowed to teach her Italian, which I have willingly consented to. Mary is well pleased at these semi-weekly visits to town, as she is so solitary without your companionship that she considers any change agreeable."[47] Mr. Searle also instructed Charles before he entered Harvard.

In 1841 one of their French instructors was Joseph Henry Guenebault.[48] Several of their aunts also tutored them in French, notably Fanny Hayne, wife of Robert Y. Hayne, and Susannah (Pringle) Smith, of whom Mary wrote, "Your Aunt said that it would give her pleasure to improve you in French if you attended to her instructions with cheerfulness and alacrity."[49]

The daughters took dancing lessons from Mr. A. Boneaud and Mr. H. P. Feugas.[50] Of these instructors, Mary wrote to a son in 1841, "Your sisters . . . are also taking dancing lessons with a very excellent teacher, Mr. Boneaud, whose skill and painstaking, make us regret all of the cash that we have thrown away upon Mr. Feugas."[51]

Mary was arguably one of the best-read women in the nation and well qualified to be her children's teacher. Although denied a college education due to her gender, she made good use of the Alston family tutors, her articulate, well-read, well-educated and well-traveled relatives, and the splendid Pringle family library. She was a voracious, critical reader who not only read but analyzed hundreds of serious classical and contemporary books. She commented extensively on them in a series of personal journals she kept and avidly discussed them in letters to her children.

Her reading tastes were as wide as they were deep. She read far more history, politics, biography, philosophy, theology, and metaphysics than novels and poetry. Her taste for classical authors included translations of and commentaries on Plutarch, Cicero and Homer. Her British and European favorites included Bacon, Rousseau, Locke, Bulwer-Lytton, Walpole, Coleridge, Shakespeare, and Shelley. Among American authors, she favored Hawthorne and Cooper, as well as Charleston native sons Hugh Swinton Legaré and William Gilmore Simms.

The 1839 inventory of Col. William Alston's personal property showed a library of 250 books at Fairfield, his country seat, but failed to list his large library in the Miles Brewton house. Colonel Alston's will directed that his library be divided between his sons Thomas and Charles,[52] so William and Mary had to build their own book collection. Between 1839 and 1861, the Pringles assembled what may have been the city's largest personal library. Most of the books survived the war, but by the end of the century, when the family's only breadwinner was Alston Pringle, over five thousand volumes were offered for sale. In the summer of 1895 Alston had a pamphlet printed for Northern book dealers which listed the most valuable books, thus giving us a partial inventory of what the Pringle family library contained. He also arranged for the sale of Judge John Julius Pringle's law library for $100. Alston felt it necessary to try to sell the family's letters from George Washington and Thomas Jefferson. His sister Susan would not permit this and purchased the historic letters for herself.[53]

About two-thirds of the eight hundred titles listed for sale concerned religion, including Bible commentaries, collections of sermons, religious history and biography, inspirational, and devotional works. Although the collection reflected a strong Protestant orthodoxy, there were also works in a much more esoteric vein, including volumes on Buddhist, Hindu, Islamic, Mormon, and mystical thought, as well as others concerning Spiritualism, metaphysics, life after death and the revelations of Emanuel Swedenborg, the renowned eighteenth-century Swedish mystic and psychic.

The remaining third of the library was heavily oriented to British works, and virtually all the volumes in the catalog were listed as being published in London, Cambridge, Oxford or Edinburgh. The Pringles' classical tastes were reflected in their volumes on ancient history, Greek and Roman philosophy. There were books on English history, economics and government; English poetry and prose; American history and biography (chiefly of the Revolutionary period); and many South Carolina favorites, including William Gilmore Simms' Revolutionary War novels, Hugh Swinton Legaré's writings, and Frederick Dalcho's *History of the Protestant Episcopal Church.*

The sale brochure listed a few volumes in French, a bit of European history, several volumes on medicine and natural history, but little fiction. It is dangerous to assume that the Pringles had lesser interests in these subjects, for our knowledge of their library is chiefly from a list of what they were willing to sell, not what they kept.

Inscriptions in their surviving books show that the children each had their favorite authors and subjects.[54] Like her mother, Rebecca cherished religious and devotional works. Susan enjoyed the poetry of Elizabeth Barrett Browning, novels by Longfellow and Nathaniel Hawthorne, and was particularly interested in the works of John Ruskin, a dominant tastemaker among intellectuals of the Victorian age. She owned three of his books on architecture and painting. Alston favored Bulwer-Lytton, Byron, and Dickens; Julius preferred history and the poetry of William Cowper. The extensive Pringle library included the four-volume *Bibliographical Manual of English Literature,* a sophisticated reference tool usually found only in professionally cataloged libraries.[55]

Mary used imagination to intrigue her children and pique their interest in learning. After writing to college students Charles and James about the relative merits of Spartan and Athenian societies, she stated, "I will make no more remarks on these subjects, thinking that I have said enough to excite your curiosity without destroying the interest that you will feel when reading, by having communicated too much."[56] She also told them that they might schedule their study time with better efficiency. "Your arrangements with regard to your studies are very judicious," she wrote. "I would only make one alteration; you say nothing about rising early in the morning, now I would recommend that you should retire to bed at an earlier hour than the one you have fixed and to arise proportionately early in the morning. Let the sun find you prepared for your studies; this season is particularly suited to application after the mind has been refreshed by sleep and before it has been fatigued by previous employment, or occupied by pleasure."[57]

Although Mary's educational standards were rigorous, they were neither unreasonable nor unachievable. Her children were challenged to excel, but not expected to perform above their capabilities. She commended them when they did well and corrected them when they fell short or made mistakes—but all discipline was done gently and with a loving hand.

When it came to learning about foreign cultures, the Pringles weren't restricted to books. They also had the intellectual and social resources of a rich and sophisticated extended family to learn from. Their uncle, Robert Pringle, made his home in Paris, where he kept an elegant apartment and was a fashionable member of Parisian society. They could also learn from their distinguished relative, Joel R. Poinsett, after whom the exotic poinsettia was named, and read the vivid, first-hand accounts which he sent back to Charleston from half a lifetime of travels through Mexico, Chile, Argentina, Europe, eastern Asia, and the steppes of Russia.[58]

As they grew older, almost half of the Pringle children had the opportunities to travel in Europe themselves, as did many of their friends. There they could acquaint themselves with art treasures and antiquities of the modern and ancient worlds and visit, as Edward did, the House of Lords and dine with the likes of Thomas Carlyle, Charles Dickens, and Ralph Waldo Emerson.

Their travels to high-society watering holes such as Sarasota Springs and Newport gave the Pringles the opportunity to rub elbows not only with New England socialites, but also with intellectuals like Donald G. Mitchell, the young author who would later wed their daughter, Mary Frances, and his learned friend, Professor Charles Eliot Norton.

Their patronage of the best local, national, and continental artists gave them a first-hand knowledge of art, which were augmented with visits to the Louvre and other European museums. In all, the Pringle children were not only intellectually but also culturally literate on an international scale.

Mary's letters to her children during the 1840s and 1850s were almost entirely tutorial in nature, with scarcely a mention of what was going on back at home. She wanted to improve them, rather than give them "professions of love," of which, she thought, they had sufficient proof. Her greatest anxiety, she told them repeatedly, was to advance their learning.

When the boys went off to college, or, in Julius's case, to sea, Mary regularly sent them stacks of books to read. Her comments make clear that she had already read and analyzed all of the books before they were shipped. To Julius in 1842, she wrote, "Your Papa shipped a box, a few days since, to Baltimore, to be sent from there, by the first opportunity to Rio, it contains the Encyclopaedia of Geography, sent to you by your Grand Papa—Southey's Life of Nelson and Napier's Peninsula War, sent by your Papa and myself, and Cooper's last novel, 'The two Admirals,' sent by your brother Alston. We were much tempted to put more, in the box, each member of the family, being anxious to slip in some little memento, but as there is so much uncertainty about you ever receiving them, we thought the expenditure, in books, quite large enough to be jeopardized, at one time."[59]

About 1859, Mary wrote Charles and James, "In your last package of books you will find 'The History of the Expedition to Russia', undertaken by the Emperor Napoleon, in the year 1812, by Gen. Count Philip de Segur.[60] My beloved boys . . . it appears rather incongruous that I should fly from ancient to modern . . . but as I have just finished Griscom's 'Tour in Europe,'[61] I cannot take a better opportunity of recommending it to you. He, at all events deserves the reputation of a liberal and intelligent traveler, who has let nothing escape his observation that was worthy of the attention of the benevolent and enlightened philanthropist."[62]

One of her most-quoted sources for the conduct of life was the letters of Philip Dormer Stanhope, the Earl of Chesterfield, whose mastery of the social arts was the model for social deportment in London and elsewhere for a century after his death. His lifelong mission was to lift his illegitimate son "upon a pedestal so high that his lowly origin should not betray itself." Stanhope sought to give his son's socially inferior blood a "true blue hue by concentrating upon him all the externals of an aristocratic education."[63]

To one of her sons at college, Mary wrote, "I placed among your collection of books, Lord Chesterfield's letters to his son, which I would not only advise you to read once but many times. I look upon them as the most valuable books that can be placed in the hands of youth—it takes in every stage of education, conveying the important and interesting information in the most concise and entertaining style. He not only makes you wish to learn but puts you in the way of understanding whatever you attempt to learn. He gives the most important rules to be a man of learning and the most useful ones to be a gentleman of fashion—clearly proving that these two characters are not incompatible. To be all that I wish, you must take the precepts of Chesterfield for your example."[64]

By the time that Mary, Mr. Cotes, and assorted tutors were through with them, the Pringle boys had received an intensive, liberal education which included a thorough understanding of classical literature, a working knowledge of Greek and Latin; fluency in French, German or both; a grounding in ancient and modern history and world geography, a broad exposure to the visual arts; a wide familiarity with European and American literature; and a fine command of spoken English and English composition. On paper or in person, any Pringle boy of eighteen was fully prepared to hold his own in business or polite society or enter the finest universities in the world—which is exactly what their parents and teachers expected of them. By the time the last of the boys came home from college in 1861, the William Bull Pringle family easily ranked among the best-educated in the nation. To their great credit, none of the Pringles ever labored under the delusion that the world owed them a living.

Living a life devoted to God and raising an orthodox Christian family were central tenets of Mary's world. She felt that religion was as indispensable to one's moral life as the lungs and blood in her body. Every morning before breakfast, she held family prayers; every evening she did the same.[65] Alone, she prayed fervently and frequently for the welfare of her family and for strength to cope with the burdens of her life.

In a personal journal kept from the time of her marriage until hear death, Mary recorded her personal supplications to the Deity for help. She prayed during her pregnancies, when birth was near, in thanks for successful births, and in celebration of the children's birthdays. She prayed for God to keep them safe during their absence, their studies and their voyages, and prayed again in gratitude when they returned. She prayed when they got married; prayed that they stayed healthy, and when they were sick, prayed for their recovery. If the problem was serious but not deadly, she gave thanks for God's mercy, and if the worst came to pass, she prayed for their souls and for the insight to understand God's will in the midst of tragedy. She prayed for her marriage and for her husband and children when they disappointed and hurt her.

In concert with her times she held the Calvinistic conviction that she was a deep sinner, and often prayed for God's forgiveness.[66] She asked God for everything He could offer he in the way of help, but she never chastised Him for failing to grant her prayers. Indeed, whatever the result of her prayers, she always gave God all the credit—but never any blame. An 1862 prayer was typical. When her son, Brewton, was wounded during the Civil War, she wrote, "I thank thee, O most merciful God, for Thy protecting care, which as a mighty shield saved his life when frightful missiles of death entered his flesh," conspicuously overlooking the fact that God had not granted her frequent prayers to spare him from all harm in the first place.[67]

Although she was passionate in her religious convictions, Mary was no zealot. As deep as was her belief, she never condemned those to whom religion was not as central to their lives as it was to hers.

In the practice of religion, the Pringles were extremely conservative. They belonged to the Protestant Episcopal church and when in Charleston, attended St. Michael's, whose tall white spire rises majestically over the Four Corners of Law at the intersection of Meeting and Broad Streets. Finished in 1761, St. Michael's shared with its venerable parent, St. Philip's, the distinction of being the spiritual home for Charleston's richest and most influential families. William's father, John Julius Pringle, was a founding member of St. Michael's, and purchased pew No. 29. In 1832 Col. William Alston purchased pew No. 2 in the middle aisle on the north side of the church. Judge Edward Frost had the square pew in the northeast corner of the middle aisle, and three generations of Pringles and Frosts subsequently worshipped there.[68]

Had the Pringles chosen to draw upon their Presbyterian roots, they might have joined the First (Scots) Presbyterian

Meeting Street and St. Michael's Church.

Church, a block closer to their home. While not the bastion of wealthy planters as was St. Michael's, it was nonetheless a socially acceptable place for an upper-class family to worship.

The Pringles did not derive their religious beliefs from comparative study or direct experience. As with their house, plantations, slaves, and silver plate, their beliefs were also inherited. To paraphrase the psychologist, William James, their religion was made for them by others; communicated to them by tradition; learned by rote; confined to fixed, orderly forms; retained by habit; preached exclusively by men, and practiced chiefly by women.[69]

The calcified views of his congregants and their obsession with precedent rather than content made a deep impression on the Rev. Paul Trapier, who assumed the pulpit of St. Michael's in 1840. "I had taken charge of a congregation made up in large part of old families, priding themselves upon ancestry and attached to the church rather because of their fathers had been there rather than from enlightened acquaintance with its principles," he wrote, "and consequently bent upon going on as those before them had gone, whether there was reason for doing so or not. It was enough for them that so far back as they could remember, or as their fathers had told them, such had been the usage in St. Michael's Church. To this they would adhere though it were in itself the merest trifle."[70]

The Pringles had the intellect and resources to explore and choose from a wide range of theological options. From their own home library they could have drawn upon books on the Islamic, Hindu, Buddhist, and Jewish faiths. But the Pringles disdained Jews and probably viewed the Eastern faiths not as credible religions but as heathen cultural oddities. Given Mary's Alston lineage, their place in society, and Charleston's monolithic Christian orthodoxy, the family's choice of the Protestant Episcopal church was preordained, and it is unlikely that they ever questioned it.

Then, as now, the motive for attending public worship service included social display as well as spiritual yearning. At St. Michael's, "the church members who owned carriages generally made use of them for attending the services, but there were of course a good many who walked, and it was not uncommon to see a lady going to church followed by a negro boy carrying her prayer book; and as the churches were not heated, an old lady would occasionally be seen followed by a boy carrying a warm brick for her use."[71]

The worship services at St. Michael's were highly structured and, save for the sermon, were read verbatim from the 1789 *Book of Common Prayer*. Singing and voice responses were all printed and prescribed; no part of the service provided for emotional or spontaneous response. Within the denomination, as within the rest of society, power was exercised almost exclusively by men, and from the top down. At St. Michael's, the gospel was preached by several highly educated and socially polished divines, including the Rt. Rev. Nathaniel Bowen, the Rev. Paul Trapier, and the Rev. Paul Trapier Keith, who served until 1861. The bishop of the Diocese of South Carolina (who was as often as not the rector of St. Michael's) appointed and supervised the priests. The congregation elected only male wardens and vestrymen to supervise the parish's temporal affairs.

While Mary's church affiliation may have been preordained by her family's social position, her personal relationship with God was passionate, and sprang not only from her roots but also from her heart. Her letters and journals are filled with examples of her search for God's guidance, protection, and consolation for herself and her family. She regularly conducted family Bible study lessons in her home, and many of her like-minded women friends were invited to attend. Sarah Russell Dehon, daughter of Bishop Theodore Dehon and wife of the Rev. Paul Trapier, was one of them.[72]

There was a pretense in Southern society that men were religious. In reality, they rarely made time for it. Although William Bull Pringle served on the vestry of both St. Michael's in Charleston and St. Andrew's near Runimede, he showed little personal interest in religion. His vestry service was motivated by tradition and public spirit rather than by spiritual quest, and he appears to have attended church only for vestry meetings, public holidays, and the baptism of his children.

While staying at Runimede, the Pringles attended St. Andrew's parish church. Services there were held only from November through May, as all the major planters spent their summers in their city homes or at favorite resorts.[73]

While staying on their Georgetown District rice plantations the family had the option of attending several Episcopal churches and chapels: Prince George, Winyah, in Georgetown; St. James, Santee; and four plantation chapels in All Saints parish, Waccamaw.[74] The Pringle plantations were not near any of these churches, however, and the family probably held their own private services at Richfield and Beneventum during much of the winter.

The Rev. Alexander J. Glennie, rector of All Saints, was a close friend of the family. They occasionally attended his services on the Waccamaw peninsula. Glennie, an Englishman, was a strong proponent of catechizing the slaves and encouraged the planters to build chapels on their plantations for this purpose. Despite their large slave holdings and Mary's commitment to the religious education of her slaves, there is no record that the Pringles built chapels on any of their plantations.

As a devout churchwoman, Mary gave her children the *Book of Common Prayer* upon their confirmations, Bibles when they married, and inspirational and devotional books on birthdays and at Christmas. Shortly after their birth, each of the Pringle children were taken to St. Michael's to be baptized.

Reverend Trapier noted that many people regarded the rite of confirmation as superfluous and "meant only for children."[75] Mary ensured that her daughters were confirmed and hoped that her sons would someday follow suit. Despite her strong influence, few of the boys knelt before the bishop. Mary's letters are full of references to attending church services with her daughters and female friends—and the fervent hope that her sons would someday formally embrace the church.

Episcopalian confirmation normally takes place in the teen years after the child has matured sufficiently to make a responsible, informed decision. When James was fifteen and Mary was visiting New Haven, she wrote to him, "Let me take this opportunity, too, of suggesting to you what I have thought of many times, as I have watched over you, in our dear old pew in church—that it is time for you to consider your religious obligation to be confirmed. I would not hurry you thoughtlessly into this sacred duty, but I would only remind you that under God's grace, there is no surer means of preserving religious impressions than by strict compliance with the ceremonial observances of our church, for every new obligation is a means and method of drawing us nearer to God; if we do so with an earnest desire to merit God's favor and help. Your own serious thought on the subject will be the best preparation that you can have and your brother Alston will, I know, most willingly lend you any external help that you may require. To show me that you have taken, in proper spirit, what I have written, you must write to me *again and again*."[76] Mary was thrilled when, one year later, James took his vow of confirmation.[77]

Other of her sons reflected the attitude toward religion described by Edward's Harvard classmate, Charles Eliot Norton, while visiting the Middletons on Edisto Island in 1855. "It seems to me sometimes as if only the women here read the New Testament, and as if the men regarded Christianity rather as a gentlemanly accomplishment than as anything more serious, —as if they felt confidant that they had secured seats in the coupé of the diligence that runs to the next world, and had their passports properly viséd for St. Peter."[78]

CHAPTER SIX

Anything But Planting

"We are the first working generation after Grand papa and we shall be proud or mortified if we sustain or lose the reputation his intellect has established."

—Alston to Julius, 1842

Mary took great pride in her role as mother of a large family and proudly wrote to Julius about his newest brother, Charles, "The young one is a fortnight old today and I am walking about my chamber and recovering my strength as rapidly as I can expect. . . . I have written, lying on the sofa and resting on my elbow, as I was anxious to let you know, under my own hand, how well I am, and to boast of being the Mother of twelve fine promising children, to whom I look for all [of my] corporal happiness."[1]

As fond as she was of her children, Mary did not gush over them, nor did she hold any exaggerated notions about their beauty. Two weeks after James, the last child, was born in 1842, Mary wrote to Julius:

> I am still confined to the sofa, and write in a recumbant position, altho' I am, as well, as I can expect to be, and our little stranger, is a well-formed, strong and active fellow, with prominent and good features. Like all his predecessors, he has no claim to infant beauty, but may calculate on future comeliness. He is not particularly like any one member of the family, but bears a strong family likeness, to the whole brood of new born Pringles, altho' he is smaller than his brothers were at his age."[2]

By January 1842 Julius had been away from home for over a year, and Mary described the children to him:

> Your sister has left me so large a portion of her sheet to fill up, that it strikes me that as a twelvemonth has passed since you have been away from home, that you should like to know how the young folks have grown and improved during that time.
>
> I cannot boast of Motte's [age fifteen] growth. It has been very little, I fear. He has become stouter and has the same pretty face and beautiful teeth. Susan [thirteen], too, has grown very little. Her face has improved very much, and her complexion, now clear and healthy. She learns with great facility and has, I flatter myself, an excellent capacity.
>
> Mary [eleven] is tall, being taller than Sue, and much improved in appearance. She is very pretty, with a beautiful complexion and fine teeth. She promises to be quite handsome. She has no taste for literature, but is clever in all female occupations, sewing, knitting, etc. William [nine] is very small for his age. We all think him a very ugly fellow, but his Aunt Wm. Smith and his Aunt Brewton say that he is the best looking of the family, in which opinion Will perfectly agrees, and makes no scruple in saying so. He has very fine teeth and is quite clever, I think, remarkably so.
>
> Brewton [seven] is a great big fellow, larger in every respect, than William. No genius, but very good, with the same pretty face that you left him with. Robert [five] is a facsimile, in figure, of his Grandpapa Pringle, and to set off his ridiculous figure, we have put him in a suit of woolen jacket and pantaloons, his red cheeks are fatter than ever and is a most mischievous, perverse creature, going about, doing nothing but mischief all day long.
>
> Elizabeth and Rebecca [three] are two of the most engaging little things you ever saw. Much improved in appearance—great talkers—most amusing little monkeys. Our Charley [one] is a counterpart of Robert, who has taken him under his particular patronage, calls him his son and has been excessively fond of him from his birth. He is an outrageous creature, self willed and conceited for a youth of one year of age. He is very large and strong. Thus have I got

through the eleven, and often picture to myself our absent twelfth.[3]

The large and growing size of the family put pressure on each member to contribute. At the age of fifteen, young Motte acknowledged that for his generation, at least, the good life had a price: hard work. In 1842 he wrote to Julius after the birth of James, "Our family was already so large that the addition of one cannot convince us more forcibly of the necessity of our exertions to support ourselves but we should recollect that all large families convey an impression of weight and respectability . . . ."[4] As the Pringle children matured, they became personalities in their own right.

Alston

Of all the Pringle boys, Alston, the eldest, was the least enamored of plantation life. In 1841 Mary wrote to Julius, "the attractions of Beneventum are thrown away on master Alston, who has no skill or taste for country sports, you know, so he complains of the many little inconveniences, which we think more than compensated for, by fresh air and field sports. . . . His only game has been a few domestic birds, after which he toils morning, noon and evening. Master Willy has already learnt the secret that 'brother cannot shoot.' In truth, dear boy, our table is very scantily supplied, now that you are away."[5]

Alston was the first of the children to leave the King Street nest for college. He enrolled in the South Carolina College at Columbia in 1841. By then the college had overcome its former image as a poorly staffed, under-equipped school and had achieved high regard throughout the South for its large library, the intellectual excellence of its faculty, and the rigor of its entrance examinations. As early as 1827 scholars wishing to be admitted into the freshman class had to write and spell well, possess an accurate knowledge of English, be able to translate Caesar's *Commentaries* and Virgil's *Aenid* from Latin, and from Greek, the four evangelists and the Acts of the Apostles. The applicant also had to have a working knowledge of arithmetic.

The students were the sons of South Carolina planter and merchant elite, and although generally well prepared academically, they had a reputation of being rowdy, lax in their studies, and a plague to their instructors. Its academic reputation notwithstanding, the college was criticized for its location, as Columbia was considered to be unhealthy and "illy supplied with provisions." Worse, it was considered to be a hotbed of infidelity because of an annual series of lectures given by Dr. Thomas Cooper which questioned the authorship and theological soundness of the Pentateuch. Cooper was forced out in 1834, and by the 1840s, enrollment was climbing again.[6]

Alston did not always apply himself to his studies. In April 1841 Mary wrote to Julius, "Your brother Alston . . . has determined to study very hard now, and appears to think that he has allowed too much time to slip away unimproved. He has, indeed, much to do, as he is to graduate, you know, next December."[7]

Alston evidently turned a few heads among the ladies of Columbia, for Julius wrote him that "the time is now fast approaching when you will bid adieu to College and Columbia, not forgetting the *fair dames*, with so many of whom you used, at different times, to be captivated."[8]

In July Alston wrote Julius that their father had declared that lost study time must be made up. "Papa seems disposed (as I am myself) to make me a hard student this summer," he wrote. "He applied to old King for a course of reading for me and the old lawyer, either thro' vanity to give one an idea how much he did when young, or that he had a design against my health, wrote an eight paged letter and recommended as many books for the summer as would be a library for any reasonable man."[9] "Old King" was Judge Mitchell King, a respected Scot and a founder of Charleston's Conversation Club. The group had among its members most of the best minds of the city and met weekly to hear and discuss essays written by its members.[10]

In September Mary wrote to Julius that Alston "appears fully determined to study law and enter Mr. deSaussure's office as soon as he returns from Columbia. I trust that he will have energy and decision of character enough to be a hard student and an industrious practitioner."[11]

In December 1841, at the age of nineteen, Alston graduated from South Carolina College and in January 1842 began his formal legal education as a law clerk to William Ford deSaussure.[12] His sister Susan noted that Alston was "thrown into an ecstasy," at obtaining the position.[13] To celebrate this event, his aged grandfather, John Julius Pringle, gave him William Blackstone's four-volume *Commentaries on the Laws of England,* which for more than a century after its publication in 1760 was used as the foundation of all legal education in Great Britain and the United States.

Though an unexceptional student at college, Alston threw himself passionately into his postgraduate legal studies. Mary wrote to Julius, "He goes to Mr. DeSaussure's office, and devotes himself to Blackstone, in his own chamber, until 11 o'clock, at night, and is again up, at 6 in the morning."[14]

Alston was admitted to the South Carolina bar at Columbia in 1843 and commenced the practice of law in Charleston. In 1846 he petitioned the Court of Appeals in Equity to practice equity law.[15] He moved into the Robert Pringle house on Tradd Street shortly after his grandfather's death in 1843. In 1845, at the age of twenty-three, he married his cousin, Emma Clara Pringle Smith, aged twenty. She was the youngest daughter of Robert Mason Smith and his wife, Elizabeth Mary Pringle. Their wedding ball was held in the Miles Brewton House, and Mary wrote to Edward, "the old chandelier smiled on the scene."[16]

Susan Pringle wrote to Emma a year later, chiding her because Alston had not written her for some time. Emma replied, "You ask what has become of my husband and why I don't persuade him to write to you? Well! he struts down to the office, day after day, his Pringle pride, bowing to his perseverence, at every step. This same Pringle pride, born of Pringle blood, you know what it is, for it is a part of your composition too. . . .

In answer to your second question, I will only say, that I have just been married long enough, to realize the sad, often told, but seldom believed, until felt, fact, that before marriage, we women reign, but after matrimony, we obey. Thus, I even order him to write, but he rebels. He orders me, and I yield. Yet, Sue, you must not think, I write, only, because he wishes me. No, no, I write from inclination."[17]

Emma somehow sensed that her marriage to Alston would keep her tied down. When Susan suggested that the newlyweds make plans to visit Europe, Emma replied, "A nice plan you have formed for me. My dear Sister, do you not know, that in marrying Alston, I was wedded to Charleston too? 'till eternity."[18] Emma was right. She became pregnant shortly after the wedding and she and Alston began to rear what soon would become a large and expensive family of thirteen children.

> "I have just been married long enough, to realize the sad, often told, but seldom believed, until felt, fact, that before marriage, we women reign, but after matrimony, we obey."
>
> —Emma Pringle, 1845

The summer of 1850 Alston and his young family were residing at 18 Meeting Street, just two blocks from his birthplace on King Street. Census records show the twenty-eight-year-old attorney lived with his wife, Emma, their three children (ages four, three and one) and Ellen Tooney, their Irish-born nanny. Alston was a respected man in the community, and on Independence Day was chosen to make an oration before the Fourth of July Association in Hibernian Hall—as had his grandfather, John Julius Pringle, fifty years before.

With ten house servants, Alston presented an upper-middle-class facade, but he had few other assets, a low income, and a stagnant career compared to many of his former college classmates or to his younger brother, Julius.

In 1854 Alston took a run for the mayor's office in Charleston, and his family hoped that victory might improve his marginal ability to support his family. Edward wrote from San Francisco, "It will do his business no harm. In fact he has not got business that is worth considering in comparison with the advantage of the mayoralty. It will open the way for him to a great many things that he could not reach other wise. . . . It is his duty to his wife and children."[19]

An aloof patrician, Alston depended too much upon his membership in genteel society and too little on campaigning. He lost the election—and the mayor's $4,000 salary—to William Porcher Miles, a mathematics professor at the College of Charleston.[20] The loss did not affect Alston's sense of civic duty, for in 1855, he served as an alderman from Charleston's first ward and on the city's board of health.

That fall Uncle Robert lent a hand to relieve some of Alston's financial burden. He gave him the use of the Judge Robert Pringle house on Tradd Street and later devised a half-interest in the house to Alston, along with the furniture from his drawing room in Paris.[21] In August 1854 Uncle Robert wrote to William, "Tell him [Alston] he may have the clock and take it with him. I believe I already gave him the secretary and drawers, if I did not, I do now. Burn all the papers that might be in them. But, if he goes on having children every sixteen months, he had better move to Paris, because people here never have more than two or three."[22]

Alston and Emma evidently paid his uncle no mind, for they had four more children before the war and an additional four afterwards. This cost them dearly. In 1859 they were living on an annual income of only $2,000. Yet they had ten house servants to feed and clothe and were paying approximately $206 per year in city taxes alone.[23]

In 1857 Alston succeeded Charles Macbeth as Recorder of Charleston. The office was a lifetime position, and Alston later became the only antebellum Charleston official who also held office after the war.[24] In January 1859 Edward wrote to Rebecca, "He may be sure that something higher will come from the discharge of his duty as Recorder, and after all $2000 is not so bad to wait upon. It is more than most of his contemporaries are making at the Bar in Charleston."[25]

Julius

On September 23, 1840, three weeks after his sixteenth birthday, young Julius obtained a midshipman's appointment from Secretary of the Navy, J. K. Paulding. Midshipmen served six-year tours of duty while being trained aboard ship as potential commissioned officers.

In October 1840 his father accompanied him to Norfolk, Virginia, where the young sailor boarded the U.S.S. *Concord* to start his training. At that time, squadrons of U.S. Navy warships actively patrolled the northern and southern hemispheres, showing the flag and protecting the interests of American trading, fishing, and whaling ships. Just before Julius left home, his mother gave him a pocket Bible. On the inside back cover Mary inscribed the following prayer: "Father of light and life thou good supreme, Oh teach him what is good! teach him thy self. Save him from folly, vanity and vice! From every low pursuit! and feed his soul with knowledge, conscious peace and virtue pare, sacred, substantial, never fading bliss." Only days after his departure, she wrote:

> Could you conceive the affliction that I feel, at this cruel separation, you would be able to imagine how very dear you are to me. I almost sink under the appalling thought, that I am not to see you again for two, may be for three years. Great God! What an age, to a mother, whose happiness and pride it has been for sixteen years, to watch over you, to guard you from every ill and misfortune that my feeble power could. And let whatever may happen, my child, remember that you will always have your Mother's warmest and choicest blessing. To God's Almighty care, I resign you – never, never cease to rely upon His mercy and protection – and to appeal daily at his Throne of Grace, for strength and wisdom to support and direct you.[26]

On November 19, 1840, Julius assured his parents that he had not fallen prey to the vices and depravities common to his fellow officers.

> It affords me a kind of melancholy pleasure, to think of

> you and the happy home that I have left for so long a time, and to relieve myself, I write as often as I can. . . . I seldom have sufficient time to write my letters before he leaves the ship. I have, myself, been only once to the Post Office since Papa left and then I had the pleasure of receiving Mama's letter, assuring me that you were all well: but since then, although I have begged every one who has been on shore to enquire for letters for me, I have not received a single letter, at which I am terribly disappointed, and very uneasy: So let me beg you to write as often as you possibly can, as nothing gives me greater pleasure than to hear from you, and also to write to you every spare moment. I had nearly finished a letter to you the day before yesterday when I was interrupted by an order for the midshipmen to prepare to go on board, themselves, and to carry the men on board the Java, and remain there until the carpenters had finished the repairs in the Concord. . . . I suppose you know that the Java is an old receiving ship laid in ordinary,[27] commanded by an old drunken Lieutenant (Piercy) with an old drunken Sailing Master, who has been in her 9 years, and 12 or 14 drunken men; all of our men are removed on board, and we have to keep a pretty good watch, to prevent them from deserting or smuggling liquor on board. . . .
>
> There has been a great deal of smoking, chewing, drinking, and, last night, gambling among the midshipmen, but I have not touched a segar or piece of tobacco, tasted a drop of spirits or wine, or touched a card, since I have been away from home, and be assured, my dearest parents, that I never will; however great may be the temptation, and as I have gone through the worst part, without entertaining the least desire but also a great dislike.[28]

His father responded, "I feel no apprehension of your becoming dissipated, as I have before said, but I cannot refrain from cautioning you against gaming of all kind. Cards to those even who do not gamble is as destructive of their time as it is of the principles and fortunes of those who do. It is prima facie evidence that a young man is promising to hear him say that he never plays cards. But I must now have done with this grave matter, else you will deem my etiquette a moral lecture."[29]

And his mother wrote, "Thank you, ten thousand times, for that sweet assurance, that you gave me, in your last [letter], that you 'would never be contaminated by any association, into which you may be thrown. . . .' For my sake, be very careful of yourself, and never take off your flannel jackets, but to change them. Be always moderate, too, in your suppers, as they are the most dangerous meals, in which one can indulge. And to secure the perfect performance of that promise that you have given me, never neglect your religious duties, as long as you attend faithfully to these, you will be safe, my boy."[30]

William commented approvingly of the warm love and respect which Julius had expressed towards his parents.

> That you should entertain the feelings expressed in [his previous letter] is as honorable to you as it is pleasing to us. It is the possession of such feelings combined with an energy and zeal in the pursuit of one's object that constitutes the difference between the hero and the ruffian. In the profession you have chosen my dear son, the difference is as marked between the high and low as between the advocate and the pettifogger or the enlightened physician to the quack. You are all officers to be sure with the same professional privileges, as all admitted as lawyers have the same. But it is the conduct and acquirements that distinguish the officer of high character in your profession as in that of any other.[31]

The *Concord's* repairs were finished in December, and three days after Christmas she put to sea on what would prove to be the start of Julius's eight-year naval adventure. The first half of the *Concord's* cruise was spent on the Brazilian Station, showing the flag and building crew proficiency. During most of 1841 and 1842 she cruised off the coast of Brazil, but also visited Montevideo and Buenos Aires, which Julius voted "the most pleasant place on the Station."

In Rio de Janeiro he witnessed the coronation of the emperor of Brazil. "The palace itself is not a very handsome edifice or very handsomely furnished," he noted. As a boy from a family which knew good tableware from bad, he observed, "the plate which his Imperial Highness makes use of is very handsome, the whole service being of gold."[32]

While Julius was at sea and his letters were long in arriving, William was perpetually anxious and went to great lengths to obtain intelligence about him. "Your Papa observed in the morning paper," Mary wrote to Julius, "the arrival of a ship direct from Rio, so he went on board of her, with the hope of gaining some information of the Concord. He confirmed our reasons for not hearing from you, by saying that the Concord was at sea."[33]

On July 2, 1842, the *Concord* sailed for the island of Tristan da Cunha in the South Atlantic and then to Madagascar and the east coast of Africa to protect American whaling interests. Julius and his ship arrived on the first of September and remained about a week, settling differences among the whalers and satisfying the curiosities of the local inhabitants, who assembled around the ship in crowds of canoes.[34]

After spending a week in Mozambique, his ship set sail to inspect other Portuguese settlements nearby. On the second of October, Julius wrote that "the atmosphere was exceptionally hazy, and by our reckoning, being near the mouth of Quillimane River,[35] and wishing to obtain a good view of the land, we stood boldly and at the rate of 8 or 9 knots. On first making the land (at 2 o'clock) we got a cast of the lead in 2 fathoms water. At (ship going 8 k.) sounded in 6 fathoms, which being much less than we expected, we reduced sail, and kept the ship away, but too late, for in a few moments, she struck violently in 13 ft. water, and becoming perfectly unmanageable, forged ahead farther on the reef and grounded."[36]

In fact, they had run aground on a sand bar at the mouth of the Loango River, in the Mozambique Channel. Their situation quickly became hopeless.

> We did not remain idle, but did everything in our power for the preservation of the ship, although without at all ameliorating the situation. . . We then lightened the ship by

> throwing overboard 20 of our guns, a quantity of round shot, grape[37] etc, and starting some of the water . . . We met with innumerable difficulties, and delays, and in the beginning of November, having discovered that the ship was utterly unseaworthy from the injury she had received while on the bar, it was determined to abandon her, as it was also deemed impossible for her to recross the reef.[38]

The crew's problems increased greatly when their her captain drowned while trying to save their ship. Lt. J. M. Gardner, who succeeded Captain Boerum, acknowledged that saving the ship was impossible and chartered a Portuguese brig to take the crew back to Rio de Janeiro.[39]

Rather than being daunted by the calamity, Julius considered it an opportunity for personal and professional growth. "This cruise to the coast of Africa, although an unpleasant one, has been one of infinite service to me, in affording me the means of acquiring a practical knowledge of my profession and incurred with pleasure with all inconveniences, which were not without the charm of excitement."[40] Within the space of just a few months, Julius would be forced to put his newly learned survival skills to the test.

After his African ordeal, Julius was returned to the United States and was granted several months leave in the spring of 1843. That summer he was transferred to another ill-fated ship, the U.S.S. *Missouri*. One of the Navy's first steam-powered warships, she caught fire while anchored off Gibraltar in 1843.[41]

The captain was ashore at the time, and by the time he reached his burning ship, the flames were already lapping at the forward ammunition magazines. A journalist wrote:

> The shell-room, containing many charged shells, was in danger and the order was given to throw them overboard. This dangerous duty was assigned to Midshipmen Donald Fairfax and Julius Pringle. Many of the shells known as the Stevens shell exploded by [percussion] and had to be lifted from the magazine to the deck with great care. One of these young officers had to stand down in the magazine and the other on deck to receive them as handed up and see them

> thrown overboard. This dangerous duty was well performed." Within minutes, the captain gave the order, "every man save himself," and the remaining crew jumped into the sea, where they were picked up by a flotilla of small craft. Shortly thereafter, one of the quarterdeck guns exploded, and then the forward magazine. The *Missouri* sank quickly, and the "officers and men, bruised and exhausted, escaped in their burnt and torn clothing, and were distributed among the many vessels lying at anchor in the harbor."[42]

Just two days after the *Missouri* sank, the American ship *Rajah* was chartered to take the crew home, but a salvage party of several officers—including Julius—and thirty men stayed behind. From Gibraltar, Julius returned to the United States and made a brief visit to Charleston before traveling to Boston to join the 147-foot warship *Plymouth*. While waiting orders for the *Plymouth*, Julius was granted shore leave and spent some time visiting with Edward, who was studying law at Harvard. Julius found the Bostonians "very kind and attentive, the lawyers particularly," and continued, "I found them excessively cordial, quite the contrary from the impression, Brother [Alston Pringle] received of them."[43] Late in March he boarded the *Plymouth* and on April 3, 1844, departed on a cruise in the Mediterranean.

By the early 1840s senior naval officers had come to recognize a need for standardized, professional training for their officers. Prior to the establishment in 1845 of the U.S. Naval Asylum (renamed the Naval Academy in 1850), each midshipman was trained by the captain under whom he served, and the quality of that training varied considerably. The Academy system initially consisted of a six-year program. Those cadets who successfully completed the course were given warrants as midshipmen and ordered to sea. Graduating and obtaining a warrant did not assure an officer's commission, however, and even after six years' preparation, midshipmen would not be commissioned unless they were required by the Navy.[44]

The first class of the Naval Academy was drawn from midshipmen already at sea. Julius was one of them, and was ordered to report to school in October 1845. With his solid academic training at Mr. Cotes's school in Charleston and four years of sea duty under his belt, Julius made his family proud at the Academy. He ranked in the top third of his class in his studies, standing seventeenth of fifty in navigation, eleventh in gunnery, ninth in natural philosophy, and seventeenth in chemistry.

While Julius was studying at the Academy, major problems were brewing in Mexico. In 1845 President James K. Polk had sent a diplomat to Mexico to negotiate Texas boundary disagreements and claims of U.S. citizens against Mexico and to propose the purchase of California and New Mexico. When the Mexican government refused to negotiate, Gen. Zachary Taylor moved his troops to the mouth of the Rio Grande River. This provoked the Mexicans to send troops across the Rio Grande, and Congress declared war on Mexico in 1846.

Among Julius's classmates, war fever spread quickly, and the midshipmen chafed at the bit to get into active service. Secretary Bancroft accommodated them by advancing the examinations of the class of 1846 from November to July 1846. This enabled all the successful graduates the opportunity to go to sea at once.[45] Julius completed his classes on July 1, 1846, and stood for his seamanship examination a week later. When the class of 1846 graduated on July 11, Julius stood sixth of forty-three.[46]

Every man in Julius's class volunteered for war duty. They served with the naval battery which fought and captured Vera Cruz. The war plan included an invasion and blockade of both coasts. Despite a number of American victories, Mexico refused to acknowledge defeat, and American troops were sent to capture Mexico City. With Julius aboard, the U.S. sloop of war *Germantown* departed from Norfolk on March 15, 1847, to join Commodore M. C. Perry's Home Squadron off Mexico.[47] The ship reached Sacrificios Island on April 1, and the next day the town of Alvarado surrendered without a shot. Next the fleet sailed to Tuxpan, where a force of U.S. seamen and marines successfully landed and stormed the Mexican forces on May 18. In June the *Germantown* helped capture Tabasco, then occupied a blockade station off the Mexican coast.[48]

Julius was in the forefront of this campaign and was wounded by the Mexicans on May 16 "as he was coming down the river in an open boat, from the town of Lallascoya."[49] Mary wrote to Edward, then traveling in Europe, that "Julius's wound, though painful, was not dangerous. He was struck by two balls, one grazing his arm and the other lodging in his neck: but he was not long confined to his bed and now he looks upon his wounds as his most valuable trophies."[50]

As a reward for his service and sacrifice, Commodore Perry offered Julius a special leave of absence. He declined to take it. The *Germantown* arrived back at Norfolk on February 16, 1848.[51] Aboard Julius's ship was the body of George Rodgers, the late brother of Admiral C. R. P. Rodgers, himself a Mexican War veteran and later superintendent of the U.S. Naval Academy. Admiral Rodgers thanked Julius for accompanying the remains and for caring for his brother's trunk.

Through a bizarre twist of fate, the lives of Admiral Rodgers and Midshipman Pringle would cross again. When the Civil War broke out, Rodgers was placed in command of the frigate U.S.S. *Wabash*, and distinguished himself at the battle of Port Royal, S. C., November 7, 1861. He was later the fleet captain in the attack on Charleston, April 7, 1863, and commanded the South Atlantic Blockading Squadron conducting the bombardment of Charleston which drove the Pringles from their King Street home. During that attack, Julius' brother, Capt. Robert Pringle, would be killed by a Union naval shell fired at Battery Wagner on Morris Island, the Confederate artillery fortification where Robert fought his guns.

At the end of the *Germantown's* Mexican War cruise, Julius returned to Charleston. In September 1848 he requested and was granted a twelve-month leave, but with eight years of arduous and honorable service behind him, he felt ready to relinquish his naval career and return to the role for which he had been trained: life as a gentleman planter.

Like his father, Julius married wisely and to great advantage. In the spring of 1849 at Auburn, her father's Greek Revival mansion near Natchez, Mississippi, Julius wed Maria Linton Duncan, the younger daughter of Dr. Stephen Duncan and his second wife, Catherine A. Bingaman.[52]

Duncan was reputed to be the largest producer of cotton in the South. His net worth in the early 1850s was conservatively estimated at almost $2 million.[53] As a wedding present, Julius and Maria received Torwood, a large and prosperous cotton and sugar plantation on the Mississippi River in Pointe Coupée Parish. Located near Franklin, Louisiana, Torwood came with a beautiful house and other assets valued at $112,500, and another $100,000 in stocks and bonds, for a total gift of nearly a quarter million dollars.[54] Duncan's largess continued to flow for a decade, during which Julius received an additional plantation (Duncannon, value $180,000), a $120,000 trust for the education of his children and other assets totaling $504,342.53, for a total matrimonial legacy of at least $716,842.53.[55]

Maria Linton Duncan Pringle

Stephen Duncan, born in Carlisle, Pennsylvania, had graduated in medicine from Dickinson College in 1805.[56] He moved to Natchez in 1808 and quickly found success as a cotton planter. His house, Auburn, was eight years old when he purchased it in 1820, and in the 1830s he enlarged it with side wings. The house is architecturally important because it was the first in the South to have two-story-high columns, and it became a design prototype for two generations of classical, antebellum plantation houses.

Duncan spent a portion of each year in the North, where he had major investments. At the time of his marriage, Julius probably did not know how valuable his father-in-law's Northern birth, business and political connections, holdings, and sympathies would be in the future, but the matrimonial alliance with this avowed Unionist was to play a key role in the postwar financial survival of the Pringle family.

After their marriage, Julius and Maria left for what was to be the first of many trips to Europe. Their letters of introduction and family connections assured that they would be favorably received by high society in all the capitols of Europe.

Uncle Robert Pringle's lavishly appointed Paris apartment was certainly an early stop. Julius and Maria found France greatly to their liking. As a major cotton and sugar planter, there is reason to believe that Julius sought to bypass the American factorage firms—a bold, though not unprecedented move—and make direct business contacts in Europe, for Steven Duncan's name would open almost any commercial door on the continent.

After returning to the United States, Julius and Maria made their home at Torwood. Like her mother-in-law in Charleston, Maria returned to her mother's house to bear her children. Mary Motte, their first daughter, was born at Auburn in 1852. Julius spent the rest of the decade planting at Torwood, consulting with his father-in-law at Natchez, attending to the sale of his crops at New Orleans, and, with the eager cooperation of his wife, socializing at the finest Northern and European spas.

They spent the summer of 1853 in Newport, where they entertained Susan and Edward Pringle. South Carolina planters had been enjoying Newport since before the Revolution. There the planters enjoyed a cool refuge from the steamy Lowcountry summers. By the 1830s Newport's "Southern colony" had become fully-organized. Most South Carolina planters stayed in the large hotels or as houseguests or tenants in private homes. In the mid-nineteenth century the city was an international watering hole where the rich—like the Pringles, Middletons, and Alstons—could go to watch the super-rich hold court and practice conspicuous consumption. There, South Carolinians spent their money "lavishly, even wastefully," wrote the ascetic South Carolina textile manufacturer William Gregg.[57]

In the 1840s and 1850s, Henry Middleton, the former U.S. Minister to Russia (and known in Newport as "Russian Henry") owned large tracts of land in the city as well as his elegant summer home, "Stone Villa" on Belleview Avenue.[58] The Julius Pringles soon became regular fixtures at Newport; so much so that their daughters Susan and Charlotte were born there in 1854 and 1859. For several years after 1855, Henry Middleton, Julius Pringle, George Tiffany, and others met at the Newport home of Casimir de Rahm to "enjoy the French cooking and discuss rare Madeira."[59]

In the 1850s a movement began in the South to boycott Northern watering holes, but Charlestonians largely ignored it. Perhaps because of the strong Duncan influence, the Julius Pringles were passing every summer and much of the fall snugly ensconced there. The William Bull Pringles were still visiting regularly, apparently unconcerned about the cost or their lack of political correctness.

Julius may have been a semi-absentee owner of his cotton and sugar plantations for half of each year, but that did not mean that he neglected their management. In January 1854 he wrote to William:

> I have been fortunate in getting this year better overseers than heretofore and my places are in better order and condition than they have heretofore been. The overseer on the cotton place particularly is a very superior man—and my prospect for a good crop next year is a good one. This year owing to a bad overseer I left on my departure for Charleston in the spring and also to my not having land enough open for the new hands, my crop was a bad one. Also owing to a

> very unfavorable season—I have only made 350 bales of cotton. My sugar crop is a large one 750 hogsheads[60] and about 1500 barrels molasses.[61] Next year I shall pitch my crop for 800 hogsheads sugar and 700 bales cotton (at least) and my estimates are not generally over the mark.[62]

Julius's production of "only" 350 bales of cotton was five or six times that of a successful South Carolina sea island cotton planter. He closed his letter with a request that William borrow $10,000 for him to help pay for a $15,000 sugar mill. "My object in getting it is to take my crop off in 40 days instead of 80 which I have accepted this year," Julius wrote, adding that the mill would increase his molasses production from fifty to 100 barrels per year.[63] In May 1856 he wrote from Torwood, "I am again down here looking at cotton, sugar and corn. . . . Just sending to market today my sugar and molasses, which I am selling at such a price as to make me nash my teeth at not making a full crop."[64]

In 1860 the average large slaveholder in Pointe Coupée Parish owned about ninety-nine slaves, an average of 751 acres of improved land, and that land had an average value of $52,709.[65] Torwood, on the other hand, was exceptional. It consisted of 1,600 improved acres, employed 318 slaves, fifteen horses, twenty-five oxen and eighty-five mules to work the fields and sugar mill, and was valued at $250,000, not including Julius's personal property of $25,000.[66] Torwood was a vast agricultural machine, designed to efficiently produce huge quantities of cotton, sugar, and cash. Unlike his father's Georgetown District rice plantations, which also produced a wide variety of fruits, vegetables, grains, and meat for family and slave consumption, Torwood produced virtually nothing except cash crops and some meat. Julius was tied with his neighbor, Charles D. Stewart, for the title of top sugar producer in the parish.[67] The 1859 cash crops at Torwood consisted of 919 bales of ginned cotton (average price: $44 per 400 lb. bale; value: $40,436); 653 hogsheads of sugar (average price: $84.58 per 1,000 lb. hogshead; total value: $55,231) and 60,000 gallons (1,905 barrels) of molasses (average price: $17.77[68] per barrel; total value $33,852).

As a frame of reference, South Carolina's top sea island cotton planters each produced fifty to one hundred bales a year. Torwood produced over nine times that much. In 1859 Torwood's enormous revenues—$129,519—were four times as much as William Bull Pringle made in his best year. Julius shared his good fortune with his parents. Mary mentioned this to Edward, then in San Francisco, who wrote back, "I have no room left [on my paper]— except to say a word of Julius's timely generosity which must be of great relief to Papa."[69] Edward's remark clearly underscores his father's severely distressed financial condition.

Maria and her children spent Christmas of 1859 at Newport. In the spring of 1860, Julius and Maria visited Charleston. Rebecca wrote to Charles, "Maria is such a lovely person. She is so refined and intelligent and well connected that she threw a charm over the home circle."[70] That summer, Mary went to New York for a short visit and to see them off for France, and on the Fourth of July, 1860, Julius and Maria sailed aboard the *Adriatic*. Her brother, Stephen Duncan, accompanied them, and they planned to pay a visit to the French city of Nancy, where James and Charles were studying.

Edward

Edward was very much the outdoorsman and relished the time he spent on the plantation, where he particularly enjoyed hunting deer. In 1841 he enrolled in South Carolina College but by May 1842, William was so dissatisfied with the education his son was getting that he pulled him out of school and prepared to send him to Harvard.[71]

Edward and his father set off for Cambridge by train in August 1842.[72] Edward excelled at Harvard. In an essay entitled "Considering the Various Grounds of Difference and Divisions in the United States, is it desirable that the Union should be continued?" Edward argued that the Union should not be dissolved. He stated:

> If the extention of territories should drive any one or more states to sever the bond, that united them to our Republic an independent community of small size could not be perfectly secure in its weakness from the aggressions of powerful neighbors on this continent and the intrigues or rapicity of foreign kingdoms, to whom privileges here would be worth much injustice and such in all incidences must be the fate of those who by contemplating small evils are blind to great blessing; and such a fate we could wish to befall those who hastily and selfishly call for the dissolution of our Union.[73]

In 1845, after three years of study, Edward graduated third in his class and received his bachelor of arts degree from Harvard president, Josiah Quincy. A newspaper praised his oration, noting that Edward "exhibited the same glowing powers of conception, the same rich fancy and highly cultivated imagination which have marked his former productions."[74] He was admitted to the bar at Columbia in 1847.[75] Shortly afterward he left to enjoy his graduation present: an all-expenses-paid, two-year Grand Tour of Europe.

Edward and several friends[76] boarded the *St. Nicholas* at New York and departed for Europe in the summer of 1847. He kept adetailed journal of his experiences and wrote, "I will not dwell upon the object proposed by my voyagings. They are easily imagined. The expected effects on my character are more important than the information to be derived. I feel that the want of mixing with the world, roughing it with men the want of energy, occasioned, activity and savoir faire. This chiefly, and then to have my eyes opened to my ignorance and to be taught what I ought to know, and what to read and inquire into."[77]

With his classical education and good command of French, Edward was well-prepared to savor all that Europe had to offer. He was met at the docks of Le Havre by Uncle Robert, and from there they traveled down the Seine. Edward wrote, "I had been told that the banks of the Seine were very beautiful, but I was not prepared for the scenes of surpassing beauty and of romantic interest which I have passed through."[78]

Of all the wonders of Paris, Edward was most captivated by the Louvre, which he visited numerous times. "The first impressions on entering the Louvre are of astonishment at the boundless world of art that opens before one. I might almost say miles of pictures stretch out on all sides of you, museums of all kinds are around you."[79]Humbled, Edward wrote, "It was a new and pleasant excitement to find myself in the midst of genuine chefs d'oeuvre[80] of the art; the consciousness was enough in spite of [my] ignorance and want of taste. . . . I enjoyed exceedingly a long visit and examined with much pleasure the different pictures almost exclusively those of the Italian school. . . . The Louvre however requires infinitely more time than I have yet given. Its beauties and wonders require weeks or months of steady perseverance—think of the numberless masterpieces I have not looked at yet."[81]

At an outdoor ball, Edward was taken aback by the informality of relations between the sexes—something unknown in prudish, antebellum Charleston.

> At first I was disgusted with the freedom that characterized them, men and women hugging each other with so much mutual liveliness and absence of improper thoughts (the effect of long habit), that it is no longer offensive. At first too I was disgusted with the contentious jumpings and childish amusements of the men and women, the former especially, but though I still feel a contempt for them, yet there is so much good humor, perfect amiability and liveliness, that I begin almost to sympathize with them. The perfect propriety that prevails in spite of the looseness of morals, added to the good humored liveliness of everybody, soon overcomes our first prejudices.[82]

After six weeks of exploring France, Edward headed south for Switzerland with his friend Ravenel in tow. The rest of 1848 was spent traveling through Switzerland, Germany, Belgium, Holland, back through France and Germany to Austria, Czechoslovakia, and Italy. In April 1849, he and a friend named Cunningham made his second trip to London, a city Edward relished as much as he did Paris.

On April 25 Edward wrote, "Had the good luck to dine today at Mr. Forester's with Carlyle, Dickens, and R. W. Emerson." Edward would have known these men by their literary reputations. Charles Dickens was the famed English novelist; John Forster was an editor, biographer and proofreader of Dickens' work. Thomas Carlyle was a Scottish essayist and historian, and Edward's countryman, Ralph Waldo Emerson, was an essayist and poet. "The dinner was of course was just such as I should have asked for and proved to me as a listener extremely interesting," Edward continued. "Carlyle was the lion of the company, the oracle at the opening of whose mouth all were attentive. He is a strangely rough looking Scotchman, loose and ungainly in figure and dress and with rather a disheveled head of hair surrounding his face. . . . He talked a great deal, often exciting himself into long rhapsodies." Edward closed his notes on the evening by writing, "Messrs, Emerson, Forester and Pringle did not take a very large share in the conversation. They made good listeners."[83] In company of this caliber, most other sensible men would, like Edward, have listened rather than spoken.

After several more months spent soaking up the best that Europe had to offer, Edward took ship in the summer of 1848 and returned to Charleston. He moved in with his parents and practiced law from an office at the corner of Church and Broad Streets in the center of the city's legal district. Charleston already had a glut of lawyers and, despite being a distinguished Harvard graduate and the grandson of the legendary Judge John Julius Pringle, Edward found the legal pickings slim.

In the summer of 1853 Edward sought to gain a position on the staff of James Buchanan, whom President Franklin Pierce had recently appointed minister to Great Britain.[84] After being assured that the job was all but his, Edward found himself outmaneuvered by a New York lawyer and was offered instead a clerkship at $800 per year, which he declined.

Dejected and forlorn, Edward wrote his father, "So it is all over with me. I have just returned from my visit to the old autocrat. I am terribly cut up, I confess; greatly disappointed; because I came here full of hope, almost certain of success. . . . Don't turn me out of the house yet. My room's my own for a little while longer. Mama must submit to my monopoly of the chamber and library and Papa must make the best of my story in Broad Street. . . . I hope to have the consolation of hearing that Brother [Alston] has redeemed my want of success by securing his place. Tell him not to sell out the law books or give up the office yet—I am still a hanger on. . . . Your much abused son, E.J.P.[85]

Edward became the family's first widely read author. His work was a carefully written defense of slavery which he had started while at Harvard. *Slavery in the Southern States,* a fifty-four-page pamphlet, was framed as a rebuttal to Harriet Beecher Stowe's, *Uncle Tom's Cabin,* which had just been published.

Edward wrote that *Uncle Tom's Cabin* "contains all the arguments against slavery vivified in dramatic scenes of great power, and made attractive by highly wrought sketches, imaginative chiefly, but, we are assured, not extravagant, the whole being rendered more effective by appropriate illustrations. . . . The dramatic power of Mrs. Stowe's book will have no other effect upon the country than to excite the fanaticism of one portion and to arouse the indignation of the other."[86]

The first and second editions of Edward's pamphlet were published in 1852 under the moniker, "By a Carolinian." The third edition in 1853 identified him by name. It was published at the urging of his close friend and Harvard classmate, Charles Eliot Norton, "in the hope of inducing calmer thought on the subject of slavery than is likely to be the result of pictorial writing." Norton had taken a great liking to the Pringles, Middletons, and other members of Newport's Southern colony. In the early 1850s, the Nortons built a summer home at Newport and the Pringles, were frequent visitors. An intimate studio photograph made about 1853 shows Charles Norton, his sister, Grace, several of the Pringles, and Miss Susan Alston. Norton later returned to Harvard, where as a teacher, writer and editor, he greatly influenced nineteenth-century literature.[87]

His support for Edward's defense of slavery was based upon his personal affection for Edward, Norton's idealistic views about scholarly freedom, and the affection of his class of Harvard Brahmins for the planter elite, but not upon any fondness for the system of slavery itself. In 1855 Norton and his sister visited Oliver Middleton, son of "Russian Henry" Middleton, at Edisto Island. There he witnessed the "peculiar institution" firsthand. Although he developed some sympathy for the burden of responsibility borne by the slaveholders, he wrote, "Slavery in its mildest form is yet very sad, and it is on such a plantation where the slaves are all contented, and well cared for so far as their physical condition is concerned, where they are treated with the consideration due to human beings, so far as their relations to each other and to their master extend, that one feels most bitterly the inherent evils of the system."[88]

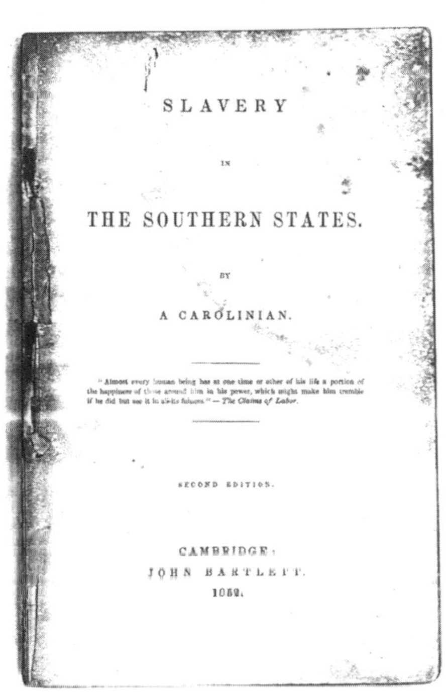

SLAVERY

IN

THE SOUTHERN STATES.

BY

A CAROLINIAN.

"Almost every human being has at one time or other of his life a portion of the happiness of those around him in his power, which might make him tremble if he did but see it in all its fulness." — *The Claims of Labor.*

SECOND EDITION.

CAMBRIDGE:
JOHN BARTLETT.
1852.

Edward Jenkins Pringle's treatise on slaveowning

Edward felt quite differently. He wrote in his preface, "I cannot imagine a more splendid career, intellectually speaking, than that of a slave-owner in a slave state, who is thoroughly awakened to the difficulty of his position."[89] In an obvious reference to Stowe and other Northern abolitionists, he said, "To preach distant reform is very cheap philanthropy,— the cheaper in proportion to the distance. The feeling of self-satisfaction exists without the necessity of personal sacrifice. Hence the temptation that betrays sometimes good men into ill-considered zeal."[90]

He anchored his thesis in the concept of *noblesse oblige,* then recited the classical antebellum litany of Southern arguments in defense of slavery:

> It was God's will, sanctioned by the Bible.
> Negro brains weighed less than white brains.
> Negroes were intellectually inferior to whites.
> Blacks themselves sold fellow blacks into slavery.
> Chattel slavery in the South was no worse than wage slavery in the factories of the North.
> Slaves on the Southern plantations were more likely to be kept together as families than were white Northern factory workers.
> Men who purchased slaves incurred a heavy obligation of social welfare and Christian duty.
> Real abuses of slaves were rare.
> Blacks were better suited to manual labor in hot climates than were whites; and finally,
> Southern agriculture would be paralyzed by emancipation of the slaves.

Few white South Carolinians of his time would have disagreed with the points he made.

He characterized Stowe's book as a "most wild and unreal picture of slavery" and wrote that her tales of owner mistreatment of their slaves were "scenes such as we have never seen or heard of." Edward held that the slave system as a whole should not be judged by its worst abuses any more than Christianity should be judged by its former uses of torture and burning witches at the stake. He also pointed out that the master of a New England mill exercised virtually the same life-and-death control over his laborers as did the Southern planter over his slaves, and that husbands often exercised similar control over their wives.

He faulted Stowe for failing to note the "profound sense of

responsibility" of the slaveholder. Equating slaveowners with monarchs, Edward asked, "Shall a king lay down his scepter, when he may be the centre of blessings to all his people?" He also noted that while Southern slaveholders were in intimate, daily contact with their slaves, Northern employers and abolitionists only rarely came into face-to-face with their wage slaves, which made it much easier to condemn chattel slavery and ignore wage slavery. "The claims of our poor are daily calling for the active benevolence of every slaveholder," Edward wrote, "while it is only the humane few at the North whose feelings are exposed to the risk of being blunted by an acquaintance with the painful scenes of poverty in the next street or next block."

Edward lamented that abolitionism was driving a wedge between the regions and wrote that "now the North and South know each other through their vices more familiarly than through their virtues." He argued that benevolent treatment of the slaves came not from pressure from northern Abolitionists but from "the suggestions of [the South's] own sense of duty."

He argued for time, during which the South could develop her own solution for ending slavery, taking into consideration the region's reliance on the institution for its livelihood. "Though slavery be not a necessary condition of labor," he wrote, "it is the only one under which the African can exist in the South. . . . This protection which slavery gives to the negro is the most humane provision that can be made for him, at least for the present."

After seeing his work published, Edward made a leisurely trip to the North in the summer of 1853, taking time to visit Saratoga (where he reported "troops of Seabrooks, Barnwells, etc."), Sharon, and New Haven, to visit his newlywed sister, Mary Mitchell; and Newport, where Susan was summering.

It was in Newport that Edward, frustrated in his attempts to earn a living in Charleston and Washington, heard the reports of great riches to be made in California. From Newport, he wrote to his father about a plan he was developing to seek his fortune. "Conversations I have had here lately have made me determine (unless you and Mama decidedly disapprove) to go to California. As long as California was in the unsettled condition of a new country, property precarious and investments hazardous, I did not have the reliance on my keenness that would justify my risking anything in it. But now I hear from many quarters. . . that secure investments may be had anywhere at .36 per cent [thirty-six percent return on an investment per year]."[91]

Edward told William that he was convinced that San Francisco would become the "second commercial city in the world" within twenty years, and asked his family to give him $10,000 or $20,000 to invest in real estate for them. He hoped to earn thirty-six percent interest on the money, retain ten percent for his services, and thereby give the family a twenty-six percent return on their investment. "You will acknowledge that this is the time to invest certainly without a possibility of losing," he wrote with the unbridled optimism of his youth.[92]

His conservative family was not impressed with Edward's plan. In September he wrote his mother to press his case. "You are as much tired as I am of my dawdling away life, doing nothing, and with no prospects of doing any thing," he wrote. He noted that the voyage from New York to San Francisco via Nicaragua was only twenty-seven days, and that the Nicaragua route was "perfectly healthy, no deaths having occurred from the transit." He lamented that a two- or three-year separation would be painful for them all, but that "If I don't do this I must be narrowed down very much in my life, for I can't go on traveling as I have done—I must give that up and take some second rate employment in Charleston, perhaps marry a poor woman and go fighting on through life. I might marry a rich woman, but I have tried in vain to bring myself to that. I would rather make this venture for two or three years, and then be able to come back to Charleston, to do whatever may suit my talents and inclinations best."[93]

Edward asked his father to raise $20,000 for him to invest, and said that he would also be writing Alston and Uncle Robert for more. He closed his letter with an urgent plea: "I feel that this thing may be the making of me—so don't dismiss it lightly you or Papa."[94] On October 29, 1853, he boarded the steamer *Adger* for New York, and on Monday, December 5, 1853, he sailed to seek his fortune in California.

His ship stopped to refuel at Kingston, where he had the opportunity to visit the city and take his usual, detailed observations. Slavery had been abolished in Jamaica in 1838 and a major part of his commentary consisted of observations about the state of free black labor there.

> On Monday I enjoyed what I have long wished for, a day in the tropics, and a sight of Cuffee[95] emancipated. . . . Now you [may] begin to laugh at the views of Jamaica, by a rabid slave holder, after six hours' acquaintance with the island. So take every thing I say, of course, with a large allowance for 'prejudices of education and mental obliguity. . . .' I enjoyed very much the sight of a whole population of negroes. They looked so familiar, I seemed to recognize familiar teeth at every corner. They look happy enough, those that one sees in Kingston; you know they are always happy, always grinning. But such troublesome beggars as they are, their great industry seems to be to beg. Strong men and women beg with as little shame as if they were asking a master or mistress for anything, and that any thing almost a customary perquisite. Cuffee is not lazy in the tropics, because he does not want money, very far from that — he will do every thing in the world for it, but work for it. And whatever labor does not give him much trouble, what is rather pleasant than otherwise, he is very anxious to do. It seems to be the paradise of every genuine negro to have some little thing to sell, which he may hawk about, and cry over and importune you to buy. Everybody in Kingston has something to sell not worth buying, and nobody anything to buy it with. When these California passengers land there seem to be but two classes, those having things to sell and those acting as runners to guide

you to the sellers, the beggars cover both classes. Cigars, fruits, cakes, jellies, baskets, every thing that can be had without labor or made with easy labor is forced upon you. But of regular industry there seem to be none. It is hardly a caricature to say that what I saw men doing chiefly was sitting down and making cigars, while women were carrying coal upon their heads to load the ship. Of course when life is so easy as in Jamaica they are happy enough; for fried plantains and yams are very good eating and while white men are working hard in Manchester for 6 and 7 shillings a week, these luxuriant negroes can get very cheap clothes to cover them. But I can easily believe from what I saw, all that is told of the latter prostration of industry in the island and the decay of all its productions. Whether men that can work ought not to be made to work if they don't choose to themselves, we shall not discuss here. . . .

I hardly wonder at the life those Cuffees lead in Jamaica, at least if they feel heat as I do. I don't wonder that plantains and yams fill their souls and that so few seem to be well to do in the world. Though amalgamation has proceeded much farther than with us, there are not many apparently rich among the mulattoes. I did not see that any obliteration of caste has been affected, black and white are still talked of as with us, even by the black; 'Massa give me a dime' is in every body's mouth; black yams and white yams are names given to the inferior and superior kinds of the great staple, the one kind being for black use chiefly, the other for white.

. . . The police officers of color were everywhere, good looking fellows, and using their authority, where their own color is concerned, with greater despotism apparently than our drivers. But enough of the Darkies. I had my eyes open — but of course I could not see much of them in one day. I certainly saw nothing to make me change any opinion. I suppose I saw the best of them. And it is saying a great deal to say that they did not look to be worse off than our slaves, except for their idleness and beggary. Whatever struck me as bright and pleasant in them I see at home — one or two unpleasant features as the result of slavery — such as the freedom of action that results in idleness, and the freedom of

> speech that results in the unbounded opportunity of begging. Emancipation has certainly loosed their tongues; a flock of parrots cannot chatter more than they do when a 'Yankee' lands among them. Whatever other virtues or vices emancipation may beget lies quite out of the range of my present pursuits. I cannot resist this chance of dwelling upon old topics — but now I shut off the last and look ahead to what is in my new line of life.[96]

Though Edward was a keen observer, it is clear that his experiences in Kingston only reinforced his views about blacks and slavery. He still felt that slaves were as well off as freedmen, and impossible that blacks be considered the equal of whites.

With his head full of ambition, his heart full of adventure, and his pockets full of his family's money, Edward arrived in San Francisco on December 31, 1853. Two weeks later he wrote to Julius, "I am more than satisfied with the looks of things. The bustle of business and the pace of life in the streets makes me very hopeful about my professional chances."[97]

He reported that real estate had gone up 800 percent to 1,000 percent in the last year, that money could be lent for three percent interest per month, and that rental property was bringing between one percent and three percent monthly return on investment. Edward tried to be conservative. "Being a new comer and unnecessarily cautious upon the old gentleman's loans, I can't get more than 3 per cent a month.[98] If I were inclined to take merchandise at half price as security or fancy stocks I could get 4 or 5 per cent." What pleased him most was the unsettled state of the legal profession. "So many great questions unsettled, so much business afloat, so many interesting cases coming up, such as a lawyer could not reach at home until gray hairs give him the presumption of experience."[99]

After a month on California soil, Edward started to realize that making money would not be so easy as he had supposed. "I have not made any great strides professionally," he wrote. "Haven't found a partner. Have made only $60 or $70 on my own hook; have driven off my first client by charging him a California fee, but think the principle is all right—here above all places no man should hold himself cheap."[100]

He tried to convince his mother what a cautious, principled man he remained. "I was offered lately a chance, almost certain, of making seven or eight thousand dollars, men of the highest position here advising it—but my conscience kept me back. Nothing is more dangerous than such a state of things as this—men are reckless, prodigal of money, making no account of it at all, pushing the virtues of generosity to an extreme that is very fascinating—but to get it, to support this happy style that is so taking with the world, they are equally thoughtless and reckless." But then Edward, never a man to take himself too seriously, continued, "Jan'y 31—I had to go to bed in the midst of my morality."[101]

The Pringle family's chief commentator on slavery also paid close attention to the status of labor in California. "The Chinamen for the three last days have been celebrating their New Year.... One night they were celebrating the anniversary of some good benevolent society and the police thought they were making a revolution, and as no explanation was possible, they seized 100 of the poor wretches and tied them together by 20s by the tails of their heads and so carried them to the lock up house. These tails they value as they do their heads."[102]

In 1854 one of Edward's friends from Harvard, John Brooks Felton, joined him in partnership. In the summer of 1855, they added another Harvard man, Adolphus Carter Whitcomb. The three partners took most of their cases on contingency—which meant that they got paid only if they won. Edward continued to draw funds on his father's credit lines, citing three percent to five percent monthly interest rates, and by the end of the year, he had at least $70,000 of family money invested in San Francisco mortgages. "Avoiding all speculation I can get 3 per cent on undoubted security. I don't mean to say there is no risk —because California may possibly prove a bubble, and the titles are not settled, the Supreme Court being venal; but the risk is not worth considering."[103]

His optimism notwithstanding, Edward's legal income continued to lag, and although he was supposedly investing the family's money at great profit, he was, in fact, a speculator, not an investor. The fact that he was still accepting an annual subsidy of $500 from his parents showed clearly that his much-touted investments were not producing anywhere near the promised returns.

Edward's law firm became known for arguing cases involving disputed land claims, notably those between newly arrived Californians and those claiming to hold earlier land grants from the Spanish government. One of the first of Edward's large Spanish land grant cases was the fabled Limantour case, in which Edward's firm argued that a large tract of land—including half of San Francisco, several islands around the bay and part of the Tiburon peninsula—was, in fact, the property of José Y. Limantour, a Mexican, by virtue of an 1843 Spanish land grant that predated later claims. Edward wrote to his father, "I have written a long letter about Limantour, because I want you to see that we have not taken hold of a desperate or bad case. The result is of immense importance to us; failure would be very damaging, success will be a fortune and I want you to see that we are justified in taking hold of it thoroughly, and in earnest."[104]

Edward and his partners felt good about the case. "We have so much confidence in the claim," he wrote, "that we have been glad to make arrangements to get a larger slice, having given up our cash fee. We now have .092 per cent of the property, which will give us each a handsome little fortune and perhaps a big one if we are lucky. . . . In consideration of having such a big fish to play, will you forgive me for expressing great doubts about my promised visit this spring."[105] He wrote, "three or four millions is not an unreasonable amount to expect to realize from the claims."[106]

The faith that Edward and his partners placed in the case

was greater than their luck. In September 1858, Limantour's documents were proven to be forgeries, and Pringle, Whitcomb and Felton withdrew from the case.[107] The fiasco was a serious financial blow to the partners, who had worked on it without fee for nearly six years.[108]

In February 1858 Edward briefly visited the family in Charleston. Still enthused about his prospects for prosperity, Edward returned to San Francisco. Late in the fall of 1858, he wrote to his father:

> I must in the end be able to redeem myself and I hope when I can meet you all again it will be with a better account of myself than I gave the last time. I hope we shall all meet then with better prospects, soberer, it is true, and less extravagant in our notions of success—but at least getting ahead and not going backwards. As long as there are so many of us to stand by each other, I am sure we ought to be strong. If you could only get the debt in some permanent shape to save the endless anxiety and ceaseless return of 60 and 90 day notes I should not feel that the amount of the debt was alarming.
>
> It is true cholera or great disaster to the crops might make us helpless—but with ordinary luck for the future and the debt put into good shape you can get along easily and I trust will soon see us succeeding well enough to make amends to you for the trouble and sacrifice submitted to for us. I suppose you are more anxious to hear how I am getting along than to have my hopes and prophecies.[109]

His references to William's high-turnover, short-term notes show that William was in severe financial distress. William viewed Edward's speculative California investments as a lottery which, William hoped, would pay off big and get the family out of debt.

Ever convinced of the prospects which California held for the family, Edward wrote to Mary Mitchell that he had "sent a sort of disorganizing incendiary letter to the old gentleman advising him to sell out his Santee estate and negroes and to make a large investment out here—and for that purpose have recommended him to tell [Donald] Mitchell to look out for some good man to go into the stock business with him." Edward sought Mitchell's advice about hiring an Easterner "who understands thoroughly the raising of cattle or sheep or both, who is very active and could take charge of a farm of eight or ten square leagues,[110] never goes to sleep and wouldn't cheat his partner very much. Such men are supposed to grow in Yankee land, more frequently perhaps than anywhere else," Edward quipped. "If you could get hold of such an one and sell out at home he could have a comfortable and easy time of it for the rest of his life and would be much richer than he ever aspired to being." [111]

In 1859 Edward again left San Francisco on a steamer bound for New York and Charleston, and this time he remained East for nearly a year. That winter and spring he visited Washington, New York, and Newport, where he stayed with Julius and Maria. In March 1860 he was still in Washington and in April, was staying "nominally at Maria's" in Newport. On September 14, 1860, Susan wrote to Charles, "Edward leaves Newport in a day or two to go to St. Louis, there to join one of his friends, a government agent, who has a public stage at his command in an overland journey to San Francisco. It will be very interesting and much pleasanter than going by steamer or the ordinary mail route, as they can stop whenever they like, and have things under their own control."[112]

In a small, cramped and jiggly hand, Edward kept an informal travel of his stagecoach journey. In October 1860 he wrote to his mother, "The sunsets and sunrises on the prairies are magnificent. But what you will like most to hear is that we have just got through that part of the country where the Indians are dangerous. When I began this letter we were in the midst of the infested region, but that was last evening and now, Oct. 11, we have just left the last of their number behind."[113]

By October 31, 1860, Edward was back at his desk in San Francisco, and reflected upon his trip. "The Indians for example though not dangerous to the stage gave a little excitement: for almost every station in the Indian Country had some story to tell of a former Indian fight; the night we arrived at Tucson the Apaches drove off all the cattle from the ranches near the town, and we saw afterwards, two rascally looking fellows in the road, looking as if they were only waiting for an opportunity to steal. But they are too cowardly to fight; only contemptible thieves."[114]

Motte

Of the family's thirteen children, Motte remains the most enigmatic. For the antebellum period, neither the family nor the public records of Charleston have much to say about him. His name does not appear on the rolls of the South Carolina College and he evidently did not have access to a university education. This was yet another omen of the family's financial distress.

In 1841, when he was fourteen, Mary wrote that "Motte is going on at the usual rate, not injuring his health by study. He says he is in no hurry about going to college."[115] When he was fifteen, he evidently wanted to follow in Julius's footsteps and join the navy. The combination of his youth and a speech impediment prevented him from doing so.

By 1849, when he was twenty-two, Motte had chosen a mercantile career and was working as a clerk for a factorage firm with offices on Adger's Wharf on the Cooper River. Factors were commission merchants and business agents. They obtained what the planter needed when he needed it and sold his crops for a small sales commission.

By the time that the census enumerators reached the Pringle family mansion the summer of 1850, Motte had married Gabriella ("Ella") Ravenel and moved to their new residence above 58 Broad Street, close to his work. Ella was the sixth child of John Ravenel and Anna Elizabeth Ford.[116] The Ravenels were also of old South Carolina planter stock, their ancestors having arrived in the first wave of Huguenot immigration in the 1680s.

Motte and Ella's first child, Anna Eliza Pringle, was born in 1851, and they ultimately had five more.

By 1852 Motte had entered into partnership with Hermann Thiermann to form the firm of Thiermann and Pringle, factors and commission merchants, with offices on the docks at 12 Vanderhorst St. In 1853 disaster struck the young firm. The partners suffered a staggering financial loss which required major financial intervention from Motte's father, his Uncle Robert Pringle, and perhaps from his elder brother, Alston.[117] From Paris, Uncle Robert wrote to William that he would be willing to mortgage his share of Beneventum and its slaves so that Thierman & Pringle could continue in business. Robert's only critical comment was, "You ought to have informed me of Motte's difficulties when they commenced."[118]

Thiermann and Pringle survived the catastrophe, but the aftereffects were still fresh in everyone's minds when Edward wrote to his father on October 3, 1858, "I hope you are able to bear life under the misfortune of Motte's failure. Falling as it does chiefly on you who were so hard pressed before, it is a great trial. But the worst is over and I feel almost as if there were a relief to you and Motte both to have had the agony of suspense and uncertainty over." Edward hinted that speculation on cotton prices might have been at the root of Motte's problems, but, perhaps in justification of his own history, stated, "the future has plenty of opportunity to redeem the past. I feel keenly *that* your trying and difficult position and am greatly mortified that my own imprudence and carelessness has cut me off from doing what I ought to be able to do to return what I owe at home." Edward closed by apologizing that he could not send any funds to help.[119]

In November of that same year, Edward, who had assumed the role of family commentator, consoled his father and tried to offer him some hope. "I do not know what to say about Motte's affairs, except to hope that in the benefit to his character, there will be some compensation for his losses. I hope the generosity of the Bank of Charleston will enable you to get along until some permanent arrangement can be made. And if Brother [Alston] gets in as judge on a good footing and Brewton is successful you may hope soon to see us all with our heads above water."[120]

To add to his miseries, Motte was laid up in bed with an infected foot in 1859. Mary wrote to one of her daughters, "Ella is like a ministering angel at his side. He can not bear her out of his sight."[121] The affliction was debilitating to Motte, and he took several months to recover, during which time he lost a considerable amount of weight. "His leg is still weak," Mary wrote. "His person and legs are but half the size they were—but his face is full and florid still. Ella looks wretchedly. She and her children must certainly be taken to Runimede."[122]

Motte's business failure severely burdened the Pringle family's already ravaged finances for a decade and threatened their ownership of Beneventum plantation. The catastrophe left Motte in dire financial straits and stigmatized by his family until his service in the Civil war overshadowed the memory of what the family had come to call "Motte's folly."

Susan and Rebecca

In the fall of 1845, sixteen-year-old Susan Pringle reluctantly left Charleston in the company of her mother and her sister Mary Frances for Pelham, New York, the site of the Pelham Priory, a private boarding school. Its headmaster was the Rev. Robert Bolton, an Episcopal priest of Huguenot extraction born in Savannah, who had established the school just a year before.[123]

The student body was composed mainly of girls from socially prominent Southern families, and it was the chosen school for several of Susan's cousins. Sarah and Ella Middleton were there with her, as were several other young women with Lowcountry surnames.[124]

Although it was common at the time for affluent Southern families to send their sons off to colleges both nearby and far away, that option was rarely exercised for their daughters.

Pelham Priory played a much different role in Susan Pringle's life than Harvard and the South Carolina College played in the lives of her brothers. Until she was sixteen, Susan's education had been conducted at home by her mother, private tutors and language instructors, but she evidently did not apply herself to learning with the zeal expected of her. As a result, she was sent to the Priory as much to remedy her lackadaisical attitude as to educate her.

Susan viewed her enrollment at the Priory as a sentence of exile and punishment. "I truly condole with you upon your incarceration," Emma Pringle wrote, urging Susan to buckle down, pursue her studies and prepare herself for life's "never decreasing duties."[125]

Life at the school was not harsh. The source of Susan's anguish was the separation from her family, not the living conditions at the Priory. Sarah Middleton wrote her mother that it was "just like a large amiable family. Mrs. Bolton is the very personification of kindness and reminds me very much indeed of Aunt Pringle. Matilda says of Mr. Bolton, 'isn't he a dear sweet old man?' and that is the opinion of all of the girls."[126]

Susan Pringle
Clarke's Studio, Charleston, 1870.

Sue complained that the rules and regulations set down by Miss Bolton were unnecessarily strict. They evidently prevented the girls from writing letters to anyone but immediate family. Mary advised her to explore with Mrs. Bolton the reason for this rule, to explain to her that she came from a large and scattered family who were accustomed to keeping in close touch by letter and to ask that the rules be eased. Mary must have thought the rules too rigid as well, for she closed her letter to Susan by saying, "If this does not answer, I must write to Miss Bolton myself."[127]

Mary was pleased that Susan had started learning Italian and with her decision not to study music, which, Mary felt, might interfere with other studies.

> I disapprove very decidedly of more than one occupation at a time. I cannot conceive that a girl can recite correctly when she is at the same moment busy with her knitting needles or her thimble. You, however, will, I trust, avoid this error, as at your time of life, you ought to be so fully impressed with the importance of an accomplished education that your improvement must depend more on yourself than on your instructors. We can have no other mode of making you learn than the one we have adopted, of placing you in a situation of attaining a finished education and of appealing to your most elevated feelings of religion, honour and refinement. Of your capability of learning, I am satisfied your mind is quick, your comprehension clear, your love of literature remarkable for one of your age, but you must exhibit application, and you must submit to control, for as Johnson[128] says, 'negligence and irregularity, long continued, make knowledge useless, wit ridiculous and genius contemptible.'"[129]

Mary constantly urged Susan to apply herself to her studies, and offered both emotional and other, more tangible comforts. "Your studies surely ought to be a pleasure to you, for if, at the age of sixteen, a young woman is incapable of zeal and ambition in acquiring intellectual accomplishments, I should be in despair about her ever being a woman of cultivated and defined minds. You have our full approbation about your drawing lessons, if it does not interfere with more important studies. I should like to have a specimen of your taste. . . . Cretia has been employed all day in making some ginger cake for you, which she has done very nicely and with much pleasure, as it was for you. I will ship it immediately."[130]

After almost a year at the school, Susan was able to show good progress and pleaded with her parents to have her four-year sentence commuted.

William wrote, "[Your mother] has so well explained her views about your plans that I need add no more except that if you promise to be very studious and will consider yourself (for a year after your return) as if [you] were in a nunnery and furthermore will make yourself very notably useful in relieving your Mama of her domestic duties, you may come at the appointed time."[131] Susan was delighted with the news and spent much of that summer in Newport, enjoying the company of her family, relatives and friends.

Eight years later, Susan was twenty-four and unmarried. A letter from Edward, also unmarried, to his mother offers clues as to why. "I am afraid you will never get either of us quite off your hands," he wrote. "She is a thousand times more fastidious matrimonially than I am. [Sue] makes herself a sort of icicle or oyster when any man approaches whom she thinks she does not fancy! Tell her I advise her as a useful moral lesson to see how fascinating she can be to the first man she meets who has dirty hands, or great thick nails."[132]

Susan and the teen-aged Rebecca spent the 1850s exercising their social skills and adorning the festivities of Charleston, Newport, and Europe. Throughout the South at that time, upper-class women regularly attended and hosted elegant parties and dances. In February 1854 Mary wrote to Mary Mitchell that Susan was

> busy over flowers forming two pyramids for the Ravenel supper table, as they are to give a very large ball tonight. After the pyramids, Sue has her dress to think of and then there is something to be contrived and made for her head. There has been a perfect stagnation in the social world around us, so I got up a party for Sue, but she disclaimed all interest in it, nothing daunted by this, I went on, and, strange to say,

> your Papa exhibited an unusual degree of zeal about it, and when the thing was fairly in agitation, Sue put her shoulder to the wheel and behaved bravely. The party (of about a hundred guests) came off most successfully, on the 22nd and, as usual, it was pronounced the handsomest party of the season.[133]

Rebecca made her social debut "with great éclat" in February 1857 at the age of eighteen. Her debutante ball was held at the Miles Brewton House. These parties were expensive, of course, and this one came at a time when money was already a major problem for the family. As usual, the Pringles chose to live the lifestyle of their fellow rice barons, even though the family coffers were virtually empty.

After Mary Frances and Donald Mitchell returned from Europe in 1855 and settled in New Haven, the birth of each child brought a new excuse for Mary, Susan and Rebecca to visit. One of the women always had to stay at home to take care of the younger boys. Those making the trip would take a steamer from Charleston to New York and then board the train for the one-day trip to New Haven. The typical Pringle trip to the North lasted two or three months and usually included time spent with Mary Mitchell in New Haven, shopping in New York, and leisurely vacations in Newport, where Julius, Maria, and the Middleton cousins held court each summer and fall.

Susan spent the summer and early fall of 1853 in Newport with her aunt, Sallie Middleton. She made friends with Mr. and Mrs. Henry Tiffany and was a guest at several of their parties. In August of 1858, Mary and Sue went to New Haven and braved the scorn of the Northern abolitionists by taking their favorite servant, Cretia, with them. The visit coincided with the birthday of one of Mary Mitchell's children, and Mary Pringle wrote, "This is Minnie's birthday,[134] three years old, and the little thing is so well, again, as to be joyous and happy over the iced sponge cake that Cretia has made and the dollar tea set that I bought last evening in New Haven as a birthday gift."[135] In 1859 both Rebecca and Susan visited Mary Mitchell

Rebecca Motte Pringle in the 1850s.

and Newport, and Susan was back again in the summer of 1860 for the birth of Mary's fifth child, Susan Pringle Mitchell.

William was not comfortable with the notion of women traveling abroad. On May 23, 1854, with Susan about to join the Mitchells in Paris, William wrote to Mary Frances, "You know that it is my opinion that young ladies are in their more proper sphere at home than traveling. But, as you know too, this is not the only one of my good old fashion notions that I have been forced to yield to the spirit of modern innovation."[136] Despite the family's financial problems, William sent Susan to Europe in 1854 to travel with the Mitchells; permitted Rebecca to stay in Paris with her aunt, Sallie Middleton in 1856; and permitted her to return to Europe the next summer and tour the Rhine, the Tyrol, and visit Munich, Vienna, and Dresden with the Middletons.

Mary Frances

The chandelier in the drawing room radiated a festive glow in 1853, when Mary Frances Pringle, then twenty-two, married popular author and Yale University professor Donald G. Mitchell, thirty-one, at the Miles Brewton House. The son of Rev. N. Alfred Mitchell of Norwich, Connecticut, Donald attended Yale and studied law in New York. By 1852 he was a well-known author whose work had been appearing in the national presses since 1839. He wrote *Reveries of a Bachelor* and *Dream Life* under the pen name, "Ik Marvel," and books relating to travel and agriculture. His short stories were widely serialized in the *New Englander, American Review, Atlantic Monthly,* and *Harper's.*

In late July 1852, the debonair author heard that Washington Irving was enjoying the season at Saratoga. Mitchell had planned a summer trip to Europe, but resolved to spend a few days with his fellow writer before departing. Several members of the Pringle family were also at Saratoga that summer: daughters Mary Frances, Susan, their parents, and their niece, Susan Alston. A friend of the Pringles told Mary Frances, "Ik Marvel is here. Don't you want to meet him?"

She replied, "I don't want to meet him. If he wants to meet me, very well." Her statement indicated that she was a woman whose companionship had to be sought and earned, and this piqued his interest. After meeting Mary Frances he was impressed, quickly abandoned his European plans, and began an intense courtship. Within a few days he gave her a copy of his book, *Fresh Gleanings,* inscribing it, "This first book of my author-life being dedicated to 'Mary,' seems, in so far, a fitting gift for my friend, Miss Mary Pringle; and I shall claim from her the same charity which her namesake has shown."[137]

In August the Pringles left Saratoga for Newport, Boston, and the White Mountains of New England, trailing the lovestruck author in their wake. In the fall they returned to Charleston, where, evidently unannounced, Donald Mitchell arrived in December—only to find that the Pringles were visiting elsewhere. He repaired to Savannah, where on December 23, 1852, he wrote Mary Frances a letter which was, for all intents, a marriage proposal. "I am sure that with your true womanly discernment you know very much of my character already; and I shall tell you nothing more here. . . . I know well enough to feel sure that your hand will never go where your heart does not wholly follow; and, if you write me that you love your southern home too well to leave it ever, I will bear the disappointment as stoutly as I can, and sincerely hope (as I do now) that God may bless you always!"[138]

Mitchell's letter hit its mark and Mary accepted him as a

Author Donald G. Mitchell

suitor. He hastened to the family mansion on King Street, and on February 1, 1853, her twenty-second birthday, Donald Mitchell put his ring on her finger.

The engagement of their daughter to a Northern intellectual did not come about without some misgivings within the Pringle family. The very evening of the engagement, Mitchell wrote a close friend that William Bull Pringle "regrets that my home will not be here [Charleston], and does not favor much the idea of my living in a small town in Connecticut." But Mitchell may have had an ally in his prospective mother-in-law, who in her youth had so admired her Yale-educated tutor, John Pierpont. Mary may have worked on her husband's doubts and facilitated cupid's work.

Donald Mitchell had his own pre-marital concerns. He had held hopes of marrying a rich wife and living on her money. After finding that the lovely Miss Pringle would not come with a significant dowry, Mitchell candidly confessed, "It is with some base regrets that I give up forever the thought of obtaining through marriage a property that I might spend in elegancies; but I am sure that good judgment, honesty, and good intent, confirm the course I have chosen. I have got a life of work before me, but I feel able to do it. If luxury had been supplied to me without effort, I fear I should have done very little."[139]

In March Donald proposed a wedding trip to Europe. "I think we might pass six months in Europe at a cost of $3,000," he wrote. "This would involve a bit of trenching upon capital, but not to such an amount as would frighten me."[140] With the

European trip decided upon, Mitchell sought a consular post, and on May 24, 1853, he was appointed U.S. consul to Venice. One week later they were married at the Miles Brewton House. On June 8 Donald gave his mother-in-law a copy of *Reveries of a Bachelor*, in which he wrote, "Will Mrs. Pringle keep this little book as a token of the earnest and thankful regard which the writer feels for that dignity and truthfulness of character, which the example of the mother has so richly confirmed in the daughter."[141]

After stopping briefly in Connecticut, the newlyweds sailed aboard the *Arctic* for Liverpool on June 25, 1853.[142] After several months of leisurely travel through England, Wales, Scotland, France, Belgium, Germany, Bavaria, and Switzerland, they reached Venice, where Mitchell assumed his consular duties and the study of Venetian history.

He found the Venetians untrustworthy, the cost of living high, and the income from his position unsatisfactory: only $150 per year. Accordingly, he resigned his post in the spring of 1854 and the Mitchells moved to Paris. There, they settled down in a comfortable fourth-floor apartment at 8, Rue de Luxembourg, where their first child, Hesse, was born. They remained in Paris until mid-April 1855, enjoying the company of Donald's brother and of Mary's Uncle Robert.

Anxious at having their daughter so far away for such a long time, the Pringles implored Donald to return as soon as possible, and he promised to have her and their baby back in Charleston by the first of May 1856. "Mary will continue her visit there as Mrs. Pringle may think prudent," Mitchell wrote, "while I am on the search for some habitable quarter at the North."[143] The home he settled upon became known as Edgewood, a 200 acre farm in West Haven. They lived there for the rest of their lives, and all of their twelve children (save for Hesse and Elizabeth) were born there.

William, Jr.

William Bull Pringle, Jr., the fifth son of the Pringle family, sought to follow Julius's example and serve a tour as a military officer. In the spring of 1849, when he was sixteen, his father asked Joel R. Poinsett to help young William obtain a patronage appointment to West Point. Poinsett replied that such appointments were difficult to obtain and suggested that William's education would not, at his age, have properly prepared him for the grueling competition.

With regret, William, Jr., put thoughts of West Point behind him, enrolled in South Carolina College and graduated "with high merit" in December 1852.[144] He found a position as a civil engineer with the Blue Ridge Railroad, but the work was hard and the company was rough. His mother wrote of him, "I hear regularly, every week, from my good son William, who sticks bravely to his business, altho' his situation has not been pleasant this summer, in consequence of the low and uneducated people among whom he has been thrown."[145]

In November 1854 William suddenly came into some money, the source of which remains undetermined. As soon as Edward found out, he offered to invest it for him. Edward wrote to Mary, "Send it all out to me as soon as possible and I will accumulate the interest for him and make him a rich man in five years. If he does not touch it before then he will be well educated and well prepared to enjoy his wealth. I can make it reach $50,000 in 5 years perhaps $100,000: if things turn out well. . . . I hope Bill's wealth is a sign of the rising fortunes of the family."[146]

The lure of France beckoned William in the summer of 1856, and his father consented to the trip. By the spring of 1857, when he was twenty-four, his father helped him establish a new rice mill on the Santee. William took up residence at Richfield plantation. Armed with his engineering background, his father's financial backing, and a basic knowledge of rice planting, he began work on his new mill. In the summer of 1857 he traveled to New York to look for machinery. By November, the mill was in operation.

Young William had the same bad luck at business as several of his older brothers. In the spring of 1859, Mary wrote, "Poor William has met with many disasters in his mill enterprises, yet it is yielding a very large income, and, but for his monied embarrassments, would be eminently successful as an investment. A few days since, William, by advice of friends, ventured to buy 4,000 barrels of rough rice to have pounded at the mill. He sent it on a sailing vessel and, fortunately, had it insured, for the vessel sprung a leak and her cargo was materially injured, may be, will be a total loss. The insurance will, we think, cover William."[147]

That same year, his black superintendent, Hector, was severely injured in a accident. Mary wrote that "he was drawn in by the machinery and had one of his legs so mutilated that it was necessary to amputate it below the knee, his other leg was much crushed, too, and his whole body jarred and bruised." In closing, Mary showed clearly the dual nature of her views about slaves: that they were chattel property, but should be treated with compassion. "There is every hope of recovery, yet the injury is an immense loss to William, as he was his most valuable negro. Your Papa valued his services in the mill at $3,000."[148]

Hector did not immediately improve, and a few days later, Mary wrote to Edward, "Hector has been obliged to submit to a second amputation, above the knee, as symptoms of mortifications [gangrene] appeared about the wound. Your Papa witnessed the operation and was much impressed by the stoicism of the sufferer. He talked cheerfully and even gaily, whilst the physicians were preparing for the operation. Before performing which, they administered chloroform, which rendered him so insensible that he was not aware of the operation until it was all over."[149]

In June 1859 William, Jr., became seriously ill. Julius, then in New York with their father, sent Alston a telegram: "Father left Sunday evening six (6) o'clock will reach Charleston two one half (22) o'clock AM Wednesday. How is William."[150] His condition worsened, and his father recorded his last moments, in which William deplored the burden he had added to the family's financial problems. "Oh Papa how is it that your children embarrass you so," he said. "I have lost thousands. How can I settle it?"

His younger brother Robert, who was at his bedside, said, "Don't worry yourself, you have lost nothing. I will settle every thing."[151]

Surrounded by his parents and several brothers and sisters, William, Jr., died of peritonitis in his bed at the family home on Wednesday morning, June 29, 1859. Mary wrote of him, "He was the purest spirit of us all."[152]

Although the mill had been profitable, young William had not been able to overcome "the difficulties of his heavy embarrassments" and his father was forced to take over the operation of the mill himself."[153]

Brewton

Brewton followed his elder brother into South Carolina College. After his graduation in 1855,[154] he returned to Charleston and found a position in a counting house. On March 10, 1856, William, Jr., wrote to Susan, "I am glad to hear of Brewton's ball-room and counting-room efficiency, why! what a business-man and what a buck the fellow has become, with his clerkly air of the morning and his flirting with the girls at night—watch him, Sue, and beware lest the gay Lothario should elope and warn him, Sue, lest like his unfortunate brother, his heart should be involved and *broken*."[155]

Shortly before the war broke out, Brewton joined into partnership with John Gravely[156] to form the firm of Gravely and Pringle, a hardware business located on East Bay Street.

Robert

Robert also attended South Carolina College, and after his graduation in 1856,[157] took a clerking position in his uncle's factorage firm, Coffin & Pringle, on Adger's North Wharf. On August 18, 1856, Julius wrote to his mother, "Bob is very well fixed – he will have good training in Coffin and Pringle's. That will be much better for him than coming out to San Francisco and uncertainties. If he takes care of his business and makes himself useful he is sure of success."[158]

Robert made a good impression with the firm in his first year. In 1857 the partners wrote him a congratulatory letter. They noted that his work had been "entirely satisfactory," and that although it was not their practice to pay their clerks for the first year, they wanted Robert to select one of the six watches they had sent as a token of their esteem. They closed by offering him a pittance of a salary: $200 per year.[159] The fact that Robert, the college-educated son of a major planter had to accept such a pathetic salary underscored both the lack of choices available to him and the financial desperation of the family.[160]

Charles and James

As with the eldest sons, the youngest also attended Harvard. Charles traveled to Cambridge in the summer of 1857 with Susan, who was to drop him off before going to New York and awaiting the telegram announcing that Rebecca had arrived in New York from Paris.

As a Californian, Edward had some definite opinions on the course of study Charles should follow. On May 19, 1857, he wrote his mother, "He must study the modern languages: French and Spanish. By the time he is twenty-five [1866], we shall have annexed Cuba and the whole of Mexico; and Americans will have to speak Spanish."[161]

Charles passed his Harvard entrance examinations and by September 13 was settled into his new quarters. He wrote a letter to his mother, describing his Apollonian personal habits.

He told of his large, comfortable room, and noted, "you would be astonished too to see in what nice order it is kept, no paper about the room no books thrown about and not more than two chairs out of their places."[162] The next week, he wrote again. "The studying so far has been easier than what I was accustomed to at home; I can either study all my lessons in the day and have all the evening, or I can study at night and have the whole day except the three recitation hours."[163]

Early on, Charles evidenced the moral fiber for which the Pringles were known. When a student was falsely accused of making fun of a tutor, Charles stepped forward, confessed, and took his punishment. He warned his parents, "The Pres[ident of Harvard] will write about it."[164]

William determined that Charles should leave Harvard at the end of his second year and travel with his younger brother, James, to study in Europe. James had also wanted to attend West Point—perhaps as much for the free education as the desire for military service—but he did not succeed in gaining admission. The cost of sending him to college weighed heavily on Mary's mind.[165] In the summer of 1858, she had written, "One of my most serious anxieties is that a painful necessity may oblige your father to deny you the advantages of a collegiate education, to throw you, with an uncultured mind, into the routine of laborious life, when you will have time only to work, but none to cultivate your intellect."[166]

Edward wrote his mother with the opinion that Charles and James should not attend the same school. He believed that if they were in separate schools, each would be forced to learn the language quicker, and both would learn self-reliance.[167] In the summer of 1859 James was sent to the Eglise Consistoriale Réformée, a small, private school in Dijon, a provincial capitol in France's Burgundy district. On July 21 Uncle Robert wrote William that "I think for the present it is a very good place for James, but before he returns home he had better study in England some time, either with some learned man who takes a few scholars, or at Oxford. I shall not mind the expense. I told

James to take fencing, dancing and gymnastics lessons."[168]

A few months after James arrived in Dijon, Charles traveled to Edgewood, Cambridge, Newport, and New York, from whence he departed for France. He arrived at Le Havre on Saturday, October 1, 1859, and made his way to Paris that evening. There he found Uncle Robert in poor health. James joined them that evening and the two boys spent the better part of the next week exploring Paris.

On Thursday they both traveled to Dijon and took up their studies. "James says it is a very dull place," Charles wrote, "but so much the better for study. He does not appear to like Mr. and Madame [Pertuzon] as much as at first, and says I will not do so either. Thus far, however, I like them very much, and hope to learn French very quickly."[169]

Mary noted with regret that James and Charles's success in Dijon had inspired other Lowcountry planters to send their children to the same school. "We are sorry to find people following our example about Dijon. Pringle Ravenel will go there after graduating this spring and Daniel Huger is to send one of his young sons, about 17 years of age, in a few weeks. . . . We are absolutely distressed."[170] It was obvious that Mary didn't want her sons distracted from their studies by their hometown friends.

In the spring of 1860, Charles and James had asked permission of their parents to change schools, and their mother replied that Charles was old enough to choose his own profession and make appropriate choices for his schooling. James, on the other hand, was told to stay at Dijon for another year. Ultimately, Mary and William relented to letting both sons make their educational choices for themselves. Mary warned them, "I pray you, my sons, to be wise and provident in your deliberations; for the future of your lives is involved in your present pursuits. Your Papa has generously afforded you advantages he can ill afford and the use you make of them is the only return you can make him for his generosity."[171]

By September Charles and James had opted to study in Berlin. Susan was only mildly impressed with the city. "From what

I have read of it, I should imagine it must have many attractions, but I have been told by persons who have spent some time there, that for foreigners, it is a very dull place, as far as society is concerned, but for that, I suppose you will not care, as you only go there for study."[172] Also in the city were several of the Ravenel boys, and the small knot of young Charlestonians undoubtedly followed with great interest the family and newspaper accounts of the powerful forces which were starting to reshape the lives of their families back in Charleston.

CHAPTER SEVEN

Trials and Triumphs

I have made a noble sacrifice today. . . . To enable your Papa to purchase "Pleasant Meadows" plantation... I have consented, nay, magnanimously offered, to let him sell the lower portion of my lot—my dear hereditary land.

—Mary Pringle, January 10, 1854

The decade before the Civil War was prosperous for the state's Lowcountry planters. Like their fellow rice princes, the Pringles continued to live well and spend freely. Out of habit and family tradition, they maintained the elegant lifestyle of the great planter families they entertained, dined, danced, and attended church with. Until the first shots were fired at Fort Sumter, they continued to buy the most elegant clothes, travel to the finest spas, summer in Newport, and send their sons to the best schools or off for tours of Europe.

There was one problem. Like the orchestra aboard the *Titanic,* which continued to play while their ship sank, the Pringle family conducted life in perennial denial of their financial reality. When the bills for their extravagance came in, William Bull Pringle did not have the money to pay them. Despite rice production which peaked at over one million pounds per year and brought them an annual income of more than $30,000, the family was staggering under the weight of its debts by the middle of the 1850s.

In 1852 Alston wrote to his mother that he wished his parents could be relieved of some of their concerns. He lamented that he couldn't help financially, but wrote, "as I can't do this, and as you would not let me if I could, I can only advise you and him just to rest for this summer, to dismiss all care of children, crop and debt and gather fresh energy for the work yet before you."[1]

Serious a problem as it was, overspending was not the sole source of their financial problems. William's wallet was also under pressure from four additional directions: over- investment in mortgaged land and slaves; Motte's business disaster, which required a financial bailout; the financial catastrophe of William, Jr.; and the failure of some of the California mortgage investments which Edward managed for the family. To add to his troubles, only one of William's nine sons chose planting as a vocation, leaving him to manage his far-flung agricultural holdings virtually unaided. By Christmas of 1860 the family was spread out, with members living in Connecticut, California, Paris, and Berlin—and debts so large and pressing that Mary was constantly depressed.

When William decided to purchase Pleasant Meadow plantation in 1854, he was forced to get his wife's consent to sell off the back half of the King Street lot in order to raise the money. The loss of half of her ancestral homestead was a powerful emotional blow to Mary. She wrote the following bitter lines to Mary Mitchell, then in Italy:

> I have made a noble sacrifice today, for the advantage of my children. To enable your Papa to purchase "Pleasant Meadows" (Hunts' plantation adjoining Richfield) which is for sale at $18,000. I have consented, nay, magnanimously offered, to let him sell the lower portion of my lot—my *dear hereditary land*. Would it be wrong to drop a tear, when I am all by myself, to this act of duty. Papa says, the Jew brokers[2] called me "a sensible woman"—it makes the Governor think me one. I know I am almost inclined to think so, myself. Even with this sale of the lot (if we are able to make it on our

> terms, viz., a pretty high price) the new purchase will very much increase our debt. . . . I have stopped to wipe away a tear; here, my child, my precious darling child, God be with you. I love you, with my whole heart. May your child be to you, all that you have been and are to me . . . .[3]

Ten days after he purchased Pleasant Meadow, William had the back half of the garden surveyed and subdivided. The northern half was sold to Edward North Thurston, a Charleston merchant; the southern half went to Cleland Kinloch Huger, another merchant. Each lot brought the Pringles $7,000. The $18,000 purchase price for Pleasant Meadow would not have included the cost of field hands required to operate it. Even if only fifty were required, at an average cost of $500 each, the slaves would have cost an additional $25,000, making a total cost of $43,000. Subtracting the $14,000 realized from selling the two building lots, this still left a deficit of about $29,000, which William undoubtedly had to borrow. Edward wrote that he mourned the loss of the garden, and proposed that in ten years, the richest two of the Pringle children should buy back the property.[4] That never became possible.

In the early part of the decade, Mary seemed to enjoy William's affection for her. In 1853 she wrote Mary Mitchell about the summer she had passed in Charleston. "I have had but one fault to find with it," Mary related, "that it has passed too quickly away—the days have not been enough for all I had to do—and my old husband has become so fond of me, that he cannot bear me out of his sight—; this is somewhat a nuisance, I confess."[5]

By the middle of the decade, strains were showing. In "A Wife's Prayer for Her Husband," Mary asked God to help her husband realize that "his spiritual and temporal concerns depend upon the faithful and conscientious performance of his duty, that he may not be seduced or discouraged by any temptation, whatever."[6]

While still a newlywed, Mary praised the conjugal state. After thirty years of marriage, however, the luster had worn thin.

By the late 1850s she was writing that "women can so seldom establish a fame on their own reputation, that they must be satisfied with the second grade of enjoying it from a connection with a great man."[7] She also spoke of finding happiness through giving birth to a man of genius and reflecting in the glory of her sons' future literary work.

By the end of the decade a distinct bitterness had crept into Mary's journal. In one essay she quoted a tale from Exodus which describes an incident during the migration of the Jews to the Holy Land. They had been without water for several days and came upon a body of water at Marah. When they found the water too bitter to drink, they murmured against Moses. Moses prayed to God, who sent a tree that, when cast into the water, made it sweet to drink. Mary's journal essay was an analogy to this story.

She wrote that we have "personal waters of bitterness" and named three. The first was temptations—passions which get the mastery of us and "burn like lava if kept down. . . . Our duty," she wrote in Calvinist fashion, "is to deny ourselves."

The second was domestic waters of bitterness—afflictions and troubles connected with our families, such as the death of a family member. "Jealousy, discord and strife often invade the family circle, she wrote. "Affection dies out, selfishness takes its place." And then there is the child on whom a family has "spared no toil" who turns out to be cold and ungrateful.

Finally, there are the "worldly waters of bitterness," which arise out of our connections with the world, such as when one is reduced from affluence to want or when one's reputation is sullied.

It is difficult to determine which temptations she may have struggled with, and which child was "cold and ungrateful"; but her reference to "domestic waters of bitterness" points to her relationship with her husband. And her "worldly waters of bitterness" clearly refer to the heavy burden of indebtedness under which they had been struggling. The toll on Mary was evident to her children, as Susan wrote to Rebecca in 1859,

"I have become accustomed to her worn and thin face."[8]

In addition to the family debts, city taxes were a constant pressure. The Miles Brewton House had an assessed value of $18,000 in 1859, which resulted in an annual tax levy of $270. Added to this were the taxes on $490 in interest income, thirty-four house servants, the barouche and another carriage, and three horses, for a total of $471.75 per year.[9] Late in 1858 legal actions apparently were underway to attach or seize the family home, and the family did some fancy deed shuffling in an attempt to protect it from creditors. Mary transferred the title to William, Jr., on November 10, 1858. Seventeen days later, he conveyed the property to his father.[10]

As their financial problems deepened, tensions in the household continued to rise. In 1857 Mary snapped at Rebecca over a trifling concern that in better times would never have produced an outburst. "You are very good to write so frequently, my darling, but please, always write to me on thick white paper—tell Mrs. Izard I thank him [i.e., Mr. Izard] gratefully for watching over your expenses, but that I pray her to indulge me in a sheet of *thick* white paper because I am a poor old woman whose sight is dim, and an unfortunate old woman whose patience is easily disturbed, so I am sadly tried by your vile, blue, thin paper, particularly when you write in the wild, desultory style that you have done from Paris."[11] Mary's self-description suggests that her spirits had been in decline for some time.

In an 1857 letter to his mother, Edward reflected that now nearly all the family members had grown up, he longed for a family reunion. "I thought that science was annihilating space so much that we should always be within hailing distance of each other. But it seems that even rail roads and telegraphs cannot keep up with the temptations and inducements to wander off. Perhaps the opening of China may tempt the next adventurer of the family; and we will look upon my California abode as only a half way house." He closed by expressing the wish that "We'll hope to be all together again next Christmas."[12]

The great family reunion was held just before Christmas 1859.

Mary Mitchell, two months pregnant with her fifth child, and her four young children arrived at the Miles Brewton House in November. When an ailing Uncle Robert arrived, Rebecca wrote with alarm, "Uncle Robert's feebleness shocked Papa and all of us extremely; but the charming sunshine has already done wonders for him and he looks and says he feels like a different man. He is staying with us."[13]

Uncle Robert stayed on for a while at Runimede after Christmas and traveled with William to Richfield in December. Although suffering from rheumatism, he invited Mary Mitchell and her family up to Beneventum "and has prepared himself to entertain a succession of company, having brought a carpet for his dining room, and a supply of groceries," Mary wrote. "His character and temper are much softened, but alas, alas! *he does 'not consider'* though he is old, weak and suffering, he seems studiously to shut out all thoughts of eternity."[14] By July 1860 Uncle Robert was back in Paris and in "pitiable" condition. William's cheerful and generous bachelor brother died in his Paris apartment on October 26, 1860. His body was returned to Charleston and buried in St. Michael's churchyard.

In April 1860 Mary and William accompanied Julius and Maria to New York, where Julius and Maria departed for France. William, chafing to return home, left for South Carolina; Mary, Susan, and Cretia went on to New Haven to attend the birth of Mary's newest grandchild, Susan Pringle Mitchell. After visiting Newport for what would be her last time, Mary returned to Charleston early in September 1860. At the age of fifty-seven, after a wearying decade of disappointment and financial calamities, it was probably for the best that Mary did not know that her most fearsome trials were still ahead of her.

CHAPTER EIGHT

The Peculiar Institution

It [slavery] is of itself revolting enough to every Christian and humane bosom, and does not certainly require the aid of misrepresentation to render it more distressing; as in some situations, and under peculiar circumstances it cannot be done away with.
—Mary Pringle

Throughout the 1850s, the overriding national issue was the abolition of slavery. As rhetoric on both sides became more vehement, Americans began speculating on a possible "war between the states."

What did the Pringles think about slavery? Save for Mary and her son, Edward, who defended the institution in print, it is difficult to know. Although family members frequently mentioned individual slaves, we have to deduce their views about the system of slavery from a limited number of references. Why did the Pringles write so little about the system? The answer is simple: slavery was as much a part of their lives as the air they breathed, the water they drank and the blood in their veins. Among themselves, slaveholding was such a totally shared experience that no one needed to mention it—except when the system was challenged by outsiders.

Mary held radical views for the wife of a prominent planter who owned over three hundred slaves. Although she felt that Negroes were an inferior race incapable of achieving intellectual equality with whites, she nonetheless felt that slavery was indefensible from a Christian point of view. In a letter written during the late 1840s, Mary stated her revulsion over the "peculiar institution." Though she could hardly be a front-row Abolitionist and still maintain her position as a planter's wife and member of their elite society, Mary wrote the following to her sons Charles and James, then studying in Europe:

> Another agreeable little work has just been published, by young [Samuel Taylor] Coleridge, entitled "Six Months in the West Indies".[1] It is very worthy of perusal, as it appears a candid and impartial statement of things such as he really found them, during a visit of six months. He expresses himself on the subject of slavery with noble independence and just humanity. It is of itself revolting enough to every Christian and humane bosom, and does not certainly require the aid of misrepresentation to render it more distressing; as in some situations, and under peculiar circumstances it cannot be done away with. Our own State, for instance, is so thinly populated with whites, and they are, from habit and the warm climate, so indolent and inert as to be entirely incapable of performing the necessary labour for the culture of our land, which is not only of the most laborious kind, but from locality, creates a mortal disease which renders it impossible to import laborers from distant climates, as habitude[2] in the earliest infancy is alone possible to render one invulnerable to its direful effects.[3]

Mary's feelings about keeping slave families united were reflected in an 1856 letter she wrote from Runimede, describing the marriage of a slave from Drayton Hall to another from an adjoining plantation:

> We all met there [at Drayton's chapel] for Mr. Drayton's usual service to the blacks. First we had service, then the communion, to whites and blacks, and then we had a marriage ceremony; and young servant Penny was married to one of neighbor Ramsay's[4] men – You recollect Penny, I dare say, as being one of the two young girls whom we used to instruct before her baptism. She is, you know, an orphan, but so good a girl, that we all felt a pleasure in assisting her.

> Her fellow servants, too, were zealous in lending a hand to deck her decently, so she appeared in a neat white dress and plain handkerchief, her bridesmaid stood by her side and they had the wedding ring, with all the paraphernalia of a veritable marriage ceremony. All passed off solemnly and was calculated to impress seriously both owner and slave, yet it should make us reflect how we sanction a connexion that we may not, ourselves, be able to preserve, in cases of marriage between slaves not belonging to the same owner. We may feel confidence in this instance, however, as we are sure our good neighbors would always be ready to assist us in keeping Stepheny and Penny together.[5]

In the late 1850s Mary wrote to Charles and James, then in Europe, "Your melancholy feelings will no doubt be excited by finding the places of several of our faithful domestics vacated by death, those who were wont to perform with such cheerfulness your commands, joining with their duty the willing spirit and with lively good-nature endeavoring to amuse your childish humours, or to pacify your wayward inclinations. I hope you will always think of them with gratitude, nay, even with respect."[6]

Cretia, the butler Mack, and other servants often asked to be remembered to distant Pringle family members, and in 1859, Old Peggy inquired of Rebecca, "And Miss Becky, how her?" "Ah! She must miss you sadly," Mary wrote.[7]

The Pringle servants often expressed concern for their masters and mistresses. After their brother, William, Jr., died in 1859, Rebecca, in Charleston, wrote to Susan in Newport, "I wished an abolitionist could have witnessed the behavior of our negroes—it is so striking—instead of the usual boisterous greeting when Mama walked through the yard, they approached her with quiet silence and with apparently the deepest pity and feeling shook her hand. Some enquired about her health, but most of them shook her hand without saying a word."[8]

Edward, who moved to California in 1853, was the chief social commentator of the family. Because of his new perspective, his eye was keener—or he felt freer to comment—and he wrote more often about the relative merits of slavery. From his detached vantage point, Edward wrote that there were institutions of human employment worse than slavery as practiced in the South:

> If you ever had any doubts about slavery, come look at the Indians here and see how the reign of the white man is demolishing them. You can't imagine in all the range of creation a greater contrast than you see here between the restless, steam engine California population and the helpless race of Indians that is melting before them. The Chinese are industrious and hard working but Brother Jonathan[9] won't let his celestial neighbors work except in the worn out diggings and bad places, and there Chinadom grubs out a sustenance. But the "wild man of the woods" as Cooper[10] would call him, wanders about with his bow and arrow where Brother Jonathan has driven away all his game but sparrows, and he begs or steals a little and dies.[11]

The Rev. Alexander Glennie, who served as the rector of All Saints parish church in Georgetown District, was a close friend and frequent guest of the Pringles and an energetic proponent of religious education for the slaves. By the 1850s Glennie had inspired the building of thirteen plantation chapels around Georgetown. Educating the slaves was also a tradition in the family of Mary's great aunt, Eliza (Lucas) Pinckney. Eliza taught her slaves to read "in the hope they might teach others; she herself on Sundays read and explained the Bible to them and taught they to pray. Her devices for encouraging them in neatness, morality, and industry, she taught to her children and grandchildren, who were all known as kind and well-beloved owners."[12] Through these examples, Mary came to see the religious education of her servants as part of her Christian duty. Her girls joined in this responsibility. Mary wrote of Rebecca's daily routine that "it was pleasant to see her surrounded by her little class of colored catechumen, as usual, after breakfast, this morning."[13]

Many Lowcountry planters were opposed to the religious education of slaves. Susan M. Fickling wrote, "The master had a real and genuine fear that Christian slaves would demand inevitably that political, social and religious equality which would not only reduce their economic value, but would endanger those conventions which were deemed necessary for the effective control of the Negro population."[14]

Nevertheless, slaveowners had several reasons for providing religious education. Earnest Christians like Mary felt a moral obligation to bring their slaves, whom they regarded as heathens, to Christ. The typical large planter was generally more pragmatic. He looked to scriptures such as Ephesians 6:5, which commanded, "Slaves, obey your masters according to the flesh, with fear and trembling in the sincerity of your heart, as you would Christ,"and saw the opportunity to portray the master-slave relationship as God's holy will. He also found great usefulness in the concept that mortal toil and suffering here on Earth would be richly rewarded for eternity in Heaven, and hoped that the Bible's moral teachings would help reduce the incidence of theft and telling falsehoods by the slaves. Finally, he saw religious education of the slaves as ammunition against Abolitionist claims that the slaves were being denied access to the Bible. The religious education of the slaves for these reasons was a highly perverted use of religion, but one which cast the patriarchal planter and his family in a sanctified light.

The Pringles appear to have treated their household servants reasonably well by local standards of the day and did not appear to overwork them. However one must never forget that life in the nineteenth century was often brutal, and that much more so for the slaves. Two "gagging irons" noted in Mary Pringle's 1834 household inventory were iron muzzles which could be locked over the heads of slaves to keep them from talking, eating, or drinking the master's food while it was being prepared.[15] Further, no Alston or Pringle ever considered any of the servants to be even remotely capable of becoming their equals.

A slave gagging iron, or muzzle.

Pringle family members were not above mocking their slaves and their fancy livery uniforms. Mack, the butler, was a favorite of Edward's, and for one reason or another, Mack was photographed and a copy sent to Edward in San Francisco. He wrote, "And old Mack! How magnificent he is! I have laughed over him a dozen times. I keep him in the office that I may exhibit him as a specimen of the "Institution." How natural the old fellow looks. . . . Tell him his white cravat is a miracle—that there is nobody so well dressed in California. I wish you had sent some more of the servants—Mauma, and Cretia and Ishmael."[16]

Although the Pringle family's house servants do not appear to have been abused, their shortcomings came under greater criticism than if the same offense had been committed by a white person. In 1856 Mary shipped some special sweets to Mary Mitchell. In her next letter, the daughter wrote, "Who packed my delicious sweetmeats? Old Mack? Shake him, scold him for me!! Only think but *three* arrived unbroken, the others were smashed literally—the *beautiful* mushrooms, the nice pumpkin chips covered with fine, fine broken glass. It *did grieve* me to see such a sad havoc. The big white jar of green marmalade, the yellow jar of orange, and one small white jar of yellow marmalade were the only ones that escaped. Why did not Mack put more straw?"[17]

In 1860 the Pringle's household service staff had ballooned to thirty-two.[18] These consisted of nineteen black adults (eleven men, eight women) and thirteen children (six boys, seven girls) to maintain the house and serve six white Pringles—an astonishing 5.33 servants for each white family member. The inordinate size of the servant staff suggests that the Pringles did not want to break up slave families, even though they may have had little work for them to do.

Because the house servants reflected the family's public face and the field hands did not, the King Street service staff were clothed in handsome fashion compared to their country brethren. The Alston house servants wore "dark green broadcloth coats and vests trimmed in silver braid and red facings with trousers of green plush."[19] The Pringle house servants were also uniformed. Edward described Old Mack dressed in a white cravat, white pants, gold studs and a gold ring. Alicia Middleton noted that Mrs. William Bull Pringle's coachman and footman were dressed in a livery of dark green corded with yellow.[20] Mary Pringle Frost wrote that Hercules, the coachman, wore "a well-made costume of 'planes'—white woolen material, somewhat costly. Our grandfather [William] asked why he wore this heavy suit in summer. He answered: 'Kye Boss, ain't you know e bin too hot to wear tin ting.'"[21]

From a white slaveowner's perspective it might seem that the house servants had a much more desirable life than the field hands. The house servants "considered themselves in a class entirely apart from the field hands," wrote one planter. "No worse threat could be made to them than that they would be sent to work in the fields."[22] They had lighter work, lived in better quarters, got better food and clothing, and had more freedom of movement than did the field hands. Mary's maid, Cretia, frequently accompanied family members on trips to New York, New Haven, Newport, and California, and a black servant named Sue lived in France with Mary's son Julius and his family.

In 1856 Mary presented Cretia with a special gift: a large, leather-bound Bible inscribed, "Mary M. Pringle. March 9, 1856—To her good and faithful servant Cretia."[23] It is difficult to determine whether this gift indicates that Cretia had been taught to read (a practice illegal before the war), as Mary makes no specific mention of whether or not she taught her slaves to read. In her will, Mary also left Cretia a woolen shawl, a dress and $100.[24]

Either the Alstons kept incredibly detailed records of their hundreds of slaves or Cretia's mother was a special favorite, because Mary was able to locate and carefully copy Cretia's birth date, marriage date, and the birth, marriage and death dates for Cretia's children and grandchildren into the gift Bible. Mary continued to enter the vital statistics of Cretia's family into the volume until 1861, spelling their family name, "Stuart." Cretia's descendants spelled it, "Stewart."[25]

Slaves did not necessarily share the perspective that the life of a house servant was preferable to that of a field hand. The latter, it is true, had harder labor, but when their task was finished their workday was done. Unlike the house servants, they could get away from their masters and mistresses, relax, tend their own gardens, fish or simply enjoy each other's company without being subject twenty-four hours a day to every whim originating from inside the big house. In addition, female field hands were less subject to the sexual demands sometimes made of female house servants by the master or his sons.[26]

As mistress of the house, Mary assigned the servants their work and issued supplies. She and her older daughters used patterns to lay out and cut the cloth for their dresses, which were then put into a red workbox in the sewing room for their seamstresses to sew.[27] Every Monday morning she handed out soap and cleaning cloths. Every day, she gave out the following allotment of towels: one Osnaburg[28] to the cook, one Osnaburgs for the plates, two tea towels, one white towel for the glasses and three Osnaburgs a week for the knives. The daily issue from the storeroom included one and a half quarts of whole rice, one pint corn grist, one pint rice flour, a spoonful of lard and one quart of rice every Monday for starch.[29]

The Pringles issued clothing to each house servant twice each year, at the start and end of the annual migration from the city to the plantation. The summer clothes and shoes were handed out in May, and the winter issues in October. Mary did not

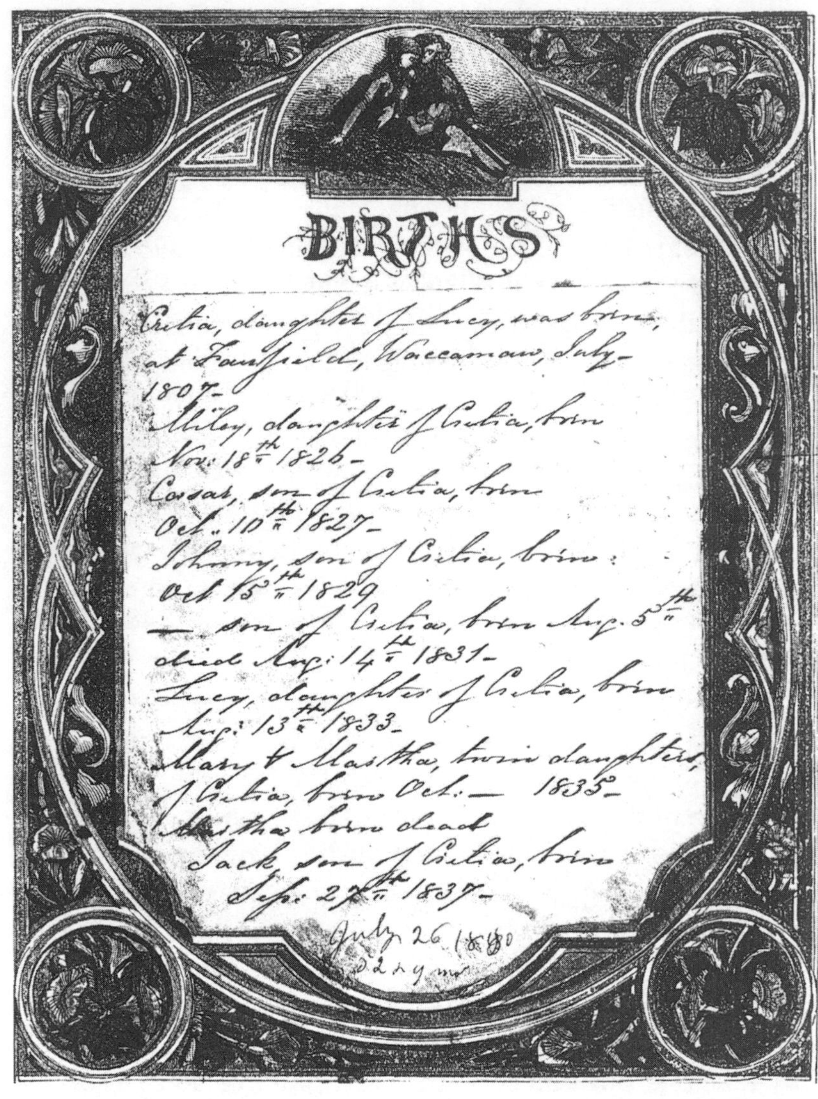

BIRTHS

Cretia, daughter of Lucy, was born,
at Fairfield, Waccamaw, July
1807—
Miley, daughter of Cretia, born
Nov. 18th 1826—
Caesar, son of Cretia, born
Oct. 10th 1827—
Johnny, son of Cretia, born:
Oct 15th 1829
— son of Cretia, born Aug. 5th
died Aug. 14th 1831—
Lucy, daughter of Cretia, born
Aug: 13th 1833—
Mary & Martha, twin daughters,
of Cretia, born Oct. — 1835—
Martha born dead
Jack, son of Cretia, born
Sep: 27th 1837—
July 26 1880
52 & 9 mo

Births page from Cretia's Bible

record the clothing issued to the women, but the typical clothing ration in the early 1850s for a male Pringle house servant was as follows:

Summer: two shirts, one pair pants, two vests, one coat, one livery coat and vest and two cravats. Winter: two shirts, one or two pairs pants, one vest, one coat, two cravats, two pocket handkerchiefs and two pair undergarments. Shoes were issued seasonally on an as-needed basis.[30]

Some servants received more than this minimum, and then, as now, rank had its privileges. Over a period of eighteen months in 1850 and 1851, Hercules, the coachman, received four pairs of shoes, eight shirts, six pairs of pants, three coats, four vests, two cravats and two handkerchiefs. Thomas Turner, the former jockey, was the beneficiary of superior bedding. In 1836 Mary noted that he had a mattress, two pair of sheets, two pillowcases, a pair of blankets and two counterpanes.[31]

An entry in one of Mary's household journals gives a clue as to what the house servants had on their plates. When the family made their annual migration to the Santee in the winter of 1850, four servants were left behind to mind the house and,

Slave quarters on a Santee River rice plantation

literally, "keep the home fires burning." Mary issued them the following rations and supplies: three bushels small rice (the eye of the grain), three bushels grist (ground corn meal), one bushel small rice extra, one bushel whole rice, one Westphalia ham, thirteen logs lightwood (resin-rich pine, used as kindling), three barrels chipped lightwood and a barrel half full for Mack['s] parlor use.[32] The fact that Mary did not mention firewood suggests that a plentiful supply was always on hand. Other than this one notation, the Pringle family records are mute about the food given to the servants, but it is fair to assume that they enjoyed at least the basic meats, vegetables, and starches produced on the family plantations.

Although their legal status as chattel was fixed by law, the servants at the Miles Brewton House appear to have been well clothed and adequately fed and housed by the standards of the times. Their provisioning reflected the wealth of their owners, and well-fed, liveried servants were, like their family portraits, a form of the competitive social display practiced by the affluent planter families. While always at the beck and call of their masters, the Pringle house servants at the Miles Brewton House appear to have lived better than some of their contemporaries, a fact that they may or may not have appreciated.

CHAPTER NINE

Soldiers, Slaves, and Refugees

The grape shot and musket / And the cannons lumber loud / It's many a mangled body / The blanket for the shroud / It's many a mangled body / Left on the field alone / I am a Rebel soldier / And far from my home.

—"Rebel Soldier," a traditional Civil War song

In late 1860, with the election of Abraham Lincoln as president, a war between the North and South seemed inevitable. Although a few politicians still urged compromise, passions were so inflamed that no further concessions, no further accommodations were possible.

The 1860 Democratic Convention had been held in Charleston in late April. When a pro-slavery platform was rejected, delegates from eight southern states walked out. Two months later they met in Baltimore to form the Southern Democratic Party with John C. Breckenridge as their standard bearer.

Mary wrote to her two sons in Europe, hoping that "good may come out of the great evil that has been overshadowing our Republican Union, and that the danger that has threatened its dissolution will only serve now to strengthen it." Her hopes were not realized.

On December 20, 1860, the delegates to the South Carolina Secession Convention voted to secede from the Union. Six days later, Maj. Robert Anderson moved his federal troops from Fort Moultrie on Sullivans Island to Fort Sumter in the throat of Charleston harbor. The South Carolina militia quickly took over Fort Moultrie and converted it into a defensive position. On

January 9, 1861, Citadel cadets stationed on Morris Island fired on the U.S. ship, *Star of the West*, which was attempting to resupply Fort Sumter. This was the beginning of open hostilities; there was no turning back.

In January Mississippi, Florida, Alabama, Georgia, Louisiana joined South Carolina in seceding from the Union. Their representatives met in Montgomery, Alabama, in early February to form the Confederate States of America. On February 18, 1861, Jefferson Davis was inaugurated as president in Richmond, the new nation's capital.

Shortly thereafter, Mary wrote to the boys that the elections of Davis as president and Alexander Stephens as vice president of the Confederate States of America "have given entire satisfaction." She reported that Alston had gone to see the nearly completed floating artillery battery which was to be used against Fort Sumter. To reassure them, she wrote, "Do not distress your selves with apprehensions, my sons, God is over all, 'not a sparrow falls to the ground without his knowledge'. We are anticipating but one battle and that will be over before this reaches you."[1]

On April 12, 1861, the first shot was fired at Fort Sumter, and two days later, Major Anderson surrendered his troops. The war was on. A month later, Mary wrote to Mary Mitchell in Connecticut, telling her not to attempt a trip to Charleston to retrieve her daughter, little Hesse. Mary warned her daughter that the risk was too high, but assured her that Hesse was being cared for with great tenderness.

As fast as they could scramble back home or disengage themselves from their civilian pursuits, the young Pringle men returned to defend their homeland. By April 1861 Robert had obtained a commission as an artillery officer. In July James followed suit. In September Charles obtained a commission in an infantry unit, and in November Motte was commissioned a captain in the Confederate quartermaster's department.

Returning to Charleston was dangerous for the Pringles who were abroad when the war broke out. These included

Julius, who was living with Maria and family in Paris; James and Charles, studying at Berlin; and their cousins, Poinsett, Lynch, and Julius, sons of John Julius Izard and Jane (Lynch) Pringle, who were studying at Heidelberg.[2] Jane Lynch Pringle and Mary, her daughter, were also in Europe at the time and snuck back past the enemy ships and soldiers at great personal risk.[3]

If Southerners returned through Northern ports they were subject to arrest. Union ships were also blockading the Southern coastline. In the fall of 1861 William Ravenel of Charleston—a relative of the Pringles—described to his son, J. R. Pringle Ravenel, trapped by the war in Paris, the perils of attempting to return. The letters were smuggled out of Charleston on blockade-running ships owned by John Fraser and Co., bound for Nassau, Havana and thence for Europe.

Ravenel told his son that he would be imprisoned if he were caught coming through a federal port. He had made arrangements with his British factors to provide his son with funds while he was deciding how to return. He noted that John Julius Izard Pringle narrowly escaped capture while returning through Canada, but that even that option was no longer viable. He advised his son to remain in Europe until a safe plan could be determined, and added, "If you should be induced to venture home, to erase every trace of your being a citizen of So. Ca. and have nothing in your trunk or about your person to indicate where you are from. You will be most rigidly searched at almost every point so be careful in the extreme."[4]

James and Charles made their way home by July 1861. A friend recorded that three cousins of the Pringle boys made it back in February 1862. "They seem to have had adventures enough," she wrote. "Walked, waded and rowed in boats, if boats they could find; swam rivers when boats there were none; brave lads are they. One can but admire their pluck and energy. Mrs. Fisher, of Philadelphia, née Middleton, gave them money to make the attempt to get home."[5]

In March 1862 Brewton enlisted in the infantry, and Alston

served for some undetermined time as a militia officer. From a surviving photograph we learn that Julius seems to have served in uniform for at least a brief time. Shortly after the fall of New Orleans to Union troops in the late spring of 1862, his actions and whereabouts create interesting mysteries. In all, seven of Mary's eight sons volunteered to serve in battle. The only one who never wore Confederate gray was Edward. Although tormented with guilt at his relative safety and comfort, he remained in San Francisco with the family's blessing to supervise their investments.

The fall of 1861 found the family preparing for dire events. In November a massive Union fleet sailed past Hilton Head Island and entered Port Royal Sound. The family responded by packing up their silver and sending it to Columbia for safekeeping before they moved to Richfield on the Santee. Scarcely were they out of the city when on Wednesday night, December 11, 1861, the most devastating fire in the history of Charleston got its start in a sash and blind factory on Hasell Street near the Cooper River at about 8:30 P.M. By the time it was brought under control it had leveled a swath of 540 acres all the way west to the Ashley River. Losses were estimated between five and seven million dollars. "The wind, which was blowing strongly from North-Northeast, increased almost to a hurricane," said the official report. "The flames rose to a terrible pitch, and in a few moments, notwithstanding the most gallant efforts of an efficient fire brigade, were communicated to the adjacent buildings. . . . Building after building caught, and became, as it were, one vast sheet of flame."[6]

Immediately afterward Alston made a startling revelation to his mother: "I forgot to say, that I have not insured your house. I received Papa's letter the day I think before the fire and as he was uncertain about it and the premium was $75 and I had only a little over $100 and he had not sent me any money to do it with I thought I would wait a day or two till I could write about it. In the mean time the fire has come and all the insurance offices of any account are broken, so that there is no use to insure for they cannot pay. By waiting I have saved $75."[7] Fortunately, the fire never burned far enough south on King Street to threaten the Miles Brewton House.

From Richfield William tried to maintain production on his rice plantations, but fears quickly rose about the feasibility of his plan. The Confederates had erected Battery White to defend the entrance to Winyah Bay, but that and a roving coastal patrol was all the protection they could muster.

Two Union warships blockaded Winyah Bay in December 1861. From Richfield Rebecca reported hearing heavy firing the morning of January 7, 1862, and wondered what it meant. Federal ships were frequently seen off the coast, and landing parties often came ashore to search for food and supplies and to break up the salt vats.[8] Occasionally enemy landing parties were captured, but the lightly armed planters and their underdefended coast were no match for the massive firepower of the U.S. Navy.

As tensions mounted over the possibility of a major coastal attack, William made plans to evacuate the slaves from his plantations and move them inland. On January 22, 1862, Mary wrote to Robert from Richfield,

> Our servants, and some persons around, heard last night sharp and quick discharges of great guns. We cannot understand what they were, for the night was dark, and the servants say the firing came until 1 o'clock this morning. Horrid visions rise up in my mind connected with those few villainous deserters who may have given the enemy such accurate information that they may have fired upon you in the dark, and killed many sleeping men in their tents. This thought of mine, *like many others*, excites much ridicule. Your Papa quite agrees with you, in apprehending no danger to Georgetown or this River, yet he has been induced to make prudent arrangements for the removal of the negroes from this place, as well as from Beneventum, and the planters, without exception, have done the same thing.[9]

On April 22, 1862, Union warships entered Winyah Bay.

By May they were steaming up the North Santee, South Santee, and the Waccamaw, blowing up abandoned fortifications at will, torching plantations and rice mills, confiscating crops, and affording slaves the opportunity to flee their owners. A New York newspaper reported that on May 21, a Union gunboat ascended the Waccamaw River ten miles above Georgetown, and "meeting no resistance, he brought off eighty contrabands. The rebels were leaving their plantations, driving their negros before them in all directions."[10]

In Charleston, the harbor was under blockade and threat of shelling from Union gunboats. But even in mid-April Mary was still holding out hope of returning to Charleston for the summer so that she, William, Sue, and Mary could be close to the sons who were serving in the army nearby. "Very many families have been away all winter, more in the interior and they will remain away and many more are going away, as the burnt district, it is supposed, will make the place unhealthy," she wrote. "Your Uncle H [Arthur Hayne] and Aunt E [Elizabeth Hayne] have been all winter in Colum[bia] and your Aunt Brewton [Rebecca Brewton (Alston) Hayne], with Margaretta, at Rock Cell."[11]

The continued presence of Union warships blockading Charleston and patrolling the coast off Georgetown convinced the family that the city and the Lowcountry plantations were in imminent danger. At the end of March William was still at Richfield. He wrote, "The accounts from every point lead to believe that a battle is imminent. We must look with great anxiety for the result as it is calculated to have great influence on the future. The removal of [our] troops from this neighborhood has created an uneasiness among the folks. But I never thought they afforded protection. The experience of Port Royal convinced me that all weak posts within reach of the enemy's vessels should be abandoned as they serve as traps for our men to be killed in or taken prisoners, giving the enemy the eclât of victory."[12]

The arrival of Union gunboats on the Santee and the federal blockade of Charleston forced the end of the annual planters' migration. Instead of returning home to summer at King Street or traipse off to Newport, the Pringles, like all the other Georgetown District planters, had only one viable option for saving their slaves, furniture, and other personal property: move inland.

On June 4 a Charlestonian wrote in his diary, "People are moving in crowds from the city. Carts are passing at all hours filled with furniture. The talk on the streets is when do you go; where are you going. Every one take care of himself and the enemy take the hindmost."[13]

William underscored his apprehensions with action: in April 1862 he leased a farm in the interior of the state.[14] By the end of May or early June 1862, Mary and her daughters had returned to Charleston and packed up all their treasured furniture, linens, china, and servants for shipment inland.

The residents of the Upcountry were extremely gracious to the Lowcountry refugees. "We are one Confederate family," wrote the editor of the *Confederate Baptist*, "and it is the duty of every one of us to use his heart, head and hands to serve his country and his neighbor as himself, and particularly those who have given up their homes for the honor and welfare of the State and Confederacy."[15]

By July 1862 the Pringle women had reassembled near Society Hill in Darlington District, about 110 miles north of Charleston. There they leased a plantation for $2,000 per year from Sarah Williams, the widow and second wife of Col. John Nicholas Williams, a son of former South Carolina governor David Rogerson Williams.[16] In 1864 the Pringles rented a plantation for $600 per year from J. T. Murdoch.[17] From 1863 to 1865, most of the family's letters were datelined "Dukeville, near Society Hill" and "Friendville." Dukeville was a plantation owned by Isaac DeLiesseline Wilson, a Society Hill planter and South Carolina legislator.[18] Friendville was a plantation nearby. They were also noted as having lived at the John D. Witherspoon House in Society Hill. The Frost family took refuge at the parsonage of the Welsh Neck Baptist Church, and Darlington District hosted scores of other Lowcountry families.

Large pieces of furniture, such as beds and clothes presses which could not be transported to Dukeville, were left behind in Charleston. Rugs, draperies, and smaller pieces of furniture were stored at Friendville. On the Santee and Black Rivers, William rounded up his slaves and those belonging to the estate of Uncle Robert. The menace of Union warships forced William to abandon his rice crop and leave all his property exposed to the "depredation of the enemy and to destruction by fire and the weather," a loss estimated at $8,000. Uncle Robert's estate also included a share in the line of steamships running between Charleston and New York, but William noted in December 1862 that "all of the said ships but one, the *Nashville*, have been detained by the enemy, in consequence whereof the said estate has suffered loss to the amount of $16,000."[19] Without access to his plantations, William was forced to buy food for his family, slaves, and livestock. A receipt dated October 31, 1863, noted purchases of peanuts, corn, and other goods and staples totaling $815.32.[20]

The war drastically reduced the flow of letters between the Northern and Southern branches of the Pringle family. Mail delivery became slow and erratic. Letters from New Haven which normally reached Charleston in ten days now took three or four months—if they arrived at all.[21] Among those intercepted by federal authorities was one from Edward in San Francisco. He wrote his mother in August 1862: "I suppose a great many letters have gone where they can tell no tales. . . . Who knows what fate this may have?"[22]

Eight letters written by Mary Mitchell to the family in Charleston in the summer and fall of 1862 were confiscated. Each was contained in a black-bordered envelope. Five of the seven were addressed to Charleston, So. Carolina, C.S.A.; and none bore any postage stamps, indicating that they were being sent by a private messenger who had been caught.

The year 1862 forced enormous challenges upon the family

and their slaves. They were forced to produce crops of food on lands completely foreign to them, with the added handicap of having to plant in the heat of late summer. By Christmas they feared they might never farm their rice lands again. The pressure of creditors and the need for seed, tools, and equipment to farm their new Darlington District property led to a painful decision: Runimede must be sold—at any cost.

Although Runimede produced a variety of table foods, it was primarily a country retreat— a luxury that a family of war refugees could scarcely afford. On February 19, 1863, Mary wrote from Dukeville that "our dear, beautiful old Runimede," its stock, provisions, furniture, and slaves had been sold to Charleston banker George Alfred Trenholm[23] for $59,000 in Confederate currency. The price consisted of $20,000 for the property[24] and $39,000 for the slaves.[25] A condition of the sale was that the slave families be kept together.

The family's financial position worsened and the only recourse was to continue selling off assets. In May 1863 William attempted to sell Beneventum, which he owned jointly with the heirs of his brother Robert's estate. With Union gunboats regularly steaming up the rice rivers, buyers were scarce. The plantation was offered to Trenholm, but he could make no more purchases."[26] On June 30, 1863, Alston wrote to an aunt that Beneventum's exposed position had made it difficult to sell, but Theodore D. Wagner, a Charleston merchant, had been persuaded to purchase the land and slaves for $52,000.[27]

In June 1863 the slaves from Beneventum were moved 100 miles inland to Marlboro, South Carolina. There they were held while awaiting division among the heirs of John Julius Pringle. The rest of the Beneventum property was sold at auction. William noted that "the debt that I owe to the Estate for money lent to me by Robert shall be paid out of my share of the proceeds of the sale of Beneventum. It amounts to about $14,000 as the account will show."[28] On September 11, 1863, William described the sale:

After postponing for a week beyond the time first ap-

> pointed to go to Beneventum to rally in some measure from the severe and prostrating blow we have received I proceeded to perform the painful duty which circumstances had required of me. My feelings were not at all soothed by the scenes and occurrences I there encountered. Around me were reminiscences of our dear brothers who have gone before me and of our venerable parents with whom too many of the articles were associated. From these the home of our brothers in happier days I was about to bid adieu for the last time amid a vulgar crowd (some intoxicated) overrunning the house. . . . My manhood almost forsook me and I was afraid I should have been obliged to give up in despair. But thank God I rallied and accomplished what I had to do and had gone for.
>
> The sale was completed but I am sorry to say fell short of Parker's estimate. . . . The account sales not having been yet sent me I can't yet tell you what they amounted to but I think a little over $9,000.[29]

In November 1863 William made a visit to Richfield. All the slaves had been moved, except, wrote Mary "some half a dozen old and infirm, who are left to keep ward and watch over the deserted buildings." From the division of his brother Robert's estate, of which he was executor, William received sixty-six slaves. He used part of the proceeds from his share in Beneventum to pay off some of his debts. Mary wrote to Julius, "Your Papa has paid all of his debts that could be paid, that is, to all who would receive Confederate notes. But, as we are now living without interest from our property, we must encroach on capital, or incur debt again. The mill [at Beneventum] cannot be sold, as its position is so exposed."[30]

In the summer of 1864 Mary wrote that disease had ravaged the family at Society Hill. "Your Papa and sisters are well," she wrote to Julius. "I have just recovered from an illness of 4 weeks, from dysentery. Your Papa continues to be very unfortunate with our negroes, having lost some of our most valuable with typhus fever. Our grave yard, since we have been here, is marked with 26 graves, most of these, prime young negroes. Our crop, too, is not promising."[31] The young Pringle men who went to war were no more fortunate than their aging, refugee parents and sisters.

Alston

Alston's lifetime appointment as court recorder gave him only the slimmest financial security, and when the war broke out, he had his wife, Emma, and nine other mouths to feed. He obtained a lieutenant's commission in the 16th Regiment, S. C. Militia, which permitted him at least some assurance that he would not have to serve too far away from home.[32] Alston and Emma were still in Charleston in November 1862 when he wrote to Susan, refugeeing at Dukeville, that he "found your thoughtful and acceptable present at Motte's . . . although I was somewhat at a loss by what underground railroad they had reached me. I keep watch sometimes in my cold dressing room and your warm socks take the place of the fire which few of us can afford to have."[33]

William Alston Pringle.
Clarke's Studio, Charleston, c. 1863.

By mid-1863 Alston was still in Charleston, but had evacuated Emma and their children from their Tradd Street house and sent them to Columbia for safety.[34] When Sherman's army marched towards Columbia, Alston and his family joined his parents and two sisters at Dukeville, in hope of avoiding the pillage which the Union troops were carrying out along their route.

Julius

Julius and Maria left the United States and returned to France in July 1860, presumably leaving Torwood plantation in the care of his overseer and under the general supervision of Maria's brother, Stephen Duncan, Jr. Their father, Dr. Stephen Duncan, a staunch Unionist, departed Misissippi at the start of the war, leaving the care of his properties to his son.

The younger Duncan "enlisted among the sixty-day men, served the term, and on account of some disability, resigned the service and returned to Natchez."[35] His brief service and minimal disability left him conveniently free to concentrate on planting. He did this so profitably that by 1873 he was free to leave the operation of his plantations to others and spend the rest of his life a wealthy, globe-trotting expatriate in Europe. He made his headquarters in Frankfurt-am-Main, Germany, but traveled extensively and often kept the company of his brother-in-law, Julius, in his travels to Paris, London, and Louisiana.

In the first months of 1861, Dr. Duncan deeded Duncannon plantation near Natchez and its slaves ($180,000) and over $300,000 in Southern bills receivable to Julius. These large and fruitful properties were too valuable and the management too complex to leave in the hands of overseers, so Julius carefully plotted his return through the Union blockade. It is unclear how he returned, but he did so sometime in 1862. Julius established his base of operations at Torwood, his cotton and sugar plantation in Pointe Coupée Parish, Louisiana, while Maria and the children remained behind in Paris at their home at 4, Rue Balzac.

The extent of Julius's Confederate military service is uncertain. No record of service in South Carolina, Louisiana, Mississippi, or other Confederate units could be found. At some time near the start of the war, Julius was photographed in an

John Julius Pringle.
Clarke's Studio, Charleston, c. 1862

ill-fitting uniform at Clarke's Studio, in downtown Charleston. He appeared nervous.[36]

He may have been in southern Louisiana and involved in the fighting in 1862—or maybe not. On February 28, 1862, Susan wrote to Edward, "I tremble for our poor brother Julius, who I fear may have been with Gen. Van Dorn in the recent battle."[37] Maj. Gen. Earl Van Dorn, a West Pointer from Mississippi, was commanding Confederate troops in southern Missouri in 1862. On February 22 his forces at Springfield, Missouri, were attacked and driven from the city by Brig. Gen. Samuel R. Curtis.

On August 13, 1862, Edward wrote to his mother, "Poor Maria is most anxious to hear from Julius, as she has not heard for a long while. I have begged a mutual friend, who hears from New Orleans to enquire where he might be. There is so much indignation felt in Mississippi against New Orleans that there is no communication between Natchez and the city; but this friend's brother is in Mississippi and she heard of him through New Orleans and they know Julius."[38] The next week he wrote, "And about Julius, what has become of him and his corps in the taking of New Orleans. How gallantly Vicksburg has held out!"[39]

New Orleans was a major port and military center for the Confederacy and Union troops eagerly sought to capture it. The battle of New Orleans took place in the spring of 1862 when a Union fleet commanded by Adm. David Farragut carrying troops commanded by Gen. Benjamin Butler sailed into the lower Mississippi River. The Union army entered the city on May 1, 1862, and held it for the duration of the war. The loss of New Orleans, gateway to the Mississippi Valley and the Confederacy's chief cotton-exporting port, was catastrophic.

The fall of New Orleans put Julius's plantations behind enemy lines and presented him with a great dilemma. As the son and grandson of South Carolina rice planters, and with seven brothers in Confederate uniform, Julius would have had little innate sympathy for the Union cause. However, with his father's finances already in ruins, Julius was the only son with the ability to earn money for the family during and after the war. As a wealthy cotton and sugar planter in Louisiana whose property was now controlled by the enemy, he stood to lose his plantations, work force, and income if he did not make some accommodation with the federal occupiers. He had strong connections to the Duncans and could get strings pulled with the Union forces to permit him to return to his lands and restart planting. But if he took up planting with the blessing of federal forces, would the family in Charleston think that he was collaborating with the enemy? From the Confederate standpoint, he would have been.

Just three months after the fall of New Orleans, an amazing report reached the Charleston family. On August 26, Mary Mitchell wrote to her mother that she had received a letter from Maria in Paris, saying that Julius was in New York.[40]

The Pringles must have been stunned. Julius in the heart of the Union at the height of hostilities? In their minds, this turn of events may have thrown Julius's loyalty to the Confederacy into serious question, but the plot continued to thicken as the war dragged on.

By November 1863 Julius was back at Torwood and was expecting the arrival of Maria and the children from France. That month Mary Mitchell wrote to him, "I am sorry to find that dear Maria will be obliged to give up her happier foreign home, but you and she must feel grateful, in these times of bereavement, that you have had all your children spared to you, and only your property to mourn over."[41] Mary was evidently unaware that Julius had already made his peace with the Union occupiers and had reclaimed his house and land.

Aloof and seemingly unconcerned about the war, Julius wrote in his hunting journal:

> The winter of 1863-64 was a very severe one, and in Point Coupée, where I was at that period, the ducks were unusually abundant and I had capital sport on Old River, Lake Moreau, etc.[42] It was rather difficult though, as the Yankee troops were raiding over the country and I was obliged to be very cautious. I managed however to kill a large quantity of game of various kinds—chiefly deer—two or three wild turkies—turkies were very scarce in that neighborhood —a great variety of ducks—such as ducks and mallard—pintail—shovellers—green-wing teal—blue wing teal.[43]

Mary confided to Julius that she had heard that Dr. Duncan had taken the federal oath of allegiance. "God forbid that we should ever hear that of you. No allegiance, I pray, from mine to the murderers of my son Robert to the foes of my household."[44]

When it came to the subject of Northern sympathizers, Mary was in an extremely awkward position. Julius was married to the daughter of a Unionist and living in Union-occupied territory. And to add insult to injury, Mary wrote to Julius in July 1864, "We have heard that Maria is at New Port. Would be that she were here with us, would that she were any where beyond the Northern line, but alas!"[45]

Julius spent the rest of the war supervising production at Torwood. He was quite successful. The journal of Stephen Duncan, Jr., noted that Julius earned $37,871 in 1863, $27,058 in 1864 and was drinking claret and champagne by the end of the war.[46]

Michael Wayne, who studied the Natchez planters, wrote that "Southern men with northern interests were the first to come to terms with Federal authorities during the occupation. It was in their homes that Yankees found shelter and society, and it was they to whom officials turned for advice in restoring stability to the region. Predictably, their behavior and professed Unionism won them favored treatment. They were allowed to lease their plantations at great profit and were given access to markets for their cotton. In the end their financial position was scarcely diminished by the conflict."[47] This description seems a perfect match for Julius.

Well before the end of the war, Julius was in full possession of all of his lands, back in full production, and enormously wealthy. By September 1865 he, Maria, and their family had reached their European home and were comfortably re-established in their old quarters. He received his federal pardon sometime late in 1865, shortly after Dr. Duncan and his son, Stephen, received theirs.[48]

Edward

Edward remained in San Francisco for the duration of the war, but the knowledge that he was safe while his family and friends were exposed to danger ate constantly at him. He knew at least one Charlestonian living in San Francisco who answered the Confederate call—and died for the Lost Cause. He was Thomas Porcher Stoney, whose father, Peter Gaillard Stoney, and five other sons fought in the war.[49]

In an August 1862 letter to his mother, Edward wrote, "I don't know when I am most anxious to be with you—when I hear of your trials and sacrifices, or when I am proud of your successes. But though I gnash my teeth at my evil star in being here, I know I am right, so far, to have stayed. I have not been able yet to unravel the tangled meshes that business here has inevitably gotten me into."[50]

Feeling Edward's anguish, Mary Mitchell wrote to Julius, "Poor Edward! He chafes terribly at his exile, yet is convinced that he has done right, and indeed Mama and all write to reassure him frequently."[51] By November 1862 an inaccurate rumor was circulating that Edward's finances had improved. Mary Mitchell wrote to Alston in Charleston:

> A gentleman who has recently seen [Edward] says his prosperity is now worth at least $250,000! so our good Brother's hopes are bright now, with the prospect of giving a good account of his stewardship. Tell Mama he proposed, in his last letter, that the family should emigrate, and I am delighted with the suggestion and Mr. M[itchell] too thinks favourably of the plan, and we have it under serious consideration, as E[dward] says his long residence and position there will enable him to give us a good start, and our being there might be of service to him and release him all the sooner. And again, dear Brother, in the event of the unhappy success of Lincoln's wicked intentions, our going there might be the beginning of a place of refuge for those who are dearest to us, or on the other hand in the event of the much hoped for success of the C[onfederate] S[tates] we should quietly find ourselves knocking at her door. I am trying to persuade Mr. M[itchell] to go and take a look. There are some friends in New Haven, outcasts like me from the Confederate States, and I could always have one of them come stay with me in his absence or they would forward all letters, should I go suddenly.[52]

Motte

On November 16, 1861, Motte was commissioned a captain in the Confederate army and appointed Assistant Quartermaster for the Department of South Carolina, Georgia, and Florida. His experience as a factor and commission merchant was good preparation for the job, which he described to a new commanding officer as "the supplying of forage, the means of transportation, and quartermasters stores for the troops in this State. I am besides charged with transportation of troops and supplies by steam boats to the different posts in the harbor and all transportation generally, and the erection of barracks, store houses and hospitals."[53] On November 18, 1862, Motte was promoted to the rank of major and the position of quartermaster, reporting to Gen. P. G. T. Beauregard. He held this position

Jacob Motte Alston Pringle.
Oil paints over a copy photograph, n.d.

until the end of the war.

Motte served most of his tour of duty in Charleston. In 1862, while assistant quartermaster, he drew a private quarters allowance of $27 per month for three rooms at $9 per month plus an additional sum for firewood. This pay was given because no official quarters were available. Until the fall of 1863 he also drew a forage allowance for three private horses in his service. In the fall of 1863 and early 1864, after his promotion to major and after assuming the position of quartermaster for all of South Carolina, his quarters allowance was increased to $15 per room for four rooms. Although there is no direct evidence, it is logical to conclude that these rooms—and the headquarters for the Quartermaster Department for the Confederate Army in South Carolina—were one floor of Motte's home, the otherwise-empty Miles Brewton House, and that the horses of his staff were stabled in its stalls.

Motte's duties demanded great ingenuity and attention to detail. On any given week, he received and disbursed anywhere from $10,000 to $250,000 for the everyday supplies of a large army. In the civilian world small mistakes rarely result in much harm, but in wartime they can lead to catastrophe. On the night of August 30, 1863, Motte ordered the steamer *Sumter* to transport troops from Charleston to Morris Island and to return exhausted troops back to the city. However he failed to notify the commanders at Fort Sumter and on Sullivan's Island that a friendly vessel would be returning in the early morning from the direction of the enemy. At 1:30 A.M., the batteries on Sullivan's Island opened fire on a vessel they took to be hostile.

The *Sumter* was sunk. Five men were killed instantly; several others were wounded and about twenty drowned.[54] Major Pringle was severely reprimanded for his negligence. Gen. Beauregard wrote that "the loss of the boat and of several valuable lives were necessarily the consequence of his oversight, and should admonish him that vigilance and presence of mind are as indispensable as zeal and energy to those placed in responsible positions."[55] He added that it was only Major Pringle's "valuable services in keeping up nightly communications with Morris Island from the 10th of July last to the 7th of September, especially during the night of the evacuation of the island, alone shield him from trial by court-martial."[56]

By the end of the war, Motte had substantially redeemed his military reputation. With the exception of the *Sumter* incident, he had proven himself an able quartermaster. At war's end Brig. Gen. Roswell S. Ripley wrote of him, "The duties of the quartermaster's department were excessively laborious on account of the limited means of transportation, and it is a matter of congratulation that with such means they were so well performed."[57]

Mary Frances

"Don't let us talk war," Mary Mitchell wrote to Susan in July 1861. "We feel sure of each other's love and sympathy outliving all wars, but keep and love tenderly our little fugitive, as a hostage until something turns up. Do write often, and don't let our little one forget us or think of us as Lincolnites.[58]

The "little fugitive" was seven-year-old Hesse Mitchell, Mary Mitchell's first child, who had been trapped in Charleston by the outbreak of the war. By the summer of 1861, Mary and Donald realized that it might be a long time until they saw their beloved daughter again. "Heaven only knows what we are all coming to," Mary Mitchell wrote.

> Even my hopeful nature now almost despairs. God help us all, we must all pray most earnestly, for never was a Country in more want of Heavenly guidance than our unhappy America. Our darling child we may not now see for a long, long time, but, dear Mama, I know you will all love and protect her, even more, perhaps, than in better times, and look upon her as a pledge of love and sympathy between our two households. . . . Do write me when ever you can, and even if you do not hear from us, don't doubt our hearts, but be assured that *no condition* can ever blunt our love and affection for all our dear Southern friends and relations—and don't let our little daughter learn to think of us as belonging to the 'enemy'. Teach her to love us as always. In all love to her and all the rest.[59]

What was to be the family's first wartime tragedy started to unfold at Richfield on December 11, when Hesse Mitchell complained to her Aunt Rebecca of a headache. After playing in the barnyard that day, she still complained of the headache, so Mary gave her a "blue pill" and bathed her feet in hot pepper tea. When the headache didn't recede, she was given another foot bath and put to bed.

In the following days, Hesse became sicker and was given another blue pill. A day or so later, she became depressed, drowsy, and started vomiting. The family sent for Dr. White of Georgetown. White declined to make the sixteen-mile trip due to his own recent illness, and the family then sent for Dr. Bailey who lived closer. He prescribed medicine for her, but "thought her indisposition very trifling." Mary took her pulse, found it "unnaturally slow" and asked the doctor if Hesse's problem might not be an "affliction of the brain." In the next days, he visited her twice a day. The head pains increased and she started to twitch. Mary "treated her promptly for convulsions." After a temporary respite, the convulsions returned, and Mary "alarmed the house."

"We did all we could," Mary wrote, "[We] covered her with mustard, after a warm bath to her feet, our darling grew worse and we thought her dying." The doctor was again summoned, and he pronounced her affliction to be an "attack upon the brain," which he later called "tubercular meningitis." He shaved her head, bathed it with cold water, but by this time, Hesse had already lost her sight. Paralysis of her right arm followed, after which she lost her ability to talk. All the neighbors rallied around the stricken family, but the doctor had no cures, and Hesse's final prayer, "I hope God will make me well," was not answered. Surrounded by family and friends, death relieved Hesse of her agony two days after Christmas 1861. The funeral was held at the Miles Brewton House. The small coffin was strewn with white camelias and violets. The Rev. T. J. Girardeau, formerly pastor of the Church of the Messiah on the North Santee River, read the service. Hesse was buried in the Pringle family plot in St. Michael's churchyard.

A grief-ridden William Bull Pringle wrote Mary a letter describing the tragedy. Not wanting the crushing news to leap out of an impersonal envelope, William chose a close friend, Collin M. Ingersoll of New Haven, to break the sorrowful news to the Mitchells in person.

The following day, Mary Mitchell wrote, "that sad, sad letter was given me last night—and our little Hessie is dead! . . . I feel, dearest Mother, that this blow *is* meant to humble my wicked contentment in this world's happiness; and to draw us nearer to God, and to make us think more of Heaven, where the brightest Flower of our Flock has gone to bloom."[60]

On January 4, 1862, a letter arrived from Robert, who was serving at Battery Wagner on Morris Island.

> I had been in hopes of receiving a letter from some of you before this, giving the particulars of our dear little Hessie's end, and previous sickness. What makes it peculiarly hard for me to realize is, that on last Saturday night [December 28, 1861], the very night after her death, I had a most remarkable dream. I was staying at Clarkesville, Georgia, and on Sunday morning I awoke oppressed with the effect of this dream, which was that Hessie had died, and that I had been permitted to carry her body on to Mary [Mitchell] under a flag of truce from General Huger. Was it not a remark-

able circumstance? for I had never even heard of her being unwell.[61]

The families in New Haven and South Carolina grieved over Hesse's death for many months, but soon, concern for their soldier-sons—and for Donald Mitchell—took precedence in their thoughts. Emigration to France, Canada or California became a topic of frequent discussion, especially when Mitchell, then forty, was declared eligible for the Union draft. In an intercepted letter to her mother and sisters penned shortly after Charles' death, Mary Mitchell wrote:

> Today we had nearly decided to emigrate, to Canada or to France, but a certificate of exemption from this wicked drafting, given by our sincere friend and Doctor, has determined us to linger a little longer, until we might get off with less sacrifice, and until Mr. M. can learn of some chance of finding bread elsewhere. As to my husband's being drawn into this hateful, unchristian war, that is out of any question. I should sooner have him die in jail than help on such a cause, and God knows his heart is too pure and Christian to be so sacrificial. . . . My head swims and my hands tremble so, since this news and the general anxiety I suffer in these days that I can hardly write coherently. . . . I do not send you E[dward]'s letter for fear of their committing him in these days of terror and sure arrests to Fort Warren,[62] but be assured they and his heart are all that you could wish, my dear parents. . . . We are drifting fast into war and mobs at the North and my ambition is too great even to losing our cherished little home where until now all has been so bright and hopeful. The poor blacks how I pity them! God forgive me for the revenge and vindictiveness that the devilish spirit of your aggressors lead me into feeling. May a merciful God continue to help and save you all until your aim is accomplished. Always in vision of hope. M.P.M.[63]

The Pringles and the Mitchells continued to explore the possibilities of emigration. In December 1862 Mary responded to her daughter's proposal to relocate to California. Mary wrote that although California offered the opportunity for a fresh start,

Mary Frances Pringle Mitchell in mourning clothes after the death of her daughter Hesse in 1861.

the great expense of moving the Mitchell family would virtually strand them there. She also confided that she regarded Edward's move to California a failure, thought his schemes were "visionary," and felt that his five years there were a near complete waste.

Until the last Mary Mitchell remained a Confederate firebrand. "Secession may have been foolish in the beginning," she wrote, "but the simple evacuation of Sumter would have spared so much sacred blood and too would have restored the Union in a Christian and humane manner. But alas! the savage barbarity and uncivilized warfare that money and conquest have led the Federals into, make me feel every day now that the Rebels are the only Americans who can have any feelings of pride. I never hesitate to call myself a rebel, and find I am treated with all the more respect for doing so. The war has made the U.S. hateful to me, and I wait and watch for the time when I and mine may be able to emigrate to some land of Peace —but poor people must keep quiet when exchange is at such ruinous rates."[64] Embittered and embattled, Mary was forced to remain in New Haven and was not able to reunite with her family until the war ended.

Brewton

During the war, most of the Pringle sons served in or near Charleston. Brewton served in the 4th Regiment, South Carolina Cavalry, better known as the Charleston Light Dragoons. It was a state militia unit which traced its roots to 1733 when it was known as the Charleston Horse Guards. Composed of Charleston aristocrats, the Dragoons were not offended when referred to as a "kid glove" company. "When in camp the Dragoons were 'in clover,' for most of them at this period of the war were in prosperous circumstances, some were wealthy; their messes[65] were well supplied by foraging in the neighborhood, and by provisions sent from their homes; their servants, of which each man had at least one, were good, and some of the cooks excellent."[66]

At the start of the war the unit consisted of their commander, Capt. Benjamin H. Rutledge, three lieutenants, five sergeants, four corporals and eighty privates.[67] The Dragoons first saw service in the spring of 1861. They remained a state militia unit until mustered into Confederate service on March 25, 1862. Private Miles Brewton Pringle enlisted that day. His cousins, John Julius Izard Pringle and Duncan Lynch Pringle, enlisted in the Dragoons a few months later.[68]

Brewton first saw action at Pocotaligo, a junction on the Charleston and Savannah Railroad. In July 1862 Robert reported that Brewton was looking well and in good spirits. On October 22, 1862, approximately 2,600 federal troops attacked the 400 Pocotaligo defenders, seeking to cut the rail line between Charleston and Savannah. After nearly a full day of fighting, the enemy withdrew to their gunboats after sustaining about 300 casualties. The Dragoons suffered one man killed and nine wounded, including Brewton, who had been shot in the lower leg. "His wound is a slow one and the bullet has been extracted," Susan wrote to Robert at Battery Wagner.[69] His wound immediately made him the center of attention of the family, but he ultimately paid a high price for the distinction.

Brewton received a medical furlough for several months while recovering. During the winter of 1862 he stayed with the family at Dukeville, where he was treated like a hero. By the first of January 1863, Brewton appeared sufficiently healed to return to his unit.

He spent the summer and fall of 1863 as a private with the Dragoons, who were ordered into Charleston in August. They camped at the Washington Racecourse—where Colonel Alston's thoroughbreds once thundered down the turf—out of the range of Union gunfire. The Dragoons relieved the 5th S.C. Cavalry and served as couriers between two of the harbor's busiest artillery batteries, Wagner and Gregg, on Morris Island. Battery Wagner, the larger of the two, was the duty post of Brewton's brother Robert. Gregg, about three-quarters of a mile up the beach, was the military home of James. The dangerous assignment gave Brewton the opportunity of seeing his brothers frequently, but at great risk to his own safety.

After the withdrawal of Confederate troops from Morris Island in September 1863, the Dragoons guarded the land approaches to Charleston until April 1864, when they were ordered to join Butler's Brigade, a new addition to Robert E. Lee's Army of Northern Virginia. With them marched the three Pringle Dragoons: Brewton and his cousins, John Julius Izard Pringle and James R. Poinsett Pringle.

The aftereffects of Brewton's wounds evidently flared up. After fierce fighting at Trevylian Station on the Virginia Central Railroad, Brewton was treated on June 13 and 14, 1862, at the Receiving and Wayside Hospital, or General Hospital No. 9 in Richmond, Virginia. His case was severe enough to require his transfer to Jackson Hospital in Richmond, where he stayed for eight more days. In August he again was sent to the hospital. This time the Office of the Medical Board of Examiners for Furlough and Discharge examined Brewton and found him "suffering from the effects of a gun shot wound of the right foot, received at battle of Pocotaligo, October 1862, which has rendered him incapable of performing the duties of a soldier in the field. We therefore respectfully recommend that he be detailed for [light] duty as within applied for, for six months."[70] The records are mute about Brewton's whereabouts during his last six months of service, but on May 3, 1865, he was paroled at Charlotte, North Carolina.

Robert

Robert wasted no time in joining the fight. By April 9, 1861, he was a second lieutenant serving as aide-de-camp to Col. (later Maj. Gen.) John Dunovant.[71] He was commissioned first lieutenant of Company B, 15th (Lucas's) Battalion, South Carolina Volunteers on June 6, 1861, and signed on with his comrades for three years.[72]

Robert served as adjutant of Lucas' battalion. They were first stationed at the Moultrie House, a three-story hotel on Sullivan's Island, which provided an excellent view of the harbor. On July 10, 1862, they were moved to Battery Island, where Fort Pickens protected the mouth of the Stono River. The battalion was moved across the Stono to Coles Island that fall. Also known as Fort Palmetto, it overlooked the entrance to Stono Inlet, just south of the tip of Folly Island.

Robert Pringle. Quinby Studio, Charleston, 1862 or 1863.

Lieutenant Pringle won his promotion to captain on December 20, 1861. The battalion was ordered to evacuate Coles Island and move upriver to Fort Pemberton, just below the Wappoo Cut, on May 10, 1862.

On January 17, 1862, Robert wrote from Coles Island that "I hold a very handsome position being the senior captain of Lucas' Battalion and consequently the next artillery officer to Lucas. If any thing were to happen to him the command of the

Batteries will devolve upon me."[73] Routine duties occupied him for months. Six months later, he wrote, "I am having a dreadfully dull time now. There is no excitement of any kind, no prospect of attack, and no diversion or amusement to kill time. If we only had some energetic man at the head of our battalion, how different our prospects and condition would have been. But there is little use in regrets that cannot mend matters."[74]

In October 1862, Robert was sent to Greenville to recruit men for his battalion.[75] At the end of November he wrote to Sue:

> Yours of the 25th inst. came to hand only today, together with the socks and only one bottle of honey. In future I beg that you will direct all packages to me directly, and not to the Quartermaster, as it seems to be a practice in that office to levy upon all goods shipped to their care. I have received all the socks and feel very much indebted to both Beck and yourself. They are exceedingly comfortable and nice, and the trouble they must give you to make is the only reason why I would not ask for a half dozen more. There is only one objection to them, and that is that my foot feels queer at having any thing so respectable on it; if you were to see the ludicrous appearance of some of my old ones, with toes where the heels should be, and heels where the toes should be, you would laugh. But these times teach us economy. . . .[76]

On July 19, 1862, Gen Roswell S. Ripley ordered Company A of Lucas' battalion moved to Battery Wagner. Ripley appointed Capt. John H. Gary commander.[77] Robert, the senior captain in the battalion, was chagrinned that he was not chosen for the command. Major Lucas assured him that the choice was due to Gary's friendship with Ripley, not any shortcoming of his own.

On July 25 Robert was ordered to relieve Company A. So arduous was the duty at Battery Wagner that the troops were rotated every four days. During his tour Robert

won the confidence of all of his superior officers. He lost

two men to the accidental discharge of a torpedo [floating mine]. On his return to the Fort he resumed his usual duties forthwith, notwithstanding his fatigue. All his officers were also present at the first dress parade after their return from Battery Wagner, which is *very* unusual. On the 16th instant [August 1863] Capt. Pringle was again ordered to Battery Wagner to relieve Company 'A'. Capt. Gary had been mortally wounded on the 12th and in speaking of it Capt. Pringle after expressing the greatest regret at Capt. Gary's fate, remarked that he thought his chances for surviving the second tour of duty very good, for it would be remarkable for two captains to be injured successively.[78]

With great relish at finally being chosen the battalion's chief of artillery, but with his predecessor's fate clearly in mind, Robert sat down and composed a set of clear and businesslike instructions for his brother Motte to follow in case the worst should come to pass:

I am off again for Battery Wagner, and will repeat my wishes to you, so that in case I should "go under", you will know what to do. Enclosed you will find two accounts, the one with the State of So. Ca. please give to Maj. Lucas with a check for the balance on hand say $29.57. The other please send in to the Adjutant and Inspector General at Richmond, asking for instructions as to what disposition must be made of the balance in hand say $28.79.

Pay to Lieut Colhoun[79] or the senior officer of my company $30 in full of company fund.[80] Pay to the same officers $75 to be paid Private J. N. Fitts of my company, it being balance of some money given to me to keep for him.

I owe Edgerton Richards and Co. about $100.[81] Cary, Stuben, Dawson and Blackman each small amounts. Yourself for segars, I believe, $15. I think that these are all my debts, except the $500 I owe you which I will come to soon. You will find a check for $935.92 enclosed being the balance of my account in bank—and in addition Lieut Lucas owes $100 on a bet that Charleston would not fall by the 17th inst. From this statement you will perceive, that after my debts are paid, there will still be a balance of some $5 or 600 on hand. With reference now to the debt I owe you, take the share and if it worth par, pay yourself by appropriating it. If below par, make the difference good out of my funds.

After all my debts are paid, give Mama the balance of the money, and tell her, that it is my appropriation towards paying for the miniatures of William, Charles and little Hesse.

Do not think that I anticipate being killed from this business like manner of arranging my affairs, but I think that every one ought guard against all emergencies.

In case I should be so unfortunate I have only one request to make, and that is, that my own family will write no obituary of me. In the words of another, my worst torture at this moment, is the overestimate which generous friends form of me.[82]

On the 19th of August 1863, Alston went across the harbor to Morris Island where he visited Robert and James. He found them both well and in good spirits. Mary was concerned for Robert's welfare and wrote him from Friendville, hoping he was safe, sending him her love, and wishing him God's protection. After surviving shelling after shelling from the federal monitors in the harbor, however, Robert's luck had worn dangerously thin.

On August 21 Robert was serving as chief of artillery at Battery Wagner. That morning, while he was directing fire at the enemy, federal monitors were shelling Wagner vigorously. Their shells were fired at a low elevation, so as to ricochet twice upon the water, the last time about twenty-five yards from the shore. They exploded just over the parapet of the battery. One of these shells struck a school of mullet and hurled one into the gun chamber. Robert picked it up and laughingly remarked, "I have got my dinner!"[83]

Moments later, at about six in the evening, a soldier notified him that one of his guns had been disabled. "I will attend to it," he said with a smile, and he made his way to the parapet of the battery. Just as Robert entered the chamber of the disabled gun, the next- to-last enemy shell of the evening exploded directly in front of him, inflicting mortal wounds. Robert's shattered body was carried back to the bombproof shelter which served as battery headquarters.

There he was treated by the battalion surgeon, Dr. Henry B. Horlbeck.[84] "He was put upon a table and I examined his four wounds and discerned at once that there was no possibility of his recovery," Horlbeck wrote. "The fragment of the shell that struck him in the pit of his stomach passed entirely thru his body, coming out at his back, while another fragment had shattered his arm just below the shoulder, cutting the artery."[85] Dr. Horlbeck later wrote that the surface of Robert's upper chest and face were "filled with granulated iron forced under the skin, the particles being mixed with the powder of the shell to make the effect more horrible."[86]

When the surgeon told Robert that he had not long to live, Robert's only concern was for his family. Major Lucas wrote that "though his wounds were dreadful and many, a quarter of an hour of perfect collectedness of mind was mercifully granted to him. This he employed in loving messages to those dearer than himself."[87] In the waning minutes of his life, as his blood drained out onto the floor of the bunker, Robert lamented to Dr. Horlbeck, "It will kill my poor mother," and his last words were, "Tell my father and my mother that they know how I have loved them, and I die loving them still, and I hope we will all meet in Heaven."[88]

That evening at about 6:30 P.M., after the shelling stopped, the Signal Corps flags on Morris Island telegraphed the news of Robert's death to the silent, desolate city. Alston was standing guard duty on the Southern Wharf that night and saw both the shelling and the signals, but had no idea what he was witnessing.

"James' account was, that when the fight had closed for the evening, he and another officer had gone into the surf to bathe, and as they came racing out of the water in the highest spirits, he met a messenger from Battery Wagner, who told him Robert was mortally wounded. He put on his clothes and hurried up to Wagner, but when he got there, his brother had been dead for half an hour. A rowboat was on the point of leaving for the city. James put Robert into it and brought him at once up, fortunately, as otherwise, he could not have reached town until daylight." Alston continued, "We took him from the boat, put him in an ambulance, and carried him into the silent King St. house. There we exposed the ghastly, cruel wounds, and Brewton, James and myself, assisted by the weeping servants, took off his bloody clothes, and laid him in the South Parlour."[89]

James and Alston brought Robert from the wharf to the house. Motte was away from town, transporting troops, and could not return for the funeral.[90] Before laying out Robert in the south parlor, his body was rested on the stone steps of the portico, where the blood seeped into the porous stone. Well into the twentieth century, the blood stains could still be seen on the portico and the floor boards of the south parlor.[91] Alston searched the house for a cane sofa to use as Robert's funeral bier, but was unable to find it. The brothers brought down Susan's bed and laid him out on that.[92]

Alston telegraphed the news to the family members at Dukeville, cautioning them against attempting to come to Charleston. "Do not increase your natural grief by the regret that you were not here. These things—all things are in God's Hands. Our enemies may again shell the city at any time," Alston wrote them, and "when it next comes it will be serious."[93]

Alston continued, "I sent a written invitation to the officers of the battalion to attend from the house. Lucas, Colhoun and Ford came. Mr. Sass called last night to express his sympathy, and I invited him to the house. This morning James Pringle, John and Williams Middleton,[94] and his friend Cliff Smith, came to the house. Madame Girard[95] sent a wreath of roses and geraniums, and Cousin Elizabeth's servant, Maria, came and assisted Lucretia, and made two wreaths from the garden. Motte, Brewton, James, Julius, Poinsett and myself bore him down the steps of the old house for the last time."[96]

The funeral was held the next morning, on Sunday, August 23, 1863, and the Rev. Stephen Elliott read the service.[97] Alston, Motte, Brewton, James, Julius and Poinsett bore the coffin to St. Michael's, and a "weeping collection of friends and fellow citizens laid it under the gray stones near where our little children lie. I was not there," wrote Mary, "nor his Father, nor his sisters."[98]

A notice on the front page of the Charleston *Daily Courier* lamented his loss. "This is a time for hasty greetings and brief farewells. Graves are hastily dug and as hastily filled, covering from the eye the precious, mutilated remains of patriots and heroes, bitterly lamented. Brief and imperfect must be the hurried tribute which we can now pay to their memory."[99]

The envelope, with Mary's annotation, which contained the notification of Robert's death.

Major Lucas wrote of Robert and his fallen predecessor, "They were the life of my command, and I could have better spared thirty men."[100] In memoriam, Mary wrote in the family Bible, "Killed on the 21st of August, 1863, in Battery Wagner, whilst repelling an attack upon it by the United States Naval forces, Capt. Robert Pringle of the Confederate Artillery Service. 7th son of William Bull and Mary M. Pringle—26 years of age." Following a grim, time-honored tradition of naming forts after fallen heroes, a new artillery emplacement on Dill's plantation on the east bank of the Stono River was named Battery Pringle in Robert's honor on August 29, 1863.[101]

Hunkered down in their bombproof shelters, but having suffered only relatively light casualties, the remaining men of batteries Gregg and Wagner continued to be bludgeoned by overwhelming firepower from ironclads and land-based Union siege guns. By September 6 enemy soldiers had advanced to within yards of the batteries and General Beauregard directed their evacuation. Union troops moved in the next day, only to find the batteries empty.

Charles

By the summer of 1861 Charles and James had returned to Charleston from Europe, finding their way through the Union blockade. They both promptly enlisted. A misunderstanding about obtaining an officer's commission for Charles sparked a major rift between the Alston and Pringle families that summer.

In August Mary's brother, Charles C. P. Alston, along with William H. Peronneau, Edward P. Ravenel, and Charles Pringle, obtained permission to raise an artillery company to serve on the coast, but only the first three were initially given officer's commissions. William Bull Pringle visited Governor Pickens and arranged for Charles to get his commission, but he left the governor's office with the impression that Alston and Ravenel had been negligent. "I have to thank God that I have made friends in the community ready to do for me in the failure of my natural friends or relatives that justice and kindness I ought to have a right to expect from them," William wrote.[102]

Charles Alston took offense at being called neglectful and charged William with making a false accusation. Mary wrote to her brother, "You feel, I trust, as grieved as I do at the painful circumstances that have occurred. I will allude no further to them, but I pray you to allow me to assure you that nothing can ever affect my feelings of affection to you." Then, by example, she encouraged Charles to help stop the dispute and heal the wounds. "We are too old, my dear Brother, to venture on any thing that would disturb our dying moments, and, as I would, then, stretch out my hand to you in all love, so let me do it now; as it is most certain we will have to give an account of all things before the judgment seat of Christ."[103]

Nevertheless, Charles Alston and William Bull Pringle continued to trade letters of accusation and rebuttal, and other relatives joined in the fray until the family battle lines were clearly drawn: the William Bull Pringles against the Charles Alstons. So bitter was the clash that young Lt. Charles Alston Pringle wrote the following letter to his uncle:

> I send you the enclosed $40. It is the amount you presented me with when I was about to depart for Europe. With it I purchased a ring which I have worn as a token of the kind feeling I then flattered myself you entertained for me. But as I have just experienced at the threshold of life, a degree of hostility and persecution from you and from your family that rarely falls to the lot of anyone, unoffending as I have been, I return the enclosed, as I otherwise I would have to wear the ring as a memento of one who, instead of the kindness I thought I had a right to expect from him as my Uncle, my Godfather and my namesake, has exhibited only singular opposition and injustice to me.[104]

Charles was appointed brevet second lieutenant of Company E, later Company H, of the 1st (Butler's) Regiment, South Carolina Infantry. On September 26, 1861, he was appointed second lieutenant of Company E. In the spring and early summer of 1862, he was serving at Church Flats and John's Island when he suddenly became ill.

On June 23, 1862, Charles's servant, Thomas, was given permission to travel from Camp Evans, on John's Island, to visit Charleston. The message he brought to King Street was grave: Charles was sick with a serious fever. Two days later, the failing soldier was brought to the Miles Brewton House, where he was nursed by Alston until William and Mary could come down from Dukeville on the 28th. A friend of Susan's wrote, "Susan says many will be comforted by hearing that what calmed him, at length, was prayer, a bright smile beamed on his face as he saw us kneeling at his bedside, and the delirium passed away. He comforted our aching hearts in his last moments by his trust in the merits of Christ and the fervor with which he joined us in prayer or began it for himself ."[105] Second Lieutenant Charles Alston Pringle died of typhoid fever in the Miles Brewton House on June 29, 1862, at the age of twenty-one years, five months.[064] He was buried in St. Michael's churchyard.[107]

James

In July 1861, shortly after returning to Charleston, James was appointed a second lieutenant in Company E, First Battalion, South Carolina Artillery. Six months later he was promoted to first lieutenant. He had a dangerous job: artillery officer at Battery Gregg, located at the tip of Morris Island, less than a mile from Battery Wagner. In the late summer of 1863, when Union gunboats were heavily shelling both positions, James wrote to his mother from Battery Gregg:

> I believe today is the 17th, my dear Mother, but not knowing certainly I cannot date my letter. I am likewise just as ignorant whether it is Thursday, Friday or Saturday. The position of things in the island remains pretty much in status quo, except that the Yankees are progressing

James Reid Pringle in Confederate dress uniform. Photographer unknown.

vastly with their batteries, and day by day are annoying both this post and Battery Wagner by a severe shelling. I have laid the flattering unction to my soul, that I have imbued my hands in their blood, as yesterday I was fortunate enough to burst several shells just in the midst of a large party of them and immediately after one of my shots, two caparisoned[108] and riderless horses started at full speed down the beach and were stopped at Battery Wagner. I have become now perfectly callous to two things, with which I hardly ever expected to be intimately acquainted with, viz., shells and dirt. In reference to the last tell Sister Susan I hardly ever expect to get clean again, being thoroughly encased in filth. I absolutely now revel in it and hardly ever think I will attempt to wash. Fleas, sand, dust, bugs of all kinds are my constant attendants. Last night, though raining in torrents, we were compelled to go get our guns ready for instant action, as there was strong reason to suppose that the enemy would land between Fort Wagner and our post in barges and then charge our battery, but the night passed and they failed to come.

I am afraid, on second consideration, I have told a fib, when I mentioned above that I had become accustomed to shells, for to confess the truth, I was most terribly frightened the day before yesterday. A communication had come to Gen. Talliafero[109] which I took from the courier, mounted his horse and started to Battery Wagner to deliver. The enemy had not yet commenced shelling, but soon after my arrival they opened fire. Knowing that I had to return, I felt rather uncomfortable, as the intermediate ground between the two posts is always pretty heavily raked.[110] However, I started on at a pretty hard gallop, trying to pay no attention to the whizzing noise around me, and managed to preserve my equilibrium pretty well, but when about half over as it seemed to me that never endless road, I heard a most infernal howling just behind and an 11 inch [artillery shell] rushed furiously past me, at only about 4 feet distance, and then burst just in front, enshrouding me, as Jupiter Olympus, in smoke, and flame; my horse threw himself on his haunches and quivered, but horse and rider soon recovered themselves, and then rushed frantically down the beach. Since that time I have never volunteered again as a courier, as you may well suppose. If you can manage to decipher this letter, it is more than I expect, as I am writing with a stump of a pencil in a most uncomfortable position. Love to all, Your affectionate son, J.R.P.[111]

James was considerably luckier than his brother artilleryman, Robert. He survived the shelling and eventual retreat from Morris Island. He was promoted to captain in January 1865 and was paroled at the end of the war.

St. Michael's Churchyard. White stone, top left: memorial to Mary and William Bull Pringle. Inscribed paving stones, clockwise, from top left: William Bull Pringle, 1800-1881; Capt. Robert Pringle, 1837-1863; "Uncle Robert" Pringle, 1793-1860; and Lt. Charles Alston Pringle, 1841-1862.

In the first weeks of 1865, a demoralized Pringle family sat gloomily at Dukeville, counting their losses. Charles and Robert lay cold in their graves and Brewton was suffering severe emotional aftereffects from the war. Mary, William, and their daughters were safe but nearly destitute. Foraging Union soldiers were expected any time, looking for food and any booty which could be carried off. Runimede and Beneventum were gone, and although many of the slaves from Beneventum and Richfield were still with them, others had died or run off in search of freedom. At Richfield, the freedmen of Georgetown District had stripped the plantation house of everything usable. It seemed as though William and Mary's family had little left except their house on King Street—and their own steely resolve. On February 11, with her faith stretched to the breaking point, Mary turned to her Bible, opened it to John 16:24, and recorded its message in her personal journal: "Ask, and ye shall receive."[112]

By February 18, when the last Confederate defenders had departed, rumors flew that unoccupied houses in Charleston would be confiscated by Union troops. This prompted a flood of women and children to race back to the city and lock themselves in. The Pringles, 110 miles away, had little choice but to huddle together at Dukeville and pray for the best. On the 19th, the troops of the 21st U.S. Colored Troops took possession of the city. Several days later the 127th New York Volunteers joined them, and the two units took over the administration of the city. As their British predecessors had done eighty-five years before, they chose the Miles Brewton House as their headquarters.

CHAPTER TEN

A Bitter Homecoming

Our dear, old homestead, built by our ancestors, owned by my grand-mother, inhabited by my Father and my Mother, my own birth place, the roof under which my thirteen children drew their first breath of life, has passed out of our possession.

—Mary Pringle, February 22, 1865

When federal troops marched into Charleston on February 18, 1865, and seized control, the Pringles became stateless persons: citizens loyal to a country which no longer existed and outcasts from the nation whose army occupied their house and ruled their lives. The loss of two sons to death, of their house, plantations, slaves, and lifestyle filled Mary and her family with feelings of impotence, bitterness, and rage.

The elegant and refined Charleston of antebellum times had been reduced by war to a barren, gutted derelict. The great fire of 1861 had cut an ugly swath of desolation across the peninsula, taking with it every scrap of wood, cloth, and foliage in its path. More disasters in February 1865 added to the desolation. Explosions and a firestorm started with the deliberate burning of the Ashley River bridge. Another fire near the Cooper River and an explosion at the North East Railroad terminal in the center of the peninsula caused "crowds of frightened women and children, white and black," to run wildly through the streets.[1]

A visitor to the city in April 1865 described "tall chim-neys, grim and charred, the dilapidated walls, overgrown with moss, the cellars, rank with grass, weeds and thistles, the streets without pavement, and ankle-deep with sand."[2]

The venerable Mrs. St. Julien Ravenel, descended from generations of native-born Charlestonians, also painted a grim picture. "Everything was overgrown with rank, untrimmed vegetation. . . . Not grass merely, but bushes, grew in the streets. The gardens looked as if the Sleeping Beauty might be within. The houses were indescribable: the gable was out of one, the chimneys fallen from the next; here a roof was shattered, there a piazza half gone; not a window remained. The streets looked as if piled with diamonds, the glass lay shivered so thick upon the ground."[3]

The steeple of St. Michael's, the Pringle family church, had been the aimpoint for federal gunners and had taken at least one cannonball. Another blew out part of the rear wall, destroying the altar and seven of the ten commandments engraved on stone tablets in the sanctuary.[4]

The Union blockade and its strangulation of cotton and rice exports destroyed planters and merchants alike and left the stores empty of merchandise and food. Charleston's bustling harbor, which had served as the focal point for the state's thriving antebellum economy, lay silent and empty, filled with the corpses of sunken ships. Gen. Carl Schurz, a prominent Abolitionist, Republican, and friend of Abraham Lincoln, served the last month of the war in South Carolina. Schurz wrote, "There was no shipping in the harbor except a few quartermasters' vessels and two or three small steamers. We made fast to a decaying pier constructed of palmetto-logs. There was not a human being visible on the wharf; the warehouses seemed to be completely deserted; there was no wall and no roof that did not bear eloquent marks of having been under fire of siege guns. . . . The crests of the roofs and the chimneys were covered with turkey-buzzards, who evidently felt at home, and who from time to time lazily flapped their wings and stretched forth their hideous necks."[5]

After seizing Fort White in Winyah Bay, the federal gunboats *Mingoe* and *Pawnee* steamed cautiously up to

Georgetown on February 23. Both the fort and city had been abandoned, and the federal troops raised the Stars and Stripes from the tower of city hall on February 25. By the end of March, former slaves on the river plantations had been notified of their freedom, but their former owners were required to feed them for sixty days.[6] Those charged to make food available—the planters—were often unable to take possession of their land, and when they could, frequently found that all food supplies had been stolen. In short order, freedmen discovered that their first new freedom was the freedom to starve.

In St. Andrew's Parish, where the Pringles had spent so many idyllic winters, Runimede, their elegant country seat, had been burned to the ground by Union soldiers. A committee of three Episcopal clergymen surveyed the desolation and wrote, "But three residences exist in the whole space between Ashley and Stono rivers. Fire and sword were not enough. Family vaults were rifled, and coffins of the dead were forced open in pursuit of plunder."[7]

During the war, with the refugee planters and their remaining slaves unable to farm their lands, the production of food for the table and the market dropped to disastrously low levels. Charlestonians from all walks of life faced the risk of starvation. The Bureau of Refugees, Freedmen and Abandoned Lands, commonly known as the Freedmen's Bureau, was organized in March 1865 to administer the distribution of the abandoned lands and regulate work contracts between the planters and the freedmen. It did so from 1865 through 1868, when South Carolina was readmitted to Congress.[8]

Each week, on alternating days, the Freedmens' Bureau issued rations of food to the destitute by race. One historian noted that "actual hunger was found as late as 1867, and many formerly wealthy were for years undernourished."[9] An observer recorded a typical scene:

> "'What is *that white* woman doing here?' asked a Northern visitor, looking upon the line of people waiting for food.

> "'My dear sir,' replied Mr. Williams[10], 'that woman, four years ago, was worth half a million dollars, and lived in a fine mansion on the Battery.'"[11]

Although the Pringles and their close relatives had little money during this time, they did have some, and their names are not found on the surviving rolls of those accepting rations from the Freedmens' Bureau in Charleston or Georgetown.[12]

On the rice plantations, deserted as they had been for the better part of three years, little useful was left. Charles Heyward reported that "as a plantation, Rose Hill [on the Combahee River] had ceased to exist. Several breaks had occurred in its neglected river banks, and the tides flooded the rice fields at will. No crops were grown. On the highlands, the fences were down, and all of the cattle and hogs had disappeared. Fire, as well as water and depredation, had done its work. With the single exception of the houses in the settlements, nearly all of which were empty, all buildings of every description were burned—barns and stables, blacksmith and cooper shops, even the hospital. In the unused barnyard tall weeds grew, and of the threshing mill only the square brick chimney remained."[13]

By November 1865 the Freedmens' Bureau had seized many rice plantations in Georgetown and Horry districts as "abandoned lands." These included Keithfield, Friendfield, Strawberry (Field), Marietta, True Blue, Hagley, Turkey Hill, and Ingleside, along with three Alston estates: Rose Hill, Forlorn Hope, and Clifton.[14]

The forced emancipation of William's 300 slaves represented the loss not only of his entire labor force but also of approximately $150,000 of his capital.[15] Most of the planters, including William, had invested heavily in Confederate bonds. When the Union forces marched into Charleston, William was still holding at least $47,400 in worthless Confederate currency and $7,300 in Confederate bonds.[16] His debts, however, all survived the war fully intact and dogged him until his death. By war's end, all that the family had left of value was their house on King Street, the possessions they had ferreted away in and around Dukeville, and each other.

The 54th Massachusetts Infantry regiment that marched into town was headed by a black soldier bearing a banner inscribed "Liberty." Federal troops searched every house to ensure that all former slaves knew of their new freedom. At the same time, Union soldiers looked for firearms and booty.[17]

On February 28, 1865, federal military commanders ordered the citizens of Charleston to take an oath of allegiance to the United States or forfeit all rights to passes or other favors—such as ever seeing the insides of their homes again. The order also noted that anyone who feared that their person or property would be molested should prominently display an American flag "in a conspicuous position," and that anyone causing harm or damage to these properties would be punished.[18]

Like his British military predecessors, Clinton, Balfour and Rawdon, Brig. Gen. Alexander Schimmelpfennig, commander of the 127th New York Volunteers and the 21st U.S. Colored Troops, chose the Miles Brewton House as his headquarters.[19] Later, Col. John Porter Hatch[20] occupied the house, using the drawing room as his office. His adjutant used the withdrawing room.

Ironically, it was a senior Union commander who caused the only structural damage to the Miles Brewton House related to the Civil War. Jacob Motte Alston wrote that Colonel Hatch knocked a hole through the azure, coved ceiling and through the pediment of the second-story portico so that the "beautiful stars and stripes which the North desecrated, might float over the time honoured mansion."[21] The exterior damage to the pediment caused by Hatch's handiwork has been carefully preserved by all subsequent owners of the house.

With the war not yet ended and their house being used as enemy headquarters, the Pringles at Dukeville could do little but cling to each other, try to hide their stored house-

The damage to the pediment caused by Lt. Col. John Porter Hatch.

hold goods, and food from predatory Yankee foragers, and wait for news from Charleston. Their depression and anguish showed clearly in the February 22, 1865, letter which Mary wrote from Dukeville to Mary Mitchell in Connecticut:

> I need no longer keep up the veil of concealment between my wretchedness and your loving heart, my beloved daughter, for our proud, old city stands humbled, and so, you know, I am wretched. The flames have swept over it, but what matter that. The Northern papers will have told you all-, and so I may be spared the sickening history; now hardly need I tell you how I feel, as the truth presses on my heart, that our dear, old homestead, built by our ancestors, owned by my grandmother, inhabited by my father and my mother, my own birth place, the roof under which my thirteen children first drew the breath of life, has passed out of our possession.
>
> Ah! how sacred, every spot in it, was to us; that South Parlor, where all of our holy dead were laid, and where the dark spot of blood still shows, where was stretched the bleeding body of our "Christian Hero"[Robert]: strange feet will tread carelessly over it, never knowing

> that a mother's lips had pressed upon it-, whilst her heart, even in its torturing grief, beat fondly and gratefully as she, even there, remembered his gallantry and that he had never caused her a pang of sorrow or of disappointment.
>
> How well "our little child" [Hesse Mitchell] understood the value of the old home. She had learned as she wandered over it at my side to know that the greatest treasures in it were the things most valued by my sainted Mother. When attracted by any object, she would say, "did this belong to my blessed Great-grandmother?" And the graves of our dead, all forsaken, too-; only violets and roses and geraniums mark our sweet little ones' grave—and there is not even a name engraved upon the grey pavement[22] that covers dear Robert. The Battery[23] that stands the most appropriate monument to his memory, will, I suppose, no longer bear his name. Well-, well-, all-, all- is in disappointment and wretchedness. Pray for us. [24]

The family at Dukeville was in the direct path of Union troops, who gleefully liberated anything they could carry. With Lee's surrender at Appomattox still a month in the future, federal troops were under no orders to restrain from looting. By mid-March Yankee soldiers were roaming freely throughout Darlington District. From Society Hill on March 19, 1865, Rebecca wrote Brewton a report of the Yankee plundering:

> I suppose you will be anxious to know how we fared with those wretched thieves who visited us in the shape of Yankee soldiers. Our situation, being off the main road, was a great benefit to us—only one party entered the house—they robbed our trunks of what they pleased—searched our drawers, ate our breakfast and then put our silver spoons into their pockets. There was fortunately a captain with them—a creature named Roberts—who comparatively restrained them. They took off poor old Julia [a horse] in spite of our efforts to save her, put three bags of flour on her, made Ge[illegible]y mount her, and took him off. He has not yet returned, and we fear he will not now be able to do so.
>
> The first party visited us on the Saturday after you all

left us, and another, some cavalry, came on Monday morning, but happily they did not enter the house—talked insurrection with the negroes, and went off. None of them were insulting to us nor to Papa, though they constantly demanded his watch. Our heaviest losses have been at the plantation, and there they were very great. Hercules[25] hid the horses successfully for two days, but it is said one of the negroes betrayed them, and the Yankees sought them out. So they all are now in Yankee hands, like everybody's, except Mr. W. Evans' and Mrs. Williams'.[26]

They took from Papa's plantation every four footed animal, and destroyed everything but the unground corn for which the negroes pleaded. They robbed the negroes of everything, taking their shoes from their feet, and handkerchiefs from the women's heads. They took off thirteen of Papa's negroes. Scipio was on his way to James, but they captured him. . . .

They took off a large number of negroes from this neighborhood, and a large number of animals. They have plundered every one of everything most valuable. Every bottle of Papa's and Julius'wine is gone—all of our beautiful china and glass that was stored in Coker's store[27] is gone and the Axminster carpet and the stair case and entry carpets were cut up for saddle clothes for their stolen horses.[28]

The people in the village had an awful time—the wretches were walking in and out of their houses from sun rise till sun set. It was a most terrible ordeal for all of us, and God knows how we will be able to endure another such trial. It was a mercy you were not here. The poor people about here told that the men of the neighborhood were in the swamps and the Yankees swore vengeance against them—searched the swamps in every direction—captured them *all*—they afterwards released those who were not in the army.

Cousin Alston[29] turned up all right with the poney all right too, a week after all the confusion—he had been behind the Yankees at Lynch's Creek.[30] He has gone off to report at Newberry.[31] We are fearing more raids up here—the Yankees have burnt the railroad up to Kingstree,[32] we hear. Our servants behaved admirably, and we hid our provisions very successfully, else we should now be starving. We are in a sad plight, being cut off from all communication with the outer world. We have no idea where our army is. We hope to have the rail road again established but we fear it will only bring the Yanks after us. Brother[33] is now here, but leaves in a few days for Spartanburg to join Governor Magrath. Bob[34] leaves shortly for Glenn Springs,[35] where the Governor established a camp of instruction for boys of 16. All unite in love.[36]

Fearing the imminent arrival of Sherman's troops in Columbia, Alston had moved Emma and his family to Society Hill on February 6. But even in out-of-the-way places like Dukeville, federal soldiers discovered most of the homes and their larders. On March 30, Emma wrote to her mother:

Nor have we escaped, as we hoped to do in this secluded spot, for these wretched creatures, turned out of their way, we heard, to visit Society Hill, as they were informed that it was well supplied with provisions, which they hauled out, stealing what they wanted, and destroying what they did not want. We are situated three miles from the village, on a by-road, and I flattered myself, our house would not be discovered. But they found us out, and paid us two visits of about a half hour each. However, they were not insolent to us, and after stealing several of our things before our eyes, departed to commit other depredations on our neighbors. They broke open Aunt Hess's trunk, and took from it many articles of value, which belonged to her dead, and thereby associated with some of her dearest memories. Horses, mules and several negroes, were carried away from Uncle William's plantation but fortunately they left some of his provisions there; and indeed almost every one has suffered, some more, some less, and in various ways by this depredation. But one man was killed in this vicinity, and no violence offered to ladies, and I feel almost grateful to the Almighty, that more atrocious deeds were not enacted here. We have lost Allit, and Maurice (Caesar's son), who were either carried, or went off with them, and Alston fears his whole

> law library, which was in Columbia, was burnt. Immense losses to us, though comparatively small, to what others have lost.[37]

With the war lost, the family wanted most to regain their house and plantations, but the new order demanded a stiff price for either. In the Beaufort area, federal forces confiscated and distributed to freedmen the "abandoned" lands they captured in November 1861 and sold twenty-six plantations in 1863. On January 15, 1865, General Sherman reserved the sea islands and plantation lands between Charleston and the St. John's River and the abandoned rice fields for the former slaves.

In 1861 Congress had imposed a tax of $29 million to help fight the war; South Carolina's portion was $363,570. In 1862 the tax law was modified to add a penalty of fifty percent if a state (such as those in the Confederacy) obstructed collection of the tax. The law further provided that if the tax was not paid, land could be seized and sold to satisfy the federal tax lien. The federal government was able to collect this tax from William Bull Pringle in 1866, when it charged him $1 each for his two watches and $4.80 for his silver plate. His son Motte paid $30 for his $600 income, $3 for his three watches, $1 for his piano and $13 for his silver plate.[38]

On June 9 Alston wrote the Mitchells a report on the family's bewildering state of affairs:

> Papa, Motte and I left Society Hill a few days ago and went to Georgetown where we took the oath of allegiance. After arranging his business at Santee, Papa returned to Society Hill and Motte and I came on to Charleston to endeavor to pay the taxes on and get possession of our houses. We had not yet been able to pay the taxes but then succeeded in getting into my house,[39] shattered as it is. Papa's house is occupied as Head Quarters and I am afraid that there will be some delay before we can get possession of that.
>
> As we are absolutely without money and as we must

have some to pay our taxes and purchase a few necessities, I have drawn two bills on Edward in San Francisco at 15 days sight payable in American gold, each for $500. These I have negotiated with C. C. Leary, a New York banker who proposes settling here at 20 per cent premium. As I do not yet know what prudence I can write to Edward I will thank you to telegraph him at once advising him of the bills so that he may be prepared to meet them. I will thank you also to write to him immediately by mail either enclosing this letter, or informing him of the bills. I am sorry that we have had to draw so soon and without notice upon Ed—but it is a matter of extreme importance that we endeavour to save our lands.

I am not sure that the Santee lands will be worth the taxes paid on them, so that every thing which we will have left will be our city property—we can presume even that. I cannot now enter into particulars of our condition, our prospects are as uncertain and dark as it is possible for them to be. We are constantly discussing a general immigration of the whole family but we do not know if we can accomplish it. We cannot account for not having found letters waiting for us in the Post Office here from Julius, Edward and yourself. Pray write to us at once at this place.

What has become of Julius? I am uneasy about him. If he is in New Port send him this letter or a copy of it. Send a copy also to Edward if you think it can be done prudently. But by all means advise him of the bills at the earliest possible time. I think that Motte and I will remain here for some time as there is much which requires our attention. Write to this point always and as often as you can for even if we are not here we can arrange to have our letters sent to us. Write to us about Julius and his family. I am quite uneasy about him as it is now several months since we have heard of him.

The family is all congregated at Society Hill waiting events. God knows what is to become of us. Papa looks very well, but Mama has just recovered from sickness and is not yet quite as strong as usual. One of my children little Rebecca is, I fear, too ill now to recover.[40] She seems

> to have some pulmonary disorder which the country doctors cannot understand. I am anxious to be in communication with Edward as there is much that I should like to consult him about. Write to him about the bills by two or three mails as to secure against miscarriage of the letters and telegraph also.[41]

Alston's banking arrangements illustrate the family's financial plight and the scarcity of capital in Charleston after the war—situations which would not change appreciably over the next four years. In 1860 Charleston could boast of nine banks with $11 million in capital; in 1883, the six surviving banks had only $1.1 million to put to use.[42] At war's end, the only family members who had access to any cash were Edward, who had managed the family investments in San Francisco with mixed success since 1853, and Julius—the alleged traitor—who by 1850 had completely eclipsed his father in wealth. It would be these two branches of the family—the "California Pringles" and the "rich French Pringles," as their descendants called them, who saved the South Carolina Pringles from starvation and dispossession after the collapse of the Lost Cause.

In the immediate postwar period, Northern carpetbaggers with ready cash, such as C. C. Leary, could make fast fortunes for the simple reason that they had the one thing that ex-Confederates did not: Union greenbacks, backed by gold. Jacob Motte Alston described carpetbaggers as "the very scum of the earth, who came in flocks like carrion crows to affiliate with 'scalawags' or renegade creatures of the South. Their stock in trade was limited, save in deception and the art of swindling."[43]

The banking transaction which Leary provided the Pringles worked as follows. Leary, in Charleston, accepted from Alston two "sight drafts" (the functional equivalent of personal checks) for $500 each drawn on Pringle accounts in San Francisco which were held in Edward's name. Leary paid out the $1,000, less his stiff twenty percent fee, to Alston in federal currency, which the family could then use to pay the property taxes imposed in 1861 by the federal government.

Alston's pleas for information illustrate the great communication difficulties which still existed. His letter also shows the family's assumption that Julius was likely soon to be back keeping Yankee company at Newport—if he was not already doing so. On June 24, 1865, William wrote to Julius from Society Hill:

> Your kind and affectionate letter of the 6th June reached us only yesterday. Be assured we fully appreciate your generosity of offering us pecuniary assistance although you are in the same category of ruin that we are. What we are to do I can't yet tell. We are poor indeed but hope to struggle and sustain those who are absolutely dependent upon me, without again taxing you. We have disciplined ourselves to so much privation for the last three years that I hope we shall make out with but little.
>
> We were much gratified by hearing that you had joined Maria and the children particularly that you had found her well. For the last accounts we had of her health were unfavourable and we had been but recently expressing apprehensions about her as well as yourself, so long has it been since we heard from you. I cannot tell you how much pleasure it would give us to see you all. It is the only kind of happiness your Mama and I can look forward to see and embrace those we love so much. I am sure we will be proud of and amused by the little folks. I hope by some arrangement we shall all be able to meet again before they go abroad.
>
> What our plans are it is impossible to say at present. Your brothers and myself having determined that our only course is to make the best of the evil, have all taken the hateful oath of allegiance and calculate to go to Charleston.
>
> But the Yankee General Hatch has taken possession of our house and will not quit it.[44] We have offered to pay the tax but they have closed the office until November. Hatch who is said to be a greater thief than Butler will throw every impediment in the way of getting the house. If we do not get it, I can't imagine what we shall do. Your brother and Motte are now in town, looking out for some

occupation to provide the means of living for their destitute families. We are badly off but my heart sickens when I look into the future of your brother Alston's large family of eight children his five growing daughters going bare footed and without the means of education.

The prospect of improvement of matters in this state is so forlorn that we would all like to quit if we could find an asylum where we could meet with moderate prosperity. But alas we know not where to turn. James, who had the good fortune to pass through battles, has resolved to make an effort to try to do something collecting up a small amount of greenbacks and taking in his carpet bag the portion of William's silver[45] he drew he is going to New York, perhaps for California to seek employment in some capacity however subordinate.

And my decision with all the distresses staring us in our faces we do not add to them by the self reproach it is yours now so bitterly I will not reproach you for doing so ourselves but remind you that there seemingly is an unkindness in you to add self reproach to the suffering of those of us who have so much to bear and suffer. It would be folly now that the result has been disastrous not to regret that secession was resorted to. But the tyranny and despotism and cruelties which our enemy has practiced is sufficient to convince one that the evil could not have been long avoided that it was natural for men to desire to escape from such a despotism which like the sword of Damocles was hanging over us, threatening destruction. However not to argue a confusion you might as well feel self reproach for the loss of your crop by the overflow as that we should feel self reproach for our ruin by secession.

As God saw fit to destroy your crop (unprecedently) by worms last year and this year by the flood so as he accomplished his ends by various means he has seen fit to destroy the prosperity of the slaveholders by means of the Yankees. . . .

I can not but reverence a cause in which such men as Lee and Jackson and your own brothers sacrificed so much so cheerfully. As well might I reproach myself for assisting one who attempted to take possession of my land altho' I

> be impoverished by the expenses of litigation. However let us be done with the past and look to the future. To no one in the South was Secession more distasteful than to Jane Pringle[46] yet when it was done she strenuously sustained her sons in their devotion to the cause and tho' losing the finer and sharing our lot of ruin no one hears from her a word of reproach of our people, but she has gone to her plantation surrounded by the Yankees passing through' what women [illegible] never been subjected to and is, strenuously exerting herself to save what she can from her wreck. Our negroes are generally remaining with us here. When I employ them (those of the plantation) to the low country I shall attempt planting upon the new system. Love to Maria and all of the young folks.[47]

In saying of Julius, "you are in the same catagory of ruin we are," William was going out of his way to be polite. Julius had the opportunity to restart planting in an orderly fashion two years before his father could even think of doing so—and with the blessings of the Union army. In addition, Julius had lavish accommodations abroad, ready access to labor and hard currency, and virtually no debt.

By the end of June 1865 the family had serious doubts that they might ever regain possession of their house and lands. Out of desperation they started to contemplate the unthinkable: abandoning their ancestral properties forever and leaving South Carolina.

So totally was their lifestyle destroyed that hundreds of bitter but unvanquished ex-Confederates abandoned their native states and moved to the Southwest and West. Others forsook the United States entirely and moved to Latin American countries, enticed by liberal offers of land. A few South Carolinians emigrated to Canada and Mexico, and some from Edgefield and Chester emigrated to Brazil. Among the Pringles' personal acquaintances, the family of Gabriel and Anne (Mazÿck) Manigault left for Canada in disgust in 1869.

In letter after letter throughout the next four years, the Pringles debated the pros and cons of emigrating to California and starting a new life as ranchers on the Western frontier. On June 26, 1865, Mary wrote to Julius:

> the negroes are still occupied in cultivating the place we rent up here, we must remain until the crop is gathered in, besides, we are not in possession of our dear, old homestead, and may be never will be. We all feel that Carolina is no longer a home for us. I and your sisters are intensely anxious to get away from it. Your father thinks we must leave, yet I fear he will not have energy for that enterprise. As Edward has some funds of ours in his hands, we should naturally think of a removal to California, but a strange misgiving possesses us, that Edward. may not have been successful. What, then, will become of us? We turn, shuddering from thinking. . . . In seeking a new home, we will consult only as to which place will best suit our unprovided, unmarried daughters.[48]

Two weeks later, she wrote, "We form no plans yet because we know not what our resources will be. We must first endeavor to reclaim our house, about which there is much doubt, for if the odious confiscation act against those with more than $20,000 is enforced, our land and house will be forfeited and we left absolutely destitute. Were I alone to suffer this, I would only *laugh at it*, but my unmarried daughters, *their fate does trouble me*.[49]

On August 25, 1865, William wrote to Edward from Society Hill:

> Your letter of the 17th ultimo gives us cause for much serious reflection. The temptation to emigrate must be very strong to induce two sexagenarians with so many ties living as well as dead to possess them to lay our bones in a distant land. For such a step I do not think the prospect in California sufficiently favorable or probable to tempt us. But the future and our prospects here are so dreary and hopeless that I know not but that self preservation will compel us to fly from our dear old State in which case California shall be the haven we shall make for.
>
> The tyranny despotism and oppression and injustice to which we are subjected is beyond the conception of

any man who has any other conception of right than might. We are regarded and treated as a prostrated and powerless people whom our rulers and subsisters clothed with little brief authority use to pluck from us every thing that might assist us to rise from our prostrated condition. Last night account came from Charleston that a certain General Saxon[50] who is charged with such matters is on the 1st October to proceed to confiscate all the houses in Charleston which were not occupied when Charleston was evacuated and to divide into lots of 40 acres all lands within 40 miles of Charleston and to sell them to negroes. This one item is sufficient to give you an idea of what we are undergoing.

When General Gillmore[51] was about to shell the city he warned all noncombatants to quit it. How could your Mama and sisters remain in our house after such warning and with the shells falling all around? We will make what we can of it. I have taken the oath and applied for pardon.[52] But it is said that will not protect it. Ours is one of numerous like cases. If our house taken from us, the question will be settled that we will immigrate. The house is the only useful piece of property we have. God knows if the Santee lands will ever be available. We are kept out of the house by occupancy of it as "Head Quarters."

I wish that you had been more expressive and precise in your statement in reference to your means. You say that you have lost a great deal in the mines. But that gives us no idea of how much you have lost or what you have left or how much cash you can command in this hour of need. Emigration is costly and can't be undertaken without funds. James had made up his mind that he had better go to California. But the want of means is a great stumbling block, and he can't determine if he can until after a short visit I will soon make to town where I will see if I can raise the means. My only means are a portion of $2500 sent by Julius to pay taxes (not yet paid) and for the present wants. The $2000 you provided was taken by your brother Alston. His necessities being as great as mine. Thus son we will require all you can command. What embarrasses me very much is your indebtedness of $5000 with interest

> to your Uncle Robert's est[ate]. I am entitled to one half. The other is to be divided between the other heirs. Now altho' they have not of late made enquiries about it, I know that is their necessities. They look to it as a resource. Your Aunt Smith being entirely destitute will now regard her share as a small fortune. I hope therefore that you will make every effort to let the heirs share their half of the amount. I can not my dear son, but say that you have been very remiss not sending your accounts. If you have been unfortunate in your investments and speculations (these last were wrong) it is better to make a plain statement of the case and state what are your hopes and prospects of paying our liabilities.[53]

In order to regain possession of their house, the back taxes had to be paid and the federal military commanders had to find another location for their headquarters. Historian Edward McCrady visited Alston Pringle one day in the 1890s when the judge lay sick. During his visit, he remarked: "Judge, it will probably surprise you to know that I have been in this chamber before."

"Ah! how was that?" he said.

McCrady related that while on parole as a Confederate officer, he had reported to the federal office and was shown to the withdrawing room, off the drawing room, which was occupied by the adjutant. Gen. Oliver O. Howard[54] had his office in the drawing room. Judge Pringle listened with great interest and told McCrady that he, too had come to the same office to request the restoration of his father's plantation. While Alston was waiting for Howard, he had observed some mutilation of the wall. When the general remarked that he seemed interested in the room, Alston replied, "Yes, General, I am, considering that this was my mother's bridal chamber, and that in it, I was born."[55]

By the middle of the summer the family was packing their household goods in anticipation of returning to Charleston. On July 12, 1865, Mary made careful inventories of the family linens, table linens, red and yellow damask curtains, quilts, glassware, and their four sets of china: common white, red, India, and French.

On July 23 Mrs. J. J. Pringle Smith wrote Mrs. William Mason Smith that Alston "has possession of his house and expects to move down in October," but noted that William and Mary did not yet have their house back.[56] William went to Charleston again in August to talk to the federal authorities, but to no immediate avail. On September 13 Mary wrote from Dukeville to Rebecca, "I am impatient as you are to be in town and as soon as Alston's family remove, I shall begin my preparation to leave this place. I will not wait to remove my furniture, but take a mattress for each of us, lie on the floor and be content with a morsel for food."[57]

By September 18 the family had realized their dream. On that day, Emma Pringle Smith wrote to her sister, Mrs. Williams Middleton, "The King Street house has been delivered up to Uncle William."[58]

After finally regaining possession of the house, Mary called together the remaining servants and told them that she could not afford to retain them. The exception was Cretia. On October 5 Mary wrote to Mary Mitchell from Alston's house on Tradd Street:

> A negro guard are still on duty in our coach house. On my first visit, about a dozen were seated before the door, howling, by note, a hymn—they did not even draw up their feet as I passed. I would have tread upon them but that I would not soil my own, by touching theirs. I have our faithful Cretia in town with me, having communicated to her our great family calamity—; she takes it as her own as she has done all of our sorrows.
>
> Some ten days before I left Dukeville, I said, "Cretia, you have consented to remain in my service, but it strikes me that when we remove to town and you see all of your fellow servants in their own lodgings and your own sons all established in a home of their own, you will feel unhappy and regret your engagement."
>
> She said, "Mistress, leave that to me, where you are, it is my pleasure, to be."
>
> I said, "You must let me tell you, if you find yourself unhappy, say so to me."

She burst into tears and said, "Mistress, I feel, in my heart, the desire to be with you and the young ladies."

I give her $8 a month, knowing that she had no funds when we came to town. I offered to advance her first month's wages. . . .

She said, "do, Mistress, do—you know what is best for me." I brought Will[59] down, too, to help, in arranging things. Your Papa promised him $12 for the month. He seems out of spirits and out of sorts. I do not know why. It will never do to hire any of our own, as they will never learn their new responsibilities in our employment. I have promised to shelter Lucretia, Daphne and Hannah until poor, little Hannah gets over her trouble.

The weather is delightful and I am beginning to reconcile to the surroundings. I pass the Black garrison now with only a feeling of contempt, yet today, when in passing Gen. Bennett[60] he bowed to Brewton, I did feel my poor old head turning friendly up, and my lips had a spasmodic sensation at being so firmly pressed together. I am trying, too, not to shudder, when I see a crowd of negroes collected at the door of Alonzo White's[61] old residence (corner of Meeting and Tradd Streets) to stare in with delight and admiration at the wild dance going on within among the Freedmen and Freedwomen. If there were no judgments to come, no cold, starving Whites approaching this old city of ours, would be a Paradise to these thoughtless, improvident people. It is a Negro City—crowds are passing to and fro—every one looking so bright, so happy, so triumphant. Those whom I know, greet me with the most simple-hearted cordiality.

I am diligently searching for house servants. When I asked the two applicants the business of their husband, they both said, 'soldiers'. I soon dismissed them. Ah! how differently I feel to the miserable creatures called soldiers whom I now meet in our streets, than I did to our true hearted, noble, defenders of times gone by whose very presence was wont to make my heart bound with pride, hope and respect and reverence, but the instruments now with swords at their sides, produce a loathing that I feel when looking at a venomous reptile.

> I do not feel thus because our slaves have been emancipated—; were that act alone the consequence of the War, I would have no complaint to make. I do not feel thus because two of my most noble sons have been laid in the grave; these things I consider direct events from a Divine Providence—, but I feel so because a heartless, mercenary people, after a victory has been gained, try maliciously to crush the unfortunate victims who lie helpless under their power. Would Lee or Jackson have placed their foot upon a prostrate foe?
>
> As nations are more powerful, so should they be more magnanimous than individuals. The ruin, desolation and wretchedness that surrounds me have led me into this train of thought. Let me be diverted from it by thinking of the happy home you have so vividly brought to our minds. For fear of listeners in the family laughing at my oft-repeated tale, I would lower my voice as I went over it to every visitor who appeared at Dukeville.[62]

The general looting carried out in Charleston by black and white federal troops alike resulted in the loss of large quantities of Charleston's finest furniture, furnishings and artwork. Although the Pringles had taken most of their portable belongings with them, the larger pieces had to be left behind. As of February 18 those pieces were in great danger.

Just after the end of the war, Jacob wrote, "the capacious [drawing] room was sparsely furnished (the antique damask covered chairs and sofas which had been snugly stowed away in a transport bound for the North, but which through the information given by an honest negro, were rescued from the freebooters, had not yet been placed where they belonged.)"[63]

On October 8, 1865, Mary wrote a prayer of supplication, asking that God grant a family member (undoubtedly William) "patience and humble resignation to Thy will" in dealing with the stress of exile and the predations of the Northern troops.[64] On the 10th, Mary started cleaning the house, and wrote to Rebecca, who was visiting the Mitchells in New Haven:

This great trouble makes others appear so trifling, yet I cannot help rejoicing that the nasty, offensive negro guard has been swept from our door. The officials most readily acceded to Alston's desire to have them removed. I keep watch and ward over my empty halls. We cannot have our furniture transported from Society Hill. The old matrimonial bedstead, with its paternal legends of a century, has been stolen. The dumb waiter of an elder date still is also gone. The large press[65] in Edward's chamber, the press from the back parlour and some from the housekeeper's room gone. There is no chair or sofa or table left in the house.

Old Scipio and Cretia are in their own chamber, that has been much improved by Yankee power. I have a yellow woman[66] engaged to cook, wash and market at $8 per month—, so I have declined Daphne's services, but will shelter her and her family in their present difficulties. Ishmael is engaged to cry fish about the streets at a percentage[67] I see little prospect of getting a man servant, as they like the atmosphere of hotels better than those of private residences. Motte expects Ella and his family down on Monday. Sue's time is not yet fixed. I yearn to have her at my side.

Mrs. Julius Pringle[68] has taken her passage in the steamer "Moncka" for tomorrow. As I have already told you, Mary goes with her. She had an interview with Gen. Bennett about the restoration of Mr. Eustice's land from the claims of the northern legatee Eustice. It was, at once, promised her. She then gave Bennett a bird's eye sketch of the negro question. He told her, he had just seen instructions from Washington that all the negroes were to be placed under a seven years apprenticeship on their former owners plantations and made to cultivate them.[69] She said, "they will not work."

He replied, "they will be made to work."

"Then a strong military power must enforce it."

"That will be done."

Georgetown, he said, had just been included within his jurisdiction. She shows her northern nature in her feelings to the wretched negro, whom, she avers, she hates, and will cheat and grind to dust through starvation and labour. She accepts them, on Yankee terms, as equal freemen, equal human beings who are to cope with her and so she will cheat him when she can, oppress him, as she has power; using him only as an instrument for her own purposes. If they want education—find shelter—help—they must appeal to the people who have made them Free men and Free women. She almost called your good, old father a fool because he thinks with pity of the poor wretches whom he has nourished and sheltered for long years. I cannot help respecting him for it, ever, as I think and feel that he will ruin himself and children by it. I am wanted at King Street now to superintend the cleaning there. I am doing it as thouroughly as if I were removing the contamination of a serpent's trail.[70]

On the 20th Mary recorded another prayer, entitled "On Returning Home," thanking the Lord for delivering them back home:

O most Gracious Father, who hast preserved us in Thy mercy withersoever we went and has brought us home in safety, we pray Thee give us grace that, like Jacob when brought again to his Father's house in peace, we many now acknowledge Thee truly to be our God," she wrote. "Let us not feel it was our own strength or our own wisdom or the ordinary chances of life, but Thine arm and Thy love that hath preserved us. Make us now to feel that although home and rest be pleasant to the body, there can be no home for the soul, no rest for the wearied spirit when Thou art not present, and no peace in the home which Thou hast not blessed. Send us faith again, merciful Lord, to our course of domestic duties, and our walk of Christian usefulness, with renewed diligence and thankfulness of heart that our return to our earthly home may be the [illegible]-nest of a nearer approach to our Heavenly Home, where we may finally enter into that rest which remaineth for Thy people, through the merits and intercession of Jesus Christ our Saviour. Amen.[71]

For several reasons, the entire family did not return to Charleston at once. Susan remained at Society Hill until the end of the fall. There she kept watch over the rented house and plantation and the family's furnishings until the railroad lines were repaired and railroad cars could be found to ship their goods back home. Stagecoaches were used to connect the broken lines, and improvised roads made travel a "rough and tumble affair."[72]

After Robert E. Lee surrendered to Ulysses S. Grant at Appomattox on April 9, 1865, the weary Pringle soldiers—Motte, James, and Brewton—returned home one by one as they were paroled. Motte's last reported position was in Raleigh on February 15, while presumably underway to Richmond, Virginia, for reassignment. James was last reported on Sullivan's Island in July 1864 and was still serving as captain of Company H., 1st Regiment, South Carolina Artillery in February 1865. He was paroled at Greensboro, North Carolina, sometime after April 26, 1865. Brewton was on light duty with the Charleston Light Dragoons at the end of the war, still suffering the aftereffects of his wound. His mental condition was rapidly deteriorating. He was paroled on May 3, 1865, at Charlotte, North Carolina.

The brothers probably rendezvoused at Society Hill in May or June, where the crop of 1865 had to be looked after. Alston retained his position as city recorder and resumed it after the war. William did not regain access to Richfield until the fall of 1865, and, at age sixty-five, would have needed all the help he could get from his sons to try to impose some sort of working order on the abandoned, weed-infested plantation. Rebecca was sent as the family's emissary to the Mitchells in Connecticut, leaving only Mary, at age sixty-two, to clean the huge, old house and make it suitable for habitation again.

In the late summer of 1865 Jacob came to Charleston. He wrote, "My dear Aunt Hess had just returned to her home. The beautiful chandelier, which had been in place for over 100 years and which could not well be carried off, was, strange to say, uninjured, and the frames of the portraits still clung to the walls. . . . During the Civil War it was impossible to remove the large frames of these portraits so [the portraits] were taken out and carefully rolled and sent to me in Columbia for safe keeping, with valuable silver, old wines, etc., etc. I will here add that although I lost so heavily by the burning of the city, I saved all that was committed to my care; so you see, there is something in 'luck.'"[73] Jacob continued:

> Our meeting was, of course, a sad one, but all had become accustomed to sadness—it was our normal condition, and 'from our enemies defend us' was about the only prayer uttered. A little cot in the drawing-room was my sleeping place and one can well imagine with what sad feelings I compared the past with the present. Of course the floors were bare, for the beautiful Axminster carpet which had been woven for the room in one piece, had been removed, but was captured by the enemy, at Cheraw[74] and cut up for saddle cloths. I was pretty tired and sleep soon relieved me of harrowing thoughts. During the night I heard something fall, and the feathery sound of wings around the very large room. I deemed it imaginary but knew not that some new *devil*opment had been practiced in the time-honored building, so I went to sleep and await what the morning would unfold. And when the 'sun came peeping in at morn' I was surprised to see a large crow quietly circling around the arched ceiling, which was painted to represent the sky, with fleecy clouds interspersed, rendered the scene all the more natural, as the bird vainly tried to rise higher and by doing paid a high compliment to the artist. . . .
>
> As I strolled through the extensive gardens, where huge shells, unexploded, were scattered around and where the rank weeds out-ranked the beautiful flowers—fit emblems of the existing state of affairs—I keenly felt the immense change which like a pall, had spread over the entire country—but in Carolina above the rest.[75]

On October 13, Mary was still living with Alston in Tradd Street while cleaning the King Street house. There she wrote to Rebecca:

> There is no prospect of our former exile Sue's getting down, if she is to wait for cars for our furniture, etc. I have written to suggest her coming down with Willie[76] and a bundle of bedding and leave the rest of our fortune under armed guard at Friendville (where it has been removed to facilitate operations) until cars can be secured. I have reminded them, dear Rebecca, that your fortune is in your trunk, mine is in my plate chest, so I ordered it brought down by Express. You had better be careful with risk yours in Yankee soil or Yankee funds. It is a rotten concern. Diamonds have always an intrinsic value. You had better let no plans be determined before you invest. The report of the seven years apprenticeship of our negroes revived even my hopes about Carolina property.[77]

As of October 18, when Mary again wrote to Rebecca, cars were still not available.

> It is time for the removal of our negroes from Society Hill and after they go, we will have no means of transporting our luggage to the depot, or rather, station, for we have no depot now. Your Papa and James should be off for Santee, but they cannot leave our luggage unprotected at Dukeville or Friendville. . . .
>
> Bonetheau[78] has sent the miniatures to criticize. Our Robert's is so very excellent that I exclaimed, 'thank God' as I opened the case. Our Charles' is not as successful; the upper part of the face is very good; with my suggestions, he will improve the likeness, I trust. I have sent him our William's ambrotype and 'our little child's' photograph that he may make miniatures from them. I must have them, so I will sell silver to pay for them or beg Julius or Edward to give me the money.
>
> I am getting the old home clean, that I may remove to it, when Sue comes. . . . Edward's letters hold out hope. I am almost convinced by my own judgment that Alston should remain where he is. His position is more desirable that money could make it in California. If our hopes are realized, he will be able to educate and maintain his daughters. His sons must work wherever work is to be found. Col. Hayne and your Aunt are selling furniture in

> Columbia, altho it is at a very low rate. I have written to beg them to come down to me when we get in our house.[79]

On October 24, Mary, Brewton, and two friends walked to St. Luke's Church, where at the door they met Mary's brother, Charles C. P. Alston. She was thrilled to see him, and learned that he had returned to town alone, as his home was still being held as a "military necessity." Mary continued:

> But, as a better spirit is dawning upon the minds of our oppressors, it may before very long be restored to its owners, houses, fortunately, not being like chairs, tables etc removable to Northern states. A few days since, Bob saw a cart on the wharf, taking a handsome dining table to a ship. On the box in which it was incased, was written, "Family relics, from Rebeldom." The more correct notification would have been, "Evidence of Rascality."
>
> 12 O'clock. I am seated in our old North Parlour, on a foot stool recovered from a fortune teller, awaiting my dear child's arrival;[80] the street door wide open to welcome the living. In my heart stands the images of my dead, whose mortal remains were borne through it, the one in the calm majesty of the Christian man's sanctified death, the other, all bathed in blood, the blood of a Christian Hero. . . .
>
> I am not bold enough to think of my darling son James' going to California. I can only pray the All Wise Disposer of events to influence him as is best for his salvation, his honor, his usefulness. If your Papa were willing to go, I would do it so gladly, particularly as Rebecca tells me Mr. Mitchell may think of taking our precious Edgewood family there, too. What a blessing it would be to have my old age cheered and comforted by them.
>
> Since I have been in town, desolation and misery have so pressed upon me that in writing to my sister Elizabeth, I begged her and the old colonel[81] to come down to me and stay so long as they found it comfortable and convenient. Her reply moved the very depths of my heart; she thanked and blessed me and most gratefully accepted my invitation, saying she had thought of asking us to allow her to occupy our two basement rooms. I have not yet

> told your Papa what I have done, he is too generous, I know, to disapprove of it. This is no time to be prudent, but to consider, 'he who seeth his brother's have need and shut his heart against him" etc. etc. Yes, I should give the shelter to my sister and her husband. They will come down the 1st November I will put them in the warm, sunny, back parlour. Mary and Mr. Mitchell and children (some of them) in the North Chamber and drawing room; one of the girls with Sue, one with Rebecca, the two boys in my chamber, and your Papa and I will sleep D.V. in our old dressing room. I will not have Mary come without her husband and children."[82]

Despite four years of hardship, sorrow and deprivation, Mary, as always, closed out the last days of the year thinking only about the comfort and welfare of her children and relatives, and not herself. Given the hardships she and her flock had yet to endure, her determination and selfless attitude would be critical factors in the survival of the Pringle family in a ruined, post-war Charleston.

On April 14, 1865, the fourth anniversary of the surrender of Major Robert Anderson's Union forces at Fort Sumter, a jubilant party of gloating Northerners arrived in Charleston aboard the steamer *Oceanus* to celebrate the raising of the Stars and Stripes over Sumter's pummeled ruins by Major (now Major General) Anderson. A great many speeches were made, and one of the speakers accused Maj. Motte Alston Pringle, the Confederate Quartermaster at Charleston, of deliberately blowing up the Northeastern Railroad Depot and its military supplies, killing scores of poor people seeking food there.

> The accounts of the explosion vary somewhat, as to the premeditated slaughter which was effected there. By a few, it is claimed that no intention of massacre can be charged upon the principals in the deed. But in the light of all these recent developments . . . the most probable

> account is that which is the most generally believed, to wit: that when the Rebels were forced to evacuate the city, they resolved to blow up this dépòt, where the Confederate supplies were stored. The poor people were told to go there and help themselves. Soon a crowd, consisting mostly of slaves, was gathered there. Major Pringle had mined the premises, and was not to be kept from, nor delayed in his purpose, although so many lives would be destroyed. By some it is averred that two or three warnings were given. Grant that there were, does this palliate the deed? Who but a fiend incarnate, would have given the order to apply the match, until he knew that all the innocent and helpless were safe from harm? The train[83] was fired, and in an instant three hundred—according to some authorities four hundred—human beings were blown into eternity. Not long after this occurrence, this Pringle was captured by colored troops, belonging to our army, which insufferable indignity to his royal Carolinian blood, so frenzied him, as to betray him into the best act of his life, as concerning mankind, the blowing out of his brains with a pistol.[84]

Writing a century later, historian E. Milby Burton gave a more sober account of the tragedy than the Northern tabloid journalists of 1865. Drawing on official military records and contemporary newspaper accounts, he wrote that early in the morning of February 18, people rushed into the depot to help themselves to stores of food abandoned by the fleeing Confederate troops. The depot also contained a large store of damaged gunpowder.

Throughout the city, supplies of cotton were being burned in their warehouses and in the public squares to keep them out of the hands of the enemy. "Some small boys, who found that black powder would make a blaze with lots of smoke when thrown on the fire, amused themselves by carrying handfuls of it from the depot, where it was stored, to the cotton. Some of the powder trickled through their fingers when they were carrying it," Burton wrote, "leaving a trail back to the depot. Somehow it was ignited, and before anyone could extinguish the fire the entire depot was blown up, along with about 150 people. Probably an equal number were burned."[85]

The accusations made against Motte by the Northern zealots were as ludicrous as the fabricated account of him blowing his brains out with a pistol. Motte was well known as a kind, ethical man and had distinguished himself as a diligent and principled military officer. Not only would he not have done anything which would endanger so many of his countrymen, it would have been physically impossible for him to have given the order. The explosion in Charleston occurred on February 18. Motte had been ordered out of Charleston on February 14 and had arrived in Raleigh, North Carolina by February 15.[86] He did not blow his brains out and die a distraught, deranged man in the custody of Union soldiers. In reality, he died at home in bed in 1886, twenty years after the war ended.[87]

CHAPTER ELEVEN

The Rice Paupers

We have slept, again, under our own roof, although it was on a mattress thrown on the floor. We have eaten breakfast on plates borrowed from our Freedwomen, sitting at a narrow old table found in a corner, sitting on boxes turned on their sides.

—Mary Pringle, October 25, 1865

It is scarcely possible to comprehend the wrenching social, economic, and agricultural changes which Lowcountry rice planters and their former slaves experienced after the end of the Civil War. South Carolina lost a greater percentage of men to the Confederate cause than any other Southern state: 12,992 of the state's men died in uniform - some twenty-three percent of the arms-bearing population of 55,046.[1] The sacrifice of the Pringle family exceeded even this horrific statistic, as they lost Robert, Charles and Brewton—one-third of their sons—to the war.

Emancipation of the state's 400,000 slaves sounded the death knell for the cultivation of rice in the Lowcountry. The freedmen, having tasted life out from under the threat of the whip, were reluctant to have contact with their former masters. As a result, the formerly lush plantations were abandoned to the rice birds and the alligators. Four years of war turned the Lowcountry rice princes into paupers.

In Charleston, the once-elegant Pringle residence on King Street was in shambles. Empty picture frames stared blankly from the walls, and three years' worth of dust and grime coated Mary's formerly immaculate house. Gas for the lights was unavailable and matches too costly to use. Mary resolutely clung to her faith in God and offered prayers each day. "She had lost two noble sons in the defense of Charleston and all that she was worth, save the house I am writing of," wrote Jacob, "and yet this noble woman, who followed so closely in the footsteps of her sainted mother, and patriotic grandmother, offered up to the Throne of Grace her earnest and pathetic prayers for those who had despoiled her of her all; and thanks and mercies still left in her old age. Men may be brave, honest and true—but a noble woman is the crowning work of God."[2]

The weary survivors who slowly regrouped their lives in post-war Charleston were a far cry from the self-indulgent, free-spending pre-war residents. The King Street household had been reduced to five demoralized and nearly penniless adults. William Bull Pringle, now sixty-five, and Mary, sixty-two, were bone-weary from the hardships of four years as refugees. Susan, thirty-six, and Rebecca, twenty-six, were still at home, along with the invalid Brewton, now slipping into dementia. The rest of the family was dispersed among residences in Charleston, Georgetown District, Connecticut, California, Louisiana, and France.

Their income having ceased, the Pringle family was in no position to let any of their assets lie unused—not even the coach house. "Our pride is being humbled by the tendency of the establishments around us, they are almost all being converted into stores for the convenience of negroes," Mary wrote. "Three storey houses are to be made into shops to entice the negroes as they come into town from the surrounding islands. Alas! Alas! my dear old paternal homestead is by this innovation lowered to one half of its value; an application was made for our coach house to be converted into a 'dry goods store'!!!"[3]

The Pringle family never lacked determination and, ruinous as their condition was, they were enormously relieved when they regained possession of their house. On October 25, 1865, Mary wrote:

> Our dear Sue is with me. We have slept, again, under our own roof, although it was on a mattress thrown on the floor. We have eaten breakfast on plates borrowed from our Freedwomen, sitting at a narrow old table found in a corner, sitting on boxes turned on their sides. Having possession in four straight backed wooden chairs that the vandals stole from some church aisle and left in my house. These inconveniences will not continue long as we are to have our furniture soon, the car with it being on the way down. Your Papa and James were to go on their weary journey to Santee yesterday.[4]

With the house again in their possession, the next goal was to regain control of Richfield. On November 10, 1865, Mary wrote that James had met Gen. Rufus Saxton, assistant commissioner of the Freedmen's Bureau, and asked about the family's Santee lands. On a second visit, Saxton told James of his "utopian plans" for educating the Freedmen and sharing the crops with them. Mary thought the whole idea ridiculous, and wrote, "after the negroes have passed through a cold, starving winter, the remnant left will then have learnt that they must work to be fed and clothed, and will come in for a share of the benefit of their experience."[5]

The freedmen had come to believe that their emancipation would entitle them to forty acres of land and a mule. Then they learned that the vast majority of the land would be restored to the planters, not parceled out to them. Worse, if they did not sign labor contracts and go back to work for the planters, they could be forced out of the houses they had occupied for generations—if not by the planter himself, then by the very Union army soldiers who had liberated them. Initially, most of the labor force refused to return to work, and only the threat of starvation and constant intervention of federal troops coerced them back into the fields.

The freedmen were notified that the former property of the planters was to be respected. The following notice to the freedmen at Camp Main plantation on the Santee on August 8, 1865, is typical of those issued in Georgetown District:

> The Freedmen and women residing upon the plantation of Mr. T. S. Horry in Georgetown District are informed that, although their freedom has been secured as a result of the war, the lands, buildings, furniture, and animals, including the swine, still belong to the planter, and that they have no right or title to them or any of them, except by purchase, gift, or in some other way obtaining a right of ownership. The property not being theirs, if they injure or destroy it, they are liable to be punished.[6]

William Bull Pringle and Frank Frost made a small crop of rice at Richfield in the fall of 1866, but their letters say little about it. The planters were obliged to provide subsistence for the workers until the crop was brought in, and the freedmen were to receive one half of the crop as their share.[7] The labor contract signed June 3, 1865, between William Bull Pringle and nine freedmen was typical of those used on the Santee:

> This agreement entered into between William B. Pringle of Richfield and other plantations on North Santee of the one part and the undersigned freedmen and women on the other part witnesseth that the latter covenant and agree with the former industriously and faithfully to tend and cultivate his lands on his Richfield and other adjoining plantations on North Santee River in the mode and manner usual on rice lands putting and keeping the banks and trunks in good order and they will in all respects conform themselves to such reasonable rules and regulations as may be prescribed by the said William B. Pringle, who shall have the right to direct at all times either by himself or his agent the nature and extent of the cultivation. The freedmen and women promise to behave with propriety, to avoid all drunkenness, disorder and immorality and they are forbidden to carry guns, pistols or weapons of war. All animals entrusted to them shall be carefully tended and prudently worked and cared for. The kind of work to be done and its faithful performance to be at all times ordered and arranged by the said William B. Pringle or his agent. Any deviation from the terms of this contract

> may be punished by the removal of the offender and his family from the said plantations. In return for these services the said William B. Pringle agrees to furnish the remaining subsistence till the gathering of the crop and to give the said freedmen and women half of the crop of rice, corn, peas and other provisions prepared for market after taking from the bulk before division the seed for the next year. This agreement to remain in force until the 1st of January 1866. On leaving the plantation the laborers and carpenters will give up the hoes, tools and all agricultural implements previously furnished.[8]

The freedmen who placed their mark on the document were Paul Wragg, Hector Williams, John Deas, Susannah Pinckney, Patey Green, Andrew Chisolm, Peggy Washington, Sarah Diley, and Charles Keith. None of them had chosen the surname Pringle. The contract was approved by Lt. Col. J. C. Carmichael, of the 157th New York Volunteers, who was serving as the commander of federal troops in Georgetown.[9]

In January 1866 Gen. Daniel E. Sickles ordered the freedmen to make valid work contracts with the planters or leave their land within ten days. When some of William's former slaves refused to sign contracts with him, he ordered them off the property. In retaliation, they put the torch to the big house at Richfield, burned it to the ground, and refused to leave the plantation.[10]

William informed General Sickles of the outrage on January 18, telling him that he was also in fear of losing his $50,000 steam-powered rice mill. Federal officers directed that those freedmen connected with burning the house be brought to justice, and that those who did not sign valid work contracts be gone from the property within twenty days. In the spring of 1866 Col. B. H. Smith, commander at Georgetown, noted supervising the signing of work contracts between freedmen and many of the major planters of the district, including William Bull Pringle.[11]

On June 23, 1866, Mary wrote to Julius:

> Our last report from Santee was very unfavorable, as regards the rice crop . . . negroes who had refused to contract at $12 per month now gladly accept food at the rate of $6 or $7 per month. . . . I am so distressed at our being thrown entirely on your generosity that I have suggested to your Papa the renting our house in Autumn and our move into a very small one, just large enough to accommodate our small family of five. He readily consented doing so. I do not know what other retrenchment to make, as every other domestic arrangement is conducted on the most economical scale. I drink too much coffee, maybe, but it is the simple nourishment that habit has made necessary to my health.[12]

Beset on every side by radical change, the family drew together and tried to make the best of a bad situation. "They gathered their children and grandchildren and friends into the drawing room on Sunday evenings," recalled Mary Pringle Frost. "Coffee and small cakes were served. Cretia baked the cakes on Saturday in the Dutch oven. The grandchildren were not supposed to have coffee, only cake, but our grandmother surmised that they would like coffee, and so they were served."[13]

In August 1866 Edward made a serious proposal to encourage his parents to emigrate. "Jim and I have been talking over it so much and are so full of it that I cannot help laying the matter seriously before you," he wrote.

> A year spent out here would give a great impulse to the health of all of you, Sue and Brewton as well as Mama and yourself. The climate here is so invigorating, the country so interesting, and the pleasure of seeing us would, I suppose, be so great, that I am sure the visit would be of common benefit to all of you, quite worth the sacrifice that it would cost. I have not urged it seriously as long as I could see no shape to give to the plan. But now that Beck is going to marry a famous agriculturalist who she says is a man of such wonderful energy, he could relieve you of the care of Santee, then there would be nothing in the way but the expense. And let us look at that. I am ashamed to

> make any plans or promises when my own affairs are in such arrears. But the great pleasure and advantage of having you all here will cost comparatively little in comparison with the benefit to you and the comfort to me. The great rub would be the passage money which for four would probably be $1000, including from Charleston to New York. Twelve hundred in gold would pay all expenses out. Once here, living would be cheap. We all know how to economize. I can get a furnished house belonging to a friend and beautifully situated such as would delight all of you for $125 a month. The other expenses we could make as light as we pleased. Three hundred dollars a month would certainly cover all expenses of living— probably $250. How much could you rent the King Street house for? The rent of that added to what Jim and I necessarily spend here would support the family easily. . . . Don't regard it as an expense, for if you can rent the King Street house, the expense of all of us united here need not exceed our present Charleston and California expenses. Come with Alston Hayne. . . . But what I care for above all is to have Mama and yourself refreshed and rejuvenated by a change from the terrible past. I beg you to give all this a serious consideration and to answer me. Come as soon as you can.[14]

Emigration was also on the minds of two of Mary's Hayne nephews, and two sons of Senator Robert Y. Hayne ultimately did move to California. Dr. Arthur Hayne left South Carolina just after the war. He was followed a short time later by his brother, Col. William Alston Hayne, his wife, Margaretta Stiles Hayne, and their children. The Haynes settled in Montecito, just over the foothills from Santa Barbara. Alston Hayne devoted himself to planting citrus fruits and became a pillar of the new American community there.[15] Yet the Pringles still held onto Richfield and this, along with the advanced ages of William and Mary, kept them tied to Charleston.

In their choice of marriage partners, the Pringle women proved themselves good judges of character. Rebecca, chose a hard-working physician and Confederate war hero, Dr. Francis LeJau Frost.

What proved to be a tender, lifelong romance between Frank and Rebecca began at Society Hill. During the war, Frank had met Rebecca's brother James. When both were on furlough, James asked his mother if he could bring Frank with him to Society Hill. Mary agreed that it would be a good occasion because they were having a pig for dinner. Frank fell in love with Rebecca at first sight, and vowed to himself that if his life was spared he would return and marry her.

Frank Frost in 1880

Frank was a descendant and namesake of the Rev. Francis LeJau, an eighteenth-century Anglican missionary priest in St. James Goose Creek parish and the grandson of the Rev. Thomas Frost, an Episcopal priest and former rector of St. Philip's Church in Charleston. His parents were Judge Edward Frost and Harriet (Horrÿ) Frost. Judge Frost was a Yale graduate, a St. Andrews Parish cotton planter, state representative, U.S. District Attorney, chairman of the vestry of St. Michael's, and president of the Blue Ridge Railroad.[16] A staunch Lowcountry man, the judge once berated an Upcountry legislator for failing to see the merit in one of his proposals because the man had "never smelt salt water." Although he had an ample income from his planting interests, he nevertheless continued to serve on the bench, "spending the greater part of his life at hotels, holding courts and taking down the testimony of rude and ignorant men."[17]

Frank Frost had been born in Charleston in 1837. He was educated in Charleston's private schools and graduated fourth in his class of forty-seven from South Carolina College in 1859.[18] Next he enrolled in the Medical College of South Carolina at Charleston. He was among the first to rally to the trumpet's call when war seemed imminent and enlisted as a private in the Washington Light Infantry, a local volunteer unit, just two days after Christmas 1860.

Rebecca's wedding broke with tradition—she was not married under the family chandelier. In a letter dated November 2, 1866, Rebecca described Brewton's unstable mental condition to Frank, which forced the family to change the wedding location from the house to St. Michael's church.[19] Frank replied that all that was important was that they were married—not where. He spent the fall preparing the Camp Main house for her arrival. "I anticipate with rapturous pleasure the 11th Dec," he wrote. "I think that by that time, with Lizzie's assistance, I will have the house quite comfortable for you. And when we be come up, after marriage, I will bring a supply of groceries so that you will have nothing to do but take possession. And with your trousseau[20] and mine complete, you may

Rebecca Motte Pringle Frost, 1880

enjoy a long season of elegant leisure, with all the dignity that you please."

Rebecca's trousseau came from France, a gift of Julius and Maria. It consisted of beautifully woven underwear, sheer, initialed handkerchiefs, white embroidered stockings, and a beautiful basque wedding dress.[21]

On December 11, 1866, at 8:30 P.M. Frank and Rebecca were married by the Rev. Paul Trapier Keith in St. Michael's. After the ceremony, the wedding party returned to the Miles Brewton House, where the chandelier in the drawing room was lit and a festive celebration was held. When Frank found that the Frost and Pringle nieces and nephews had not been invited, he sent messengers for them, and "the children arrived gleefully."[22]

The poverty of both families put severe constraints on their gift-giving. Frank gave his bride a handsome cup and saucer in lieu of a wedding ring. William Bull Pringle gave his daughter $75. Rebecca was grateful, knowing that he had lost virtually everything in the war. Mary gave her a Bible.

Frank and Rebecca spent their wedding night in the withdrawing room, next to the drawing room, where the reception had been held. The notion of a long, expensive honeymoon such as Mary Pringle enjoyed with Donald G. Mitchell, or as Julius took with Maria, was out of the question.

❧

One of the painful effects of the war was the separation of the Pringle and Mitchell families. As soon as hostilities ended, one of the first priorities was to reestablish contact. In the summer and fall of 1866, Rebecca and Susan each paid visits, and in the summer of 1867, William and Mary permitted themselves the luxury of visiting the Mitchells. Encountering the jarring difference between postwar life in Charleston and New Haven led William to pen the following account to his sister, Elizabeth Smith:

> If anything were wanting to make a poor Southerner feel more keenly the desolation of our own home he would

> only have to make a visit to this land of improvement and progress and contrast it with what he leaves at home. I had determined upon coming to the North to shut my eyes as much as possible to prosperity in which I can feel no interest, but I felt would drown the evil passions of one's natural anger and jealousy. But the truth is too glaring to be blinded to. We reached the boarding house in New York at 11 at night and left it at 11 the next morning. In a short walk to Mr. Mitchell's office and in our passage to the R.R. cars (for this place) I was obliged to see enough to convince me that in the ratio that the war has been ruinous to the South it has been promotive of the prosperity of the North. Life is so different here from what it was with us. When I see the busy active progress wherever I turn my eyes I am forced to summon what little religion I may have to my aid and hope that Providence has something better in store for us hereafter.[23]

William and Mary stayed with the Mitchells for several weeks, sharing the love and affection they had been denied by their seven-year separation. Upon their return to Charleston, Susan took their place at Edgewood for several months.

Back home, Mary turned her full attention to the financial survival of the family. In March 1867 William had received $10,225 as his share of his brother Robert's estate, but the family's debts quickly swallowed up the whole sum. With their sole surviving plantation producing no profit, Mary explored every possible means of making money.

The threat of homelessness was very real for many once-wealthy members of Lowcountry society. Shortly after regaining possession of their house, the Pringles opened their hearts to Mary's homeless sister, Elizabeth, and brother-in-law, former U.S. Senator Arthur P. Hayne. William, Mary, Rebecca, Sue, and Brewton retreated to the second, or drawing room floor. The Haynes moved into the ground floor.

Before the war, the Haynes had lived well. In 1841 they sold their Charleston and Georgia properties and passed their summers in Newport and their winters on the Waccamaw. They were living in Columbia when Sherman's troops arrived. Although Hayne was over seventy years old and had served in the U.S. Army, the Haynes were cursed, shoved and robbed of everything that could be carried off by the Union soldiers.[24] When Arthur Hayne died in 1867, the Charleston *Courier* noted that he was "among the severest sufferers by the sad reverses and calamities of the times." Elizabeth Hayne died later that year.

The Pringles also rented out the entrance floor, experiencing many a problem with their tenants. In the spring of 1867 Mary wrote to Rebecca:

> By great management and ingenuity I counted up my outside rents at $600, including the housekeeper's room and library. The housekeeper's room was engaged by a most respectable workwoman, with a policeman for her husband. She had worked for three weeks daily in Sue Huger's family.[25] The Hugers recommended her most highly. The woman could make $6 a week the year round. Some two or three days after she took possession, I smelt spirits on her breath. I had great misgivings, but did not whisper them. I saw the woman every day. She said she was ill and could not go out to work. At last Sue Huger came to see her about her work. Walking up from the [room] she said, 'Aunt Hess, what is the matter with the woman?' The secret was out: the woman was drunk for a whole week!!! She is sober since yesterday and has resumed her work. Her husband is quite a respectable person. I have given her notice that she must leave, so my rents have fallen, and worse than this, your Papa says I shall not let stragglers come in the basement again. How can I make money now? I am so distressed.[26]

On March 6, 1868, Mary noted that the coach house had been rented out. She confided to Susan that "I am a walking advertisement, humbly whispering to my friends that my apartments are vacant. I fill up my leisure moments in thinking who I should like to have; may be I have told you all of this already. My head, however, is so full of it that you may expect a re-capitulation of the misfortune by every mail."[27] Mary also fretted that because the old house badly needed paint and repairs, she would not be able to attract the proper type of tenants. Luck was with them, and in December, she was able to write:

> Our tenants are in—queer folks—'twill be hard work to get on with them, but we will try to be patient, for they are stricked people. I am much touched by the poor daughter. She is, I am told, quite accomplished and an admirable girl; but o, so ugly and timid, so sad. She has been put in our beautiful South parlor as her chamber, her bed against one of the large mirrors, her sweet toned piano opposite to it. On Sunday evening, her soft voice is heard, singing, 'Rock of Ages' and 'I Would Not Live Always', and every evening she sings with her door closed. The mother is ensconced in the North Parlor, the paralytic old man, with his Bible at his side, is shut up in Edward's chambers; the son, a young man, in the library, and our small breakfast parlours, their only sitting room. They have few friends and few acquaintances, they say. They live like our rats in the old home, gliding away to hide themselves if we come upon them suddenly when our bell rings for prayers. Their kitchen door is not unlocked. The daughter however is up. I wish I could get her up to talk to us. She is very grateful for every little attention, yet shrinks from it. Her name is Bess. Her young sister died about six weeks since, and she has been broken hearted since. She and her brothers only are left. They are good pay, volunteering to pay quarterly.[28]

Every space capable of generating income was pressed into service. In 1871 Mary wrote to Rebecca, "I have rented my coach room to the Jew Lewis[29] and he has fitted it up as a store. The goods are being placed on the shelves today. Your Papa most officiously, told Lewis he could hire the place for $4 per month, when I was holding it at $5. W. laughs at us for renting it out at so low a rate. We think now we could have got $10. We had another Jew applicant immediately after your Papa had rented it to Lewis."[30]

By 1868 Mary was making orange marmalade, which she shipped to Mary Frances to sell in New Haven. "She says, 'it went off like a pop-gun,'" Mary wrote. "She doubled my money and I have received it safely. Like Sue, I have re-invested and will send off a second supply in a few days. I have already money enough for the marble to mark where our little Angel Child[31] lies—and have written to explain to Mary the motive of selling the marmalade.[32] She later complained, "The dreadful Yankee women do keep us very long out of our money. Preserves sent on in October have not all been paid for yet. I wonder if they mean to cheat us?"[33]

In 1870 Mary gave serious consideration to making a business of selling terrapins. These turtles abounded in the creeks and rivers and were considered a great delicacy in the North. She wrote to William, who was evidently visiting the Santee, "I met Mrs. Hayne yesterday, who begged me to enter upon the terrapin investment. She will pay for one half of the expenses for one half of the profit, so please secure a monopoly of the creatures, for we will make a handsome profit. Tell Rebecca she may enter into the transaction if she will help me, and you too, old man, shall come in, if you give me the chance of making a penny."[34]

Susan was now forty, but still "girlish enough, with her rosy cheeks and soft brown hair." She set herself to work making bouquets and corsages from the flowers in their garden. The Frost children helped her gather pansies, roses, pinks, violets, and geranium leaves, which she wired together. The bouquets were sprinkled with water, placed into a large sweetgrass basket, taken to the Charleston Hotel, and sold by Tony, their aged gardener. There were no professional florists in town and the bouquets were eagerly purchased by visitors from the North for twenty-five cents each. On a good day, Susan could make as much as ten dollars, and the flower sales went a long way in helping pay the taxes on the house.[35]

Renting rooms and selling marmalade and flowers brought in much-needed cash, but it was the unflagging generosity of Julius and Maria which saved the Charleston Pringles from economic disaster. As of the late 1860s Edward had not yet been able to recover the family's money he had lost through his speculative investments, and was not in any position to aid the Charleston family. Julius, on the other hand, was a rich man by war's end. As soon as communication was again possible with Charleston, Julius started sending money to help the destitute family. In May 1867 Mary wrote to Julius in gratitude, "Yours of the 1st May came safely to hand, with the check for five hundred dollars. God bless you, my good son, for your great liberality to your old Father and Mother. A crop at Santee this year will relieve you from the heavy tax we have been upon you the two last years.[36]

The expenses of running Richfield were high each year, and Frank Frost calculated in 1868 that the next year might net William only $1,500 after expenses. William owed a Mrs. Singleton[37] $8,000, the interest on which was a severe drain on the family. Mary wrote, "Mrs. Singleton has offered to compromise about her debt. She says she will take $6,000 cash for the $8,000 due; this is tantalizing, but we cannot do it, for to borrow with no prospect of being able to repay is dishonest."[38] Rebecca wrote to Susan in November 1868, "If Papa was not encumbered with that horrid Singleton debt, he could live on the fifteen hundred with the rent of the first floor, but that debt presses heavily upon him."[39]

William had no working capital and was forced to borrow money each year to prepare the next year's crop. After the sale of the 1867 crop in September, Mary noted that he had borrowed $20,000 at seven percent interest for the next year's expenses.[40] Desperate to raise money in the spring of 1868, William sold the engine and pounding machinery from his North Santee rice mill to David Risley of Georgetown for $3,000.[41] The mill had been valued at $50,000 before the war. The same year William was so concerned about his precarious financial position that he deeded the title to the King Street house to his son, Alston, so that it would not fall prey to his creditors.

Frank had 250 acres into production at Richfield in 1868,

175 of which were devoted to rice. That year Richfield produced 4,400 bushels of rice, 400 bushels of corn, seventy bushels of peas and beans and 320 bushels of potatoes.[42] Under the vastly changed postwar conditions he faced, Frank averaged twenty-five bushels of rice per acre. These statistics clearly show that the glory days of the rice barons had come to an end.

The high cost of indebtedness continued to dog the family's every footstep. In May 1869 Mary wrote to Susan, then in New Haven, that Julius had sent William $700 to be used to enable William to make a trip to Edgewood and see his daughter and grandchildren. Instead, Mary wrote, "the old man has paid the $700 out on interest of debts, and stands again pennyless. But nothing must be said to our dear Julius about this, as he has recently besides the $700 paid a debt of $6,200."[43]

As if financial ruin were not enough, Mary's postwar letters paint a grim portrait of her marriage. In a letter to Rebecca dated March 6, 1868, Mary wrote:

> Yesterday was the anniversary of my wedding day, forty-six years ago! Your Papa celebrated it by a beautiful and abrupt silence at the very commencement of a scold he had begun to give me for my promiscuity in spending small sums because they were in my pocket book. I had not a simple excuse to give, but most fortunately for me, a transient thought of the wedding day flashed over my mind, and I used it as a plea for mercy. His old heart was at once softened and his bitter tongue silenced, and he absolutely brought me some sticks of candy from the supply he was purchasing for the Niggers. Heaven knows what is to protect me now, when ten cents slip through my fingers.[44]

A photographer from Boston provided the family with a bit of entertainment in May 1868 when he arrived to photograph the exterior and interior of the Pringle home.[45] Two of his views have survived. Mary wrote a detailed description of the event to Susan, who was then visiting Edward in California:

The exterior of the Miles Brewton House, 1868.

The whole home family were in a whirl of excitement yesterday. The information was circulated that the photographer was to be before the old house at half past eight o'clock. We sent for the Judge[46] and his son Julius, Motte and his son Willie. Eliza and Mary Motte slept here to be ready for the crisis. The Tradd Street girls[47] flocked

Emma Smith Pringle, Mary Pringle, and William Bull Pringle in the drawing room, May 1868.

around; we sent for Motte's. Emma walked in saying she knew Willie would like to find her among the crowd; an express was sent for Ella. Cretia was put in position. Caesar was told to take a place in the courtyard. Mary Stuart[48] asked if she were called. I had to tell her no. [As] everything was ready, a ragged, old Negro passing on the pavement was left standing there, two stray children found places there, too. The old house stood still and so was fairly represented, but Caesar beckoned to Cretia and so was turned into a blot and the whole thing failed. Another attempt was made, and, they say, more successfully.

Then the drawing room was surveyed, the best positions selected for your Papa and me. I put on my best cap. I tried to look placid, not too sad, not gay, you know how it always is, a hideous caricature of a hard featured old woman. My feelings were really hurt. Your father behaved very amiably. Emma and Ella and some of the children were very good. Your father too was good. Little Julius exhibited a marvelous docility but three minutes are so long to keep one's limbs still, the eyes fixed, the mouth just as it ought to be, so the poor child flounced at last and nothing was to be seen of him but his white cambric shirt so this was spoiled. 'Twas too much for your father's patience; he began to rebel. After remonstrance and consultation it was resolved that the effect of such a crowd destroyed the appearance of the room so the children were all turned out. Alston moved he could spare no more time from his business; Motte said once for such a penance was enough, so they went off. Your Papa, Emma, Ella and I were left in the room; none of us had courage to look at this impression so left it to the photographer's decision. Your Papa positively asserting that the price of the photographer twice over (think of him) would not induce him to play the fool again.[49]

The realities of Reconstruction and the new social order were frequently the subjects of Mary's postwar letters. What she wrote reflected the deep bitterness she felt over how their world and privileged position had been snatched from them. To Julius on May 7, 1867, she wrote:

Dr. Frost is managing our affairs judiciously, and the Freedmen are behaving well, being beyond the influences of Northern emissaries. In the cities, they are busy in mischief. Senator Wilson[50] appeared in our midst, haranging the Blacks, recapitulating the origin and cruelty of slavery; lauding the philanthropy that had torn them from oppression, impressing on them the position, 'they now held as equals in freedom to the Governor of South Carolina or the Mayor of the City of Charleston' -- and appealing to them to unite with the Republican party in maintaining the government, holding out the privilege of their being able to purchase lands from the government, as the age of the large plantations had passed away and the age of farms, been established. The next day it was announced that the street cars were open to the public. The 'Niggers', of course, crowd into them, and the White people, not being citizens, keep out of them.

I thank God that some of my children are away from our ruin and humiliation. I would give up the great happiness of seeing you, could you give up all your interest in this ill-fated country. I gave up Edward and James cheerfully, and would send Sue to Edward, to be employed as a scribe in his office, if your Papa would consent to her going out with Alston Hayne's family. This arrangement made, I would be content to lie down and die, amidst the ruins of our old home. Alston is so tramelled by his large family that he dare not think of forsaking his four brothers, as his eldest sons are receiving salaries. Motte is content to fight on with his chimera[51] of planting, and Rebecca is cheerful under her new happiness, so I need not be waiting here to see the failure of their plans and hopes. Your Papa is willing to stand still; he folds his hands and generally awaits the break up. I am not so patient. Motte's family is with us, as his house is rented out for $400 for the summer. Your Papa and I hope to sail for N.Y. en route for Edgewood on the 1st June.[52]

Mary was an avid observer and commentator on the political landscape which whirled around her. Like many other South Carolinians, she held special contempt for Brig. Gen. Daniel Sickles, who had been appointed military governor of the Carolinas in 1865. On September 7, 1867, Mary wrote of him, "Commands are belching forth, a last salute to Sickles. I spit upon him. [Gen. Edward] Canby[53] is making a favourable impression by his unostentatious deportment, walking about in a plain citizen's dress. The 'Nigger's' probably will not appreciate him as highly as they have done Sickles, whom Alston's nurse says he is the 'justices man in the world'. An old woman sitting on the pavement as he drove by her, said 'I neber see a man hab so many carriages as Gen. Sickles, he must be a king.' Well I am glad the Nigger King no longer drives among us."[54]

Mary's tolerance for Canby had evaporated by May 1868, when Canby appointed William McKinlay, a freedman, to the city council. Mary said to her husband, "no gentleman should sit on the board with him."[55]

Although Mary was disgusted by the current state of affairs and felt threatened by the freedmen, she held out hope that some form of the old order would eventually be restored. In the summer of 1868, she wrote to James, "there must be a change, such an administration cannot continue. An inferior race cannot have the supremacy over a superior, more intelligent and cultured people. It is a terrible trial to be passive under a mob government, yet we must wait, that this evil may correct itself. The crisis is, I believe, at hand; the presidential election will bring on the issue; there will be risk in it, no doubt, but the Democrats once in power, the government of the Southern states will be re-organized, although individual ruin and misery may never be repaired. . . . You cannot imagine the total prostration of certain classes."[56]

The election of 1868 was the first time since the end of the war that Charlestonians could vote for their mayoral candidate. The election gave the men of Charleston—white and black alike—the opportunity to choose between the Democratic candidate, Henry Deas Lesesne, a conservative Charleston attorney from an old Huguenot family, and Gilbert Pillsbury, a radical Republican reformer from Massachusetts.

Pillsbury was one of the many idealistic abolitionists who

came to the South to "right the wrongs of slavery" after the war. Born in Hamilton, Mass., he was educated at Andover Theological Seminary and graduated with high honors from Dartmouth in 1841. He came to South Carolina as an agent of the Freedmen's Bureau. He first worked at Hilton Head, but later came to Charleston, where he and his wife took an active part in educating the freedmen.[57] For Mary and Charleston's old guard, the mayoral race was no contest. On November 10, 1868, she wrote to Sue:

> While the rabble of poor, ignorant negroes; the vile, corrupt and intriguing white men are crowding our streets, and our good and broken-spirited citizens have rounded themselves up to a contest of principle, in which involves the most momentous political events of our old city. I seal myself today again, I am glad you are away, whilst this municipal election is taking place. The Honorable Henry Lesesne is the Democratic candidate, Pillsbury the radical candidate. These two men are as different in character as light is from darkness, but then, each one suits his party best.
>
> I walked out yesterday afternoon with Motte and Ella. I was afraid to go out alone, as much excitement had been created by the two days of legislation. As we were walking, we overheard the conversation of two tipsy negro men. One said, "well, we will put old Pillsbury in tomorrow; we have fixed the Presidential Election. Tomorrow we will put in Pillsbury." I hate to think of it, so I keep up the most perfect hope that Mr. Lesesne will be elected. What will be our condition if Pillsbury is? Young Mackey[58], you know, is Sheriff. He has appointed a negro jailer. But if I tell you only of these things, you will no longer desire letters from me, but how can I think of anything else today.
>
> . . .Your Papa has just come in. No indication of disturbance. The negroes are noisy and in great crowds. Our citizens are fully aroused. Every man is doing his duty. Men old and sick totter from their homes to cast a vote for Mr. Lesesne. If his election is lost, it will be an indication that we can do nothing to save ourselves. The negroes are stimulated by the Radicals posting notices that

> if Pillsbury is defeated, the negroes will be put in bondage again and slavery reestablished. How can one censure poor, ignorant animals for being under the influence of such assurances.[59]

Mary's worst fear came true: Pillsbury was elected by a majority of only twenty votes. "My heart is sick," she wrote.[60] A Pillsbury family history later stated that Pillsbury "was very popular with the people, and at the close of his administration, they presented him with a gold watch and a gold-headed cane suitably inscribed."[61] "The people," could only have been Charleston's freedmen and their Republican allies, for Mary and her ex-Confederate neighbors would have been more likely to flail Pillsbury with a walking stick than present him with one.

Mary wrote that many Charlestonians had dismissed servants who spoke openly of their Radical affiliations. She also stated, "I am somewhat suspicious of our man Caesar, but as I have no proof against him, I am quiet, simply reminding him when he is going to market, to 'be careful from whom he purchases meat for me, as I will not have it bought from a Radical Nigger.' Tell Sue I am much, very much afraid that our dear, good Cretia is a down right Radical. She seems to chafe very much when I venture to repeat to her some flagrant Yankee outrage."[62]

Cretia's husband, Scipio, had been liberated by Union troops and carried off while the family was refugeeing in Darlington District in March 1865. He rejoined his wife at the Pringle compound on King Street shortly after the war ended. He was sixty years old when he died of a pulmonary hemorrhage the morning of June 25, 1868. His funeral service was held in the yard, and he was buried in the Rikerville Baptist Church Cemetery.

"Cretia is much grieved," Mary wrote. "The funeral service was in the yard. At the conclusion of it the men formed a line on one side, the women on the other and the coffin was borne slowly through them chanting a solemn dirge. The old, worn, wooden crutches were carried after the coffin and buried in the grave with it."[63]

In February 1868 Sue, with Cretia in tow, left Charleston for San Francisco, with the intent of staying with Edward and James until May 1869 while she scouted the area as a possible place for the family's emigration. With Rebecca spending much of her time with Frank on the Santee, Mary was left alone in the big house with no one save William, whose health was slipping and whose presence was now only cold comfort to her. Just after Susan departed, Mary wrote to Rebecca, "You cannot think how I miss you, my darling daughter. I could not enter that cold, gloomy, silent North Chamber yesterday. I kept the doors shut, but this morning I had to go in to gather up your baggage. The fire was still burning and the smell of anise brought such a vivid memory of the shaking of that sagacious little head that I could but smile through my tears. I wish you would never go away from me. I do miss you too much. 'Tis strange to feel what a large place that little baby held in my heart and thoughts and time. I feel as if I had nothing to do, no chocolate to warm in the morning, no baby to run to see, no hurrying over little domestic cares because I wanted just to look in and see that you were well."[64]

William and Mary were both concerned about their health, and Mary noted that William's mind wandered. In 1869 William fell ill, but recovered. Mary wrote to Susan, "What an infinite mercy, made the more impressive by your precious Father having been rescued by God's power from the very brink of the grave. Ah! what a blank in our lives his having been called away would have made to everyone of us, but to me, to you, to Alston, the dear presence, the hourly counsel, the guiding influence would have been a thing missing through every hour."[65]

William filled his days with his grandchildren and did whatever he could to help Frank Frost keep Richfield supplied. As late as 1870 William was still making trips to Richfield. On March 5, 1870, their forty-eighth wedding anniversary, Mary wrote to him at Richfield,

> This is the day for writing to Rebecca, but the thoughts and feelings associated with it draw my whole heart to you, the beloved husband of 48 years. The progress of these long years has been marked by exquisite happiness, much hope, proud successes, and oh! what bitter sorrows, grievous disappointments, crushing reverses and with so dark a future before us that the bright spots of former days can hardly be kept in memory through the gloom of the present. 'Man erases for happiness from what happens, but God promises peace, happen what may.' Let us strive for that peace; then we may hope. . . . I fear you landed in unfavorable weather on Friday. I trembled at the thought of you getting down the side of the steamer into the little boat. I trust you found our dear ones at the Camp all well."[66]

The older she grew, the closer Mary drew to the church. During the Lenten season of 1871, she noted, "I go to church three times a week besides Sunday, and in this week, daily, true, I am tempted when once in the open air, to linger out, and find myself up King[67] after service instead of at home, and when I do come home, I meet visitors and so the morning passes."[68]

❧

For three decades before the war, the family never had less than twenty servants in the yard. By 1866 they could afford only three. In April 1871 Mary wrote to Mary Mitchell about her daughter, Minnie Mitchell, then about to depart Charleston for New Haven. "I have considered it right to advise Minnie to deviate from your directions about the servants' presents. Two dollars are quite enough for Cretia, and $1 for the cook and $1 for the waiter. These comfort our domestics; somewhat a contrast to the fourteen we were want to have. I find my domestic duties *much less* without the crowd."[69] A few months later, Mary's staff was reduced to two. In July 1871, Mary wrote to Rebecca:

> We have just informed Thomas that we cannot keep

> him after the end of his present month. I give him up as a matter of principle, for people in charity should not keep three servants. We are to manage now with Cretia and the cook Amalia. We must learn to yield to circumstances, aye, what trifles these are to the great trials of our wretched lives. This coming back to the old, desolated home, has almost killed us. I have never seen your Father weep, as he has done in this return to our dreary abode. We walked up the stone steps through the sad, silent entry, up the side stair case with the slow, solemn steps of people following the dead, again in the drawing room. I bade them point out the spot where my dear son was laid. I did not touch my foot upon it, it was too sacred for a mortal foot to tread upon; I only looked at it with clasped hands and a bowed head. James, my joyous, bright, happy, beautiful son, laid dead there. I have not yet stood where my five children lie buried. I shrink, I do confess, from the new grave there, but I will go there soon, for until I do, I feel that I am leaving something undone.[70]

A short time later, Cretia announced that she was going to move out of the servant yard and live with her son Johnny, whom Mary characterized as "an aristocratic carpenter." She was willing to work during the day, she informed Mary, but that proposal did not meet her approval. Mary wrote to Mary Mitchell in New Haven, "It was a great shock to me, for Cretia is the comfort—animal comfort—of my every day life. None of these demoralized negroes would make up my chamber fire at daylight in the morning (Cretia does it, indeed, before day light) or give me as much cold water as I like to bathe in all the year round. I was much startled at her communication, yet endeavored not to show it."[71]

William's account with his factor, James R. Pringle & Son, for the year 1870 shows that with two exceptions, the family purchased little more than the basic necessities of life in the post-war years. Gone were the days when the Pringles charged petticoats, gloves, bonnets, toys, candy and other fancy goods to their account. Instead, they now bought only the basics: coal, petroleum oil, sugar, molasses, potatoes, flour, salt, lard, herring, coffee, tea and soda biscuits. William did indulge himself in two areas: smoking and strong drink. His factor's records for 1870 include payments of $63.65 for 200 pounds of leaf tobacco, $11 for brandy and $157.80 for an astonishing 128 gallons (three barrels) of whiskey.[72] If consumed in one year, this would have amounted to 1.4 quarts of whiskey (about two bottles) per day.

In 1871 the William Bull Pringle family suffered their final indignity: they were forced to sell Richfield. The plantation, which had cost $160,000 before neighboring Pleasant Meadow was added to the tract, was sold to James B. Morrison and Samuel J. Lofton for $10,000.[73]

The sale came as a crushing blow to the family, for without rice lands, the Pringles ceased to be planters—and lost one of the most important parts of their identity. On November 30, 1871, Mary wrote to Rebecca, "You and Frank have both been startled, I know, about the sale of Richfield, yet will be relieved about it, as you have both told me that Frank cultivated it only on our account, which was always a painful reflection to your Papa and to me. Thus, I thank God it has been sold. The low price of $10,000 alone, secured the sale. Julius will feel now that we do *sometimes* take his advice, for his advice was from the beginning to sell at $10,000, at $3,000, indeed to give it away rather than to cultivate it. The $10,000 will enable us to pay our debts, and debt was the terrible bugbear of my life. Once out of debt, and I can be content on 'dry herbs.'"[74]

Frank wrote to his father-in-law, "In relinquishing finally all connection with Richfield, I beg to express my profound sense of obligation and gratitude to you for the uniform course of kindness, liberality and confidence with which you have always treated me. This will ever form in my mind one most pleasant link and association with the place, which no reflections of wasted energies or blighted hopes can ever mar or efface. Very affectionately yours, F. L. Frost."[75]

By 1872 William and Mary were both feeling their age. Mary wrote, "Your Papa is 72 years old today. I passed my 69th year. How can we think of the next winter. And we are both feeling weak enough to die this very day. Your Papa impatient to do so, *he thinks*. I am quite too full of sin to desire to be called to my account. 'God, have mercy upon me, a sinner,' and help me to be ready when He knows it is best for me to go. Weary as I am, I will await His good pleasure."[76]

In the summer of 1873 William described how he wanted his estate to be distributed. He made optimistic provisions that Mary and Susan be supported by his estate and that they be entitled to live in the family home for their lifetime. Upon their death, he directed that his estate was to be equally divided among his children; the children of any deceased child taking their parent's share. Because of Edward and Motte's financial disasters, which had so drained the family, William made special provisions for them.

"In making the division," William wrote, "I direct that the sum of twenty three thousand dollars which I lent to my son Edward and the sum [not mentioned] which I have paid for my son Motte shall be taken into account with interest thereon and said sons shall be entitled respectively to a share of my estate only when refunding the said amounts with interest, it being my will that the said sums shall be taken and regarded as a part of the assets of my estate, so that in the division of my estate each of my children shall have an equal share thereof. It is a matter of regret to me that the disastrous result of the late war should make this provision in relation to my sons Edward and Motte a matter and act of justice to the rest of my children and I trust that by a blessing of Providence this requirement may not be impossible or oppressive."[77]

❧

Perhaps the most painful decision William and Mary had to make in their lives revolved around Brewton's condition. His unpredictable mental behavior had become too heavy a burden for the elderly couple to bear. In 1866 William and Mary agreed to commit Brewton to the care of the South

Carolina Lunatic Asylum. The records of the Asylum state that Brewton was admitted around the first of December, 1866. The cause of his disorder was listed as exposure and illness during his Confederate service, and he was described as having typhoid dysentery before his attack of insanity. The records state that he had been insane for eighteen months before admission, was subject to religious delusions, and was slightly disposed to injure others. The records are mute as to his treatment.[78]

Hard though the choice had been, Rebecca noted the positive effect that Brewton's absence had on Mary. Late in 1868 she wrote to Susan, "I deferred writing to you till I came to town, that I might tell you how I find Mother and Papa looking. They are both just as you left them. Mother more full of energy and elasticity than ever, it seems to me. Few young people can whisk about as she does. She surprises me hourly—the fact is her health has so much strengthened since the weight of poor Brewton's condition has been removed from her presence."[79]

In December 1868 Alston Pringle and Motte Alston traveled to Columbia for business and visited Brewton. They "found him in a still more sad condition than when Alston last saw him, but he was neatly dressed. Since they left him, he has written the best expressed letters that I have received from him since his absence. He alluded with pleasure to the visit of his brother and cousin. In his last letter, he addressed me as 'beloved Mother', the previous one, 'Blessed Mother . Ah! that I could comfort him. Now that his case is hopeless of cure, I consider it my duty to keep him at my side, but alas! your Father and brothers differ from me." For Brewton's Christmas present that year, Mary prepared iced cakes, covered with French sugar plum frosting.[80]

Brewton languished in the Asylum until the summer of 1874. On July 28 of that year he came home to spend his final months of life at the Miles Brewton House.[81] Rebecca wrote of her mother, "It is such a comfort to her to be able to nurse poor Brewton, and it seems such a comfort to him to be able to be at home. Mother says his patience and resignation are most touching. He never asks but for a little cool water and never objects to any thing. How untiring a mother's love is!"[82]

Miles Brewton Pringle, the cheerful, gallant "bold Dragoon," died quietly on Wednesday morning, December 2, 1874, in the house in which he had been born thirty-nine years and five months earlier. The cause of death was listed as myelitis: inflammation of the spinal cord or bone marrow.[83] He was buried in St. Michael's churchyard.

The next week, Mary wrote to Mary Mitchell, "It is but a week today since my dead was taken away before me, yet the days seem as long as weeks, though the dear life appears still breathing around. I wander in the silent, empty chamber, with the sad, solemn feeling with which we approach our dead; that North Chamber [the withdrawing room] where so many young mortals first drew the breath of life, where so many weary Pilgrims laid down the coil of human misery. My son Brewton was my only child who breathed his last there; the others suffered and died in my own bed. . . . You must consider me as just moving on and on to the resting place which so many are already at rest, there to await the solemn summons to appear at the judgment seat, where we can expect acceptance only through the merits and intercession of our Merciful Redeemer, who having felt our infirmities, knows how to pardon them."[84]

By December 1874, at the age of seventy-one, a mourning Mary Pringle wrote to her daughter in New Haven about her loss. "The stone has been placed over my beloved son Brewton's grave, so I venture to church, D.V., on Sunday next. I did intend going last Sunday, but I dared not venture so near the uncrossed grave. How I do miss the sacred duties at my son's bedside. I try to think only that he is at peace, but my heavy heart turns to its deep sorrows. God help me, pardon me and take me."[85]

CHAPTER TWELVE

The Ghost Planters

I have a heavy heart about my business, my hindrances and discouragements are so great. I see no good prospect for the future, and am very fearful of failure at both places.

—Frank Frost to Rebecca, 1871

As rice planter Edward B. Heyward drove through the Lowcountry pinelands in the summer of 1868, he made a startling prediction to his young traveling companion: rice planting in the Lowcountry could be profitable only as long as the present generation of former slaves was still able to work. That, he estimated, would last for no more than twenty years. Heyward advised his friend to sell his plantation when that time came and give up planting.[1] His prediction proved astute. By 1890 planting rice on the Santee was no longer profitable and almost all of the old planter families had given up the crop.

The antebellum rice planters of old Georgetown District (restyled during Reconstruction as Georgetown County) did not all return to their plantations when the war ended. Some never came back. Mrs. Eleanor Ball (Simons) Lucas, widow of John Hume Lucas, abandoned Hopsewee in May 1862, and rice was never grown there again.[2] Some were still in federal prison camps in the North. Many had been killed or disabled, and some were too old or infirm to plant and had no sons to take over for them. Others had moved into the interior and decided to stay there and plant cotton. Many were destitute and took whatever work they could find in Charleston. Still others left for the Southwest and California and a few—like Maj. Gabriel Manigault,[3] were so demoralized by the collapse of the Confederacy that they eventually abandoned the United States entirely.

Those planters who attempted to restart rice planting on the Santee after the war found that life had been radically transformed. Most of the plantation houses had been stripped of everything useful, including their doors, window sashes, locks, and keys. Supplies of food and seed had disappeared. At nearby Chicora Wood, which belonged to former governor R. F. W. Allston, the freedmen had ransacked the plantation house in their search for money and booty. His daughter Elizabeth wrote, "It was a scene of destruction, and papa's study, where he kept all his accounts and papers . . . was almost waist-deep in torn letters and papers."[4]

Those who returned worked tirelessly to rebuild their plantations and restore what they could of their antebellum lifestyle. They faced formidable obstacles. Labor was expensive and no longer under the control of the planter. Rice fields were overgrown and the ditches clogged. Farm implements were worn out, broken, or stolen. Capital was nearly nonexistent and interests rates were high: up to three percent per month. Prime rice land, which had sold for $250 per acre before the war, was now valued at only $40 to $50.[5] With their economic backs broken by the emancipation of their slaves, the aftereffects of losing the war and the weight of their debts, the rice planters of South Carolina struggled in vain for the rest of the century to breathe life into their plantations again.

The change from slave to free labor was a huge monkey wrench in the cogs of plantation society. As early as 1863 South Carolina's planters began receiving gloomy reports of labor strife to come, as letters filtered back from Union-occupied areas such as Natchez. Stephen Duncan, Jr., who managed Julius and Maria Pringle's Mississippi cotton plantations while they were in France, wrote to his father, "It may seem a light matter to manage five plantations, but I don't think it there is anything more arduous, trying and vexatious. The Negroes who remain are to receive for able bodied men 9$ per month, women $7, children $3.50 and others in proportion to their capabilities. But all this arrangement will be knocked in the head. Mr. Mellon and Mr. Yeatman have been appointed to manage a system of labor and I have seen a draft of this plan which will be issued in a short time. A more abominable and infamous set of regulations were never concocted, and the desire seems most evidently to ruin the planter and place the Negro upon a near equality with the White man."[6] By the end of the year, however, Duncan wrote to his father, "The plantations under my control have done pretty well notwithstanding the disadvantages attending the new system of labor. . . . It requires a good deal of Macchiavellean diplomacy to get along with them, and were it not remunerative it would be unbearable."[7]

With slavery abolished, the black laborers of the Lowcountry had to be wooed and bargained with—a concept wholly alien to the aristocratic planters. Large, capital-intensive plantations could no longer be worked in a cash-starved economy. Many were broken up into small farms and rented to freedmen for a share of the crop. On undivided plantations, such as Camp Main and Richfield, freedmen also worked for shares of the crop. William never forgave the freedmen for burning his house and fumed constantly at their new privileges and status. In contrast, Frank Frost earned their trust at a relatively early date. His home at Camp Main was not molested, and he was able to secure as many hands as he needed.

With the control of the labor supply in the hands of freedmen and their Northern allies, the planters of Georgetown County looked for new labor options. In 1869 the Georgetown Agricultural and Mechanical Club endorsed the idea of using Chinese labor to replace the freedmen.[8] The California Pringles—Edward and James—had studied the possibility a full three years earlier. On August 9, 1866, Edward wrote to Rebecca, "If any thing comes of the suggestion, I am going to see what can be done in the way of sending Chinese laborers to South Carolina. I have been thinking of that for a long time and I intend to write to Papa and Motte about it. Perhaps Motte can make a business out of it and perhaps Dr. Frost may help to work up the problem. I have already spoken to Chinese merchants here about it and I will see what can be done."[9]

Due chiefly to immigration restrictions, the Chinese labor proposal never bore fruit, and getting freedmen to do the ditching remained a problem. Every year, the ditches had to be cleaned of the plant growth which would prevent proper water drainage, essential to producing high yields of rice. The amount of labor required was enormous—each acre of rice field required about 650 feet of ditches, and a typical rice plantation of 250 acres meant nearly thirty-one miles of ditches to be cleaned.[10]

After the harvest of 1867 was completed, Frank wrote that a number of his men still refused to go into the ditches unless they were paid higher wages. The problem was common all along the Santee. On November 22, 1867, he wrote to Rebecca, "Your father and I have been to see Hazzard[11] today to learn about his contract with an Irishman to do his ditching at $2.50 per acre. We are so much pleased with the idea that we are quite in the humor of making the same arrangements if we can find anyone to undertake it."[12]

William M. Hazzard wrote that Mr. Middleton was using a combination of Irish and Negro labor in his fields.[13] Theodore D. Ravenel, who went to work on the Cooper River rice plantations in 1881, wrote that Irish laborers would come down from the brickyards on the Hudson River about December first and work at ditching until the first of April. "We had to get them because our prime men had all gone off for higher wages," Ravenel wrote. "The Irishmen's work always cost more and was never entirely satisfactory."[14]

Frank's father, Judge Edward Frost, did not agree that foreign labor sources could solve the postwar labor problems. On December 2, 1867, he wrote, "I have not much confidence in the character of the white labor which can be obtained in the South. They are the refuse of N[orthern] laborers—disorderly and faithless. Of several trials, I have known none to succeed. Bad as our negroes are, I think they are more reliable that the white laborers who come south for employment. I cannot advise you, because I do not know the temper of the negroes on Santee. But I would suggest to you that if they will contract on the same terms as white laborers, it would be safer to employ them.... Without steam pumps or wind mills to dry the fields, the cultivation of rice must languish. That custom of cleaning ditches by working them, waist deep in mud and water, cannot be continued. Compulsory labor alone continued it, during slavery."[15] Ultimately, the Santee planters abandoned their attempts to use foreign labor and resigned themselves to work out their disagreements with the freedmen.

The day after their wedding, Rebecca and Frank Frost drove to Camp Main in a buggy, accompanied by Aleck Raphael, their cook, who walked.[16]

Frank was still recovering from his service in the war. On June 1, 1861, he had entered Confederate service as an orderly sergeant in Company H, 1st (Maxcy Gregg's) Regiment, South Carolina Volunteers. While in that command at Suffolk, Virginia, Frost went to Richmond and took the examination for the position of assistant surgeon. He chose as his thesis the timely subject, "Pyoemia or Blood Poisoning, as Resulting from Gunshot Wounds."

In the fall of 1861 he received an officer's commission and was promoted to the rank of assistant regimental surgeon and returned to Gregg's regiment. Frank had previously served as an enlisted man, and upon his return, he was not received warmly by the regimental surgeon, Dr.

J. W. Powell. Frank's skill in attending to the wounded prompted Powell to change his mind and recommended him for promotion to full surgeon.[17]

In January 1862 Frank was at Camp Huger, in Suffolk, Virginia. He wrote to his brother, Richard, "In this army life one can make no allotment of his time for certain duties; this is particularly the case with a surgeon; he is more or less busy all day and has little time that he can call his own; for he may systematize the affairs of his own department as far as is practicable, still he cannot foresee the accidents of the day, and there is no telling at what hour of the day or night some man is going to have his head broken or to have the colic, which are occurrences not at all uncommon. I am almost afraid to go to bed at night, so much do I dread having to get up and dress to visit some provokingly sick man."[18]

That same month, Frank wrote to his mother, thanking her for the clothing and blankets that she had sent. He noted "I weigh 143 or 4 pounds, that is about 6 pounds more than I ever did." He then complained about the erratic mail service. "I am sure that you do not receive all of the letters that I write. You speak of hearing from me on an average once a week; I write much oftener than this, almost every week I write home twice, and sometimes three times."[19]

Each Confederate officer was entitled to have a body servant with him at the front, and Frank took a trusted slave, Robinson. "Robinson begs to be remembered to you and sends his love to his mother and other people in the yard," Frank wrote.[20] "He seems to be very well satisfied here, he is comfortable, is well fed, and has become very well acquainted and known about the camp. His chills have not returned since the first attack. I am giving him quinine and whiskey to drive them from his system. He serves me very well and makes a good servant. The Col. and the rest of my mess are well pleased with him. I keep him busy all the time white washing my house and cleaning it up, or digging ditches about it or something else to keep him employed, knowing how necessary it is that he should not be idle."[21]

In the fall of 1862 Frank took the examination for surgeon and chose for his thesis, "The Aetiology, Pathology, Prophylaxis and Treatment of Small Pox." He was successful, was named a surgeon, and promoted to the rank of major. He took part in the battles of Gettysburg and Boeteler's Ford, and the later campaigns in Virginia, Maryland, and Tennessee, serving under Generals Lee and Jackson.

After gallant action on the field he was assigned to Lt. Gen. Ambrose Powell Hill's 3rd Corps, Army of Northern Virginia, where he served as Hill's personal and staff surgeon. At the Battle of the Wilderness in May 1864, Frank was shot through the right shoulder, nearly losing his arm and his life. After his wound healed, he got the call to become the surgeon of Gen. Martin Gary's brigade, the 7th South Carolina Cavalry. There, despite the fact that he was only twenty-seven, he was found to be the senior surgeon of the brigade. He served with Gary for six months until he was recalled to join General Hill. While with Gary's brigade, which was guarding Richmond, Frank distinguished himself by establishing a series of temporary field hospitals. It was noted that Frank "was beloved by the gallant men who experienced his valuable work," and "on the long and tiresome march, Dr. Frost frequently trudged along the rugged road and let some brave soldier, with bare and bleeding feet, ride on his horse."[22]

While Frank would do anything to assist a sick or wounded soldier, he despised shirkers. One night while in Gary's command, Frank assembled Christmas dinner for his sick soldiers. The smell of fresh food proved too powerful a lure for some malingerers, who showed up at the dinner tent. Frost immediately had them returned to active duty.

General Hill was killed on April 2, 1865, during the siege of Petersburg, and Frank was transferred to the staff of Lt. Gen. James Longstreet, who, with Lee and the rest of the Army of Northern Virginia, surrendered their arms in April 1865. Frank was finally able to lay down his scalpels and bone saws and make his way home.

On April 25, 1865, Union General John Porter Hatch issued an order which commanded the white inhabitants of Charleston and Georgetown Districts to take the oath of allegiance, after which they could return to their plantations, tell their former slaves that they were free, and make work contracts with them. On May 29 President Andrew Johnson issued a broad pardon to most of the former Confederates, on condition that they swear an oath of allegiance to the Union. The act excepted former Confederate generals, high officials and those now worth over $20,000, who had to apply for individual pardons.

Frank took the oath on May 30, 1865, at the headquarters of the Northern District, Department of the South at Charleston, witnessed by an officer of the 55th Massachusetts Volunteers, a Negro infantry unit. On July 30 he rode to Georgetown to attempt to regain possession of Camp Main plantation. The next day, from the house of Mr. Miller,[23] his overseer, he wrote to his father:

> I wrote a few lines from Darlington to you. I left there with Wando[24] in the buggy on Friday morning, driving uncle's old horse. We made easy stages of 28 miles per day and arrived at Georgetown on Sunday at 12 P.M., and from there rode out here the same afternoon, yesterday. After talking and consulting with Mr. Miller until late last night, we determined to make an early start for Georgetown this morning to learn what the authorities there would do for us. I was disappointed in their reception and expressions. They tried to make various objections to our making any contract at all or laying any claim to the place for the present at least. Had the same old story about the negroes planting and working the crop and then consequent rights—told me that the plantation had been possessed by the Government as abandoned property etc—of its having been confiscated together with all the lands on Santee except Mr. Hume's place.[25] All of these various points we complained from one office to another, showing Gen. Beal's[26] order allowing extension of time, your letter to Col. Dyer and the counter forfeiting

order, until finally they agreed that the lands had neither been confiscated nor abandoned and promised to send a captain to the plantation with Mr. Miller[27] and myself tomorrow to superintend the making of a contract. So that I will go into Georgetown early tomorrow morning to take this captain in the buggy, accompanied by an escort on horseback, to the place, there to meet Miller, to make the contract. Then probably spend the night there as the ride back to town and then back here (41 miles in all) will be too fatiguing for either the horses or ourselves.

I am a little afraid that the negroes may make some objection and that we may have trouble and not be sustained by the military. The disposition to be made of the 50 negroes from Darlington, their stealing of rice, killing of stock etc is a question too difficult for them and one which I am afraid they will keep clear of. You will be disappointed when I tell you that I learn of Mr. Miller that of 2,000 bushels rice thrashed last year by him there is not now a grain left, the whole having been squandered by the Yankees and the negroes, one or two boatloads were sold by the latter at 50¢ per bushel. Of 1500 bushels in the straw but little is left—the Darlington people having been feeding out and distributing it to the whole river. We do not know definitely what rice in the stalk is left there; but I expect very little and the value of the corn—

Mr. Miller says that there are now 10-12 sheep, 40 or 50 hogs, pigs and 4-5 cows on the place, all of which the negroes have claimed and are caring for as their own. I would make an attempt to sell what little rice remains and all of the stock on the place, but the market is so glutted with all of these things, at a mere nominal price that I believe we will make by allowing the negroes to continue their stealing and selling what they leave at full market price at a later period.

Rough rice is selling for only 50¢ and butchered beef at 8 to 10¢ and a very limited sale for the latter. I have not yet been to the plantation, not having had time and thinking it best to feel the Yankees first and learn their propensities. I am afraid that the negroes are more or less unruly and insubordinate and that they will object particularly to Mr. M's return to the place. They cannot understand why that now that they are free they should have any white man over them any longer, and are altogether opposed to it. Mr. M. has heard them say they are willing to suffer uncle Thomas,[28] but that they wish and mean to have nothing more to do with Judge Frost.

... Mr. Miller does not enter so fully into the proposition of resuming charge as I would like. He is evidently a little afraid of the negroes. He says that I must tell you that he will do all that he can tho' he is not at all disposed to stay on the place. He says that the negroes object entirely to any white person being on the place at all. I will probably stay here a week longer to see things straightened out, to get Mr. Miller established in authority, and then will return to Darlington, or maybe go to Society Hill for a day or two.[29]

From Camp Main, three days after the Christmas of 1865, Frank wrote a detailed description of conditions on the Santee to his mother:

I am the only white person on the whole river except Mr. Maxwell,[30] twelve miles off, near South Island. I find the temper of the negroes better than I had expected. The very great majority of them are however evidently very much disturbed at my presence on the place. They look upon me as one who has come to interrupt the entire freedmen from any restraint whatever, which they have enjoyed for past nine months.They had hoped too to possess this land. The dispelling of this delusion distresses them no little. And their discomfiture is much more increased when I tell them that they are to work just as they used to do, or leave the plantation. They cannot understand how it is that the Yankees would set them free and give them no lands; how it is that they can have been born and raised on the soil and yet not inherit it upon becoming free.

Old Titus, Santee the driver, and two boys, Prince and Marcus take very good care of me. They provide my meals regularly and do other such service as I may desire. My fare is good; rice, potatoes, milk, pork, or wild ducks, which latter I procure myself. I also have tea and sugar, which I brought with me. I stimulate my attendants by giving them occasionally a plug of tobacco, or some sugar and coffee, procured in Georgetown. For a bed, I have nailed together four boards so as to contain a bundle of straw, and on this I have two blankets and an oil cloth. When the weather is very cold I sleep with all of my clothes on and with the addition of an extra pair stockings and my India rubber overcoat. So you can see I manage to make myself quite comfortable on small means.

There is no furniture whatever in the house except 2 old timed affairs, desk, book case and drawers all combined, and an old sideboard from all of which the drawers have been taken. In my room I have this old sideboard, and a table and 2 chairs, which I have borrowed from the people. The house is in very good condition; except that some of the locks and all of the keys have been removed; 2 doors have been broken, and 1 sch. sash carried off.

Since I have been here I have divided each crop as they made. Our share, 1/3 of whole, amounts to 80 bushels corn, 15 bushels rice, about 3 bushels potatoes and some fodder. The negroes made little, and of that they stole freely I cannot but think. They and the Yankees together have killed every animal on the place except 4 cows and 3 calves. I amuse myself chiefly in hunting ducks, of which there are great numbers here. I sell most of them in Georgetown, to meet various expenses. I regret much that I cannot get them to the family there. They would be a great treat to them. The change to them from beefsteak to wild duck would not be only most pleasant, but economical. I have killed 28 in all. I have been out turkey hunting twice, though without success. I have been going to Georgetown twice a week to confer with the Yankees there about the negroes, to get letters from Papa, and look for my baggage, which, after long expectation of it, came only yesterday.

It is impossible to say what we will do next year. The negroes are entirely indisposed for anything like regular, systematic work. What they want is to be let alone. The

> Yankees assure us that if they do not make contracts that they will turn them every one off the plantation. This is the only hold that we have upon them. We may by this measure force them to work. If we only had the money to pay wages, I think that we would operate more successfully. As it is we will be obliged to work the crop on shares with people. Papa writes to say that there is to be a meeting of all planters at Georgetown next week to confer with each other and the Yankees as to the future of planting. He will then come down here and remain I suppose until something definite is decided upon and done. When he comes I will, of course, do what I can for his comfort. . . .
>
> On Saturday I hope to have a Yankee one man guard with me. He may stay in the house with me; though may be at the Parsonage,[31] which I would prefer. The negroes have been trying to have a merry time of it. They have been dancing with little intermission, day and night, on the different plantations in turn. To night they are still at it with great vim, on our place, though the Christmas is over. I hear the ruckus and the shooting very distinctly. I hope that this will be the last of it, and that they will then think of work.[32]

To the extent that the rigors of planting would permit, Frank courted Rebecca under the eaves of the Miles Brewton House. Guests were generally received and entertained in the South Parlor, but Frank and Rebecca were considered very bold: after exchanging pleasantries with the family, the two withdrew to the North Parlor across the hall.[33] Frank asked her to marry him in the summer of 1866, and she accepted. She refused to have an engagement ring, for she knew that the Frost and Pringle families needed the all their money just to pay their living expenses.

Sarah Middleton and other of her women friends congratulated Rebecca on her engagement. From California, her brother, Edward's perspective was a bit more sober, noting that Frank was nearly penniless. Sensing true love, Edward gave his consent—with the stipulation, "tell him you are a great deal too good for him. . . . I'll promise to struggle as much as possible against the jealousy which brothers must always have of a 'feller' who comes in and takes away a sister, as much beloved as you are."[34]

In the fall of 1866 Frank shuttled between Darlington, where he superintended the cotton and corn crops on his father's plantation, and the Santee, where he worked to restart planting on the Frost and Pringle plantations. Frank's life was hard, and every day on the plantation was a day away from the true love of his life: Rebecca. Every time he came to Charleston or returned to Santee, the trip took two days on horseback. He wrote to Rebecca:

> I left town as determined at 10 A.M., [Oct.] 8th. After a tedious journey, I arrived here yesterday at 11:30 A.M., without event or accident. 8:15 P.M. Here I have been interrupted by a visit from Maxwell Lucas[35] of 1.15 hour.
>
> On account of the heaviness of the road and of my load, I was unable to travel more than twenty-nine miles the first day; so there I stopped, about an hour after dark, and spent the night with sufficient comfort, by the warmth and light of a large fire.
>
> My reception on the plantation has been pleasant and satisfactory. The people all seem glad to see me, and express a readiness to work and be orderly. As an earnest sign of their temper and intentions, I have received today from different parties the following articles: forty-six eggs, three fat wild ducks, three pints of beautiful honey in the comb, a plate of nice fresh butter, one-half peck of potatoes, besides new rice and peas, and plenty of milk which I get from plantation cows. They have all been to see me today, some before I had got out of bed, and others I received dishabile.[36] I give them to understand that I expect them to work and at once; and that I will care for and feed them. They assent to the proposition. The thought of greasing themselves once more with bacon seems to fill them with happiness. They have suffered most severely this past summer and have felt the necessity of some one to represent them, to feel an interest in them and to supply their wants; and they seem to hail me as that merciful party. I think that I will have no difficulty engaging as

many as I want, mostly of our own people. I will begin work on next Monday, the fifteenth.

Day after tomorrow I expect to go to Georgetown to get a supply of provisions, tools etc. for temporary use, until I can get a full supply from Charleston. My dear Love, since parting with you on Sunday night there has hardly been a moment of the day or night that I have not thought of you, and with the utmost tenderness. I do so long to be with you again. I feel as if I had been absent a long time. You are suggested to my mind by every thing that's pleasant; by almost every thing that I see, or that transpires. I thank you very much for your goodness in giving me your likeness. It is a source of much comfort and enjoyment to me. I look at it and look at it, and it so intensifies my wish to see you that the feeling amounts almost to pain.

This separation, if possible, must not continue much longer, for it makes me very impatient and uncomfortable. Since I have been up here, marriage seems much more practicable than it did before. The good temper of the people makes me hopeful of the future. I am already revolving in my head plans for the thorough cleaning and refitting of the interiors of the house, the rebuilding of fences, cleaning up of the premises and other things which may conduce to the good appearance and comfort of the place. With a moderate expenditure of means I think that we can live here very comfortably and abundantly, and be able to offer such inducements to our relatives and friends as to secure visits from them and so supply the only want which I fear you may feel, that of congenial company. If I had you here with me I feel as if every thing would look bright and promising; and I, at least, would be contented and happy.

I have a plenty to eat, much more than I have an appetite or relish for; for as long as I am absent from you I find no pleasure in any thing.

The mosquitoes are exceedingly troublesome—even in the day there is no peace from them, and but for the kindness of Lucas in lending a net, I would be unable to endure them a night at all. I never have known them, by a greater degree, as bad as they are now.

You will infer so much from what I have written that I may as well come out and tell you that I am staying on the plantation. When I arrived here I found that both of the Lucas were absent, and so the Parsonage abandoned, and that they had determined to remove to their homestead today. So if I had gone there I would have been alone and most inconveniently distant from my business. Do not allow yourself to be uneasy about me; for I am quite comfortable and well and with every prospect of continuing so. I take regularly eight grains of quinine a day, double the quantity that I took at Fairfield—the additional four grains entirely for your benefit and comfort. Do continue your daily fill until the sixteenth.

11th, 9.30 P.M. I was so interrupted last night, and so repeatedly today, that I have been obliged to continue this letter at short intervals to day; and it is now so late, that I must bring it to a speedy close, as I have to write to your father to night before returning to my homely, though comfortable couch of straw. You are so continually in my mind, and it gives me so much pleasure to communicate with you, even in this unsatisfactory manner, that I feel as if I could write almost indefinitely; but a regard for your patience and goodness must make me desist. If I can get things well at work next week so as to see my way clearly, I will probably return to Charleston week after next to arrange for the permanent conduct of the plantation to remain as short a time as my business will admit of. I hope that you have my likenesses and that they give you as much pleasure as yours does me. Do take every care of yourself; and if you should get sick, let me know at once so that I may come immediately to see you. The two Lucas have just left, having spent the evening with me. My dear, dear girl, I can never express my feelings of love, esteem and regard for you. You have my earnest, constant and enduring love. You are linked in most intimately with every thought, hope and aspiration of my life. Everything seems bland and without interest except as associated with you.[37]

Unlike William, Frank got along with the freedmen. He noted that he expected to start work at Camp Main with about twenty hands. "They still seem disposed to work and do so well that I am much encouraged," he wrote. "I am quite hopeful of a good result. I find too that there is by no means as much repair and work needed as I had expected; and that the people have made a much better crop than I had supposed, and that they are honest on harvesting and storing it according to the contract. I have no reason to think that they have stolen any of it; and the two foremen assure me that they have not."[38]

Frank Frost was one of the first of the planters to return to the Santee. By the spring of 1867 there were only a handful of others. His letters mention Gen. Arthur Middleton Manigault, of White Oak;[39] his brother, Maj. Gabriel Manigault; one or more sons of Elias Horry, IV; a Mr. McCants[40]; George Ford[41]; Francis W. Johnstone, of Annandale[42]; Frank's brother, Richard D. Frost, of Fairfield; two of the five sons of Dr. Alexander Hume, of Hume's Cat Island and Frank's neighbor, William Rivers Maxwell.

"Mr. Max" owned White Marsh, which produced 1,485,000 pounds of rice in 1860—but only 1,740 bushels in 1868. In January 1868 Frank Frost went to see Maxwell and found him away at Georgetown. "He is preparing to leave here to move to Darlington to live with his and our families," Frank wrote. "The plantation is almost abandoned."[43] Walter Middleton returned briefly in 1867, but Frank noted that he had "abandoned his planting and given up his whole interest to his brother Arthur, his prospects were so hopeless. Walter is to go north with his father for the summer."[44]

When Frank and Rebecca Frost arrived on the Santee on December 13, 1866, they were one of very few white families on the river. One planter wrote, "The stillness of the Dead Sea overspreads the land. No boat or vessel seen on the river. No sound of a mill in operation—nor of a flail on the threshing floor. All is painfully quiet and silent. The negroes work as much or little as they please. I have met with no incivility whatsoever. But they cannot bear [the overseer] Singleton, nor would they any manager, and he is obliged to submit to the tacit disregard of his orders. . . . The whole scene is sad and sickening."[45]

Frank's aunt, Mrs. Elizabeth L. Parker, made the Camp Main house as cozy as possible. Mary Pringle Frost remembered it as a spacious house with two rooms on each side of a hall, a piazza and a garret with dormer windows.[46] One of the Frost daughters remembered "a beautiful live oak with grass sloping from its base."[47] Elizabeth Parker had obtained a carpet and other furnishings from Frank's mother. In the fall of 1867 Frank had their servant Aleck paint the house white and the shutters and banisters green. "Yesterday he began dusting and painting the dining room and will continue until he completes the whole of the inside; so that in course of time I hope that the house will look very nicely and be very comfortable."[48] A few days later he apologized for its condition, writing that it was "very small" and that the carpets were "very scant and shabby."[49] Frank also established a vegetable garden behind the house, which he tended as time permitted. The summer and fall of 1867 were lonely times for him. With the exception of an occasional short trip to Charleston, Frank lived alone at Camp Main until after the birth of their first child, William Pringle Frost, in December 1867.

Rebecca, like her mother and sister Mary Frances before her, became pregnant almost immediately after her wedding. Domestic servants were readily available on the Santee but the money to pay them was scarce. In September 1867 Frank reported that a freedwoman was eager to work as a seamstress for Rebecca for $3 per month. That same month, Rebecca engaged a washerwoman for $4 per month. With money in short supply, Rebecca conserved every penny. She explained to Frank how she had minimized the cost of the baby's layette. "Susan sold my cord bracelet for $25 — $10 of it I have directed her to spend in piqué[50] for our little one's cloak; the other $10 I think of expending on a blanket shawl of which we will all feel the comfort — a family purchase. The other $5 we may spend in a crib. I saw some very nice looking ones for $5 and $6. Mother said it is the best use I could put the bracelet to—far better than keeping it locked up. I made a sale of something for $2, so that in reality, baby's comfort cost only a dollar."[51]

In November, Frank divided the rice crop in the first week of December and began shipping it to Charleston aboard the schooner, *Three Sisters*. With the crop disposed of, Frank was finally able to turn his thoughts to Christmas and the imminent birth of their first child. From Camp Main on December 18, 1867, he wrote to Rebecca about his trip:

> I arrived here safely yesterday afternoon at 12:30. I got to the 32 mile house the afternoon before at sun down. I am very well pleased with Fanny, except that she is too foolish about getting into steamboats and flats[52]and crossing bridges. I had a great deal of trouble with her in this matter. It took four men to pull her onto the steam boat and four to pull her out and she lunged very violently both times; and to get her onto the flat I had to blindfold her: otherwise, she is gentle and a horse of fine action, showy and endearing. . . .
>
> I am now most painfully anxious about you, my dearest, only wife. I trust and pray that our merciful Father may safely deliver you of a sound and perfect child to the glory and praise of His name, and to the inestimable comfort of us, his weak and sinful servants. I am so painfully anxious to be with you, and yet duty detains me here. How I wish that you could be over your troubles and return to me! I feel that we could be so happy and contented here together. I do truly long and yearn for that happy day. . . I wish to make a handsome Christmas present to your mother, and also to make a present to Mamma and to Susan and my sisters. Do think of what we shall give them. I think it proper that we should do this; particularly for your mother; for I feel very grateful to her for her kindness to you. Do you not agree with me? I think we may becomingly spend twenty to twenty-five dollars for presents, to include some candy etc. for the children and a present to my goddaughter. I am afraid that I will not be able to get any game to send you. I will if I can. I will send some eggs by Friday's steamer.[53]

The Frosts' Christmas present arrived five days late. At 7:40 in the morning of December 30, 1867, William Pringle Frost made his debut. He was first of the fourth generation of Miles Brewton's descendants to be born in the withdrawing room of the family home on King Street.

Just two days after the birth of their son, the pressures of planting forced Frank to return to Camp Main. "I truly hope that you are well and our dear little one," he wrote. "I will miss you now more than ever, dearest. I thought that I loved you before, but now our sweet little fellow brings you nearer ever to me and makes me love you, if possible, even more than I did before. My whole heart is yours, dearest, and I think of you and our boy almost every moment of the day and night."[54]

The pregnancy had been hard on Rebecca, and several of the letters she wrote after the baby arrived were written in a weak and faltering hand. On January 15, Rebecca wrote to Frank that he should come, as planned, to get her on January 25. "Susan has taken baby into the drawing room. Mother promises to let me dine at the table on Sunday. On Friday, I hope to be able to put on my dress. How glad I will be to find myself strong and able to walk about once more. Baby will charm you by his improvements. But I yearn so intensely for my husband."[55]

William Pringle Frost was christened on February 5, 1868, and he and his mother stayed at the King Street house until the end of spring. In early June, Frank took them to South Island, where the little boy was the darling of the planters and their wives who summered there. Yet country life never held any charm for Rebecca, who flourished in Charleston and longed for California. In mid-June she wrote to Sue, in San Francisco, "How far off we do seem to be from each other. South Island must seem like some inconceivable spot in creation to you in San Francisco. I am thinking of you all the time, and trying to imagine your surroundings. Frank and I are impatient for your letters. I often wish we were in California and look forward to a move there at no distant day— if Mother and Papa join you. I tell Frank we must undo our fastenings here too. Poor Mother Frost is trembling over the fear of Frank's being enticed there. . . . Frank will be in no hurry, but quietly await the development of affairs with us. Every one predicts a general emigration of all the Pringles. All say it is but a matter of time and our friends say that they feel very bitter towards you for being the pioneers of all the rest of us."[56]

At the age of twenty-nine, Frank was already weary, a man who bore an enormous burden on his shoulders. Not only was he responsible for taking care of his new wife and son and growing rice on the Frost and Pringle plantations but for furnishing the two Charleston households with food. The Frost family properties which Frank supervised consisted of Camp Main plantation and its plantation house on the South Santee, additional rice fields on Toby Creek, and a house on South Island, all belonging to his mother, Harriet Horrÿ Frost.

In addition to his planting responsibilities, Frank was the only physician on the Santee for a radius of many miles. Of necessity, he was often forced to see his patients after putting in fourteen-hour days on the plantation. Rebecca wrote, "Last Saturday Frank did not get home until half-past eleven and we dined about twelve—midnight. Pringle and I dine at about three and then I dine again with Frank. He has a very troublesome patient in our neighborhood . . . and he sends for Frank no matter how late he comes at night. Frank's not charging for medical services makes him very unreasonable, and their calls upon him interfere seriously with his business in the morning."[57]

The work of rehabilitating Camp Main and Richfield was so arduous that Frank spent virtually the entire year on the plantation. Rebecca spent the winter there, except for the time she went into confinement prior to the birth of her children at the Miles Brewton House. This meant that, on average, Frank and Rebecca were separated for eight out of twelve months each year.

They coped with the enforced separation with correspondence. Frank's long and frequent letters to Rebecca made it clear that she was his inspiration. "She is an infinite blessing and treasure to me and our dear little ones," he wrote in 1871. "She is a woman of very rare excellence of character; and with age, develops in all Christian and womanly virtues and goodnesses, and day by day commands more and more my highest respect and esteem and admiration and my purest and most elevated affections. I prize her infinitely as my wife, but above this even, do I prize her in the most sacred character on earth [as] mother of my children. She is so full of good sense and of sound judgment and of holy affections, that I feel that her character is the sure guarantee that her children, thro' her example and training, will possess the same high qualities and traits."[58]

Rebecca was as industrious as her mother, and spent much of her time at South Island making aprons, petticoats, and dresses for her son, Pringle. "These little ones require such a number of clothes to keep them nicely," she wrote. "I cannot bear to have Pringle dirty, so I have to keep busy to get him a sufficiency of clothes—and I wish him to be neat by education, for boys are so rough by nature that they need all the refining influences we can give them."[59]

She taught her children to revere their elders at an early age. In 1869, when Pringle was two, she wrote to Susan, "I always teach Pringle to kiss his grandmother's letters and yesterday as I took yours and mother's letters out of the envelope he took them out of my hand, and with the most cunning look, pressed them to his lips .... As soon as Pringle is old enough you must take him that he may grow up with a memory of his grandmother and grandfather."[60]

The crop of 1866 was a pale shadow of prewar years and Frank had little to show for the year's work, but he kept the Frost and Pringle families from starving. Their survival of that awful year was enough to give them cause for thanks, and the two families somehow managed to find the courage to carry on.

By the spring of 1867, Frank's life had settled into a pattern which would last for a decade. Frank and the other Santee planters lived on South Island during the summer to escape the heat, mosquitoes, and deerflies along the river, and returned to their plantations or town houses in the winter. In the summer of 1867 he wrote to his brother, Henry,

> I am again on my almost daily routine of travel to the plantation. The ride is long and irksome and the annoyance from the heat, sand flies and mosquitoes very great and what return I may get I cannot say. My expectations of my success here are by no means as flattering as those of yourself and Papa; indeed I often think that I will make nothing at all. . . . I hope that I may realize your expectations; but I do not think it. In the mean time however I am determined that if I do fail it shall not be my fault, and so I keep hard at work all the time. The crop gives promise of only a very moderate yield. I do not think more than 3,500 - 4,000 bushels. Out of this all the heavy expenses of the plantation are to come which are so great as probably to consume the whole of it, unless it sells at very high price, $3.00--and this I cannot expect.[61]

He reported to Rebecca that Aleck gave him regular morning baths in her old tub, followed by breakfasts of boiled chicken, hominy, tea, bread, and butter, and described a dinner of boiled chicken, hominy, boiled okra, boiled onions, potatoes, and bread, "all with butter sauce and very nice."[62] Frank's regular reports to his absent wife—usually written daily—paint a vivid and detailed picture of postwar life on the Santee:

> I left here early this morning and visited both plantations. I found every thing going on as usual. The rice has advanced a great deal since I last saw it. It is now fully headed over nearly the whole of the two tracts, has turned brown and is hanging down. On uncle's place I think it is in advance by 4 or 5 days of that on Richfield, altho' the former was planted a week later. This is owing,

I suppose, with Hector and the difference in treatment: the one having been kept flowed during the whole of its growth, and the other kept dry. Another singular circumstance I noticed on Camp Main, that the second planting, 10 days later than the first in advance of the first and will probably be cut first. I don't know how to account for this; for both have received the same treatment. The whole of the Camp Main crop, except two fields, will be ready for the [rice] hook within three or four days of the same time. It will all come in a rush upon us; which I am afraid will make it necessary to hire hands and even to stack and leave in the field to be brought home when all is cut down and stacked. This is not so much the case with the rice crop; the fields on the main will ripen together, but the other fields will follow in convenient succession.

. . . Today we had for dinner, which we have just finished, okra soup, 1 pair wild ducks, shrimp pie, potatoes, onions, guinea squash [eggplant], rice, etc. I think I will leave to take Aleck in hand and make him reduce his present style. I brought three ducks from [the] plantation yesterday, killed by one of the people. I did so wish that I could get them to you. I could not enjoy them today; for I know that you would have liked them so much. It makes me sad to eat the nice peaches which Mr. Maxwell gives me from his trees, and tells me to eat them and think of you.

We learn that the Emilie will not make a trip here for a month and that the St. Helena[63] will probably not come. It is important for me to know if this be so or not so do ask your father to enquire about it and do you let me know all that he can learn; for if the steamer is not co come up, I will have to make arrangements to go to you by land; and this I am inclined to so any how. I think that with a fresh horse at 32 mile house, I can make the journey in one day, leaving here at 3 A.M. I may leave the horse and buggy at Mt. Pleasant[64] in charge of a servant to care for, while I go over and stay three or four days with you. In coming back I will go to McClellanville[65] the first day, spend the night there with Mazÿck and come on to the plantation next day in time to attend to business, and so will lose only one day each way. Be sure to write me about the steamer. If she comes next week I will probably send down to you some butter and chickens and maybe some eggs, green corn, water and musk melons and some guinea squashes. The second crop of vegetables and melons is just coming in, so I have a plenty of green corn and guinea squash and larger water melons than we have had this season. Do not tell your mother of these things for I may not be able to send them. But I will almost certainly send down something, so get your father to enquire at the boat for things, that is should the steamer come up again. In case she does not, you must send all of the letters by mail. Yesterday, Wednesday, we got the papers of Tuesday, the day before.

I hope to come down to you about the end of this month. I may go before that time; for my absence from you is most painful and there is not much to do on either plantation until the harvest, about the first week in September. Now that I think more of it, it is quite likely that I will leave here on Saturday or Friday, 23rd or 24th, and be with you the afternoon of the day that I start from here. If no accident happens, I think that I can easily make the drive. Do write to me, my dear wife; for I long to hear from you, how you are and of our dear little one, does the sweet little fellow jump now? and does he give you much uneasiness?[66] I love you with the whole strength and energy of my heart, my good, sweet one. Your devoted husband, Frank.[67]

The crop of 1867 was also meager by pre-war standards. On September 15, 1867, Frank wrote to Rebecca, "I have now forty-five acres of my best rice cut down and twenty-five acres tied and staked in the field. A great part of it was lying in the rain and water for six days.There will in consequence be no doubt great loss by shelling off in the field and by stain,[68] besides by the birds. I have been so thrown back in the harvest that the rest of the crop is over ripe and the birds are still eating it. . . . If we have any more rain, it will be the ruin of us all.[69] Three days later, he wrote that he was working from before dawn to dusk, but that things were "getting along well" and he hoped to have some rice thrashed and to market by October. "The crop has suffered somewhat by the bad weather, and a great deal by the birds," he wrote. "They are as bad as they can be, and it requires the utmost effort to keep them from making total destruction of the crop."[70]

Frank estimated the loss to birds at two to three bushels per acre. Mary put all of Frank's predictions and revised predictions into perspective in a letter dated September 24, 1867: "Frank reports our harvest as progressing successfully. He thinks it will quite come up to his estimate of thirty bushels per acre, making a yield of 4,000 instead of the old ones of 34,000!!!, and at a cost of ready cash three times as much as when the lands were worked by slaves."[71]

When it came time to harvest, Frank moved his residence from South Island to the Parsonage, which was located closer to the fields. Moving onto the plantation before the first hard frost was a dangerous decision, and despite the fact that Frank was taking quinine, his work in the fields greatly distressed Rebecca. On September 26, 1867, Frank wrote assuring her that he was taking every possible precaution. "I will sleep on the second story, and I do not think will be in any danger there. I will keep the windows all shut and build a fire in the room at dusk and use all prudence and precaution. I expect to begin to thrash next Monday and it will be very important that I should be there on the spot early and late. The ride back and forth I find very fatiguing, and consumes four hours each day. I am worn out every night when I get back here and am good for nothing but bed, and yet I am usually up until ten in writing or overlooking accounts."[72]

The rains started just after forty acres at Camp Main and thirty acres at Richfield had been cut and was laying in the stubble, making it impossible to tie or stack any of it. When the last of the 1867 crop at Camp Main and Richfield were threshed, the yield fell below even Frank's most conservative estimates. He had been hoping for 4,000 bushels and a profit of $1,000 to $1,500, but Camp Main produced only about 3,000 bushels.

The marginal crop had a predictable effect on Frank. In October he wrote that he had "lost spirit and become depressed. I do not like the thought of beginning again, to go through the same hard and disagreeable work, with all the worry and anxiety of mind that I have had with the prospect of finding myself at the end of the year just as I was at the beginning. I have worked hard and attended faithfully to my duties on the two places. I do not think that I could have done more; and if I have accomplished nothing, it is natural. I should fear the same result for next year; for I do not know what more I can do than I have done. . . . I have been getting on so well with the harvest and thrashing, ahead of any one else and to met with this unexpected fall in my estimates affects me most depressingly."[73]

William traveled to Richfield for an inspection early in November 1867 and was greatly depressed by its condition, the labor problems, and the small size of the crop. Frank wrote, "The refusal of the negroes to ditch disturbs him very much, even more, he says, than the failure of the crop; as it diminishes hope for the future. We have been at Richfield all day, witnessing the yoking of the wild oxen, talking with Hector, etc. Your father is now in better spirits than he was. I gave him for dinner yesterday: roast fowl, Irish and sweet potatoes, rice, bacon and eggs and ale and butter; for breakfast: hominy, poached eggs, mackerel, waffles, coffee and butter, and for dinner to day two roast ducks, sewee beans, rice, potatoes, ale and butter. Fortunately he has a good appetite and enjoys everything, and last night he slept very soundly. He suffered so much by sea, that he has determined to return by land in the buggy, will probably start next Tuesday afternoon."[74]

Frank and the other Santee planters coped with their isolation in a number of ways. One was the organization of their own mail service; the other was providing their own entertainment. In the fall of 1867 Frank Frost, William Maxwell, George Ford, and two other planters banded together to form a North Santee mail delivery co-operative. Each planter in rotation furnished a messenger, who picked up the mail twice a week in Georgetown and once a week from the steamer landing at South Island. The messenger then delivered the mail to the five plantations.

Removed by two day's travel from the society of Charleston, the Santee planters of necessity become masters of entertaining themselves—and they were willing to travel considerable distances to do so. By the fall of 1867, weekly dances had been reestablished at Plantersville, between the Black River and the PeeDee, seventeen miles from Georgetown. Frank noted that all the young people in the area looked forward to attending them.

On January 15, 1871, while Rebecca and the children were in Charleston, Frank wrote of the successful party he had held.

> The company, consisting of over 40, seemed to enjoy themselves exceedingly, and were reluctant to leave at 2:30 A.M. . . . I had the big hall cleaned out of everything except the old sofa, scoured, waxed and brilliantly lighted, with my big shop reflector and other lamps, for dancing. For ladies reception room, had our chamber and bed put in the nicest condition, and the same with the company room for the gentlemen. Had the supper table in our dining room. I must go to church now, will finish afterwards. Monday morning, 7 A.M. My very dear wife, to resume, I went to church yesterday. Mr. Lucas read our usual services to an unusually large congregation, and the service and music were very pleasant. I then went to dine with Mr. Trenholm[75] and met there Miss Emma for T. Mr. Johnstone and Mr. Macbeth; and we had a very pleasant party. At dark as I was about to go it was proposed that we should go over to the Hazzards and pay a visit there. I could not decline and so went, and met a very large company there, all of their own large household, and nearly all our gentlemen on the River. We stayed there singing and laughing until 11 o'clock, when I returned with the Trenholm party, and upon ordering my horse, found that he had been a long time put up and that all the servants had gone for the night, and was told that I would

have to spend the night. I did not at all wish it; for I was very anxious to come home to write to you. However, I had nothing else to do but to stay, and so I did. . . .

Well, to continue about the party, after finding myself involved, I determined to make the best of it, and so I went to some trouble to clean up the house and put it to rights, and then the next thing was to get up music and the supper. For the first I got two fiddlers, a man with sticks[76] and one with a tambourine, and they made very lively, if not very melodious music, and quite enough of it, in quick and very good time. For supper I had the good fortune to stumble on oysters that Tony Smith had at South Island. I got a good supply of these, and had them opened, and Aleck & Wando stewed them in milk very nicely. Aleck made a nice custard too, which was much admired by all the ladies for its good quality. And then I got some bread from Georgetown made some sandwiches, so that with the oysters, custard, sandwiches and rice cakes that you sent me I had a very nice supper, at not much expense, which greatly astonished every body as something so superior. I had to borrow some plates, custard dishes, silver etc. from Mrs. Middleton, Mrs. Johnstone & Mrs. H[orrÿ]. The table really presented a very handsome appearance. I have been congratulated repeatedly upon the great success of my entertainment. The only regrets on the part of myself & of all present were that you were not here.[77]

Bringing in a successful harvest in 1868 was no easier than in the previous year. In January, the weather and tides were so unfavorable that ditching had to be suspended for most of the month. By the first part of April, Frank was planning to plant 160 to 165 acres, and observed, "I think that our property must be better than last year, certainly we can hardly do worse."[78] On April 23 a heavy, three-day freshet struck the Santee, overflowing the river banks and putting the swampland six feet under water. On April 26 Frank wrote to his father:

I had planted about 125 acres, the entire crop except Middle Island[79]; 40 acres, which latter not yet planted. Of

> the 125 acres I presume that 35 acres, open trench, will be totally lost; 35 acres, open trench, and 30 acres, covered, in great peril; the balance, 25 acres, open trench, may survive without material injury. I have been using all effort and energy to make a crop this year, and considering the difficulties of high river, etc., was getting on well, with prospect of making a fair crop. I would have completed the planting by 30th inst., except 8 acres, which I intended to plant in June. How utterly changed is the prospect now! It makes me gloomy and almost hopeless. If we had seed to replant, we might recover from this severe misfortune. I have none but about 100 bushels on hand, intended for Middle Island. To replant the land that will be devastated will cost in seed and labor not less than $1,000. Without considering this expense, the time lost to the fields will not be less than two weeks, and the amount of extra work required on banks, etc. will not be less than 1 week's work of the whole force. Half of the barn yard is flowed, great part of the bottom corn land and water is three feet deep in the weather ho[use].[80] I can go in a boat over almost any part of the rice lands. I hear that Hazzard & Middleton are also flowed.[81]

The crop was damaged, but Frank's worst fears did not materialize. After the water receded, he found most of the young rice seedlings intact and commented that the corn crop had benefited from all the rain. On June 18 he wrote, "I have nearly completed the first hoeing of rice and the second of corn and am preparing land, one acre, for slips.[82] I will soon be on the second hoeing of rice and I hope to complete it in fortnight. The crop I think is better than last year, certainly earlier and less grassy. The freshet and continued high river have injured it very much and greatly interrupted the work and management of the plantation. I have about 160 acres rice planted, 20 corn, 1-1/2 potatoes.[83] The people are doing tolerably well."[84]

At Richfield, Frank's work resulted in a respectable yield of 4,400 bushels from 175 acres, or 25.1 bushels per acre.[85] Yet the overhead was high, and on October 30, Mary wrote,

> "I was not born to a country life, and will not consent to have our children become country men. My whole nature abhors this. I consented to live on the Santee only because I knew it was something transient; but to settle down to a country life in the South, or indeed anywhere except very near a city, I will never agree to."
>
> —Rebecca Frost, 1869

"The doctor returned to his weary duties this morning, after having spent a week with us. He and your Papa made a calculation last night as to the proceeds of the crop. Some rice has been sold. The proceeds of the whole crop, after expenses have been taken out, will only be enough to pay the interest of our debts and we will have nothing to live on."[86]

By the spring of 1869 Rebecca was pregnant again and weary of country life. The accommodations at Camp Main and South Island were a far cry from those on King Street, and Frank's plantation duties often kept him at work from 3 A.M. until 11 P.M. In February 1869, she opened her heart to her mother. "You need not be afraid of Frank's emigrating," she wrote. "We have not the means, and no longer wish to live in the country. I was not born to a country life, and will not consent to have our children become country men. My whole nature abhors this. As to planting cotton in the middle country, the suggestion horrifies me. I consented to live on the Santee only because I knew it was something transient; but to settle down to a country life in the South, or indeed anywhere except very near a city, I will never agree to. If Frank gives up these plantations I hope he will be able to invest the little money he has in Charleston, as we can afford to go nowhere else."[87]

The previous three years on the Santee had been hard on Frank's health. He narrowly missed being crushed to death in a rice mill accident which left him incapacitated, bedridden and dependent on morphine pain killers for weeks.[88] In the spring of 1869 he came down with fever. Rebecca wrote, "Frank's health broke down completely. I was quite miserable about him, but I am grateful to the gracious God for his restoration—but the attack of malaria together with the unsatisfactory results of his labors have determined him it is time to look beyond these boggy rice fields. I know he has worked enough on them to make more than he has done were the lands capable of improvement commensurate to what has been done on them—but the condition of the surrounding country causes labor to be almost wasted, as the waters rush in and wash away all the work on the banks. The tides sweep in and out at their pleasure and the labor has become more and more scarce. No one but a person in daily contact with the details of rice planting can imagine what a harassing, unsatisfactory struggle it is."[89] A few days later, she wrote, "I will be thankful for anything that will oblige him to give up planting."[90]

The 1869 crop was also a disappointment. Frank only broke even at Camp Main and Richfield. The crop of 1870 was about the same. In the winter of 1870, Rebecca left Frank at the plantation to return to the family's birthing place on King Street. Mary Pringle Frost was born there on March 15, 1871. On April 1, Frank wrote to Rebecca, "Yours of yesterday I have received. You are so good and precious that I love you more and more every day. I do long until I am sick to have you back with me. This life of separation wears and tears me and keeps me most miserable and uncomfortable in body and mind. I am glad to hear such good accounts of our precious little ones; and your fancied likeness of the little girl to my sainted father touches me deeply. I am here to direct some repairs to our house and to put the premises and grounds in order against your coming. I have a heavy heart about my business, my hindrances and discouragements are so great. I see no good prospect for the future, and am very fearful of failure at both places."[91]

Frank and Rebecca's first vacation in five years came in the summer of 1871, when they left their children with Mary and took a leisurely trip to New York (where they visited the Breevort House, the hotel where James died), New Haven (where they visited Mary Frances for a week) a two-week excursion in Canada, and back to New York, where a family friend took them to Delmonico's, one of New York's finest restaurants.[92]

By late September, Frank & Rebecca were back on South Island, but left Pringle and Edward, their two sons, in Charleston with their grandmother. On September 22 Mary wrote that Edward was acting "like a skylark," but that she was concerned about reports of yellow fever in Augusta. Several days later, Edward started to show signs of being ill. Mary wrote to the Frosts, "Sue's predictions about our precious little Edward's having fever has been realized. We had to send for [Dr.] Geddings last evening, as Edward had a decided fever, indeed, I believe, as Sue does, that he had it the night before his skin certainly indicated it, but his spirits were so bright, his appetite so excellent, that I really felt ashamed to send for the doctor. But last evening, towards tea time, the brave head fell down, although the indomitable spirit avowed one no sick. We sent for Geddings, who came promptly and said, 'he had a good deal of fever.'"[93]

When the news reached South Island that Edward was sick, Frank and Rebecca left for Charleston, and Rebecca remained there to nurse him. With the harvest in full swing and in need of his supervision, Frank was forced to return to the island. In the days which followed, Dr. Geddings treated Edward with calomel pills, powders, and blisters, but all to no avail. On October 18 he complained of nausea and looked jaundiced. The doctor ordered that a blister be put on his stomach.

The next day Edward's fever returned and he lost strength, so Dr. Geddings was again summoned. "He encouraged us on the 18th," Mary wrote, "but after his last visit, that ominous brown-coffee coloured fluid came up, staining the pure lips of our little one. Dr. Francis Parker[94] was watching with us, he pronounced it "black vomit.' At four o'clock the lamb was gathered in the fold. In my own great sorrows, I have wondered how I could have wept such bitter tears as I did over my own little child and I have thought surely one should not weep at the death of a young child, but should think only of its having been sheltered from many sorrows."[95]

Edward Frost died of yellow fever on October 19, 1871, at the age of two years and four months. He was buried in St. Michael's churchyard. Rebecca had the grave of her twin sister, Elizabeth, opened, and laid Edward next to him. Like many parents who lose a young child, Rebecca feared that in some way she may have been responsible for his death. In November, she wrote to Susan, "Oh how sad to see him [Pringle] all alone in his crib. We were so proud of the two together in that crib. I feel now, that I was too proud of the blessing and too unmindful at the same time that I owed my sweet children to God's goodness alone. I so seldom remembered that they were only lent to me. I never thought that one might be taken. Now I feel that none may be left."[96]

When the Pringles sold Richfield in November 1871, one major load was taken off Frank's back, yet he was still saddled with Camp Main. He longed to abandon rice planting, but although it brought him little profit, it provided both families with food. Other careers offered their own risks,.with little better certainty of profitability.

The longer Frank worked at making a success of planting, the greater grew Rebecca's desire for him to abandon it and move the family back to Charleston. Rebecca and Frank ultimately spent most of a decade wracked with indecision and torn between conflicting goals. Rebecca's devotion to Frank impelled her to spend every possible moment with him on South Island and Camp Main. Yet she also longed to spend as much time as possible in the Miles Brewton House with her sister and elderly mother, where her children could grow up in a sophisticated, urban environment.

After living a Spartan life for all nine years of her marriage, Rebecca wrote Frank this wistful letter in late 1873:

> I wish I were with you. We would have such a nice day together. Nevermind, I am going to be back with you soon, and then I mean to keep house so nicely for you and

> fix up every thing so nicely. You will cede me a few days to get over demoralization and then you'll see how much good a change does a body. There are so many things I would like to have—a nice pony carriage for instance—new carpets, new curtains, and above all a nice horse for your use. Of course I don't expect any of these things, but I might as well indulge in the wishes. You'll say not, but the poorer we get, the more I mean to aspire, so as to keep our heads above water. If you knew how I long to feel your dear arms around me you would never doubt that your love alone is all I need for happiness. I am only telling you of these wishes to tease you, dearest. I am so happy in your love. When I think of you—that you are my own dear husband—I do feel so happy, I don't care for anything else. I can't feel so uneasy about the future as you do, for the thought of the wealth I possess in you makes me feel I would be throwing away such a blessing. No, no, as long as your dear life and love are preserved, I will not be over anxious.[97]

The next four years saw no improvement in Frank's crops, and his neighbors had little better success. One by one they bit the bullet, admitted defeat, retired from planting, and took whatever they could get for their lands. In the fall of 1876 Frank suggested that it would be unwise to continue to plant Camp Main. Rebecca wrote to her mother, "I must say ten years on North Santee has given me such a horror of country life in South Carolina that I would rather go through any personal privations in a State that has some future before it for there our children would grow up among a prosperous community, which alone would be an advantage, while anywhere, and everywhere in South Carolina, negroes & decay are the prominent features."[98]

Half of Rebecca's wish was granted that year. Frank's weary resignation from planting finally came in the winter of 1876. After a decade of toil, he was forced to admit that further efforts to cultivate rice on the Santee would be futile. Frank abandoned all work at Camp Main and sold his remaining rice, oxen, hogs, plantation tools, and equipment to William M. Hazzard of Annandale plantation.[99] Frank and Rebecca moved their family back to Charleston before Christmas. From San Francisco, Edward again repeated his call for them to come, but Rebecca's dreams of starting a new life in California never came true.

CHAPTER THIRTEEN

A Seven-Bottle Man

Father would have given his life for the Confederacy, but not his fortune.
—said of Julius by his daughters.

Of all the Pringle children, Julius was the only one to increase his wealth and carry it through the war. In 1860 Julius had real estate holdings valued at $500,000 in Pointe Coupeé Parish, Louisiana, and the family made frequent visits to Newport. However, with war on the horizon and the Newport colony starting to turn a cold shoulder to Southerners, Julius began to move his family and most of his money to France. They fell in love with their new home and found the Biarritz of Napoleon III and Empress Eugenie gayer and more exciting than life in the old South. By 1861 they had become expatriates.

With the war all but over, Maria and the children returned from France. By March 1865 the family was united again at Torwood. Later that year Maria and the children made a visit to Newport to relax among their Northern friends[1] before returning to Paris with Julius in July.

In January 1866 an acquaintance in New Orleans wrote, "Julius Pringle is here, and thinks he has succeeded in making good cotton crops with his negroes, most of whom remained. He has been planting all the time, the Yankees all around him."[2] In 1870 Julius's 1,200-acre Pointe Coupeé parish cotton plantation produced 350 bales of cotton and small quantities of other crops, valued at $40,600. Torwood continued to be one of Julius's chief sources of income, and well into the 1880s was producing 500 to 600 hogsheads of sugar a year.[3] In 1868 Julius inherited approximately $150,000 from the estate of his mother-in-law, and by 1870 he was one of the richest men in the South.

"Father would have given his life for the Confederacy, but not his fortune," one of his daughters later stated. Julius's pragmatism saved his fortune—but sullied his honor in the eyes of some family members.

At Biarritz, on the Bay of Biscay in the south of France, Julius built a splendid, three-story mansion known as the Villa Pringle. He stocked it with family portraits, fine furniture, and a large library full of calf-bound, classical and contemporary books, including Darwin's 1830 *Journal of a Naturalist* and his 1860 *Voyage of the H.M.S. Beagle*. The Pringles soon became known for the brilliance of their parties, and "their villa was considered one of the most gracious homes in Southern France."[4] Julius also kept a small summer home at Versailles and retained at least two black servants, presumably from his Mississippi or Louisiana plantations.

Sue, a servant of John Julius Pringle. Photographed in Paris, 1869.

Described by a relative as "a Sybarite and *bon vivant*," Julius could well afford to be self-indulgent, but he was never selfish. He shared his good fortune with his destitute family in Charleston. In addition to money, Julius sent apples, cheese, and sugar from Torwood, and his presents were received with enthusiasm. His quarterly financial support was "magnificent," Mary wrote in 1865. "He has sent it, thank God, for we could not have lived without it. Then he sent a delicious barrel of sugar house sirup, the nicest I have ever tasted. Your Papa almost lives upon it, it so relieves his cough, that is often terrible."[5] In the fall of 1866 Mary thanked Julius for his generosity. "Ah! my precious son, may the good God reward you a hundred fold for your great generosity to your old father and Mother."[6]

The magnitude of Julius's largesse is evident in the letter William wrote to him in 1869: "Whereas I have from time to time in my pecuniary difficulties received from my son John Julius substantial aid to the amount of $25,000 or $30,000 and whereas he always generously disclaimed any desire or expectation to have it returned to him, I cannot but feel much regret that the great depreciation of my estate and my consequently impoverished condition made it out of my power to repay him that which he so liberally bestowed upon his dear Mother and myself. May the Almighty in his goodness make him experience in his children what a blessing good children are."[7]

Julius's generosity was not limited to sending cash and food. He also enlisted his sister Mary Mitchell to outfit the Charleston Pringles with a new wardrobe, for which he picked up the tab. His mother wrote:

> The children were wild with delight; such dresses, such hats, such ribbon, such veils, had not been seen in the Confederacy for four long years—hoops, too, and boots for the little naked white feet. Our judicious Mary's expenditure of your gift was entirely wise—every article was *just the article* we each wanted, and not content with taking all the trouble that the purchase must have given her, she added to it from her own poor purse, by sending presents, too—the very shawl from her own shoulders was folded and sent to me, never suspecting that I would detect it. You were very dear to know the particular things your Papa wanted most; that light, beautiful overcoat will enable him to lay aside the coarse, uncouth, striped one

> that Brewton received from the company store for soldiers and gave to him. The cloth will make a genteel sack and vest to wear with the pants Motte gave him last winter, and thus enable him to discard the dress coat, with its long, narrow shirts, that was purchased some 25 years ago. The Eau de Paris he considers a *most delicate* attention. When James told him how young and fresh [he was] looking, he said, 'I dare say, it is owing to his use of the Eau de Paris'. The girls and I like our delicate cologne much better. Then you have supplied us with delicate toilet soap, too—Confederates surely never possessed such luxuries before.[8]

Julius also reconnoitered the shops of Paris for the materials to restock Sue's garden. "I procured your garden seed, some artichoke, migonette, hearts-ease, and a great variety of pinks, carnations, anemones, ranunculus. You can plant them in the open ground; frost will not kill them," he wrote.[9]

John Julius Pringle in France, about 1880.

Despite Julius's kindness to his parents, his relationship to the rest of the family had changed by the end of the war. Whether it was his lack of apparent service to the Confederacy or the suspicion that he may have collaborated with the enemy in Louisiana, there was now a detectable coolness between Julius and his brothers and sisters. As a result, Julius and Maria seldom visited Charleston, and the Charleston family never visited them in Louisiana.

A generation later, Mary Pringle Frost's rambling and disorganized family history, *Chronicles and Reminiscences,* was published. The 1939 book gushed about their heroic ancestors and doted on William and Mary's children, save for three who had, in the author's eyes, fallen from grace: Brewton, who spent his last years in the South Carolina Lunatic Asylum; Motte, whose business failure and blunder with the C.S.S. *Sumter* had embarrassed the family; and Julius. The book did mention Julius's Mexican War wound but ignored his heroism aboard the U.S. S. *Missouri* and said nothing further about him. Maria and their children were not even named and his postwar generosity was ignored.

After the war ended, Julius developed his own variation of the planter's annual migration. He spent May through September in Europe and September through May at "The Snipery," his Louisiana hunting preserve located in the bayous of St. Mary's Parish, near the village of Glencoe.[10] From there he managed Torwood, Duncannon, and Reserve plantations, all of which he had received from his father-in-law.

Maria and John Julius Pringle in France in the 1880s.

In South Carolina, the annual migration of the rice planters coincided with the appearance and disappearance of the mosquitoes. In Louisiana, Julius's arrival and departure coincided with the annual migration of the snipe, a small shore bird which flourished there. Each fall, Julius would leave France and travel to London, where he would spend a week or two. He would then go to Liverpool, and board a luxury liner, such as the *Russia*, *Java*, *Scotia* or *Scythia*, for a deluxe passage to New York and from thence to Louisiana. The snipe season lasted from about November 1 through the middle of March.

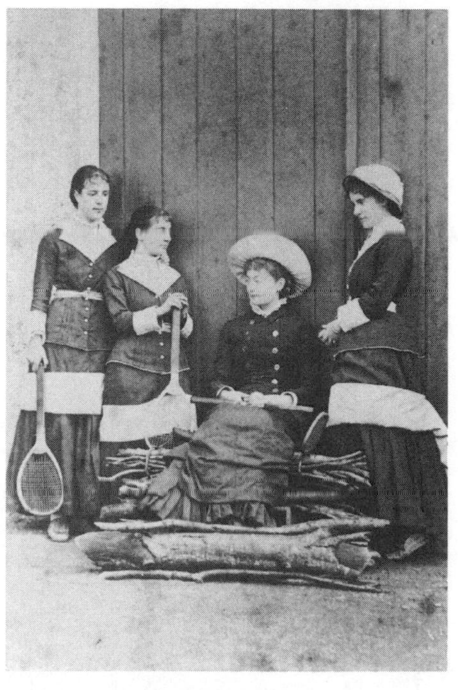

Julius and Maria's daughters in France, 1880s.

After assuring that his crops were properly planted, he packed his trunks in May and made his annual visit to the East Coast. Some years he stopped to see the family in Charleston; others he did not. When he did so, he stayed several days, then made his way back to New York and sailed back to Europe. June through late September was spent with his family in Paris, Versailles, and Biarritz, on shooting trips to England and Scotland, or to many other fashionable European destinations. He maintained contact with his friends in Newport, which he visited three times in the 1870s despite the lingering anti-Southern prejudice there.

Julius and Maria had six children: Catherine ("Cassie") Duncan, Mary Motte, Stephen Duncan, Maria Duncan ("Maizie"), Susan, and Charlotte Duncan. Only Charlotte married, and she had no children. Following steadfastly in the American tradition, Julius refused to provide dowries for his daughters.

Maria and the children traveled extensively around the continent, played tennis, attended numerous social functions and formed part of the core of Biarritz's community of expatriate Englishmen and Americans. To a daughter in Paris, Julius wrote:

I am glad to hear that Lent has put a stop to the festivities which you all seem to have indulged in so freely. [I] miss you all, particularly your Mother, who seems to have been more constant and indefatigable in her attendance at parties and balls than either you or Cassy. No wonder she is used up by the gaiety as you say she is. I can not for the life of me see what pleasure you can all take in that horrid vulgar second rate society you frequent. I think the American society in Paris is about as vulgar and nasty a thing as is possible to conceive of—a sort of 'high life below stairs.' I wish you possessed the reticence and the conservatism and the domestic resources of her Porters!!!!"[11]

In the United States, Maria and her children seldom strayed further south than New York and rarely visited Julius during his annual eight-month stay in Louisiana. In 1868 Julius's daughter Mary Motte made a visit to Charleston. Then about sixteen, she caught the attention of the French consul. "He took her out to drive, walked with her, talked with her, as he could not talk to many others. She would make appointments to meet him here when they walked on the Battery. The little flirtation gave a great zest to her visit." Miss Mary later turned the head of one of J. J. Astor's grandsons. Julius's son, Duncan Pringle made annual stops in Charleston on his way back to France each year.[12] Both Susan Pringle and her nephew, the Rev. Francis L. Frost, Jr., visited Maria and her daughters in France.

Julius noted in his shooting journals that he lived "very much alone" at The Snipery.[13] He enjoyed the life of a bachelor sportsman and planter and was quite content to spend two thirds of each year—including virtually every Christmas—with his dogs, his English and American shooting cronies and an occasional visiting relative or friend. The only record of his family visiting The Snipery came in 1880, when his daughter, Maria ("Maisie") spent the winter, and other winters when his son, Duncan, came to visit and shoot with him.[14] The Charleston Pringles were conspicuously absent.

Julius and his servants at The Snipery, late 1870s

Although Julius enjoyed hunting big game and shooting other birds, it was snipe shooting, which he called, "the trout fishing of shooting," which captivated him.[15] Snipe shooting was an established sport among the planters of South Carolina as well as Louisiana. On December 1, 1867, Julius established The Snipery at Camperdown, his father-in-law's plantation on Bayou Teche in St. Mary's Parish, Louisiana. In 1871 he moved the headquarters of The Snipery to neighboring Oaklawn plantation, and devoted the rest of his life primarily to shooting.

The accommodations at The Snipery included a large and comfortable house, stables for about six horses, kennels for three or four Gordon, English and Irish setters and pointers, barns for his wagons and quarters for about a dozen servants and their families. His hunting accessories included a large collection of shotguns, including his favorite, a twelve-gauge Purdy Hammerless Choke, from the famous gunsmiths in London; a four-wheeled dog cart from New York and a shooting wagon, to carry his guns, cartridges, and game. His

Julius, his gun bearer, and dog at The Snipery, late 1880s.

field staff consisted of a servant to drive the wagon when he was shooting, another to carry spare cartridges and the birds, and several young servants. The latter served as game beaters, who helped flush the birds from the ground, carried additional cartridges, and retrieved his game.[16]

As game birds go, snipe are among the hardest targets to hit. Duncan C. Heyward wrote, "On a cold day, one could shoot snipe for hours, for when they were started up, they would circle around the field, fly high for a while, and returning light a short distance from where they had been flushed. In the bogs they could be walked up in rapid succession, first zigzagging as they uttered a little cry, then flying straight away, presenting a most inviting mark if the hunter waited until they did so."[17]

On December 2, 1867, Julius went for his first day of shooting at the Snipery, and on December 4 he recorded his first bag of over 100 snipe. He kept meticulous records of each day's hunt in a series of hand-tooled, leather-bound logs. Between 1867 and 1888, Julius spent about one day in three shooting snipe. The other days were devoted to hunting other species of birds, managing his plantations, and taking trips to New Orleans.

There were no game regulations or bag limits in Julius's time, and a man's skill was measured by the size of his daily kill. "The birds being such migrants," he wrote, "and only in the country for a short time, I had no mercy on them, and killed all I could, for a snipe once missed might never be seen again."[18] Julius was renowned for his strong constitution, which enabled him to go afield in fair weather or foul, from dawn to dusk, and for his exceedingly keen vision, which made him a crack shot. Accordingly, his bird kills were enormous.

Over the twenty years for which he kept his records, Julius spent an average of 35 days each season shooting snipe, killing an average of 110 birds a day. On November 12, 1870, he recorded that "this morning, hearing from Victorin, the black butcher of Cypre-Mort [part of The Snipery], that there were some snipe near his house, I drove there and began to shoot at 10:30, and finished at 1:55 with 123 snipe."[19] His peak day was December 11, 1877, when he killed 366 snipe.[20]

In 1877 Julius wrote, "The December shooting was the best I have ever had, I having killed 1943 snipe in 7 consecutive shooting-days, and 2154 in the month of December in 9 days shooting. I fear the shooting will not continue much longer so good as it has been heretofore, for much of the land, old fields, etc., over which I have been shooting, having been thrown out of cultivation during the war and left uncultivated and unenclosed for some years after, are now being reclaimed, fenced, drained, and put in good cultivation."[21] In the twenty shooting seasons between 1866 and 1887, Julius shot 78,602 snipe and 3,499 other birds, for a total personal kill of 82,101, not counting the thousands shot by his hunting companions. Between 1887 and 1899, he still hunted occasionally, adding another 9,515 snipe and 727 other birds to his bag.

He also noted shooting woodcock, partridge, wild ducks, teal, rail, bitterns, curlew, plover and a variety of hawks. "I have killed a great many hawks of different varieties on these grounds, only some of which I have enumerated," he wrote. "I always kill them when I can, for they are very destructive to game and poultry."[22] Julius also hunted deer, bear, alligators, otters, terrapins and an occasional hare, raccoon, opossum, mink, and snake. He continued his annual trips to Louisiana through 1896, when the entries in his game books end.

Although Julius spent only a few days in New York twice a year, his dining habits were legendary. In an age when conspicuous consumption was fashionable, Cholly Knickerbocker, the *New York Journal-American* society columnist, wrote of him:

> Why my friend Pringle can eat and drink more than any dozen of them [younger men]. Pringle is a seven-bottle man. He drinks seven bottles of burgundy with every dinner the Lord lets him swallow, and then he sometimes feels as though he had only got the wire edge off his thirst. And eat! Well, now, Pringle knows how to eat. When he's at home on his Southern plantation he lives like a king. He's very fond of bouillon; and how do you think he prepares it? He has it made of snipe that he shoots himself, and he allows twenty-six snipe to every cup of bouillon! If it's any weaker than that he won't eat it!
>
> If Pringle has ordinary company; that is, casual callers of the neighborhood, he adds six snipe to his bouillon for each guest. But if the company is extraordinary—some important guest from New York, for instance—he uses twelve snipe for each additional cup of bouillon!
>
> Where does he get the snipe? He bags 'em, sir; he bags 'em himself. Why Pringle is one of the best

"A Seven-Bottle Man" from the New York Journal-American

> wing-shots in the country. He walks twenty miles every day of his life, and his eye is never so clear and his nerve never so steady as when he has his seven bottles under his belt. My opinion of a Waldorf cafe dude is never so contemp-tuous as when Pringle comes to town.[23]

His lavish lifestyle notwithstanding, Julius stayed fit and slender his entire life. The writings of Horace Fletcher, a philosophical New Orleans nutritionist, told how. After eating an enormous meal at Julius's home, Fletcher asked the "renowned gourmet" how he stayed so slim. "By chewing my food 32 times," Julius replied, because that prevented overeating. Later Fletcher would credit the "epicuriean philosopher" with one of the key concepts he made famous in his 1895 book, *Menticulture, or the A-B-C of True Living*.[24]

By 1888 the snipe population of Lower Louisiana was in severe decline. Julius attributed the calamity to the drainage and reclamation of farmlands, and to the increasing availability to the masses of cheap, breech-loading shotguns. These, he estimated, were seven or eight times as efficient as the muzzle-loaders previously available. Julius noted, "I continued the shooting in spite of the gradual destruction of the snipe grounds and the decrease in the number of birds. And though the birds were much less abundant than in previous years, and I made no more big bags, there were enough of them to afford fairly good sport, and I enjoyed shooting to the last."[25]

In 1898 and 1899 Julius sold his plantations and moved back to France, where he spent the last two years of his life. In 1899 he published his shooting memoirs in a 324-page illustrated book entitled *Twenty Years' Snipe-Shooting*. He died at Biarritz in 1901 and was buried in Sabaou Cemetery. He devised all his property to his wife, Maria, providing small annuities for his sister Susan and a black servant, Dolly. Maria survived him by seven years.

Four of Julius's children, Duncan, Catherine, Susan, and Mary, became legends of Biarritz. They involved themselves deeply in the welfare of the community during the First World War. According to Susan Pringle Frost, who corresponded with them regularly, the daughters drove their large black automobiles to Verdun to help evacuate wounded soldiers.[26] The sisters also supported a hospital in Biarritz, for which Mary Pringle, as the representative of the family, was awarded the Cross of the Legion of Honor in diamonds.[27] In Charleston, the *News & Courier* reported:

> The decoration was awarded in recognition of the generosity of her sisters, her brother and herself in giving towards the relief of war sufferers in the republic." The French newspaper article spoke of Mary as a "noble and generous American." The writer, the Deputy Mayor of Bayonne, France, wrote that Duncan Pringle, "who during the war was deeply impressed by the sufferings of France through her innumerable sacrifices and the consequent reparations, confessed to me his desire to give a certain sum to the civil hospital of Bayonne, the chief establishment of the region which could care for so much physical suffering and so much human misery. He then gave the sum of 500,000 francs, which at the time had the value of the franc in gold. . . . His sisters have spent their lives in caring for the unfortunate," he wrote. "With tenderness of heart they combine far-seeing judgment. Biarritz, Anglet, Bayonne, Ville Franche, our entire region has benefited through their charitable initiative.[28]

Stephen Duncan Pringle died in 1917. Catherine Pringle died in 1923 and Maria in 1940. Motte Alston Hamilton, a first cousin engaged in the cotton business abroad, was visiting the two surviving Pringle sisters when the Wehrmacht occupied Biarritz during World War II. He offered them assistance in returning to the United States, but they declined, feeling themselves more closely tied to France than to America. The red-headed German colonel he talked to was very polite and correct, and assured him that the women would not be molested. Susan died in 1942 during the German occupation of Biarritz, and Mary died in 1945. Because of their reputations for selflessness, the two spinsters and their home were never harassed by the Nazi troops.[29]

The Pringles in the Golden West

It was only when the war began and I was cut off from direct communication with home, and contemplated leaving California to join you and for that purpose desired to 'make haste to be rich' that my gambling began.

—Edward Pringle to his mother, 1868

Edward, the would-be pathfinder for the destitute Pringle family, was partially successful in his bid to get the family to abandon the rice coast. His brother James moved to San Francisco and joined his law firm in the spring of 1866. Their sister Susan came to live with them from February 1868 through April 1869.

In the summer of 1865 when he was twenty-two, James set off to find work in New York. He left with only a few coins in his pocket, a small quantity of silver plate and a few pieces of old jewelry to sell and live off until he found work. "I cannot say that I approve of his being there," Mary wrote, "but I do not feel that I have a right to object to his praiseworthy enterprise. . . . This is what we subjugated Confederates will all have to do."[1]

The New York venture did not prove successful. In the spring of 1866, James set his sights on the Golden West. He moved San Francisco and started work as Edward's law clerk. Soon he was courting Coralie, the strong-willed daughter of Samuel L. Butterworth, another San Francisco

James Reid Pringle.
1866 copy of an earlier image.

lawyer. In November 1868 Mary wrote to Edward, "I do hope James will soon get married. Tell him as soon as he is married to take the control of his own wife, and not let Mother Butterworth get the upper hand of his wife. I am a little uncertain about Cora. James must firmly and gently teach her to bend her will to his, else she will get the upper hand, and I can't bear a wife to 'hack' her husband as Brother says. I do hope it will be a happy marriage, but unless Cora looks up to James, I fear they will sometimes jar."[2]

Mary's worries proved unfounded. James and Cora were married in San Francisco on December 15, 1868. They soon had a baby boy, Henry Butterworth Pringle, [and another child]. Then, on May 8, 1871, at four o'clock in the afternoon, an urgent telegram arrived at the Miles Brewton House, notifying the family that James was seriously ill, declining rapidly, and was being put aboard ship for Charleston that day.[3] Cora and her parents were accompanying him.

A month later, James still lay ill in the Breevort Hotel in New York, with Cora, their son, and the Butterworths at his side. Frank Frost lamented to his mother:

> We are now suffering great anxiety of mind from the very sad news that we get of James P[ringle]'s hopelessly ill condition in N.Y. This disturbs us a great deal, but more than this does it distress us to think how terrible will be the blow to his old parents, now weighed down with the woes and troubles of this life. I fear that they will never survive this great sorrow. James is their favorite child, the pet and pride of their old age, and made doubly dear by

> his noble traits and development of mind and body, and by his natural association in their mind with Charles, whose mourning is ever fresh in their minds. The fatigue and discomfort of the journey will of itself wear them greatly, and I am afraid that they will be overcome by it. They surely have been sadly stricken in their old age.[4]

William, Mary, and Susan immediately traveled to New York. A letter from Susan made it clear that the New York physicians had no idea what was ailing James. She wrote, "One thing we all feel certain of, *the brain* was *not* the beginning, but the trouble of the brain was the *result* of some other disease. Just as in Charles' case, delirium was the effect of that congestive fever.[5] Disease was marked on every feature, you never would have known him, his complexion had become so strangely dark. He was so very thin. Dr. Barker's idea was, it was an affection of the kidneys. Some San Francisco Dr. though the liver caused it—but I don't believe any of them knew."[6]

James died that same day, and his body was embalmed for its final shipboard journey to Charleston. Cora was inconsolable, and repeatedly murmured, "Oh God, let me die." Sue wrote, "he will be carried home and laid among us there. Cora said she would be glad to have him there if we promise that a place beside him should be reserved for her and her children. How strange and sweet after the five long years of separation he should be brought to die in the arms of the Mother and Father he yearned so to see."[7] On June 14, 1871, James was laid out at the Miles Brewton House. The courageous, former Confederate artilleryman was interred in St. Michael's churchyard the next day.

Cora, now a young widow with one child and another on the way, was taken back to the bosom of her family, who embarked upon a two-year visit to Europe. There they were entertained by Julius and Maria and met the young French Pringle girls. Mary reported to Mary Mitchell, "Cora says, Cassie is very ladylike and refined and gentle. All of the girls made a great impression upon Mrs. Butterworth and Cora.

They say they 'never saw such well brought up children.' Mrs. Butterworth was charmed with them. Cora says Maria and Charlotte are the handsomest; Susie, the least pretty. Maria made a pleasant impression, as she always does."[8]

The Butterworths moved to Paris for the winter, where James' son, James Reid Pringle, was born just before Christmas 1871. Cora and the two boys returned to California in the late spring of 1872, where she reared her small family and remained in close touch with the Charleston Pringles for the rest of her life. In her 1917 will, Susan noted that Cora's kindness and financial support enabled the Charleston Pringles to maintain their old home.

The responsibilities of Edward's legal practice and his resolution to recoup the family funds he had lost kept him hard at work after the war. Despite recurring bouts of homesickness, Edward spent the rest of his life in California. With dogged determination, he and his Harvard classmates, John B. Felton and Adolphus C. Whitcomb, snared every case they could and worked late into the nights to make their firm a success. Although they had lost the José Limantour case, their diligence had earned them the respect of their colleagues and brought them considerable publicity. By the end of the 1870s Edward's law firm was one of the most respected in the state.

Armed with extensive information and warm invitations from Edward, William Alston Hayne, his wife, Margaretta Stiles, and their seven children emigrated to California in 1867. Alston Hayne[9] was a son of Gov. Robert Y. Hayne and a nephew of Col. Arthur P. Hayne, who was then living with William and Mary at the Miles Brewton House. Hayne was very close to the Pringles and the Alstons, and named three of his children after them. The Hayne family prospered in California and remained in intimate contact with the Pringles there. Alston Hayne's son, Robert Y. Hayne, was educated in the public schools of San Francisco, was admitted to the bar in 1874 and practiced law with Edward's firm until 1880. He was elected a judge in 1880, authored a book on trial law and was appointed a Commissioner of the California Supreme Court in 1887.[10] The two jurists remained fast friends until Edward's death.

Edward may have learned the fine points of the law in stuffy Charleston, but in California, his adventurous spirit led him to take on any kind of legal work which seemed potentially profitable. In May 1867 Edward accepted the job of surveying the 250,000-acre Najalayequa Ranch, near Santa Barbara. For his work, he was to receive ten per cent of the land. His surveying adventures read like a Zane Grey novel.

> Nearly the whole of the immense tract consists of barren and almost impassable mountains, most of it worse than worthless. On one day I was for twelve hours in the saddle and only succeeded in getting half way across the narrowest part of the ranch and with difficulty back again to avoid sleeping in the mountains. The country was so dreary that no birds or beasts seem to live in it. We saw the tracks of three or four grizzly bears but almost no other signs of life. . . . I made the excursion with a famous guide who had starved in the Rocky Mountains with Fremont and has traveled over the whole continent, and he said he had seldom seen a worse country than my domain. The owners have an idea that the mountains and the fabulous amounts of gold, silver and quicksilver,[11] but I would not give them a sou[12] for the greater part of their mineral mountains. What I look to give value one of these days to my fee is the portions of good arable land which adjoin the Town of Santa Barbara. . . . On the hill side adjoining the town is some valuable land and after a long fight my fee will I hope be productive of some real value. . . . I eat fresh olives and olive oil, mulberries, figs and pomegranates that reminded me of home, drank the fresh wines of the place which I think are the best of American wines, and saw oranges, lemons, almonds and English walnuts and even our old familiar persimmons, which I felt like kneeling to salute. And in my mountains near the town is a hot sulphur spring so delicious that I am sure it will one

day be the nucleus of a great watering place. . . . If Alston Hayne could be satisfied with so quiet a place to live in I am sure he could build up a sure fortune there.[13]

The survey of it has been a terrific job—for I find that it is twenty-two miles long, and twenty miles wide, and contains two ranges of mountains about 4,000 feet high. Of course the greater part of it is valueless: except for the minerals it may contain. But within the mountains are occasionally beautiful spots of valuable land and in its whole length it surrounds the town of Santa Barbara and derives value from that circumstance. Its location and survey involved many points of law and hence I had to go with the surveyor all over the ranch or at least as much over it as we could manage to go. I was nearly three weeks at it and have had some very rough times. It took us six days to ride to the different points necessary to make a preliminary reconnaissance. During the trip you would hardly have recognized me. The surveyor and I started with two guides, all mounted on tough mountain horses, with an attendant jackass carrying our blankets, coffee, bacon, crackers, and frying pan. We went to places in the mountains that certainly no man and no animal but a grizzly bear had ever been to before, and when we camped at night we were hungry enough to enjoy a very rude article of coffee and very fat bacon. My first night on the mountains was a little hard, but the next night and thereafter I was tired enough to sleep well with nothing but a blanket between me and the ground, and my coat for a pillow. The ground was hard, I confess, and *grew much harder* towards morning, but the sky was co clear over head and the air so pure and fresh that a night in camp has really it's luxurious side.

Occasionally high up in the mountains the soil was so rich that we could camp in a field of wild oats and make a soft bed as dainty as a spring mattress. These fields of wild oats were very picturesque, high up in the mountains, yellow as gold waving in the sunlight, and all unbroken except by lanes crossing them here and there where the grizzlys had been passing. Fortunately we saw no grizzlys though their tracks were all around us and in one place we saw where one fellow had just been climbing a honey tree and trying to poke his paw in after the honey. The tree was all marked with his claws and the bark lying at the foot.[14]

While surveying the ranch, Edward found two other ranches for sale. He purchased both for $5,000, sold one to Alston Hayne for $3,000 and kept the other, consisting of ninety-one acres with a good house. He used his good fortune to again plead with the family to join him.

> Whilst I hope that, by the aid of great Democratic victories, you will all be saved from the absolute necessity of emigration, I am always hoping also that I may be able to offer at least to you and Mama and Susan the opportunity for a short repose from the painful surroundings of negro glorification. If I can have you here long enough to let you use your judgment as to the future prospects of California we should all be able to discuss more satisfactorily what should be the 'necessity point' for a general emigration from South Carolina. We must be guided somewhat by Alston Hayne and Margaretta. She is a hero; and on better acquaintance with him I find him full of energy and with apparently great knowledge of farming. I have great hopes of his success."[15]

As enthused as he was about the farming prospects at Santa Barbara, his mother remained cautious. "I have just been reading a charming letter from our good Margaretta [Hayne] to her Aunts. I wish you could read it. The Santa Barbara homestead makes me tremble, so far away in the interior, and so beyond the conventionalities of civilized life. How brave our dear Margaretta is; how full of faith and trust; how unselfish; duty is her pleasure. May God's providence guide Alston's plans."[16]

A week later, Mary wrote to Susan, then visiting Edgewood, "Edward's account of his Santa Barbara expedition makes me shudder from the mere thought that his precious life had been placed in such peril. All praise be to God, that he was preserved. Always thinking of us, I believe he is always working for us, though so many cruelly believe that he has done us wrong. The wrong has only come through his too great haste to advance our fortunes. His Mother will always trust him, and I earnestly trust that God in His own good time will let his whole conduct appear in its true purity, as I am confident it has only been over-shadowed by misfortunes."[17]

Edward was stung by the implication that he had covered up his loss of the family funds. During his 1860 visit to Charleston, he told his mother that he had not mentioned his pre-war losses because he had felt confident that he could recover them before the family become aware of them.

> It was only when the war began and I was cut off from direct communication with home, and contemplated leaving California to join you and for that purpose desired to 'make haste to be rich' that my gambling began. . . . Let them find all fault with me for gambling (though I feel that I was not an ordinary gambler)—but I think you all find too much fault with my investments when you see that it really has only been since the close of the war and that it has only been because I hoped to repair my losses without letting you feel them. Were I to live the past over again I should not of course be as imprudent and rash as I have been but if I found myself at the end of the war in the same situation, I should still desire to keep from you all a knowledge of losses, from the hope of repairing them.[18]

In addition to his closest friends, Edward also found his bride in San Francisco's legal community. In 1868 he married Cornelia Letitia Johnson, the third daughter of Sidney L. Johnson, a distinguished member of the San Francisco bar. They shared a close and loving life together and reared a family of five sons and two daughters.

On March 18, 1868, Edward told his father that he resented the implication that his upcoming marriage might be better avoided and that marriage might make it harder for him to recoup his losses. He felt that the family's emigration to "Runnimede," as he called his Santa Barbara ranch, would be practical. "What are your calculations for the future of South Carolina?" he asked.

> I have been thinking over your labor question very much and I can't see that even a political relief to the South would give you any social or economical relief. Even when the negroes consent to make labor contracts, they seem to show very little of the results of incentive to labor. And that it seems to me, will always be the case where the planter is obliged to furnish them by way of advance with food, clothing and lodging. This has the double disadvantage of taking from them the *daily incentive* to labor which poverty ordinarily gives, and of *diminishing constantly* the interest which they have in the crop. The present system seems to me to be the worst of all systems of labor, especially as applied to a race of newly liberated. But Frost's ill success seems to be argument enough. Is there any hope in the future? Has there been any day, since the closing of the war, when property was not lower and hope fainter than the day before? And take hope away from any existence, and you double all its evils and lessen all its good. Hope may be often a fool's Paradise—but the absence of it is even a wise man's Hell.[19]

Edward's financial reverses turned tide in 1869, when he sold his ranch, "Runnimede," to a homestead association for a reported $100,000. "These associations are organized to enable clerks, mechanics, laborers and salaried persons who have no capital and only monthly salaries to buy land by paying on account a small sum, say $8 or $10 per month," he explained.

> An owner of a tract of land capable of being subdivided into say 500 small lots makes a contract to sell to an association at a price generally so large that he can afford to wait for his money for 2, 3 or 4 years, receiving it in small monthly payments without interest. The association with 500 shares at $10 each per month will receive $5,000 per month which it pays over on account of the purchasers to the owners of the land. And when the whole of the

> purchase money is made by these small installments the owner makes his deed to the association which then distributes the 500 lots among its 500 shareholders, either by lot or at an auction among themselves, bidding for the choice. In this way, laboring men, women and clerks are induced to economize and by putting aside something every month from their wages, they are able to buy lots which they would otherwise never have capital enough to pay for.[20]

While Edward eventually recouped his speculation and gambling losses, his slow success was dwarfed by the financial achievements of his original two law partners. In the post-Limantour years, John Felton's fees were said to be "enormous." His 1877 obituary stated that his California legal income over the past twenty years was nearly one million dollars. Another source claimed that he had received a one million dollar fee for a single case.[21] Adolphus Whitcomb outstripped both of his original partners. He arrived in California in 1850, made a fortune in real estate, and retired in 1867 at the age of forty. He married after moving to Paris and spent the rest of his life enjoying his wealth. When he died in 1888, his widow and two children were left to manage his $30 milllion estate.[22]

In 1873 Edward and Cornelia moved their home across the bay from San Francisco to Oakland, where they spent the rest of their lives and reared their children. The firm of Pringle & Felton became Whitcomb, Pringle & Felton, and, for a time, Pringle & Hayne. Edward's partnership with Robert Y. Hayne lasted until Hayne was appointed a California Supreme Court commissioner. Edward's sons, Edward and William Bull, also joined his firm and practiced law in San Francisco, and William B. Pringle became active in the civic affairs of Oakland.

In the spring of 1899, when Edward was a hale and hearty seventy-three years old, he was also appointed a commissioner of the California Supreme Court. Like his great-great-uncle, Miles Brewton, Edward did not live long enough to shoulder his new responsibilities. Two months after his appointment, he contracted typhoid fever. He died at his home in East Oakland, survived by his wife and all seven children. A colleague wrote, "In the death of Mr. Pringle our profession has lost one of its most distinguished members, the State an able and upright judge, and society one of its most interesting and useful members. The vacant place in the hearts and affections of his family can never be filled."[23]

Edward's widow Cornelia kept in close touch with the Charleston Pringles until her death in 1941. Her heirs donated Edward's personal and professional papers to the University of California-Berkeley, where they became known as the Edward J. Pringle Family Collection.

CHAPTER FIFTEEN

Of Rice and Ruin

Rice planting, which for years gave me the exhilaraion of making good income myself, is a thing of the past now—the banks and trunks have been washed away, and there is no money to replace them. —"Patience Pennington" (Mrs. Elizaeth Waites Allston Pringle), about 1900.

Grim is the only word which adequately describes the last ten years of William and Mary's lives. The war and its aftermath had taken a terrible toll on their family and fortune. Their granddaughter Hesse had died of a brain inflammation while in their care. Charles had succumbed to typhoid fever. Robert had been killed in action. Brewton had been driven insane. James died of a brain fever. Edward had lost much of their fortune in California. Motte lived on under the cloud from the loss of the C.S.S. *Sumter,* and some family members suspected Julius of treason.

During the war they had been forced to sell Beneventum and Runimede, their beloved country seat, which the Union Army later burned. Freedman burned the big house at Richfield in 1866, and the Pringles were forced to sell the plantation itself in 1871. Although they still had Susan, Alston, and his children to care for them, William and Mary had seen all their dreams snuffed out. It was no wonder that Mary was in a state of profound depression toward the end of her life and that William appeared to be drinking heavily.

They spent the last ten years of their lives in quiet anticipation of the inevitable.

William Bull Pringle died of pneumonia on Tuesday morning, December 13, 1881, at the Miles Brewton House, halfway through his eighty-second year. On the calendar hanging near his bedside, Mary wrote, "Blessed are the dead which die in the Lord from henceforth; yea, saith the Spirit, that they may rest from their labors, and their works do follow them. Amen and Amen."[1] He was buried in St. Michael's churchyard.[2] Worth half a million dollars in the 1850s, William's estate was valued at $89.00 when it was finally probated in 1895.

William Bull Pringle in the late 1870s.

Mary chose the drawing room as her bed chamber for her last years. There, on Saturday morning, October 4, 1884, she died. The death certificate listed the primary cause of death as "senile bronchitis" and the secondary cause as "gradual exhaustion." She was in her eighty-second year.[3] Her funeral was held in St. Michael's church, and she was buried in the churchyard next to her husband, children, and other relatives.

From Paris, Julius wrote to Sue, "Your letter of the 5th gave me news of the death of our dear old mother, and though it was not unexpected, when the announcement did come my grief was none the less. You are the one who will feel her loss the most, but it must be a satisfaction to you to remember how devoted and tenderly you alleviated her

The last known likeness of Mary Pringle, about 1880.

suffering of her feeble old age. . . . I am sorry I was not with you all to follow her to her grave as I did my dear old father."[4]

Mary Mitchell wrote to Sue, "I am so grateful that so many of my children have had the privilege of having seen their darling grandmother and the venerable old family mansion. We love to talk of her gentleness, her earnest faith and trust in God, her charity, her sound judgment and her loveliness in person as well as character. A modest mother and a true friend that rich and poor honored and revered. God help us do as she did and may her holy spirit and loving influence prove a bond of love and affection to the six that survive her."[5]

In her 1876 will, Mary had specified who would receive the most precious of her possessions. Although the depth of her love for William was never returned in full measure, her devotion never faltered. "I make no mention of my beloved husband," she wrote, "because all that I have is his, as is my whole heart, and no distribution of my worldly possessions is to be made without his approbation and consent as long as he lives. . . . I make this distribution merely as a suggestion to him as to what I consider right and would wish done." Mary left to her "faithful servant and friend," Cretia Stuart, "the large black woolen shawl and one of my black dresses and any other article from my wardrobe that my daughters do not require for themselves or for my daughters Emma and Ella." To Cretia and Betsy she also left one dress apiece, and to Cretia she bequeathed the sum of one hundred dollars.[6]

However, Cretia predeceased Mary. She remained in the employ of the Pringle family until she died of pneumonia in 1879, at the age of seventy-two. She was buried next to her husband.

Hannah, Cretia's daughter, was taught hair-dressing.[7] Cretia's daughter Amey became Edward's and Susan's nurse. Amey's first husband, Davis, was a fisherman in Charleston' "mosquito fleet," a flotilla of small, canvas-powered fishing boats owned by black fishermen. The daring and skillful pilots provided Charleston with seafood until the Second World War. Davis drowned in a squall off South Island. Amey's second husband was Caesar, a hunter, who supplied game and fish for the family. He also caned chairs and made baskets.[8] Their daughter, Mary, who married Caesar Chisolm, was born a slave in September 1851 and died a free woman in November 1922.[9] She was with Susan in the last years of Susan's life.

Mary Chisolm and her son Joseph

Alston Pringle's law library appears to have survived the burning of Columbia, where it had been transported for safety when Charleston was evacuated. When the war ended, he returned to his position as Recorder of the city court and remained in office until his death. He resided in the Judge Robert Pringle house at 70 Tradd Street and was driven to work every day by Robert Chisolm, his coachman. Robert later served as the butler at the Miles Brewton House after Alston moved there.

Alston's wife, Emma, died in 1879. In 1886 he sold the

Judge Robert Pringle house at 70 Tradd Street and moved into the Miles Brewton House with his sister Susan. He suffered from a respiratory condition which left him wheezing for the last twenty years of his life. At the age of seventy-two he died in the room in which he was born, the place where he had often expressed the wish to die.[10] He was buried in St. Michael's churchyard.

Robert Chisolm

Motte had sent Gabriella and their children to Columbia during the latter half of the war. In the summer of 1865 he wrote to an aunt, "I am about making all the arrangements I can to bring Ella to town, altho I do not know how I can feed the family. But I think it important to have the family here as their occupying the house may be the means of saving it from the clutches of the Freedman's Bureau.[11]

After the war, Motte found himself with a family consisting of "five helpless girls and one uneducated little boy. His two elder boys are educated and ready and able to work," Mary wrote. At the time, she thought that Ella was not up to coping with the challenges at hand, but she soon changed her mind when she saw how Ella cared for her son.[12]

Despite impaired health, Motte decided to take up planting after the war. Ella was his ministering angel, a role which Mary described in an 1869 letter to Susan. "Motte is better. Ella is devoted to him. I sit with him daily that Ella may take a walk. When she returns they kiss and caress each other so tenderly that I tell them only my strong maternal devotion can influence me to place myself in the most trying position of seeing how much he prefers her to me."[13] Motte and Ella resided at 13 Legaré Street. In the 1880s he earned a small amount of extra money by serving as the consul for the Republic of Argentina.[14] In 1886, at the age of fifty-nine, Motte died and was buried in St. Michael's churchyard. Ella died in 1914, at the age of eighty-six.

Susan was fifty-five years old and unmarried when her mother died. Susan resided in the family mansion until her own death in 1917. Alston moved into the house just before Charleston's devastating earthquake, which occurred on August 31, 1886, at 9:51 P.M. Susan was home at the time, and wrote the following account to her cousins:

> Brother had been quite sick that day, as he has been for some weeks, and had gone to bed early. Soon after 9 I told him good night, and went to prepare for bed myself. I was standing by the dressing table with a book open before me, and a lamp side of it when that awful thing began.
>
> The huge brick building rocked and swayed and tottered like a house of cards about falling to pieces. It is impossible to make you understand the sensation, the groans of the convulsive heaving earth, the falling of buildings and furniture, the screams of the people, the awful mysterious power that suddenly seemed let loose to rend and tear the solid buildings, make a photograph on my mind I shudder to recall.
>
> I could hardly stand, but as soon as possible I flew to Brother's room. One door could not be opened, and I had to go through the drawing room where the chandelier was literally flying about in the ceiling. It was awful, but I got at last to Brother, and found him sitting up in bed while the heavy bookcases had fallen and almost imprisoned him. We never thought of escaping but just stood there together.
>
> When the other shock came, Motte rushed around to see us pretty soon, and then when all was quiet we dressed and came down stairs, securing our money and papers

on our persons, and we took chairs and sat by the garden door, meaning, if necessary, to escape thro' them. I have always heard that in an earthquake the best plan was to stay in the house, and I am quite sure it is. Brother was too sick to go out in the night air and too feeble. He wanted me to go, but of course I would not leave him, as I said if he were to be killed, I should quite as well be killed too. So there we sat thro' repeated shocks, waiting for the morning, and when at last through the weary hours the morning came at last, what sights met our eyes— Charleston in ruins!

Yes it is literally in ruins. This dear old sacred home (I am so glad you care for it) has escaped wonderfully. The chimneys fell and the roof is much injured, great damage, of course, but nothing compared to many others. The walls are not cracked, the foundation and lower storeys stood like a rock. The yard buildings mostly in ruins, but the old kitchen, like the house, has stood it well.

On Wednesday morning, Brother found poor old Aunt Emma and her children wandering on the battery and brought them here which the poor old lady seemed to think the only safe spot in town. I as you may suppose am only thankful to shelter them. She had a wonderful escape. Was In bed in the 3rd story, and Joe, Charles, and Susie on the 2nd piazza when it began. They flew upstairs, the stairs which were rocking and swaying so that Susie fell twice. Their beautiful house is also lately in ruins, and I do think they bear it beautifully.

They go home every morning and stay down stairs, while they try to gather up their things and try and arrange matters, but the whole house is unsafe like all the battery houses. Joe is searching all over the city for a small wooden house for his mother and sister but there are really not enough houses to shelter the people, many of whom live in tents. The Smith's house is a ruin. Aunt Emma would at once take possession of the lower story here, and for a year at least live with me, but you know Mrs. Stewart has rented that until the 9th Octr. Motte's house is very much injured, but they can occupy a few rooms.

It is indeed an awful condition of affairs, but I feel I

> have so much to be thankful for, I only try to trust more truly in the good God who has helped us so wonderfully. I do believe if I had been alone in the house as last summer, I must have died, and every hour I thank God I was not persuaded to go to Mary's but staid at home with very poor suffering brother. I don't believe in running away from one's duty. Our friends have been very sympathetic and my good guardian angel Cora at once telegraphed to know if we needed funds. We have had a great many shocks since, but I think they are diminishing now and hardly [make] me nervous. But for several nights we sat up in chairs in the stone [illegible] by the garden door, and although for two nights we have some of us slept in our beds up stairs, every body feels jaded and badly and nervous.
>
> Sitting up watching for earth quakes is harrowing to flesh and spirit. As you must excuse my scrawl. I am not sure you can read it. I have so many letters to write and I am so tired.[15]

During the 1880s and 1890s, a number of relatives came to live with Susan and care for her. A cousin, James Reid Pringle and his aunt, Miss Rosa Pringle, resided on the first floor for a while. Later, her nephew, William Alston Pringle and his wife, Minnie occupied the first floor. Susan also had the assistance of her maid, Mary Chisolm, a granddaughter of Cretia and Scipio Stewart. Financial assistance was provided by Julius and Maria in France; by Cora Butterworth in California, who sent the interest from James Pringle's insurance; and by the children of Mary and Donald Mitchell.[16]

By a provision of her mother's will, Susan had a one-third interest in the Miles Brewton House and the right to live their for the remainder of her life. The remaining two-thirds ownership was to be divided equally between Alston, Mary Mitchell, Rebecca Frost, or their surviving daughters.

Mary Mitchell lived at Edgewood outside of New Haven with her husband, enjoying their country home until her death in 1901 as the age of seventy. In retirement Donald Mitchell devoted himself to the outdoor life. "His garden and his trees form his pleasure ground," a reporter wrote. "In summer, the garden attracts him. In winter wood-chopping in the forest is his pastime. He is reserved, and does not care for society."[17] Donald survived Mary by seven years. A library near New Haven was named in his honor.

After abandoning rice planting in 1876, Frank Frost moved into the Miles Brewton House with Rebecca and their children. He went into the phosphate business and spent 1878 and 1879 on the road, making sales calls for the Stono Phosphate Company. His own venture, the Ashley Phosphate Company, failed a few years later, leaving the sixty-year-old physician dependent on the income earned by their three hard-working daughters. Their two sons, Frank Jr. and William, were in college at the time.

Their daughters never married and became known as "the Misses Frost." Rebecca and Mary Frost taught school; Susan Pringle Frost became a court reporter and stenographer for the United States District Court and later went into real estate. "To our father it was a distress, and something of a mortification that he could no longer be the main stay of his family," wrote Sue Frost. "He often quoted

The Misses Frost: Rebecca, Mary, and Susan

The Frost family at their summer home in Saluda, N.C.

St. Paul, saying 'a man was no good who could not support his family. We girls turned over our earnings to him in order that he might still feel the dignity as head of the family."[18]

The family later moved to a house on Savage Street, and then to Logan Street. In 1884 they purchased a house in Saluda, North Carolina, which they enjoyed every summer. Rebecca Frost died there of cancer in 1905, at the age of sixty-six. Frank died of pneumonia at their Logan street home in 1912, at the age of seventy-five.

At Susan Pringle's death, the ownership of the Miles-Brewton House stood as follows:

Susan Pringle's one-third interest was held by her nephew, James Reid Pringle. William Alston Pringle's two-ninths share was held by his daughter Mary P. Rhett. Mary Pringle Mitchell's two-ninths share was shared between her daughters Mary M. Ryerson, Elizabeth W. Mitchell, Susan M. Hoppin, Hesse A. Mitchell, Rebecca M. Hart and Harriet W. Mitchell. Rebecca Pringle Frost's two-ninths share was held by her three unmarried daughters, Mary Pringle Frost, Susan Pringle Frost, and Rebecca Pringle Frost.

At the request of several heirs, the property was appraised. An architect and two prominent real estate agents returned a valuation of $45,000 for the house and lot, with an additional $1,250 for the chandelier, drawing-room mirror, carpet, curtains, and fireplace brasses.

In 1918 the Misses Frost offered to purchase the Miles Brewton House from the heirs for $45,000 cash. It was understood by all that the three Frost sisters would deduct their share of the inheritance from this price prior to distribution of the balance. An additional $1,950 was offered separately for the chandelier, drawing-room mirror, carpet, curtains, and fireplace brasses, for they were part of the personal property devised to seven heirs under Mary M. Pringle's will. The heirs accepted the proposal, and the sale was completed in 1919.

The funds with which the Misses Frost purchased the property came from two loans secured by mortgages provided by Mrs. William K. duPont and Ireneé duPont. At the time, Rebecca Frost worked for and lived with the duPonts as a governess. The Frost sisters sold their Logan Street house and applied approximately $10,000 to the duPont loan. During the 1920s the duPonts forgave the remainder of the loan and canceled the mortgage. They also paid for a number of repairs to the house.

The Frosts continued the post-bellum Pringle family practice of renting out rooms, and this income was used to maintain the old homestead. A 1921 Pittsburgh newspaper writer raved about the "Pringle House," as it was then called:

> Two of the sweetest and kindliest women in a land where all women are kindly and sweet, the Misses Mary Pringle Frost and Susan Pringle Frost, came into a part inheritance of the old mansion, and like some other Southern families, if you come recommended by royalty, as indeed you should be to associate with these lovely women, you may be received as a guest and be permitted to sleep and eat in this marvelous house. . . . As to food, ask Miss Mary to divulge the secrets and mysteries of 'Hoppin' John' and 'Bubble and Squeak'[19] and divers other epicurean dishes as cooked by the goodly old colored woman, Sarah. . . . And then you must have the happiest

of old colored mammies, Mary, make up your seventeenth century bed. It is worth many a two-bit piece to hear her sing, 'Nobody knows the trouble ah see,' as she rolls around the footboard." He also wrote, "One should see . . . the Frost garden in the rear of the old Pringle House to realize the fine art of flower arrangement."[20]

George Nelson, a black from the Beaufort area, became the doorman and major domo of the Miles Brewton House in 1920. Susan Pringle Frost wrote:

> Among his varied duties in the home are to keep the floors waxed, to hang the more than century old red and gold damask curtains in the drawing room and the North parlour; he also admits visitors to the house, sees that they sign their names on the register at the front door, and make their contribution for going through the house. After my sister and I have served them wine in the dining-room, giving a brief account of the house and furnishings, we turn them over to George and he takes them downstairs, through the garden and basement, and court-yard and the old kitchen; he shows the andirons, Adam and Eve, with proper reverence; and the store-room and 'gentlemen's library': and finally escorts them through the lower green gate, and shows them the mail box. Here they take their leave. George is so well known to the visitors that if they happen to call and find him not in attendance on the door bell, they always ask what has become of him. His manners are courtly, and his bearing that of a 'gentleman of the old school.'[21]

A 1944 advertisement noted that the public could tour the house daily (except Sundays) from ten to one and three to five for one dollar each.[22] Public tours of the house were offered until shortly before Susan Frost's death in 1960.

Susan Pringle Frost went on to become Charleston's first female real estate agent, a pioneer in the women suffrage movement, and in 1920 founded the Society for the Preservation of Old Dwellings, now the Preservation Society of Charleston. Rebecca Pringle Frost, the last of the Misses Frost, died in 1971. She devised the house to Mary Pringle (Ham-

Susan Pringle Frost, as president of the Charleston League for Equal Suffrage.

ilton) Manigault, wife of Edward Manigault who was the daughter of Miles Brewton Hamilton and Mary Ravenel (Pringle) Hamilton and the granddaughter of Jacob Motte Alston Pringle and his wife, Gabriella (Ravenel) Pringle. When Mary Pringle (Hamilton) Manigault died in 1987, the property passed to her son, Peter Manigault, publisher of the Charleston *Post & Courier*.

In the 1880s South Carolina still produced more than half of the nation's rice, but by 1890, the majority of American rice was being produced in Arkansas, Texas, and Louisiana.[23] With the viability of rice planting in serious doubt, the value of plantation land dropped dramatically. In 1883 a rice plantation which had sold for $65,000 before the war was sold for $1,800.[24]Flooding destroyed thirty percent of the Lowcountry's anticipated crop that year, and production dropped slipped almost every year thereafter. By 1887 so few planters remained on the Santee that the Planter's Club of St. James, Santee, was allowed to lapse. In 1903 it was reorganized as the Agricultural Society of St. James, Santee —but half its new membership consisted of rich Northerners who had bought up Santee rice plantations to use as hunting preserves.[25]

A series of severe storms put the last nails in the coffin of South Carolina's commercial rice production. Devastating hurricanes pounded the rice coast in 1893, 1894, 1898, 1906, 1910 and 1911, destroying dikes and trunks and submerging fields in salt water. The 1893 hurricane alone killed over one thousand people along the coast.

Under the pen name, Patience Pennington, Mrs. Elizabeth Waites (Allston) Pringle wrote, "The rice planting, which for years gave me the exhilaration of making good income myself, is a thing of the past now—the banks and trunks have been washed away, and there is no money to replace them."[26] The 1906 storm put an end to planting at Rice Hope, formerly the plantation of Simons Lucas. A Santee plantation of only moderate size, Rice Hope had produced 300,000 pounds of rice a year in its prime, but by 1906, South Carolina's total rice production amounted to only 418,722 pounds. Arthur Middleton Manigault, the son and namesake of his famous father, the Civil War general, planted at White Oak and Rochelle until 1907. The last of the Santee rice plantations to fall quiet was David Doar's Harietta, which ceased operation in 1908.

President Grover Cleveland visited Georgetown in 1894 for a duck-shooting vacation. The attendant publicity encouraged wealthy Northerners to think of South Carolina as a good wintering spot. By the end of 1908, virtually all the rich Santee and Waccamaw rice lands lay fallow and unused, except as habitat for many species of birds which were both sporting to shoot and delicious to eat.

The distinction of being South Carolina's last commercial rice planter fell to Theodore D. Ravenel, a Pringle cousin. He first planted rice on the Cooper River shortly after the beginning of Reconstruction and ultimately moved to the Combahee, where he planted until 1927.[28] The commercial production of rice in South Carolina ended forever that year.

Sic transit gloria mundi.

Epilogue

Mary Pringle's last surviving letter, written in 1882, reflected her characteristic generosity. It accompanied a $50 wedding present for her granddaughter, Mary Ravenel Pringle, who married Miles Brewton Hamilton in a ceremony celebrated under the welcoming chandelier of the old family homestead.

> My dearest granddaughter,
>
> Stiff as my old fingers are, I find that they have the power of holding, so I think it the safer plan to send you the little hord of gold pieces that I have laid aside for you, that you may select for your wedding day some small token to remind you that your Grandmama was thinking of you on the approaching event that is to fill up your life. May God's best blessings be ever with you, my sweet child. Trusting all things that His infinite wisdom and goodness knows the best for you, is the fervent prayer of your devoted Grandmama, Mary M. Pringle[1]

For years after the Civil War, when the Pringles and the Frosts were continually strapped for cash, virtually all major maintenance and repair of the Miles Brewton House were of necessity deferred. After a century of neglect, the house suffered from a wide array of problems. In 1987 Peter

Manigault started a museum-grade restoration of the property. A small army of urban archaeologists, art and textile conservators, architects, architectural historians, legions of specialized craftspeople and practitioners of arcane specialties, including paint analysis and paleobotany, converged on the house and contributed their knowledge and skills to the work. The author had the privilege of serving as the historical researcher for the project from 1990 to 1992.

The physical work began after two years of research and planning. Architectural details obscured, damaged, or missing for over a century were uncovered, restored, or replaced.

On Saturday night, December 14, 1991, after four years of painstaking work, Mr. and Mrs. Peter Manigault held a reception to celebrate the completion of the restoration. The house was draped with pine garlands and illuminated solely by candlelight. Just as it had for the wedding of Mary Motte Alston and William Bull Pringle 169 years earlier, the chandelier in the drawing room once again sparkled with the light of a thousand diamonds.

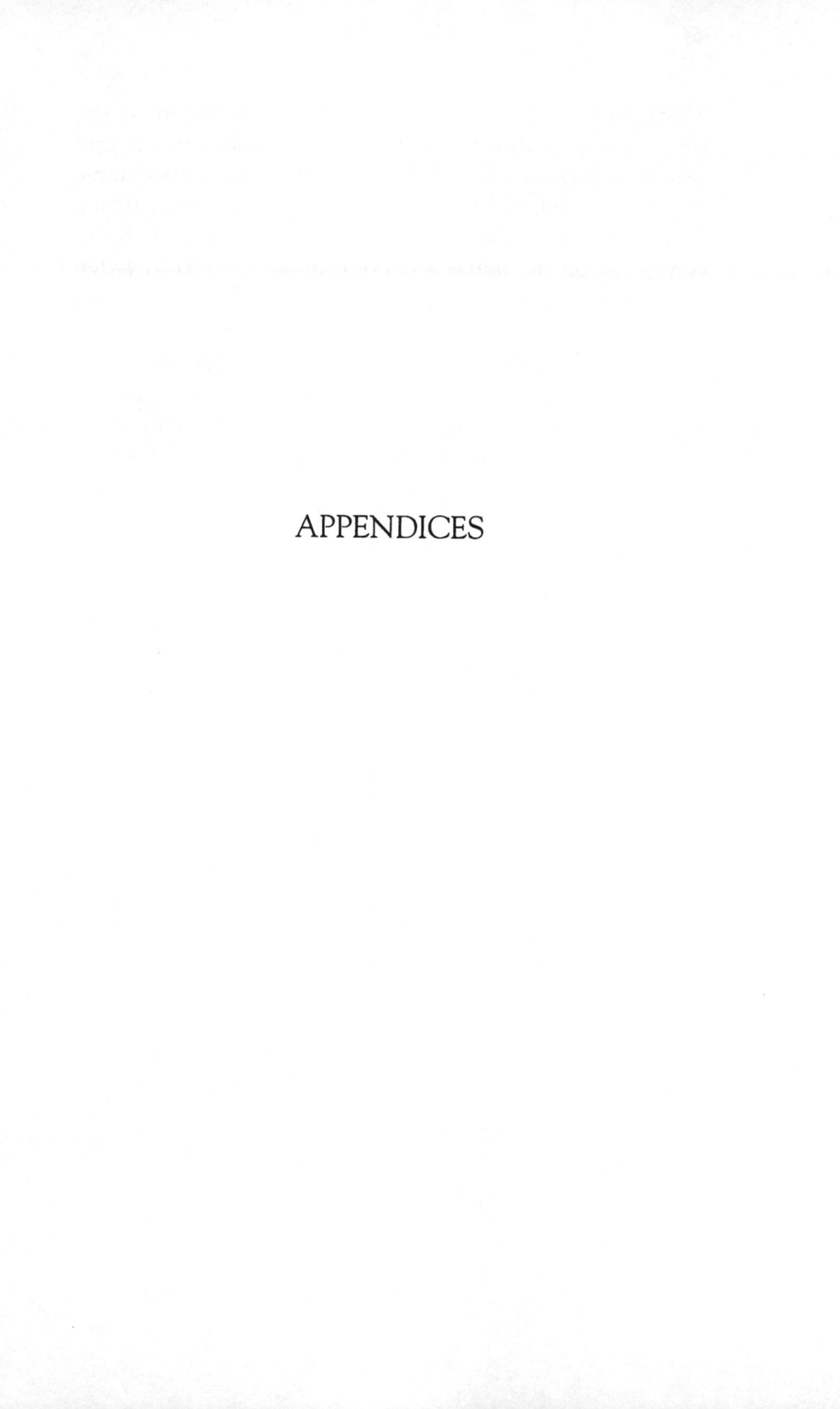

APPENDICES

Appendix I

Children of Judge John Julius Pringle (1753-1843) and Susannah Reid (1768-1838)

John Julius Pringle (1784-1807)
b. October 18, 1784
m. 1806 Mary Izard (c. 1782 November 9, 1857)
d. August 2, 1807
(Mary later married Joel R. Poinsett)

Robert William Pringle (1786-1790)
b. October 10, 1786
d. December 16, 1790

Susannah Pringle (1789-1846), of Smithfield plantation
b. January 8, 1789
m. William Mason Smith, brother of Robert Mason Smith
d. May 18, 1846

Elizabeth Mary Pringle (1791-1873)
b. May 9, 1791
m. 1808 Robert Mason Smith (1786-1847), brother of William Mason Smith
d. April 8 or 11, 1873

Robert Pringle (1793-1860), of Beneventum plantation & Paris
b. March 28, 1793
did not marry
d. October 26, 1860 in Paris, buried at St. Michael's.

Mary Pringle (1795-183__)
b. August 23, 1795
did not marry
d. between 1831-1839

Edward Jenkins Pringle (1796-1838)
b. December 16, 1796, twin of Charles James, below
m. Maria Henrietta Middleton (1802-1838)
d. June 14, 1838 aboard steamer *Pulaski* with his wife, two children, and their nurse.

Charles James Pringle (1796-)
b. December 16, 1796, twin of Edward Jenkins, above
d.

William Bull Pringle (1800-1881)
b. July 8, 1800, 70 Tradd St., Charleston
m. March 5, 1822 Mary Motte Alston (1803-1884)
d. December 13, 1881, MBH

Emma Clara Pringle (1803-1889)
b. January 23, 1803
m. 1824 Charles Cotesworth Pinckney Alston (1796-1881), brother of Mary Motte Alston, above
d. April 23, 1889

Appendix II

Children of Col. William Alston (1756-1839)

By his first wife, Mary Ashe, whom he married February 13, 1777:

Maria Alston (b. 1778)
b. February 2, 1778
m. Sir John Nisbet, November 15, 1797
m. Dr. John Murray of Scotland

Gov. Joseph Alston (1779-1816), of The Oaks plantation
b. August 15, 1779
m. February 2, 1801 Theodosia Burr (1783-1813)
d. September 10, 1816, buried at The Oaks

John Ashe Alston (1780-1831)
b. September 22, 1780
m. March 26, 1801 Sarah or Sally McPherson (1785-1812)
d. 1831

William Algernon Alston (1782-1860), of Rose Hill plantation (inherited Clifton)
b. June 26, 1782
m. 1806 Mrs. Mary Allston Young (c. 1782-1844), widow of Thomas Young
d. September 16, 1860; buried at The Oaks

Charlotte Alston (1785-1817)
b. September 12, 1785
m. Gov. John Lyde Wilson (1784-1849)
d. November 26, 1817; buried at The Oaks

By his second wife, Mary Brewton Motte (c. 1769- November 22, 1838), whom he married February 24, 1791:

Thomas Pinckney Alston (1795-1861)
b. 1795
m. Jane Ladson Smith (1800-1823), May 25, 1820;
m. Susan Elizabeth Smith, Jane's sister, June 25, 1825
d. April 29, 1861

Rebecca Brewton ("Fanny") Alston (d. 1863)
b. ?
m. Robert Y. Hayne (1791-1839), May 31, 1820
d. January 25, 1863, Pendleton, S.C.

Elizabeth Louisa Alston (____-1867)
b. ?
m. November 25, 1822 Col. Arthur Perroneau Hayne (1788-1867), brother of Robert Y. Hayne
d. March 3, 1867, in MBH withdrawing room

Jacob Motte Alston (c. 1798-1818)
b. c. 1798
did not marry
d. September 11, 1818 in a riding accident; buried at The Oaks.

Charles Cotesworth Pinckney Alston (1796-1881), of Fairfield and True Blue plantations and East Battery
b. 1796
m. Emma C. Pringle (1803-1889), sister of William Bull Pringle, May 30 or June 1, 1824
d. January 6, 1881; buried in Magnolia Cemetery.

Frances Serena (____-1802)
d. July 29, 1802

Mary Motte Alston (1803-1884)
b. June 17, 1803, MBH
m. William Bull Pringle (1800-1881), March 5, 1822
d. October 4, 1884 in the MBH; buried at. St. Michael's.

Appendix III

Children of William Bull Pringle (1800-1881) and Mary Motte Alston (1803-1884)

1. William **Alston** Pringle (1822-1895). Lieutenant, 16th Regt., S.C. Militia
   b. December 2, 1822, MBH
   m. February 6, 1845 to Emma Clara Pringle Smith (February 5, 1825 - October 8, 1879)
   d. February 27, 1895, MBH
      Anna Tilghman Smith Pringle (1845-1850)
      William Bull Pringle (b. 1847, fl. 1884)
      Robert Smith Pringle (b. 1849, fl. 1884), m. Maria H. White
      William Alston Pringle (b. 1851, fl. 1884), m. Minnie Lomax
      Mary Motte Pringle, (March 23, 1853 - April 12, 1927), m. March 3, 1880, Benjamin Rhett (December 11, 1852 - February 28, 1915), res. Mobile, Ala.
      Elizabeth Smith Pringle (1854-1871)
      Emma Smith Pringle (January 24, 1856 - January 30, 1878)
      Rebecca Motte Pringle (1857 - February 15, 1884; twin of Susan)
      Susan Pringle (b. & d. 1857; twin of Rebecca)
      Anna Tilghman Smith Pringle (b. 1859, d. by 1869)
      John Julius Pringle (1866-1872)
      Susan Reid Pringle (1867-1884)
      Anna Tilghman Smith Pringle (1869 - December 30, 1881)
      Edward Jenkins Pringle (1870-1871)

2. John **Julius** Pringle (1824-1901). Midshipman, U.S. Navy; Confederate rank & service not established.
   b. September 2, 1824, MBH
   m. March 20, 1849 to Maria Linton Duncan (January 1, 1826-October 15, 1908, buried Sabaou Cemetery, Biarritz)
   d. October 30, 1901, Biarritz, France; buried Sabaou Cemetery, Biarritz.

Catherine ("Cassie") Duncan Pringle (February 22, 1850 - October 29, 1923; buried in Versailles)
Mary Motte Pringle (January 13, 1852 - May 5, 1945, Biarritz)
Stephen Duncan Pringle (January 17, 1854 - July 13, 1917, Biarritz)
Maria Duncan ("Maizie") Pringle, (May 4, 1856 - January 15, 1940, Biarritz)
Susan Pringle (b. Newport, June 4, 1859 - January 21, 1942, Biarritz)
Charlotte Duncan Pringle (b. Newport, August 21, 1859, d. 1945, m. ___ Radcliffe of Devon, England

3. **Edward** Jenkins Pringle (1826-1899). No military service.
b. February 13, 1826, MBH
m. May 12, 1868, to Cornelia Letitia Johnson (1847-1941), San Francisco. Cornelia d. July 2, 1941 in San Francisco.
d. April 21, 1899, Oakland, California
Edward Jenkins Pringle, Jr. (1870-1944), m. Miriam Phillips Moore
Cornelia Covington Pringle (b. 1871, fl. 1899), unmarried
William Bull Pringle (1872-1916), m. Anne Isabel Hutchinson; left two children: William Bull Pringle, Jr., and Isabelle Alston Pringle
Sidney Johnson Pringle (b. 1875, fl. 1899), unmarried
Mary Motte ("Hess") Pringle (1878-1930), m. William Morris Houghton
Charles Alston Pringle (1879-1916), unmarried, d. in Mexico.
Euclid Covington Pringle (b. 1881, fl. 1899), m. Kathleen Bull and Mrs. Bert Meek

4. Jacob **Motte** Alston Pringle (1827-1886). Major, Chief Quartermaster, Dept. of S.C. & Ga., C.S.A.
b. November 9, 1827, MBH
m. May 21, 1850 to Gabriella Ravenel (1828-1914)
d. November 27, 1886, Charleston
Anna Eliza Pringle (b. 1851)

Hess Alston Pringle (1852-1861)
John Ravenel Pringle (b. & d. 1855)
William Bull Pringle (b. 1857)
Mary Ravenel Pringle (b. 1859), m. Miles Brewton Hamilton
Fannie Ravenel Pringle (b. 1861), m. James Reid Pringle Ravenel

5. **Susan** Pringle (1829-1917)
b. October 8, 1829, MBH
d. September 24, 1917, MBH

6. **Mary** Frances Pringle (1831-1901)
b. February 1, 1831, MBH
m. at the MBH to May 31, 1853 to Prof. Donald G. Mitchell (1822-1908)
d. December 5, 1901, New Haven, CT
Hesse Alston Mitchell (1854 - 1861)
Mary Pringle Mitchell (1855-November 15, 1939), m. Edward Larned Ryerson
Elizabeth Woodbridge Mitchell (1856-c. 1943), unmarried
William Pringle Mitchell (1858-1899), m. Katherine (Kate) Mower
Susan Pringle Mitchell (1860-1932), m. James Mason Hoppin
Donald Grant Mitchell, Jr. ("Stonewall")(1861-1950), m. Mary Dews Rees
Hesse Alston Mitchell (1863-c. 1936), unmarried
Rebecca Motte Mitchell (1865-1928), m. Walter Tillman Hart
Harriet Williams Mitchell (1870-c. 1939), unmarried
James Pringle (James Alfred?) Mitchell (1871-1892), unmarried
Walter Lewis Mitchell (1875-1962), m. Esther R. ("Hetty") Buckner
Harry W. Mitchell, fl. 1902

7. **William** Bull Pringle, Jr. (1833-1859)
   b. July 2, 1833, MBH
   d. June 29, 1859, MBH

8. Miles **Brewton** Pringle (1835-1874). Private, Charleston Light Dragoons, C.S.A.
   b. July 5, 1835, MBH
   d. December 2, 1874, MBH, of insanity induced by war trauma; buried at St. Michael's.

9. **Robert** Pringle (1837-1863). Captain, 15th (Lucas's) Bn., S.C.V. (artillery).
   b. July 31, 1837, MBH
   d. August 21, 1863, from artillery wounds received at Battery Wagner, Morris Island, S.C.; buried at St. Michael's.

10. **Rebecca** Motte Pringle (1839-1905)
    b. March 9, 1839, MBH
    m. December 11, 1866 to Dr. Francis LeJau Frost (1837-1912), Charleston
    d. July 4, 1905, Saluda, NC
    William Pringle Frost (1867-1891), unmarried
    Edward Frost (1869-1871)
    Mary Pringle ("Sissy") Frost (1871-1943), unmarried
    Susan Pringle Frost (1873-1960), unmarried
    Francis LeJau Frost, Jr. (1875-1935), unmarried
    Rebecca Motte Frost (1877-194__), unmarried

11. **Elizabeth** Pringle (1839-1844)
    b. March 9, 1839, MBH
    d. January 22, 1844, MBH

12. **Charles** Alston Pringle (1841-1862). 1st Lieutenant, 1st (Butler's) Regt., S.C.V. (artillery).
    b. January 14, 1841, MBH
    d. June 29, 1862, at MBH of typhoid fever contracted on John's Island, S.C.; buried at St. Michael's.

13. **James** Reid Pringle (1843-1871). Captain, 1st Regt., S.C. Artillery.
   b. October 8, 1842, MBH
   m. December 15, 1868, to Coralie Butterworth, of San Francisco
   d. June 9, 1871, Brevoort House Hotel, New York City.
      Henry Butterworth Pringle (b. 1869)
      James Reid Pringle (b. 1871)

Appendix IV

Descendants of Cretia (1807-1879) and Scipio (1808-1868) Stewart

Cretia, daughter of Lucy, was born a slave on Fairfield, Col. William Alston's Waccamaw River rice plantation, in July 1807. She married Scipio, a fellow slave at Fairfield, in January 1825. Cretia became Mary Pringle's maid and remained in the employ of the Pringle family until her death. She was living at 26 Morris Street, Charleston, when she died of pneumonia on July 21, 1879, at the age of 72. She was buried in the Rikerville Baptist Church Cemetery. Scipio was a cooper -- a skilled worker who made barrels and casks on the plantation. He was born in Georgetown District about 1808. He was living at the Miles Brewton House when he died of a pulmonary hemorrhage on June 25, 1868, at the age of 60. His funeral service was held in the yard of the Miles Brewton House. He was also buried in the Rikerville Baptist Church Cemetery.

By 1856 and after emancipation, the couple was known as Cretia and Scipio Stewart. This compilation includes all information recorded in the Bible given to Cretia by Mary Pringle in 1856. Additional information about the Stewart family and their descendants may be found in *Chronicles*, 14-16; *Highlights*, 60, 62, 65-67; and the Charleston County Death Records card file at the Charleston County Library. Their children were as follows:

1. Miley Stuart, b. Nov. 18, 1826
   Married Caesar Chisholm.
      Louisa B. Chisholm, b. Dec. 14, 1880
      Joseph Chisholm, b. Feb. 2, 1882, a house cleaner
      Frank Chisholm, b. Nov. 29, 1883
      Caesar Chisholm, b. Jan. 31, 1886
      Joele Chisholm, b. Dec. 25, 1887

Charles Chisholm, b. Oct. 15, 1889
Joseph Chisholm, b. Dec. 18, 1890
Mary Chisholm, b. Dec. 18, 1890

2. Caesar Stuart, born Oct. 10, 1827, d. July 26, 1880. Married Amey, at Runimede plantation, 1848. Amey's first husband, Davis, was a fisherman. Amey was a nurse to Edward and Susan Pringle. Their children:
   Morrison Stuart, b. August 2, 1849
   Mary Stuart, b. September 4, 1851, d. November 28, 1922.
   Lucretia Stuart, b. March 29, 1854, d. Sunday, January 12, 1941, at 9:20 PM at 29 King Street, Charleston. She was a member of Class No. 4 of Emanuel A.M.E. Church.
   Thomas Stuart, b. March 30, 1861

3. Johnny Stuart, a carpenter, b. Oct. 15, 1829; married Maria, June 15, 1856
   Charles Stuart, b. August 3, 1857
   Louisa Stuart, b. August 25, 1858
   Mary Stuart, b. March 29, 1860
   Samuel Stuart, b. December 20, 1863
   Cretia Stuart, b. December 19, 1864
   Diania Stuart, b. March 7, 1867
   Sarah Ann Stuart, b. June 17, 1868
   John Stuart, b. January 2, 1870
   ____ Stuart, son, b. Feb. 6, 1872

4. ____, son of Cretia, b. Aug. 5, died Aug. 14, 1831

5. Lucy Stuart, daughter of Cretia, b. Aug. 13, 1833

6. Mary Stuart, a twin daughter, born ____, 1835.

7. Martha Stuart, a twin daughter, born dead ____, 1835.

8. Jack Stuart, son of Cretia, b. Sept. 27, 1837.

9. Hannah Stuart, dau. of Cretia, b. Aug. 5, 1838, d. 6 April 1883. Hannah was taught hairdressing and worked on the household staff.

10. Maulsey Stuart, dau. of Cretia, b. Oct. 13, 1840, d. November 12, 1861, aged 21 years and one month.; m. William Chisholm, Oct. 1857
    George Chisholm, b. January 12, 185

Joseph Chisholm, b. Dec. 18, 1890
Mary Chisholm, b. Dec. 18, 1890

11. Alert Stuart, son of Cretia, b. Sep. 13, 1842; m. Martha
    James Stuart, b. July 15, 1867
    Harriett Stuart, b. June 30, 1869
    Mary Maria Stuart, b. May 26, 1872

12. Scipio Stuart, son of Cretia, b. Nov. 22, 1845

SOURCE NOTES

FAMILY MEMBER ABBREVIATIONS USED IN THE SOURCE NOTES:

The following initials are used to identify members of the Pringle and Frost families in the source citations. All other names are spelled out.

CP: Charles Pringle (1841-1862), son of William and Mary Pringle

EJP: Edward Jenkins Pringle (1826-1899), son of William and Mary Pringle

FLF: Francis L. Frost, M.D., husband of Rebecca (Pringle) Frost

FLF, Jr.: Rev. Francis L. Frost, Jr. (1875-1935), son of Dr. Francis L. and Rebecca Frost

JJP: John Julius Pringle (1824-1899), son of William and Mary Pringle

JP: James Pringle (1843-1871), son of William and Mary Pringle

MAP: Motte Alston Pringle (1827-1886), son of William and Mary Pringle

MBP: Miles Brewton Pringle (1835-1874), son of William and Mary Pringle

MMP: Mary Motte (Alston) Pringle (1803-1884), wife of William Bull Pringle

MPF: Mary Pringle Frost (1871-1943), daughter of Dr. Francis L. and Rebecca Frost

MPM: Mary (Pringle) Mitchell (1831-1901), daughter of William and Mary Pringle and wife of Prof. Donald G. Mitchell

RBF: Rebecca Brewton Frost (1839-1905), daughter of William and Mary Pringle and wife of Dr. Francis L. Frost

RMF: Rebeca Motte Frost (1877-1971), daughter of Dr. Francis L. and Rebecca Frost

RP: Robert Pringle (1837-1863), son of William and Mary Pringle

SP: Susan Pringle (1829-1917), daughter of William and Mary Pringle

SPF: Susan Pringle Frost (1873-1960), daughter of Dr. Francis L. and Rebecca Frost

WAP: William Alston Pringle (1822-1895), son of William and Mary Pringle

WBP: William Bull Pringle (1801-1884), husband of Mary

WBP, Jr.: William Bull Pringle, Jr. (1833-1859), son of William and Mary Pringle

WPF: William Pringle Frost (1867-1891), son of Dr. Francis L. and Rebecca Frost

Chapter 1: Mary's Charleston

1. Quoted in Wendell Garrett, "Charleston," *Antiques*, February, 1993, 269.

2. Alexander S. Salley, "Col. Miles Brewton and some of his Descendants," in *South Carolina Historical [and Genealogical] Magazine*, II: 128-52; 241-44, passim. The magazine will hereafter be cited as *SCHM.*

3. Salley, "Brewton," 130-31; also "Robert Brewton," in Walter B. Edgar and N. Louise Bailey, eds., *Biographical Directory of the South Carolina House of Representatives*, II: 98. The *Directory* will hereafter be cited as the *BDSCHR.*

4. Obituary of Miles Brewton, undated newspaper clipping [APF].

5. Leila Sellers, *Charleston Business on the Eve of the American Revolution* (Chapel Hill, N.C.: 1934; reprinted New York: Library Editions, Ltd., 1970), 145-46.

6. "Miles Brewton," *BDSCHR*, II: 96.

7. Maurice A. Crouse, ed., "The Letterbook of Peter Manigault, 1763-1773," in *SCHM*, 70: 189.

8. George C. Rogers, Jr., *Charleston in the Age of the Pinckneys* (Columbia: University of South Carolina Press, 1980), 164.

9. Mary Pringle Frost, *The Miles Brewton House:: Chronicles and Reminiscences* (Charleston, privately printed, 1939):, 21.

10. An illustration of a cheval-de-frise may be found in *Russell's Civil War Photographs* (New York: Dover Publications, 1985).

11. Bivens, John and J. Thomas Savage, "The Miles Brewton House, Charleston, South Carolina" in *Antiques*, February 1993, 298.

12. "Journal of Josiah Quincy, Jr., 1773," in *Proceedings of the Massachusetts Historical Society*, 49: 453.

13. Sellers, *Charleston Business*, 211-212.

14. "Miles Brewton," *BDSCHR*, II: 97

15. *Chronicles*, 29.

16. The whereabouts of the administration and inventory of Miles Brewton's estate remains a mystery. Although Brewton was a man of substance, these records could not be located in the collections of the South Carolina Department of Archives and History, the South Carolina Historical Society, or in family papers.

17. Salley, "Brewton," 151.

18. *Chronicles*, 37.

19. Clinton's *Narrative of the Campaign in 1781 in North America* (Philadelphia: John Campbell, 1865) makes no reference to the specific location of his Charleston headquarters. The best evidence of the British occupation of the house is physical, not documentary. British soldiers scratched a profile caricature of Sir Henry, along with several accurate renderings of Revolutionary War-period warships, into the marble mantel of the south parlor.

20. William B. Willcox, *Portrait of a General. Sir Henry Clinton in the War of Independence* (New York: Alfred A. Knopf, 1962), 322.

21. David Duncan Wallace, *South Carolina: A Short History* (Columbia, South Carolina: University of South Carolina Press, 1951), 319.

22. In 1890, Jacob Motte Alston recorded his experiences growing up in the Miles Brewton House and on the Pringle and Alston rice plantations in a rambling, 500-page manuscript entitled, "Random Recollections of an Inconspicuous Life." Hereafter cited as "Random Recollections." My citations refer to a 355-page typescript copy in the Miles Brewton House Collection. A heavily abridged version which excised Jacob's paternalistic views on slaveholding was published as *Rice Planter and Sportsman. The Recollections of J. Motte Alston, 1821-1909* (Columbia: University of South Carolina Press, 1953). It is cited as *Rice Planter*.

23. Margaret Hayne Harrison, *A Charleston Album* (Rindge, New Hampshire: Richard R. Smith, 1953), 38.

24. *Chronicles*, 37.

25. Harrison, *Album*, 38.

26. Mrs. St. Julien Ravenel, Charleston. *The Place and the People* (New York: Macmillan, 1926), 276.

27. Typescript copy of an 1877 sketch of Rebecca Motte, written by Maria Middleton, in Mrs. O. J. Wister and Agnes Irwin, eds., *Worthy Women of Our First Century* (Philadelphia: Lippincott, 1877), 266 [APF].

28. *Chronicles*, 37-38.

29. Isaac Hayne (1745-1781) was a grandson of John Hayne (d. c. 1718), the first of that family of English emigrants to South Carolina. The brothers, S. C. Governor Robert Y. Hayne (1791-1839, who married Mary's sister, Rebecca Brewton Alston, and Col. Arthur P. Hayne (1788-1867), who married her sister, Elizabeth Laura Alston, were both great-great grandsons of the same John Hayne.

30. Versions of this story disagree. According to A. S. Salley, Rebecca

Motte was "living there in 1781 with her three daughters and Mrs. John Brewton, widow of her nephew John Brewton when the British took possession of her house for a military post." She and her family were permitted to remain in the house until Marion and Lee arrived, when she was requested by the British to retire to her overseer's house near by. From this point forward, Salley's version and the one presented here are essentially the same.

31. Salley, "Brewton,"149.

32. Jacob Motte Alston wrote that combustible materials were attached to conventional arrows and fired from an African bow formerly presented to her by a sea captain [Jacob Motte Alston, Barclay Farm, Ga., to My Dearest Hessie, August 11, 1886. Jacob Motte Alston Papers, Library of Congress]. Another account stated that "the arrows did not produce the fire; that Nathan Savage threw a ball of burning pitch and brimstone on the roof." The account credited by her descendants, and by historian, A.S. Salley, stated that the arrows were discharged from a musket. This method, similar to the operation of present-day rifle grenade launchers, makes good sense, because the distance from Marion's men to the house—musket range—was far outside the range of a bow-launched arrow or a man throwing balls of flaming pitch. Salley, who collated and evaluated all written accounts of the event, cited as most accurate the version given by her grandson, Charles C. Pinckney, in a letter to the *Columbia Carolinian* dated September 27, 1855, which was corroborated by several other authoritative sources. See Salley, "Brewton," 148-51; Mrs. O.J. Wister and Miss Agnes Irwin, eds., "Worthy Women of Our First Century" [typescript in APF]; Tablet to Mrs. Rebecca Motte. Erected by Rebecca Motte Chapter of the Daughters of the American Revolution . . . May 9, 1903 (Charleston: Daggett Printing Co., 1903), 10-11 and Middleton, Jeremiah Theus, 151.

33. Wallace, *Short History*, 316.

Chapter 2: King Billy's Daughter

1. James L. Michie, "The Oaks Plantation Revealed: An Archaeological Survey of the Home of Joseph and Theodosia Burr Alston, Brookgreen Gardens, Georgetown County, South Carolina." Research Manuscript 4. (Conway, S.C.: Waccamaw Center for Historical and Cultural Studies, Coastal Carolina University, 1993), 10.

2. "Quincy," in *Proceedings*, 49: 453.

3. "Random Recollections," 3.

4. Approximately forty of Col. Alston's books are preserved in the library of the Edmondston-Alston House, 21 East Battery Street, Charleston, a museum property administered by the Middleton Place Foundation.

5. Gov. Thomas Pinckney to William Allston, Jr., May 7, 1787. "This

commission to take rank from the twenty-ninth day of October 1781 as a commission of that day was given to me being worn out. Hugh Horrÿ, Lt. Col." [APF].

6. For a full listing of Col. Alston's children and their spouses, see the Appendix.

7. An eight-volume set of M. Tulli's *Ciceronis Opera*. . . . (Paris, 1768, in Latin) belonging to Theodosia survives in the library of the Edmondston-Alston House Museum, Charleston.

8. Anthony Devereaux, *The Life and Times of Robert F. W. Alston* (Georgetown, S.C.: Waccamaw Press, 1976), 1. Jacob Motte Alston confirmed that "Whilst on [the] Waccamaw Theodosia resided in the winter months at 'Hagley'. . . and sometimes at 'The Oaks.'"

9. "Random Recollections," 19.

10. "Random Recollections," 203.

11. The birthplace of Aaron Burr Alston and the vice president's visit are discussed in Richard N. Côté, "Theodosia Burr Alston, Aaron Burr and the Miles Brewton House," research memorandum #11, April 25, 1989 [APF].

12."I have also desired that my beautiful little bust of Bonaparte be sent to Mr. William Alston." Aaron Burr, Washington, D.C. to Theodosia, n.p., April 5, 1802, in Mark Van Doren, ed., *Correspondence of Aaron Burr and His Daughter Theodosia* (New York: Stratford Press, 1929), 96.

13. Theodosia Burr Alston, New Rochelle, New York, to Dr. William Eustis, Boston, October 3, 1808. Aaron Burr and Burriana Autographs and Documents, C.P.G. Fuller Collection, portfolio III, box 2, item 15, Princeton University Library.

14. "Random Recollections," 17, 118.

15. "Random Recollections," 62.

16. The captain's logs of Warren's squadron were located and examined by Dr. James L. Michie of Coastal Carolina University, Conway, S.C.

17. Obituary of Joseph Alston, *Carolina Gazette*, September 14, 1816.

18. Harrison, *Album*, 52

19. N. Louise Bailey, ed., *Biographical Dictionary of the South Carolina Senate* (Columbia: University of South Carolina Press, 1986) 1: 62. Hereafter cited as *BDSCS*.

20. Elizabeth Deas Allston, *The Allstons and Alstons of Waccamaw*, (privately printed, 1936), 7.

21. "A Lucas Memorandum," *SCHM*, 69: 196; also George C. Rogers, Jr., *History of Georgetown County* (Columbia: University of South Carolina Press, 1970), 165. In 1920, Henry Ford disassembled the rice mill at Fairfield and re-erected it at his museum near Detroit.

22. Alston genealogical records [APF]; also "William Alston," in *BDSCS* 1: 62-64.

23. Obituary of Col. William Alston.

24. "Random Recollections," 8.

25. Lawrence Fay Brewster, *Summer Migrations and Resorts of South Carolina Low-Country Planters* (Durham, N.C.: Duke University Press, 1947), 57.

26. Deed Book E-6, 507-510, Charleston County Register of Mesne Conveyances Office. The £8,000 cited by Josiah Quincy included the cost of the house and its furnishings.

27. Francis W. Bilodeau, ed., *Art in South Carolina, 1770-1970* (Charleston: South Carolina Tricentennial Commission, 1970), 42. The portrait is on loan to the Gibbes Museum of Art.

28. "Random Recollections," 62.

29. "Random Recollections," 48.

30. William Alston, Miscellaneous Receipts, 1805 [APF].

31. "Random Recollections," 9.

32. "Random Recollections," 16; Anthony Q Devereaux, *The Rice Princes: A Rice Epoch Revisited* (Columbia: The State Co., 1973), 25; and Allston, *The Allstons and Alstons*, 68.

33. *Immotus*: calm, undisturbed; an appropriate motto for this conservative man.

34. In 1832 Col. Alston purchased pew #2, on the north side of the middle aisle in St. Michael's church, for $900 from Louisa Hunt, widow of Thomas Hunt. Deed Book E-10, 30, Charleston County Register of Mesne Conveyances Office.

35. "this period" refers to Col. Alston's final years of life in the late 1830s. "Random Recollections," 48, 91.

36. John B. Irving, *The South Carolina Jockey Club* (Charleston: Russell & Jones, 1857), IV: 14.

37. J. H. Easterby, ed., "Charles Cotesworth Pinckney's Plantation Diary, April 6 - December 15, 1818," *SCHM*, 41: 115.

38. William Alston, *Racing Reminiscences*, n.d. [APF].

39. Irving, *Jockey Club*, IV: 6.

40. Irving, *Jockey Club*, IV: 14.

41. Irving, *Jockey Club*, IV: 24-25.

42. Henry deSaussure Bull, *All-Saints Church* (N.p.: Historical Activities Committee of the South Carolina Society of Colonial Dames of America, 1948, 18-19.

43. Obituary of Col. William Alston.

44. Thomas Jefferson, Monticello, to William Alston, August 15, 1818 and October 6, 1818 [MBH].

45. True Blue: see "Random Recollections," 276-278. Rose Hill: see Allston, *Allstons and Alstons*, 80. Smithfield: see D. E. Huger Smith, *A Charlestonian's Recollections, 1846-1913* (Charleston: Carolina Art Association, 1950), 82-83.

46. Susan Pringle Frost, *Highlights of the Miles Brewton House, 27 King Street, Charleston, S.C.*, (Charleston: privately published, 1944), 18.

47. "Random Recollections," 59-60.

48. "Random Recollections," 59-60.

49. John Pierpont (1785-1866). Journal, 1805-1810, 6-7. Pierpont Morgan Library, New York, 6-7.

50. J. Isaac Copeland, "The Tutor in the Ante-Bellum South," in *Proceedings of the South Carolina Historical Association,* 1965, 40.

51. In Greek mythology, Charon was the boatman who ferried dead souls across the river Styx to Hades.

52. John Pierpont journal, 7-9.

53. John K. Winkler, *Morgan the Magnificent. The Life of J. Pierpont Morgan* (New York: Vanguard Press, 1930), 24-28.

54. John Pierpont journal, 14.

55. John Pierpont, Georgetown, S.C., to Samuel J. Hitchcock, c/o Rev. A. Backus, Bethlehem, Ct., June 22, 1806 [SJH].

56. John Pierpont, Clifton, to Samuel J. Hitchcock, Bethlehem, Ct., November 26, 1806 [SJH].

57. John Pierpont, Georgetown, SC, to Samuel J. Hitchcock, c/o Rev. A. Backus, Bethlehem, Ct., June 22, 1806 [SJH].

58. John Pierpont, Charleston, to Samuel Hitchcock, Student, Yale College, New Haven, Ct., July 9, 1807 [SJH].

59. John Pierpont, Georgetown, S.C., to Samuel J. Hitchcock, c/o Rev. A. Backus, Bethlehem, Ct., June 22, 1806 [SJH].

60. John Pierpont, near Georgetown, S.C., to Samuel J. Hitchcock, c/o Rev. A. Backus, Bethlehem, Ct., August 13, 1806 [SJH].

61. John Pierpont, near Georgetown, S.C., to Samuel J. Hitchcock, c/o Rev. A. Backus, Bethlehem, Ct., August 13, 1806 [SJH].

62. John Pierpont, Fairfield, near Georgetown, S.C., to Samuel Hitchcock, Bethlehem, Ct., January 13, 1807 [SJH].

63. John Pierpont, Georgetown, S.C., to Samuel J. Hitchcock, Bethlehem, Ct., March 19, 1807 [SJH].

64. John Pierpont journal, 10-11. Pierpont's experience of Christmas on the plantation is discussed in Abe C. Ravitz, "John Pierpont and the Slaves' Christmas," in *Phylon, the Atlanta University Review of Race & Culture,* Vol. 21, No. 4 (Winter, 1960), 383-386. Ravitz's Ph.D. dissertation (New York University, 1955) was entitled, "John Pierpont: Portrait of a Nineteenth Century Reformer." Although Ravitz misinterpreted the name of Marietta Plantation (citing it as "Monjetta"), his article and dissertation present a clear and balanced picture of the young, Northern idealist, his rapid disenchantment with plantation society, and the development of his abolitionist sentiments.

65. John Pierpont, *DAB.*

66. Draft of an obituary for Motte Alston, n.d. [APF].

67. John Pierpont, Medford, MA to MMP, September 16, 1852 [APF] and Winkler, 27. Abbie A. Ford, who wrote *John Pierpont. A Biographical Sketch* (Boston, privately printed, 1909), overlooked Pierpont's journal and much of his correspondence, dismissed Pierpont's Southern

experiences, and ignored his enduring personal affection for the Alston family.

68. North and South Islands are barrier islands on either side of Winyah Bay, which is Georgetown's harbor. It is formed by the confluence of the Sampit, Black, PeeDee, and Waccamaw Rivers.

69. In Greek mythology, Phoebus was the equivalent of Apollo, god of the sun. *Chronicles*, 48.

70. MMA journal, Yauhanee, July, 1818 [APF].

71. Carolyn G. Heilbrun, *Writing a Woman's Life* (New York: W.W. Norton, 1988), 51.

Chapter 3: Judge Pringle's Son

1.*Chronicles*, 53. Mechlin, a weaving center located between Brussels and Antwerp in northern Belgium, was noted for the fineness of its lace.

2. "Married at Edgewood," undated newspaper clipping describing the wedding of Susan Pringle Mitchell to J. Mason Hoppin [DGM].

3. *Chronicles*, 53.

4. "Robert Pringle," in Alexander Pringle, *The Records of the Pringles or Hoppringills of the Scottish Border* (Edinburgh: Oliver & Boyd, 1933), 344.

5. Upon the death of Robert Pringle, ownership of the house at 70 Tradd Street passed to John Julius Pringle (1753-1843), then to his sons, Robert and William Bull Pringle, and to his nephew, William Alston Pringle (1822-1895). After the death of his wife, Alston sold the house in 1886 and moved into the Miles Brewton House. He lived there with his sister Susan until he died in 1895.

6. "Robert Pringle," in Alexander Pringle, *The Records of the Pringles or Hoppringills of the Scottish Border* (Edinburgh: Oliver & Boyd, 1933), 344; "Robert Pringle," in *BDSCHR* 2: 542-543 and "Robert Pringle and His World," *SCHM* 76: 1-11.

7. His classmates included Richard Beresford, later a member of the Continental Congress and lieutenant governor of South Carolina; Charles Pinckney, later governor of South Carolina and a U.S. Senator; and Thomas Shubrick, later aide-de-camp to Generals Lincoln and Greene in the Revolutionary War. E. Alfred Jones, *American Members of the Inns of Court* (London: The St. Catherine Press, 1924), xi, 175.

8. John B. O'Neill, *Biographical Sketches of the Bench & Bar in South Carolina*, 2, 3-10; *BDSCHR* 3: 586-88, the D.A.B. 8: 237-238 and "Ralph Izard," in *BDSCHR* 3: 371-73; and Charles Fraser, "Tribute to the Memory of the Hon. John Julius Pringle" [APF].

9. Susan Pringle Frost also gives this reason in her "Account of the Portraits in the Drawing Room and Parlours at 27 King Street" (typescript, n.d.) [APF].

10. Judge Pringle leased #54 Tradd Street to Charleston's postmaster,

Thomas W. Bacot and it was used for a time as Charleston's post office. Pringle sold the property in 1807, and after Civil War, the property was neglected and fell into disrepair. It was restored in 1917 by pioneer preservationist, Susan Pringle Frost, Judge Pringle's great-granddaughter. Charleston *News & Courier*, April 19, 1917.

11. For a listing of Judge Pringle's children and their spouses, see Appendix I.

12. Charleston County Death Records card file, Charleston County Library.

13. No records of any collegiate education have yet been found for William.

14. "Commissioners of Free Schools," in *Descriptive Inventory of the Division of Archives and Records* (City of Charleston Department of Archives and Records, 1991).

15. South Carolina General Assembly Petitions, n.d., #4032-01. Charleston College. SCDAH.

16. James H. Smith to William B. Pringle, August 15, 1836 [photocopy from a private collection in the Miles Brewton House collection].

17. Installation certificate, July 12, 1820 [APF].

18. *Chronicles*, 52.

19. Alicia Hopton Middleton, *Life in Carolina and New England During the Nineteenth Century* (Bristol, R.I.: privately printed, 1929), 62.

20. *Chronicles*, 52.

21. MMP journal, 1822-1881 [APF].

22. Charles C. P. Alston, Fairfield plantation, to MMP, Charleston, March 17, 1822 [APF].

23. David Doar, *A Sketch of the Agricultural Society of St. James, Santee, South Carolina, and an Address on the Traditions and Reminiscences of the Parish, Delivered Before Society on 4th of July, 1907* (Charleston: Calder-Fladger Co., 1908), 29.

24. "Random Recollections," 21.

25. "Random Recollections," 140.

26. "Random Recollections," 32.

27. "Random Recollections," 33.

28. Doar, *A Sketch*, 17.

29. Mrs. Genevieve W. Chandler, interview with Uncle Ben Horry, age 87, Murrell's Inlet, S.C., August, 1937. South Carolina "Slave Narratives," Part 2, 307, in *The American Slave: A Composite Autobiography* (Westport, Conn.: Greenwood Publishing Co., 1972), vol. 2.

30. Doar, *A Sketch*, 11.

31. Anthony Q. Devereaux, *The Rice Princes: A Rice Epoch Revisited* (Columbia, S.C.: The State Co., 1973), v.

32. Obituary of Col. William Alston.

33. Obituary of Col. William Alston.

34. "Random Recollections," 158.

Chapter 4: Children of the Pluff Mud

1. According to surviving bills of sale in his papers, William bought 40 slaves from Robert Y. Hayne on January 1, 1823; 7 from John Dawson on January 21, 1823; 8 from Mary Ann B. Miles on February 28, 1826; 6 from Edward Thomas in March, 1834; 7 from Elizabeth McPherson on February 1, 1842; 11 from Charles Alston on February 7, 1844; 10 from James Poyas (executor of the estate of Isaac Ball) on January 10, 1845; 5 from Daniel G. Joye on January 30, 1846; 6 from Edward Fripp on January 22, 1846 and 7 from T. Savage Heyward on February 5, 1846 [APF].

2. Elizabeth B. Pharo, ed., *Reminiscences of William Hasell Wilson (1811-1902)* (Philadelphia: Patterson & White, 1937), 20.

3. The fate of the barouche is unknown. It was probably sold after 1865 to raise money for the family. The smaller coach, fully restored, is now preserved at Middleton Place.

4. Alberta Morel Lachicotte, *Georgetown Rice Plantations* (Columbia, S.C.: The State Co., 1955), 85-88. The front entrance was later remodeled in the Greek Revival style, probably in the 1840s or 1850s.

5. MAP, Beneventum to JJP, USS *Concord*, November 27, 1841 [JJP].

6. WBP, Beneventum, to JJP, USS *Concord*, Rio de Janeiro, February 27, 1842 [JJP].

7. Charlotte Manigault to Arthur M. Manigault, February 14, 1848. Joseph and Charlotte Manigault Papers [MBH].

8. 1850 Federal Census. Agricultural and slave schedules. Charleston District. St. Andrews Parish.

9. Jane Pringle, Greenfield Plantation, to MMP, c/o Smith & Coffin, Charleston, December 1, 1845 [M-P].

10. MMP and RBP, Beneventum, to JJP, USS *Concord*, February 27, 1842 [JJP].

11. *Chronicles*, 77.

12. *Chronicles*, 93.

13. *Chronicles*, 76.

14. "Random Recollections," 102.

15. Bannockburn was a rice plantation on the east bank of the Waccamaw River in Georgetown District owned by John Izard Middleton (1800-1887). His wife, Sarah McPherson (Alston) Middleton was a niece and frequent correspondent of MMP.

16. MMP, Charleston, to JJP, USS *Concord*, October 18, 1840 [JJP].

17. The "marsh tackey" was a small horse "said to have been brought by the Spaniards to the Low Country of South Carolina and Georgia, and bred to stock imported from Europe." Heyward, *Madagascar*, 118.

18. "Random Recollections," 92-93.

19. MMP, Charleston, to SP, Pelham Priory, November 17, 1845 [APF].

20. Bob Wilkins was one of their horses.

21. MAP, Beneventum, to JJP, USS *Concord*, April 20, 1841 [JJP].
22. "Random Recollections," 5-6.
23. "Random Recollections," 5-6.
24. Frederick Law Olmsted, *A Journey in the Seaboard Slave States, With Remarks on their Economy* (New York: Dix & Edwards, 1856), 419.
25. WBP, Charleston, to JJP, USS *Concord*, October 30, 1841 [JJP].
26. EJP, San Francisco, to MMP, Charleston, October 30, 1855 [EJP]
27. Dr. Eli Geddings (1799-1878), a distinguished professor of anatomy and surgery at the South Carolina Medical College, lost his library and fortune during the war and was forced to resume a private practice. Joseph Ioor Waring, *History of Medicine in South Carolina* (3 vols. 1964-1967, reprinted Spartanburg, S.C., The Reprint Co., 1977), II: 235-238.
28. MMP, Charleston, to RBP, Paris, June 19, 1857 [APF].
29. MMP receipt book, 1791- (vol. 1) [APF].
30. MMP, Charleston, to MPM, n.p., June 9, 1853 [APF].
31. MMP reciept book, 1791- (vol. 1) [APF].
32. Chillblains: painful swelling or inflamed sores on the feet or hands caused by exposure to cold.
33. MMP, Runimede, to SP, Pelham Priory, December 6, 1845 [APF].
34. MPM, Edgewood, to MMP, February 13, 1856 [M-P].
35. *Chronicles*, 53.
36. *Chronicles*, 54.
37. William's "worthy and lamented friend and relative" may have been his elder brother, Charles James Pringle, who was born in 1796 and about whom little else is known.
38. WBP, Charleston, to JJP, USS *Concord*, Brazilian Station, January, 1841 [JJP].
39. MMP household journal, 1850-1861 [APF].
40. MMP household journal, 1834-1865 [APF].
41. *Chronicles*, 54.
42. "Random Recollections," 58. The name of this gardener has been lost.
43. *Chronicles*, passim.
44. "Random Recollections," 59.
45. "Random Recollections," 57.
46. Interview with Peter Manigault, June 1, 1992.
47. Jacob's memory failed him in this detail. The figures on the ceiling are eagles.
48. "Random Recollections," 58.
49. "Random Recollections," 64.
50. Frost, *Highlights*, 21.
51. MMP, household inventory book, 1834-1870 [APF].
52. These textiles have been donated to the Museum of Early Southern Decorative Arts in Winston-Salem, N. C.

53. David Shields, "The Place of the Arts in the Culture of South Carolina," a lecture delivered at the Gibbes Museum of Art, January 11, 1992.

54. Margaret Simons Middleton, *Henrietta Johnston, of Charles Town, South Carolina: America's First Pastellist* (Columbia: University of South Carolina Press, 1966), 56-57.

55. Miles Brewton House collection.

56. "Random Recollections," 55.

57. Rebecca Brewton and Rebecca Motte portraits: Miles Brewton House Collection.

58. Jacob Motte Alston, Barclay Farm, Ga., August 11, 1886, to My Dearest Hessie. Jacob Motte Alston Papers, Library of Congress.

59. As of 2000, this portrait was on loan to the Gibbes Museum of Art in Charleston.

60. Paul Staiti, "John Ashe Alston: Patron of Samuel F.B. Morse," in *Art in the Lives of South Carolinians: Nineteenth-Century Chapters* (Charleston: Carolina Art Association, 1978), PSa-11.

61. Martha R. Severens and Charles L. Wyrick, *Charles Fraser of Charleston* (Charleston: Carolina Art Association, 1983), 16 and plate 5 (opposite p. 46). This Fraser sketchbook belongs to the Carolina Art Association; another is at the South Carolina Historical Society and two more reside in the Charleston Museum.

62. Alice R. Huger Smith and D. E. Huger Smith, *Charles Fraser* (Charleston: Garnier & Co., 1967), 19; also Severens & Wyrick, 71. Miles Brewton House collection.

63. Fraser's account book for 1841, in Severens & Wyrick, 140.

64. MMP, record of servants book, 1850-1861 [APF].

65. *Chronicles*, 13.

66. "Random Recollections," 87.

67. *Chronicles*, 13.

68. *Chronicles*, 26.

69. "Random Recollections," 22.

70. "Random Recollections," 26.

71. Heyward, *Madacascar*, 219.

Chapter 5: A Family of Substance

1. "Random Recollections," 86.

2. "Random Recollections," 124.

3. Inventories of Estate, H: 433; I: 470-471. Charleston County Probate Court.

4. Rogers, *Georgetown County*, 267; also Lachicotte, *Georgetown Rice Plantations* , 25. Alston descendants lived at Fairfield until 1936, when it was sold to George Vanderbilt, after which it became part of Arcadia Plantation.

5. Inventories of Estate, vol. H., 433 & 470-471. Charleston County Probate Court.

6. Brent Holcomb, "Marriage and Obituary Notices from the Columbia Free Press and Hive," in *South Carolina Magazine of Ancestral Research,* I: 97.

7. Rogers, *Georgetown County,* 339.

8. South Carolina General Assembly Reports, n.d., #1246-01 & 1406-01, SCDAH.

9. Rogers, *Georgetown County,* 316.

10. MMP to SP, Pelham Priory, March 4, 1846, in *Chronicles,* 85.

11. WBP, Beneventum, to JJP, USS *Concord,* Norfolk, Virginia, late 1840 [JJP].

12. In 1820, Rabbit Island consisted of two small islands in the middle of Winyaw Bay, two miles southeast of the mouth of the Sampit River and ten miles upstream from the mouth of Winyaw Bay.

13. "Fancy and Masquerade Ball" invitation, no date; also "Commencement Ball" invitation, Charleston, October 24, 1833 [M-P].

14. Susan L. King, *History and Records of the Charleston Orphan House* (Easley, S.C.: Southern Historical Press, 1984), passim.

15. Receipt dated March 12, 1861 [APF].

16. WBP, Charleston, to JJP, USS *Concord,* Rio de Janeiro, May 23, 1842 [JJP].

17. S.M. Middleton, Waccamaw, to MMP, Charleston, November 1, 1845 [M-P].

18. MMP, Charleston, to SP, Pelham Priory, New Rochelle, NY, October 24, 1845 [APF].

19. MMP, King Street, to SP, Pelham Priory, October 27, 1845 [APF].

20. MMP to RBP & SP, c/o Mrs. William Mason Smith, Blue House P.O., Godfrey's Savannah, December 21, 1841 [APF].

21. MMP, Charleston, to MPM, September, 1853 [APF].

22. WBP, Jr., Beneventum, to JJP, USS *Concord,* Rio de Janeiro, March 11, 1842 [JJP].

23. MMP, Runimede, to My dear son [Charles], February 20, 1860 [EJP].

24. MMP, Charleston, to SP, Pelham Priory, October 20, 1845 [APF].

25. MPM, Edgewood, to RBP, n.p., January 27, 1856 [M-P].

26. DGM to Hesse Mitchell, June 11, 1880 [DGM].

27. MMP, Charleston, to MPM, abroad, September, 1853 [APF].

28. *Chronicles,* 61.

29. William Barrow, *Essays on Education* (Philadelphia: Harrison Hall, 1825).

30. Rosser H. Taylor, *Ante-Bellum South Carolina: A Social and Cultural History* (Chapel Hill: University of North Carolina Press, 1942), 116.

31. MMP, Charleston, to JJP, USS *Concord,* Rio de Janeiro, October 28, 1841 [JJP].

32. MMP journal, 1826- (vol. 6, 31-32); also MMP to a son at college, no date, in *Chronicles,* 109-110.

33. Doar, *A Sketch,* 20.

34. "Free Schools in South Carolina," in Miller's *Planters' and Merchants' Almanac. . . .* (Charleston: A.E. Miler, 1838).

35. WBP, Jr., Beneventum, to JJP, n.p., March 11, 1842 [JJP].

36. Colyer Meriwether, *History of Higher Education in South Carolina with a Sketch of the Free School System* (Washington: Government Printing Office, 1889), 30.

37. Meriwether, *Higher Education*, 31.

38. William J. and Isaac Lesesne, "both of whom had been his scholars." Meriwether, *Higher Education*, 31; MMP, Charleston, to JJP, USS *Concord*, May 27, 1842 [JJP].

39. "Random Recollections," 102.

40. MMP, Charleston, to JJP, USS *Concord*, Rio de Janeiro, August 31, 1842 [JJP].

41. "Random Recollections," 103.

42. Septimus Cotes, Newington Rectory, Wallingford, England to WBP, March 23, 1855 [APF].

43. *Chronicles*, 93.

44. MMP, Beneventum, to Mary & Susan Pringle, c/o Mrs. Wm. M. Smith, Blue House P.O., Godfrey's Savannah, December 17, 1841. [APF] The author has been unable to locate information on Mr. Raslam.

45. The 1856 and 1859 Charleston directories list William Searle, teacher, residing at 68 Wentworth Street. Mary used the spelling, "Searles."

46. D.E. Huger Smith, *A Charlestonian's Recollections, 1846-1913* (Charleston: Carolina Art Association, 1950), 60.

47. MMP, Runimede, to SP, Pelham Priory, February 4, 1846 [APF].

48. The 1856 Charleston city directory lists Joseph Henry Guenebault, a teacher, at 156 Meeting Street.

49. MMP, Beneventum, to Mary & Susan Pringle, c/o Mrs. Wm. M. Smith, Blue House P.O., Godfrey's Savannah, December 17, 1841. [APF]

50. Mr. A. Boneaud, dancing master, was listed at 145 Meeting Street in the 1849 Charleston city directory. Mrs. Feugas and her Dancing Academy were listed at 74 King St. in the 1840-41 Charleston city directory; Mr. H. P. Feugas, a French teacher, and Madame Feugas, a teacher of dancing, were listed at 70 King Street in the 1849 Charleston city directory.

51. MMP, Charleston, to JJP, USS *Concord*, Brazilian Station, June 21, 1841 [JJP].

52. In 1838, Mary's brother, Charles Cotesworth Pinckney Alston, purchased what is now known as the Edmondston-Alston House Museum at 21 East Battery Street, Charleston. Its library contains many of the books which Charles inherited from his father.

53. William Alston Pringle, Charleston, to Dear Sissie [Mrs. Benjamin Rhett], Mobile, Ala., May 23 and July 2, 1895 [RPW].

54. Richard N. Côté and Rose Tomlin, "Inventory of Antebellum Books in the Miles Brewton House, April, 1993" [APF].

55. William Thomas Lowndes, *Bibliographical Manual of English Literature* (London, 1858-1864), 4 volumes. This immense reference work listed approximately 50,000 titles and their cost or market value to collectors.

56. MMP to her sons, no date, in *Chronicles*, 106.

57. MMP to her sons at college, no date, in *Chronicles*, 102.

58."Joel Roberts Poinsett," *DAB*.

59. Robert Southey (1774-1843), *The Life of Nelson*, London, printed for John Murray, 1813. William Francis Patrick Napier, *History of the War in the Peninsula and in the South of France* (London, 1826). 6 vols. James Fenimore Cooper, *The Two Admirals* (Philadelphia, 1842). 2 vols.

60. Philippe-Paul, le compte de Segur, *Histoire de Napoléon et de la grande armée pendant l'annee 1812*. An English edition was published in 1826.

61. John Griscom, *A Year in Europe . . . 1818 - 1819* (New York: Collins & Co., 1823). 2 vol.

62. MMP to her sons, n.d. (1850s), in *Chronicles*, 63.

63. Oliver H. Leigh, ed., *Letters to His Son. On the Fine Art of Becoming a Man of the World and a Gentleman*. By the Earl of Chesterfield (New York: M.W. Dunne, 1901), i.

64. MMP journal, 1826-, 31, 32; also MMP to a son a college, no date, in *Chronicles*, 108.

65. "Random Recollections," 66.

66. MMP journal, 1822-1881 (vol. 4) [APF].

77. MMP journal, 1822-1881 (vol. 4) [APF].

68. Bill of sale, Louisa Hunt to Col. William Alston, October 26, 1832 [APF].

69. William James, *The Varieties of Religious Experience* (New York: New American Library, 1958), 24.

70. George W. Williams, ed., *Incidents In My Life. The Autobiography of the Rev. Paul Trapier, S.T.D., With Some of His Letters* (Charleston: Dalcho Historical Society, 1954), 26.

71. Pharo, *Wilson*, 29.

72. Sarah Russell Dehon to Paul Trapier, November 1, 1832, in the Trapier Family Papers, Southern Historical Collection, University of North Carolina, Chapel Hill.

73. Albert Sidney Thomas, *A Historical Account of the Protestant Episcopal Church in South Carolina, 1820-1957* (Columbia: printed by the R.L. Bryan Co., 1957), 270.

74. The Pringles are mentioned three times in the records of All Saints parish. Mary was listed as having come into the parish in 1837 and removed in 1839. In 1840 she was the sponsor at the baptism of George Blyth Weston, son of Francis & Elizabeth Weston. In 1842, their daughter, Mary Frances, was a sponsor at the baptism of Maria Henrietta Middleton, daughter of John Izard and Sarah M. Middleton. Despite this, they do not seem to have been heavily involved in the life of the parish.

75. Williams, *Trapier*, 22.

76. MMP, Edgewood, to JRP, Charleston, August 25, 1858 [APF].

77. MMP, Runimede, to My dear son [EJP], April 14, 1859 [EJP].

78. The diligence was a French train. Charles Eliot Norton, Midway Plantation, Edisto Island, to J.R. Lowell, April 6, 1855, in *Letters of Charles Eliot Norton, with Biographical Comment by His Daughter, Sara Norton and M. A. deWolf Howe* (Boston and New York: Houghton Mifflin, 1913), II: 124.

Chapter 6: Anything But Planting

1. MMP, Charleston to JJP, USS *Concord*, Brazilian Station, January 28, 1841 [JJP].

2. MMP, Charleston, to JJP, USS *Concord*, Rio de Janeiro, October 24, 1842 [JJP].

3. MMP, Beneventum, to JJP, USS *Concord*, Rio de Janeiro, January 20, 1842 [JJP].

4. WAP, Charleston, to JJP, USS *Concord*, Rio de Janeiro, October 9, 1842 [JJP].

5. MMP, Beneventum, to JJP, USS *Concord*, Rio de Janeiro, December 14, 1841 [JJP].

6. Taylor, *Ante-Bellum South Carolina*, 118-121.

7. MMP, Beneventum Plantation, to JJP, USS *Concord*, Brazilian Station, April 13, 1841 [JJP].

8. JJP, USS *Concord*, at sea, to WBP, Jr., South Carolina College, Columbia, September 14, 1841 [M-P].

9. WAP, Charleston, to JJP, USS *Concord*, Rio de Janeiro, July 20, 1841 [JJP]

10. Smith & Smith, 8-9.

11. MMP, Charleston, to JJP, USS *Concord*, Rio de Janeiro, September 11, 1841 [JJP].

12. Judge William Ford deSaussure was a widely-respected Charleston attorney from an old and honored Huguenot family. He was a Harvard man (class of 1810), practiced law in Columbia and Charleston, served a term in the state legislature, served six years as judge of the chancery court, and was elected to the U.S. Senate.

13. SP, Beneventum, to JJP, USS *Concord*, January 20, 1842 [JJP].

14. MMP, Charleston, to JJP, USS *Concord*, May 27, 1842 [JJP].

15. Court of Appeals in Equity. Petition to practice law. Box 1, No. 50, SCDAH.

16. MMP & WBP, Charleston, to EJP, Cambridge, March 2, 1845 [APF].

17. Emma S. Pringle, Runimede, to SP, Pelham Priory, New Rochelle, NY, April [n.d.] and May 16, 1846 (same letter) [RPW].

18. Emma S. Pringle, Runimede, to SP, Pelham Priory, New Rochelle, NY, April [n.d.] and May 16, 1846 (same letter) [RPW].

19. EJP, San Francisco, to WBP, September 29, 1854 [APF].
20. City of Charleston *Yearbook*, 1881, 374.
21. Will of Robert Pringle, May 5, 1860, proved October 29, 1860 [APF].
22. Copy of a letter from Robert Pringle, Paris, to WBP, August 17, 1854 [APF].
23. City of Charleston, *List of the Taxpayers of the City of Charleston for 1859*, 280.
24. Obituary of WAP, Charleston *News & Courier*, February 28, 1895.
25. EJP, San Francisco, to RBP, Charleston, January 30, 1859 [APF].
26. MMP, Charleston to JJP, c/o WBP, Norfolk, Virginia, October 7, 1840 [JJP].
27. In ordinary: laid up out of commission.
28. JJP, USS *Java*, Norfolk, VA to MMP & WBP, Charleston, November 19, 1840 [M-P]
29. WBP, Charleston, to JJP, USS *Concord*, Rio de Janeiro, May 23, 1842 [JJP].
30. MMP, Charleston, to JJP, USS *Concord*, November 14, 1840 [JJP]
31. WBP, Beneventum Plantation, to JJP, USS *Concord*, Norfolk, Virginia, late 1840 [JJP].
32. JJP, USS *Concord*, Rio de Janeiro, to JMAP, Charleston, July 20, 1841 [M-P].
33. MMP, King Street, to JJP, USS *Concord*, Rio de Janeiro, October 28, 1841 [JJP].
34. JJP, Off Cape Henry, to My Dear Parents, March 28, 1843 [M-P].
35. Quillimane: now Quelimane, a port on the central coast of Mozambique.
36. JJP, Off Cape Henry, to My Dear Parents, March 28, 1843 [M-P].
37. Grape: grape shot, a cluster of small, cast iron balls, which, when fired from a cannon, spread in a shotgun pattern. In naval warfare, grape shot was highly effective against sails, rigging and personnel.
38. JJP, Off Cape Henry, to My Dear Parents, March 28, 1843 [M-P].
39. *Dictionary of American Naval Fighting Ships*, II: 158.
40. JJP, Off Cape Henry, to My Dear Parents, March 28, 1843 [M-P].
41. *Dictionary of American Naval Fighting Ships*, vol. IV, 390-391.
42. "A Naval Reminiscence. Ex-Gov. [Rodman M.] Price Tells His experiences Of When He Was Paymaster in the Navy. The Burning of the United States Steam Frigate Missouri at Gibraltar in 1843. . . ." Undated newspaper clipping in JJP's Game Book (unnumbered volume) [JJP].
43. JJP, Boston, to MMP, Charleston, March 9, 1844 [M-P].
44. W. D. Puleston, *Annapolis: Gangway to the Quarterdeck* (New York: D. Appleton-Century Company, 1943), 53.
45. Puleston, *Annapolis*, 66.
46. Abstracts of Service Records of Naval Officers. Records of Officers, 1798-1893, microfilm reels 6 & 8 (July, 1840 - December, 1858),

National Archives. Another record, dated July 1, 1846, ranked him 8th out of 50. Board of Examiners Records, 1846, 43, Naval Academy Archives.

47. In 1846-1847, Commodore Matthew Calbraith Perry (1794-1858) commanded the Gulf squadron during the Mexican War.

48. *Dictionary of American Naval Fighting Ships,* III: 91.

49. MMP journal, 1822-1881 [APF].

50. On June 4, 1847, Edward wrote in his journal that he had read in the newspapers that Julius had been wounded at Laliscoya. On July 1, 1847, he received a letter from Mary describing the wounds. EJP, Grand Tour Journal, 1, 34 [EJP].

51. *Dictionary of American Naval Fighting Ships,* III: 91.

52. Pringle Family Bible [MBH]; also Stephen Duncan Correspondence, Special Collections, Hill Memorial Library, Louisiana State University, Baton Rouge, La.

53. Michael Wayne, *The Reshaping of Plantation Society: The Natchez District, 1860-1880* (Baton Rouge: Louisiana State University Press, 1983), 10.

54. Stephen Duncan. Journal, 1861-1870. Stephen Duncan and Stephen Duncan, Jr., Papers, Louisiana and Lower Mississippi Valley Collections, LSU Libraries, Louisiana State University.

55. Stephen Duncan. Journal, 1861-1870. Stephen Duncan and Stephen Duncan, Jr., Papers, Louisiana and Lower Mississippi Valley Collections, LSU Libraries, Louisiana State University.

56. Stephen Duncan was born March 4, 1787, and died January 29, 1867, at Rheinbeck, New York.

57. Taylor, *Ante-Bellum South Carolina,* 105-106.

58. Bertram Lippincott, III, Librarian, Newport Historical Society, to the author, May 27, 1993. "Russian Henry": "Whitfield's," in Newport *Journal,* June 26, 1909.

59. Mrs. John King Van Rensselaer, *Newport, Our Social Capitol* (Philadelphia: J.B. Lippincott, 1905), 29.

60. A hogshead contains 63 gallons. Louisiana's antebellum chronicler of sugar production, F. A. Champomier, used 1,150 lbs. as amount of sugar in a hogshead, although he noted that there was a considerable variation from plantation to plantation. The federal census enumerators used 1,000 lbs. as their definition.

61. A standard U.S. barrel had a capacity of 31.5 gallons.

62. JJP, Natchez, to WBP, Charleston, January 17, 1854 [M-P].

63. JJP, Natchez, to WBP, Charleston, January 17, 1854 [M-P].

64. JJP, Torwood, to MMP, May 19, 1856 [M-P].

65. Joseph Karl Menn, *The Large Slaveholders of Louisiana - 1860.* New Orleans: Pelican Publishing Co., 1964, 31.

66. Menn, *Slaveholders,* 320-321. The $250,000 was the value of the land itself, not including slaves. At $500 each, his 318 slaves would have been worth at least $159,000 additional. The $25,000 in personal

property should have included slaves and the contents of his home, farm implements, crops on hand, and livestock. Clearly, it did not.

67. P. A. Champomier, *Statement of the Sugar Crop, Made In Louisiana, in 1859-60* (New Orleans: Cook, Young & Co., 1860), 3-5.

68. The price for molasses is from 1859 sales at Woodlawn plantation, Assumption Parish, La., about 100 miles from Torwood. See Barnes Fletcher Lathrop, "The Pugh Plantations, 1860-1865: A Study of Life in Lower Louisiana," Ph.D. dissertation, University of Texas, 1945, 64.

69. EJP, San Francisco, to MMP, Charleston, February 13, 1859 [APF].

70. RBP, Runimede, to CAP, March 8, 1860 [EJP].

71. WBP, Charleston, to JJP, USS *Concord*, Rio de Janeiro, May 23, 1842 [JJP].

72. MMP, Charleston to JJP, USS *Concord*, August 9, 1842 [JJP].

73. EJP, student papers [EJP].

74. Charleston *Courier*, October 11, 1845, reprinting an article from the *U.S. Catholic Miscellany*, August 29, 1845.

75. Certificate from the South Carolina Law Court of Appeals, May 12, 1847 [EJP]. Judge Edward Frost, the father of his future brother-in-law, Frank Frost, was one of the bar examiners.

76. Edward had several companions at different times during his European travels. They included Dr. Arthur Rose; Arthur Parker, Charles Shannon (from the Upcountry); and two chums whom he names only as "Heyward" and "Ravenel."

77. EJP, Grand Tour journal, 1 [EJP].

78. Grand Tour journal, 19.

79. Grand Tour journal, 46.

80. Chefs d'oeuvre: art masterpieces.

81. Grand Tour journal, 47-48.

82. Grand Tour journal, 54.

83. Grand Tour journal, April 25, 1849 [EJP].

84. James Buchanan (1791-1868) served as minister to Great Britain for several years before winning election to the presidency in 1856.

85. EJP, Lancaster, Pennsylvania, to WBP, July 28, 1853 [APF].

86. Edward Jenkins Pringle, *Slavery in the Southern States* (Cambridge, Mass.: John Bartlett, 1853, third edition), p. 6.

87. Charles Eliot Norton (1827-1908) taught at Harvard from 1873 to 1897.

88. Charles Eliot Norton, Midway Plantation, Edisto Island, to J.R. Lowell, April 6, 1855, in Norton, vol. 1, 125.

89. *Slavery in the Southern States*, 3.

90. *Slavery in the Southern States*, 3.

91. Edward meant 36 percent annual interest. EJP, New Port, to WBP, "Tuesday" (about August 2, 1853) [APF].

92. EJP, New Port, to WBP, "Tuesday" (about August 2, 1853) [APF].

93. EJP, New Port, to MMP, Charleston, c. September, 1853 [APF].

94. EJP, New Port, to MMP, Charleston, c. September, 1853 [APF].

95. Cuffee: a euphemism for slaves.
96. EJP, near Nicaragua, to MMP, December 14, 1853 [JJP].
97. EJP, San Francisco, to JJP, n.p., January 15, 1854 [JJP].
98. The old gentleman: William Bull Pringle.
99. EJP, San Francisco, to JJP, January 15, 1854 [JJP].
100. EJP, San Francisco, to MMP, Charleston, January 30, 1854 [EJP].
101. EJP, San Francisco, to MMP, Charleston, January 30, 1854 [EJP].
102. EJP, San Francisco, to MMP, Charleston, January 30 & 31, 1854 [APF].
103. EJP, San Francisco, to WBP, Charleston, January 31, 1854 [APF].
104. EJP, San Francisco, to WBP, Charleston, January 3, 1857 [APF].
105. EJP, San Francisco, to WBP, February 4, 1857 [APF].
106. EJP, San Francisco, to WAP, Charleston, March 3, 1857 [APF].
107. "The Limantour Claims. The Story of the Man Who Claimed to Own San Francisco. . . ." (San Francisco, no publisher, 1983).
108. EJP, San Francisco, to WBP, Charleston, October 3, 1858 [EJP].
109. EJP, San Francisco, to WBP, Charleston, November 4, 1858 [APF].
110. League: three statute miles.
111. EJP, San Francisco, to MPM, New Haven, February 4, 1859 [APF].
112. SP, Edgewood, to CAP, n.p., September 14, 1860 [EJP].
113. EJP, n.p., to MMP, October 10, 1860 [APF].
114. EJP, San Francisco, to SP, Charleston, October 31, 1860 [EJP].
115. MMP, Charleston to JJP, USS *Concord*, Brazilian Station, February 16, 1841 [JJP].
116. "Descendants of Judge Robert Pringle," *SCHM*, 62: 226-227.
117. On February 7, 1852, Alston sold 52 slaves to Allen S. Izard for $22,500. The reason for the sale is not known, but may have been in support of Motte. Bills of sale, vol. 6-C, 417, SCDAH.
118. Robert Pringle, Paris, to WBP, January or June 30, 1853 [APF].
119. EJP, San Francisco, to WBP, Charleston, October 3, 1858 [EJP].
120. EJP, San Francisco, to WBP, Charleston, November 4, 1858 [APF].
121. MMP, Charleston, to SP, Newport, October 26, 1859 [APF].
122. MMP, Charleston, to my dear daughter, November 25, 1859 [APF].
123. Lockwood Barr, *Ancient Town of Pelham, Westchester County, New York* (n.p., Dietz Press, 1946), 150; also Reginald Pelham Bolton, "Nanette Bolton, Principal of the Priory School for Girls," *Quarterly Bulletin of the Westchester County Historical Society*, 9, no. 4 (October, 1933), 84-85.
124. MMP, King Street, to SP, Pelham Priory, October 27, 1845 [APF].
125. Emma S. Pringle, Runimede, to SP, Pelham Priory, March 21, 1845 [RPW].
126. Sarah McPherson Middleton, Bannockburn Plantation, quoting

her daughter, Sarah Middleton, to MMP, Charleston, June 25, 1844 [M-P].

127. MMP, Charleston, to SP, Pelham Priory, November 5, 1845 [APF].

128. Presumably Samuel Johnson.

129. MMP, Charleston, to SP, Pelham Priory, October 11, 1845 [APF].

130. MMP, Charleston, to SP, Pelham Priory, November 10, 1845 [APF].

131. MMP and WBP, Charleston, to SP, Pelham Priory, May 30, 1846 [APF].

132. EJP, New York, to MMP, Runimede, November, 1853 [APF].

133. MMP, Charleston, to MPM, February 27, 1854 [APF].

134. Minnie: Mary Pringle Mitchell, the second child of Mary Frances and Donald Mitchell, who was born in 1855.

135. MMP, Edgewood to RP, August 28, 1858 [APF].

136. WBP, Charleston, to MPM, Paris, May 23, 1854 [APF].

137. Waldo H. Dunn, *The Life of Donald G. Mitchell. Ik Marvel* (New York: Charles Scribner's Sons, 1922), 240-241. *Fresh Gleanings* was published by Harper & Brothers in 1847.

138. Dunn, *Mitchell,* 245.

139. DGM to Mary Goddard, February 1, 1853; in Dunn, 246.

140. Dunn, *Mitchell,* 252.

141. MMP's inscribed copy of *Reveries of a Bachelor* [MBH}.

142. Dunn, *Mitchell,* 259.

143. DGM toWBP, October 30, 1854, in Dunn, 267.

144. *Chronicles*, 54; Roll of Students of South Carolina College, 1805-1905 (Columbia: South Carolina College, 1905), 24, and obituary, *Charleston Mercury,* June 30, 1859.

145. MMP, Charleston, to MFM, abroad, September, 1853 [APF].

146. EJP, San Francisco, to WBP, November 8, 1854 [APF].

147. MMP, Runimede, to EJP, San Francisco, April 20, 1859 [EJP].

148. MMP, Runimede, to EJP, San Francisco, April 20, 1859 [EJP].

149. MMP, Runimede, to EJP, San Francisco, April 26, 1859 [EJP].

150. JJP, New York to WAP, Charleston, telegram, June 2, 1859 [APF].

151. WBP, Charleston, to JJP, July 9, 1859 [JJP].

152. *Chronicles*, 54.

153. MMP, Charleston, to JJP, August 19, 1859 [JJP].

154. *Roll of Students of South Carolina College, 1805-1905* (Columbia: South Carolina College, 1905), 26.

155. WBP, Jr., [at Mrs.] Harden's, to SP, March 10, 1856 [APF].

156. In 1840, John Gravely operated a hardware store at 35 Broad Street and resided at the "new Hotel." John Graveley, merchant, resided at 28 Broad St. in 1855, 6 Short St. in 1856 and 19 Montague St. in 1859.

157. *Roll of Students*, 26.

158. EJP, San Francisco, to MMP, Charleston, August 18, 1856 [APF].

159. Coffin & Pringle, Charleston, to Robert Pringle, Charleston, May 15, 1857 [APF].

160. Robert Pringle, Charleston, to Coffin & Pringle, Charleston, May 16, 1857 [APF].

161. EJP, San Francisco, to MMP, Charleston, May 19, 1857 [APF].

162. CAP, Cambridge, Mass. to MMP, September 13, 1857 [EJP].

163. CAP, Cambridge, Mass. to MMP, September 18, 1857 [EJP].

164. CAP, Cambridge, Mass. to MMP, November 21, 1857 [JJP].

165. EJP, San Francisco, to MMP, Charleston, May 19, 1857 [APF].

166. MMP, Edgewood, to JRP, August 25, 1858 [APF].

167. EJP, San Francisco, to MMP, Charleston, October 4, 1859 [APF].

168. Robert Pringle, Paris, to WBP, n.p., July 21, 1859 [JJP].

169. CAP, Dijon, to MMP, Charleston, October 8, 1859 [APF].

170. MMP, Runimede, to SP, Newport, December 7, 1859 [APF].

171. MMP, Runimede, to My Dear Sons, March (n.d.), 1860 [APF].

172. SP, Edgewood, to CAP, abroad, September 14, 1860 [EJP].

Chapter 7: Trials and Triumphs

1. WAP, Charleston, to MMP, June 30, 1852 [JJP].

2. "Jew brokers": real estate brokers.

3. MMP, Charleston to MPM, Florence, Italy, January 10, 1854 [APF].

4. EJP, San Francisco, to WBP & MMP, Charleston, February 4, 1857 [APF]; also EJP, San Francisco, to MMP, June 19, 1857 [APF].

5. WBP was 53 at the time. MMP, Charleston, to MFM, abroad, September, 1853 [APF].

6. MMP journal, 1822-1881, 126 [APF].

7. MMP to "My beloved sons", MMP journal, vol. 9 [APF].

8. SP, Newport, to RMP, Charleston, October 16, 1859 [APF].

9. Charleston County Inventories of Estate, vol. H., p. 433. Charleston County Probate Court.

10. Deed Book F-14, pp. 135 & 136, Charleston County Register of Mesne Conveyances Office.

11. MMP, Charleston, to RP, Paris, July 28, 1857 [APF].

12. EJP, San Francisco, to MMP, Charleston, May 19, 1857 [APF].

13. RMP, Charleston, to SP, November 21, 1859 [APF].

14. MMP, Runimede, to SP, Newport, December 7, 1859 [APF].

Chapter 8: The Peculiar Institution

1. Henry Nelson Coleridge (1798-1843), *Six Months in the West Indies*, 4th ed., with additions (London: printed for T. Legg, 1841).

2. habitude: the habitual condition of mind or body. Mary is implying that resistance to the diseases of the rice swamps is acquired by birth from parents exposed to them.

3. MMP journal, n.d. (vol. 7) [APF].

4. In 1860, M. G. Ramsay was a small planter with 37 slaves and 130 acres of land under cultivation. His plantation was located immediately north of Runimede on the Ashley River in St. Andrews Parish. 1860 Federal Census, population, agricultural and slave schedules, Charleston District, St. Andrews Parish; also Map of Charleston and its Defences. . .Nov. 28th, 1863.

5. MMP, Runimede, to MPM, December 25, 1856 [APF].

6. MMP, Fairfield, to Beloved Boys, n.p., n.d., in *Chronicles,* 63.

7. MMP, Runimede, to SP, Newport, December 7, 1859 [APF].

8. RBP, Charleston, to SP, November 21, 1859 [APF].

9. Brother Jonathan: a figure of speech used to denote the American people, especially in the context of corruption and misrule.

10. James Fenimore Cooper, the novelist, travel writer and social critic who feared that unspoiled nature would eventually be destroyed by the encroachments of civilization.

11. EJP, San Francisco, to SP, Charleston, January 18, 1857 [APF].

12. Susan Markey Fickling, "The Christianization of the Negro in South Carolina, 1830-1860," (M.A. thesis, University of South Carolina, 1923), 4n.

13. Catechumen: a person receiving instruction in the fundamentals of Christianity. MMP, Runimede, to My dear Son [EJP], April 14, 1859 [EJP].

14. Fickling, "Chrisitianization," 2.

15. In 1756, Samuel Johnson's *Dictionary of the English Language* defined gag as "to put something in the mouth which hinders speech or eating." An illustration of a wrought iron mouth gag from the Spanish colony at St. Augustine, Florida, may be found in Albert H Sonn, *Early American Wrought Iron,* (New York: Charles Scribner's Sons, 1928), III, 234 and Plate 318, opposite 234. Gustavus Vassa, a former colonial slave, described the use of the device on a Virginia slave. See Sally Smith Booth, *Hung, Strung and Potted. A History of Eating in Colonial America* (New York: Clarkson N. Potter, Inc., 1971), 27.

16. EJP, San Francisco, to MMP, Charleston, August 18, 1856 [APF].

17. MPM, Edgewood, to MMP, February 13, 1856 [M-P].

18. 1860 Federal Census. Slave Schedules. Charleston. Ward 2.

19. "Random Recollections," 48.

20. Alicia Hopton Middleton, *Life in Carolina and New England During the Nineteenth Century* (Bristol, R.I.: privately printed, 1929), 60.

21. *Chronicles,* 13.

22. Duncan Clinch Heyward, *Seed from Madagascar* (Chapel Hill, N.C.: University of North Carolina Press, 1937), 187.

23. *Chronicles,* 12.

24. *Chronicles,* 60.

25. From 1861 through about 1872 the entries were made in another well-trained hand (though not of a Pringle family member), who

spelled the name, "Stewart." After 1872 the entries were made in several other hands, probably those of Cretia's own family, who continued the spelling, "Stewart." The Bible also contains the vital statistics of Mary Chisholm's children. See Appendix IV. Miles Brewton House Collection.

26. Charles Joyner, *Down by the Riverside. A South Carolina Slave Community* (Urbana: University of Illinois Press, 1984), 85

27. MMP, record of servants book, 1850-1861 [APF].

28. Osnaburg: a type of coarse, heavy cotton cloth used in making sacks and work clothes.

29. MMP, record of servants book, 1850-1861 [APF].

30. MMP, record of servants book, 1850-1861 [APF].

31. MMP, household inventory book, 1834-1870 [APF].

32. MMP, record of servants book, 1850-1861 [APF].

Chapter 9: Soldiers, Slaves, and Refugees

1. MMP to Charles and James, late February or March, 1861 [APF]. The first and last pages of the letter have been lost.

2. Susan Lowndes Allston, "Vice Admiral J.R.P. Pringle Named for Joel R. Poinsett," Charleston *News & Courier*, May 12, 1942.

3. Mary Pringle Fenhagen, "Descendants of Judge Robert Pringle," *SCHM* 62: 221.

4. William Ravenel, Charleston, to J.R. Pringle Ravenel, Paris, September 19, 1861 [APF].

5. Mary Boykin Chesnut, *A Diary from Dixie* (New York: Peter Smith, 1929), 186-87.

6. City of Charleston *Yearbook*, 1880, 306-07.

7. MAP, Charleston to MMP, North Santee, December 12, 1861 [APF].

8. Bull, *All Saints Church*, 38.

9. MMP, Richfield, to RP, January 22, 1862 [APF].

10. "The Reconnaissance of the Yankee Gunboats to Georgetown, S.C.," Charleston *Mercury*, June 23, 1862.

11. Rock Cell was Robert Y. Hayne's country residence near Pendleton, S. C. Margaretta was Margaretta Stiles Hayne, wife of Col. William Alston Hayne, a son of Robert Y. Hayne. MMP, Richfield, to MPM, n.p., April 14, 1862 [APF].

12. Eclât: glory or splendor. WBP, Richfield, to Elizabeth Pringle Smith, March 30, 1862 [MPF].

13. "The Confederate Diary of William John Grayson," *SCHM* 63: 142.

14. MMP, Richfield, to My dear daughter, April 14, 1862 [APF].

15. *Confederate Baptist*, May 4, 1864. Plantation files, Darlington County Historical Commission.

16. "Our grandparents had friends, the Williams', in Society Hill,

an old community further up State; with her usual cordiality Mrs. Williams took in our grandparents and our Aunt Susan Pringle and our mother." Susan Pringle Frost, "Jottings – A Brief Sketch of My Life . . . 1948." [APF]

17. Receipt from WBP to the agent of J. T. Murdoch for $60, dated April 18, 1865 [APF]. The receipt was for use of the plantation in 1864.

18. "Society Hill Home Names" in the *Hartsville Messenger*, February 24, 1938.

19. Deposition of William Bull Pringle, Darlington District, S. C., December 12, 1862. [CMSR of Capt. Robert Pringle.]

20. Receipt from J. W. Evans to William B. Pringle, October 31, 1863. [APF]

21. National Archives RG 169. "Intercepted Letters, 1861-1865," Entry 189.

22. EJP to MMP, August 20, 1862 [Intercepted Letters].

23. George Alfred Trenholm (1807-1876), a wealthy Charleston businessman and financier, also served as Secretary of the Treasury for the Confederacy. MMP, Dukeville, to My beloved son, February 19, 1863 [APF].

24. Deed Book S-14: 158, Charleston County Register of Mesne Conveyances Office, Charleston.

25. MMP, Dukeville, to my Beloved Son, February 19, 1865 [APF]

26. SP, Society Hill, to RP, Fort Pemberton, May, 1863 [APF].

27. In 1867, Wagner sold 2,087 acres containing Beneventum to William Miles Hazzard, a Georgetown Planter. Lachicotte, 87.

28. WBP, Charleston, to My dear sister, July 4, 1863 [MPF]; also inventory of rice, livestock and implements at Beneventum plantation, July 6, 1863 [M-P-F].

29. Parker was probably the auctioneer. WBP, Society Hill, to EJP, San Francisco, September 11, 1863 [EJP].

30. MMP, Society Hill, to JJP, November 11, 1863 [JJP].

31. MMP, Dukeville, to JJP, July 28, 1864 [JJP].

32. CMSR of MAP.

33. WAP, Charleston, to SP, November 7, 1862, in *Chronicles*, 84-85.

34. MMP, Society Hill, to JJP, November 11, 1863 [JJP].

35. Obituary of Stephen Duncan, Jr., from a Natchez newspaper, c. August 10, 1910 [JJP].

36. Photograph in the Miles Brewton House Collection.

37. MMP and SP, Richfield, to EJP, February 28, 1862 [APF].

38. MPM to MMP, August 13, 1862 [Intercepted Letters, LC]

39. EJP to MMP, August 20, 1862 [Intercepted Letters, LC]

40. MPM, New Haven, to MMP, August 26, 1862 [Intercepted Letters, LC].

41. MPM, Edgewood, to JJP, November 4, 1863 [JJP].

42. Old River, a segment of the Red River, and Lake Moreau were located in Avoyelles Parish, in central Louisiana, just west of the

Mississippi River and approximately fifty miles southwest of the Duncan plantations at Natchez.

43. JJP, Game Book #6, pp. 11-12 [JJP].

44. MMP, Society Hill, to JJP, November 11, 1863 [JJP].

45. "beyond the Northern line": south of it. MMP, Dukeville, to JJP, July 28, 1864 [JJP].

46. Stephen Duncan, Jr., journal, 1861-1895, p. 51 [SDSDJ].

47. Michael Wayne, *The Reshaping of Plantation Society: The Natchez District, 1860-1880* (Baton Rouge: Louisiana State University Press, 1983), 38.

48. Adam Badeau, Headquarters Armies of the United States, Washington, D.C., to Dr. Stephen Duncan, October 29, 1865 [SDC].

49. Peter Gaillard Stoney (1809-1884) planted rice at Medway plantation on the Back River in St. James Goose Creek Parish. John B. Irving, *A Day On Cooper River*, enlarged and edited by Louisa Cheves Stoney (Columbia: R. L. Bryan, 1932), 69.

50. EJP to MMP, August 20, 1862 [Intercepted Letters].

51. MPM, Edgewood, to JJP, November 4, 1863 [JJP].

52. MPM to My dear Brother [WAP], November 6, 1862 [Intercepted Letters].

53. MAP, Charleston, to Gen. A. R. Lawton, Quartermaster General, November 14, 1863 [CMSR].

54. The sinking was reported in the Charleston *Daily Courier*, September 1, 1863; *Mercury*, September 2-3, 1863.

55. *The War of the Rebellion*: A Compilation of the Official Records of the Union and Confederate Armies. Series 1, 28 (1) 689.

56. Official Records, Series 1, 28 (1), 689.

57. Official Records, Series 1, 14, 260.

58. MPM, Edgewood, to SP, Charleston, July 23, 1861 [APF].

59. MPM to MMP, August 19, 1861 [APF].

60. WBP, Richfield, to MPM, December 27, 1861 [APF].

61. RP, Coles Island, Charleston District, to MMP, January 4, 1862 [APF].

62. Located in Boston harbor, Fort Warren was used as a Confederate prisoner of war camp.

63. MPM to MMP, August 5, 1862 [Intercepted Letters].

64. MPM, Edgewood, to JJP, November 4, 1863 [APF].

65. A mess is a group of military men who regularly take their meals together.

66. Edward L. Wells, *A Sketch of the Charleston Light Dragoons, from the Formation of the Corps* (Charleston: Lucas, Richardson & Co., 1888), 4

67. Wells, *Dragoons*, 12-13.

68. John Julius Pringle (1842-1876), Dominick Lynch Pringle (?-?) and Joel Roberts Poinsett Pringle (c. 1843-1864) were sons of John Julius Izard Pringle (1808-1862) and Jane Lynch (d. 1896), of Greenfield

plantation on the Black River. The three brothers were studying at Heidelberg when the war broke out. This Julius is sometimes confused with Mary's son, the former midshipman.

69. Frost, *Highlights*, 148.

70. CMSR of MBP.

71. The officer in question is identified as Gen. R.G.M. Dunovant in Robert's Compiled Military Service Records but this is an error. No R.G.M. Dunovant served as a Confederate general, but John Dunovant (1825-1864) did. He was a major in the state forces during the firing on Fort Sumter. By July 22, 1861 he was a colonel in the 1st South Carolina Regulars (the lowest officer grade which merited an aide-de-camp) but did not become a general officer until 1864.

72. The 15th (Lucas') Battalion, South Carolina Volunteers, consisted of two companies and was mustered into Confederate service on June 6, 1861. A third company was added to the unit in November 1862. Although designated an infantry unit, Lucas' battalion always manned heavy artillery.

73. RP, Coles Island, to MMP, January 17, 1862 [APF].

74. RP, Fort Pemberton, to My dear Sister, July 27, 1862 [APF].

75. Special Order No. 39, Head Quarters, Camp of Instruction, Dept. of S.C., Columbia, Oct. 4, 1862 [CMSR of RP].

76. RP, Fort Pemberton, to SP, November 30, 1862 [APF].

77. Capt. John H. Gary commanded Company A until he was killed defending Battery Wagner on Morris Island. Edward Manigault, *Siege Train. The Journal of a Confederate Artilleryman in the Defense of Charleston.* Ed. by Warren Ripley. (Columbia: University of South Carolina Press, 1986), 310.

78. Major J. Jonathan Lucas, Fort Pemberton, James Island, to MMP, August 24, 1863 [APF].

79. Lt. (later Capt.) E.B. Colhoun succeeded Capt. John H. Gary in command of Company A, Lucas' Battalion. He served with the unit through the end of 1865. *Siege Train*, 310.

80. The company fund derived its income from the sale of excess rations issued to the company. The proceeds were used to provide for widows and orphans and for the welfare of the men. Robert had evidently received a loan from the fund.

81. The 1869-70 Charleston city directory listed the store of E. W. Edgerton & F. Richards at 32 Broad St.

82. RP to WAP, August 16, 1863 [APF].

83. Robert C. Gilchrist, "The Confederate Defence of Morris Island," City of Charleston *Yearbook*, 1884, 384.

84. Dr. Henry B. Horlbeck (1839-1901) was an 1859 graduate of the Medical College of the State of South Carolina. He served at Roper Hospital and visited London and Paris. In 1862 he returned to serve the Confederacy as surgeon of the First Regiment of South Carolina Regulars in 1862. He served until the end of the war.

85. WAP, Charleston, to WBP, Society Hill, August 25, 1863 [APF].
86. H.B. Horlbeck, Charleston, to WAP, December 4, 1882 [APF].
87. Obituary of Robert Pringle. Undated newspaper clipping [APF].
88. WAP, Charleston, to My dear Parents, August 23, 1863 [APF].
89. WAP, Charleston, to MMP, August 22, 1863 [APF].
90. MMP, Society Hill, to My beloved Children, September 19, 1863 [APF].
91. Interview with Peter Manigault.
92. WAP, Charleston, to WBP, Society Hill, SC, c. August 25, 1863 [APF].
93. WAP, Charleston, to MMP, August 22, 1863 [APF].
94. Williams Middleton (1809-1883), a signer of the South Carolina Ordinance of Secession, was the owner of Middleton Place. His cousin, Lt. John Middleton (184?-1869?), the son of Jacob Motte Middleton of Crowfield plantation, was an officer in the 1st Regiment, S.C. Artillery.
95. The 1870 federal census listed Antoinette Girard, age 70, teacher, born in Poland, as living in Charleston's fourth ward.
96. Julius & Poinsett: John Julius Pringle and J. R. Poinsett Pringle, sons of John Julius Izard Pringle of Greenfield plantation. WAP, Charleston, to MMP, August 22, 1863 [APF].
97. The Rev. Stephen Elliott (1804-1866) was an Episcopal priest who had served Ascension Chapel on the Combahee before services there were halted in 1861.
98. MMP, Society Hill, to My dear Children, September 19, 1863 [APF].
99. "Captain Robert Pringle," in the Charleston *Daily Courier*, August 27, 1863, 1.
100. Obituary of Capt. Robert Pringle. Undated newspaper clipping [APF].
101. Special Order No. 167, August 29, 1863, in Official Records, vol. 28, part II, 314.
102. WBP, King Street, to Mrs. Charles Alston, Battery, August 15, 1861 [MPF].
103. MMP, King Street, to Charles Alston, Battery, August 16, 1861 [MPF].
104. CAP, King Street, to Charles Alston, September 16, 1861 [MPF].
105. Amelia [surname lost], Mosholm (?), to DGM, August 1, 1862 [APF].
106. Charleston County Death Records card file, Charleston County Library.
107. CMSR of CAP.
108. Caparisoned: fully-dressed or outfitted.
109. Brigadier General William Booth Taliaferro (1822-1898) commanded several companies of artillery at Battery Wagner during the final attempts to defend it in the fall of 1863.
110. Heavily raked: under heavy fire.

111. JRP, Battery Gregg [Morris Island], to MMP, about August 1863 (typescript copy) [APF].

112. MMP journal, 1822-1881 [APF].

Chapter 10: A Bitter Homecoming

1. Simkins and Woody, 15.

2. Justus Clement French and Edward Cary, *Trip of the Steamer* Oceanus *to Fort Sumter and Charleston, S.C. . . . April 14th, 1865,* (Brooklyn, NY: The Union Steam Printing House, 1865), 39.

3. Mrs. St. Julien Ravenel, Charleston. *The Place and the People* (New York: The Macmillan Co., 1927), 505.

4. French and Cary, *Trip,* 121.

5. Carl Schurz, "The South After the War," in *McClure's Magazine,* Vol. 30, 6 (April, 1908), 661.

6. Rogers, *Georgetown County,* 417-418.

7. "Report of the Committee on the Destruction of Churches in the Diocese of South Carolina, During the Late War. Presented to the Protestant Episcopal Convention, May, 1868" (Charleston, SC: Walker, Evans & Co., 1868), p. 8.

9. David Duncan Wallace, *History of South Carolina* (New York: American Historical Society, 1934), III: 223.

10. When the war broke out, George Walton Williams (1820-1903) was a prominent businessman, financial counselor and a director of two railroads and the Bank of South Carolina. Although he achieved even more wealth and prominence after the war, he handled the procurement and distribution of food to the needy with such skill and benefit that "the friends of Mr. Williams regarded this beneficent enterprise and labor as the crowning achievement of his life." William Way, *History of the New England Society of Charleston. . . .* (Charleston: Published by the Society, 1920), 160-161.

11. French & Cary, *Trip,* 125-126.

12. National Archives Record Group 105. Records of the Bureau of Refugees, Freedmen and Abandoned Lands.

13. Heyward, 116.

14. George C. Fox, Agent, Bureau of Refugees, Freedmen and Abandoned Lands, Georgetown, S.C., to Lt. Col. A.J. Willard, November 2, 1865. RG 105, Entry 3210. Labor Contracts, Georgetown, S.C. National Archives.

15. Assigning an "average" price is difficult. The value of a slave was influenced by training and expected future working capacity, and the price could range between $0 and $1,500 and occasionally more. I have used $500, the value attributed to a slave by the Charleston *Daily News* when in 1867 it stated that "the $200,000,000 invested in the state's 400,000 slaves had been lost." Simkins and Woody, 12.

16. These Confederate bills and bonds were with the family papers

in 1989. There is no way to tell the quantity of other Confederate currency and bonds the Pringles may have discarded as useless after the war.

17. Simkins and Woody, 15.

18. Burton, 322-323.

19. Burton, 322. Alexander Schimmelpfennig (1824-1865) was an experienced army officer when he emigrated to the United States in 1853, and became an engineer in the War Department. He held many field assignments during the war and was sent to fight against Charleston, where he contracted malaria. He also contracted tuberculosis, from which he died in September 1865.

20. Brigadier General John Porter Hatch (1822-1901) was an 1845 graduate of West Point, a veteran of the Mexican and Apache wars, was wounded while serving in Virginia, and was awarded the Medal of Honor for his service at South Mountain. He was commander of the Coast Division, Department of the South (which included Charleston) at the end of the war.

21. "Random Recollections," 56. The hole was knocked through the peak of the pediment which tops the second floor balcony. This scar has been carefully preserved by four generations of postbellum owners and remains clearly visible.

22. Gray pavement: the gray slate used for grave markers and paving stones in St. Michael's churchyard. See photograph, p. 227.

23. Mary was supposing that Battery Pringle, at Dill's plantation on the east bank of the Stono River, would be occupied by federal forces and renamed. In fact, the battery was ignored after war, retained its name, and is being conserved by its new owner, the Historic Charleston Foundation.

24. MMP, Dukeville, to MPM, February 22, 1865 [APF].

25. Hercules was the Pringle family's noted coachman.

26. Mrs. Williams: Sarah, the widow of Col. John Nicholas Williams. Mr. W. Evans could not be identified.

27. J. L. Coker & Co. purchased John L. Hart's store in Hartsville after Hart's death on May 16, 1864. Coker Family file, Darlington County Historical Commission.

28. Jacob Motte Alston wrote, "Of course the floors were bare for the beautiful Axminster carpet which had been woven for the [drawing-]room in one piece, had been removed, but was captured by the enemy, at Cheraw and cut up for saddle cloths." "Random Reminiscences," 64. Notwithstanding his account, some of the carpet survived and appears in the 1868 photograph taken in the drawing room.

29. Cousin Alston: one of Mary's many Alston relatives.

30. Lynch's Creek flows into the Pee Dee River forty miles north of Georgetown.

31. Newberry, now the seat of Newberry County, lies 150 miles northwest of Charleston.

32. Kingstree, the seat of Williamsburg District, lies fifty miles northwest of Georgetown.

33. Brother: J. Motte Alston Pringle. His connection with South Carolina Governor Andrew Gordon Magrath (1813-1893) is unknown. Magrath had fled from Columbia to Union, S.C.

34. Bob: possibly Robert Pringle (1849-?), one of William Alston Pringle's sons.

35. Glenn Springs: a small resort town in Spartanburg County, South Carolina, 200 miles northwest of Charleston.

36. RP, Society Hill, to MBP, March 19, 1865 [JJP].

37. Emma C. P. S. Pringle, Society Hill, to Eliza C. Middleton Smith, March 30, 1865, in Daniel E. Huger Smith, Alice R. H. Smith and Arney R. Childs, eds. *Mason Smith Family Letters, 1860-1868* (Columbia, SC: University of South Carolina Press, 1950), pp. 184-185. Hereafter cited as Mason Smith Family Letters.

38. National Archives Microfilm Publication M789. Internal Revenue Assessment Lists for South Carolina, 1864-1866. Roll 1.

39. The Judge Robert Pringle House on Tradd Street.

40. Alston's eight year-old daughter, Rebecca Motte Pringle, recovered and lived another nineteen years.

41. WAP, Charleston, to MPM, June 9, 1865 [EJP].

42. Arthur Mazÿck (1883) and Gene Waddell (1983), *Charleston in 1883* (Easley, S.C.: Southern Historical Press, 1983), xvii.

43. "Random Recollections," 40.

44. "General Hatch had fixed his residence in the house next but one west of us [the Nathaniel Russell House], then belonging to Colonel Ash and which subsequently passed into the hands of its present [1929] owner, Mr. W. K. Ryan, while his military head-quarters were at Mr. Wm. Bull Pringle's house on King St." Nathaniel Russell Middleton, Jr., in *Life in Carolina and New England During the Nineteenth Century* (Bristol, R.I.: privately printed, 1929), 174.

45. This may refer to a portion of William Bull Pringle's remaining silver.

46. Jane Lynch Pringle, wife of John Julius Izard Pringle, of Greenfield plantation on the Black River.

47. WBP, Society Hill, to JJP, June 24, 1865 [JJP].

48. MMP, Dukeville to EJP [Newport?], June 26, 1865 [JJP].

49. MMP, Dukeville, to JJP, July 12, 1865 [JJP].

50. General Saxon: General Rufus Saxton was Assistant Commissioner of the Freedmens Bureau.

51. Quincy Adams Gillmore (1825-1888) of Massachusetts was a brilliant field commander who served as chief engineer in the Port Royal Expedition in 1861-1862 and led operations against Charleston, Fort Sumter and Morris Island in 1863. In 1865 he returned as commander of the Department of the South and served until December, 1865. D.A.B.

52. William's pardon was dated October 20, 1865 [APF].

53. WBP, Society Hill, to EJP, San Francisco, August 25, 1865 [EJP].

54. A champion of the ex-slave, Oliver Otis Howard (1830-1909) graduated fourth in his class at West Point in 1854. On May 12, 1865, he became the first commissioner of the Freedmen's Bureau and did much for his charges, although unable to stop corruption and mismanagement.

55. *Chronicles*, 35.

56. Daniel E. Huger Smith, Alice R. Huger Smith and Arney R. Childs, eds., *Mason Smith Family Letters, 1860-1868* (Columbia: University of South Carolina Press, 1950), 223.

57. MMP, Dukeville, to RBP, September 13, 1865 [APF].

58. Emma Pringle Smith, Society Hill, to Susan Smith Middleton, September 18, 1865 [M-P].

59. Will may have been William Chisholm, the widowed husband of Cretia's daughter, Maulsey Stuart (1840-1861).

60. General Bennett: could not be identified.

61. Alonzo James White (1812-____) started his career as a clerk in the counting house of Gibbon & Co., wholesale merchants. By 1860 he had become one of Charleston's largest slave dealers.

62. MMP, Tradd St., to MPM, Edgewood, October 5, 1865 [APF].

63. "Random Recollections," 65.

64. MMP, King Street, "For a member of the family, under a grievous affliction," October 8, 1865 [APF].

65. Press: clothes press, a freestanding wooden clothes closet.

66. Yellow woman: a mulatto.

67. To cry fish: sell fish from door to door and live in the servant's quarters in return for a percentage of his sales.

68. Mrs. John Julius Izard Pringle, of Greenfield plantation, now a widow.

69. The proposal for a seven-year apprenticeship, like many others, never came to pass.

70. MMP, Tradd St., to RBP & MPM, Edgewood, October 10, 1865 [APF].

71. MMP, "On Returning Home," King Street, October 20, 1865 [APF].

72. "Random Recollections," 63.

73. "Random Recollections," 62-63.

74. Jacob may have been mistaken, as the carpet seems to have been stored at Society Hill.

75. "Random Recollections," 63-64, 66.

76. Willie: probably William Alston Pringle, son of Alston and Emma.

77. MMP, Tradd St., to RBP, Edgewood, October 13, 1865 [APF].

78. Charleston artist Henry B. Bounetheau (1797-1877) a contemporary of Charles Fraser, worked in the city from the 1830s until after the war.

79. MMP, Tradd St., to RBP, Edgewood, October 18, 1865 [APF].

80. My dear child: Mary's daughter, Susan Pringle.

81. Her and the old colonel: Col. & Mrs. Arthur P. Hayne.

82. MMP, Tradd St., to RBP, Edgewood, October 24, 1865 [APF].

83. [Powder] train: a trail of gunpowder, used as a fuse to ignite an explosive charge.

84. French & Cary, *Trip*, 130-131.

85. E. Milby Burton, *The Siege of Charleston, 1861-1865* (Columbia, SC: University of South Carolina Press, 1970), 321.

86. CMSR of MAP, including specifically, MAP, Raleigh, NC, to Major M. B. McMaster, March 15, 1865.

87. During the research for his *History of South Carolina*, David Duncan Wallace of Wofford College investigated the claims against Major Motte Alston Pringle and found them "absurd."

Chapter 11: The Rice Paupers

1. Frances Butler Simkins and Robert Hilliard Woody, *South Carolina During Reconstruction* (Chapel Hill: University of North Carolina Press, 1932), 10-11.

2. "Random Recollections," 66.

3. MMP, King St., to JJP, November 2, 1866 [JJP].

4. MMP, Tradd St., to RBP, Edgewood, October 24, 1865 [APF].

5. MMP, King St., to DGM, Edgewood, November 10, 1865 [APF].

6. Brig. Gen. Beale, Headquarters, Military District, Eastern S.C., Darlington, August 8, 1865 [APF].

7. Rogers, *Georgetown County*, 424

8. National Archives Record Group 105, Records of the Bureau of Refugees, Freedmen and Abandoned Lands. Entry 3210, Labor Contracts, Georgetown, S. C., December. 1865 - April 1866.

9. National Archives Record Group 105, Records of the Bureau of Refugees, Freedmen and Abandoned Lands. Entry 3210, Labor Contracts, Georgetown, S. C., December. 1865 - April 1866.

10. Rogers, *Georgetown County*, 431.

11. Rogers, *Georgetown County*, 432.

12. MMP, King St., to JJP, Paris (?), June 23, 1866 [JJP].

13. *Chronicles*, 58.

14. EJP, San Francisco, to WBP, August 17, 1866 [EJP].

15. Harrison, 113-114.

16. "The Demise of the Hon. Edward Frost," Charleston *Courier*, July 22, 1868.

17. Benjamin F. Perry, "Judge Edward Frost," in Ulysses R. Brooks, *South Carolina Bench and Bar* (Columbia, S.C.: State Co., 1907), 129-132.

18. *Roll of Students of South Carolina College, 1805-1905* (Columbia, S.C: South Carolina College, 1905), 28.

19. RBP, Charleston, to FLF, Darlington, November 2, 1866 [APF].

20. trousseau: a bride's initial stock of clothes, undergarments, and linens for her new home.

21. *Chronicles,* 94-95.

22. *Chronicles,* 94.

23. WBP, Edgewood, to My dear sister (Elizabeth Smith), June 10, 1867 [MPF].

24. "Random Recollections," 348.

25. Sue Huger could not be positively identified.

26. MMP, King St., to RBF, May 7, 1867 (typescript) [APF].

27. MMP, Charleston, to SP, San Francisco, September 29, 1868 [APF].

28. MMP, Charleston, to SP, December 15, 1868 [APF].

29. Possibly Isadore Lewis, who was listed as a dry goods merchant at 102 King Street in the 1875 Charleston city directory.

30. MMP, Charleston, to RBF, South Island, November 21, 1871 [APF].

31. Our little Angel Child: Hesse Mitchell.

32. MMP, Charleston, to RBF, Georgetown, March 25, 1868 [APF].

33. MMP, Charleston, to SP, December 15, 1868 [APF].

34. MMP, Charleston, to WBP, March 5, 1870 [APF].

35. *Highlights,* 45; *Chronicles,* 76.

36. MMP, King Street, to JJP, n.p., May 7, 1867 [APF].

37. In the 1869-70 Charleston city directory, J.M. Singleton was listed as the manager of R.G. Dun & Company's mercantile agency at 5 Hayne Street.

38. MMP, King Street, to SP, in care of EJP, San Francisco, October 30, 1868 [APF].

39. RBF, Charleston, to SP, San Francisco, November 7, 1868 [APF].

40. MMP, Charleston, to a daughter, September 24, 1867 [APF].

41. David Risley (1825-1895), "a practical lumber man of Philadelphia," bought Waties Point plantation from R.F.W. Allston in 1855 for use as a lumber yard. After the war, Risley promoted railroads and lumbering. He may have wanted the rice mill's steam engine. David Risley, Georgetown, to WBP, May 1, 1868 [APF].

42. "Return of Crops, And Other Statistics, of Georgetown County, State of South Carolina, For The Year 1868," SCDAH.

43. MMP, Charleston, to SP, c/o DGM, Edgewood, May 7, 1869 [APF].

44. MMP, Charleston, to RBF, Georgetown, March 6, 1868 [APF].

45. "Random Recollections," 277.

46. The Judge: William Alston Pringle.

47. The Tradd Street girls: Alston's daughters.

48. Mary Stuart: a daughter or either of two granddaughters of Cretia and Scipio Stewart. See Appendix IV.

49. MMP, Charleston, to SP, San Francisco, May 6, 1868 [APF].

50. Henry Wilson served as a U.S. Senator from New Hampshire during and after the war.

51. chimera: an impossible or foolish fancy.

52. MMP, King St., to JJP, May 7, 1867 [JJP].

53. For five years following the end of the war, Brigadier General Edward Richard Sprigg Canby (1817-1873) "was moved from place to place in the South, being sent anywhere the administration encountered serious difficulty."

54. MMP, King St., to a daughter, September 7, 1867 [APF].

55. MMP, Charleston, to SP, May 23, 1868 [APF].

56. MMP, Charleston, to JRP, San Francisco, August 4, 1868 [APF].

57. David B. Pillsbury and Emily A. Getchell, *The Pillsbury Family* . . . . (Everett, Mass.: Massachusetts Publishing Co., 1898), 135-136.

58. E.W.M. Mackey has not yet been identified.

59. MMP, Charleston, to SP, San Francisco, November 10, 1868 [APF].

60. MMP, Charleston, to My beloved son [Edward or James], November 11, 1868 [APF].

61. Pillsbury Family, 135-136.

62. MMP, Charleston, to JRP, San Francisco, November 23, 1868 [APF].

63. MMP, King Street, to my beloved daughter [Coralie Pringle?], June 25, 1868, in *Chronicles,* 159-160.

64. MMP, Charleston, to RBF, South Island, North Santee, February 13, 1868 [APF].

65. MMP, King Street, to SP, care of DGM, New Haven, May 7, 1869] [APF].

66. MMP, Charleston, to WBP, March 5, 1870 [APF].

67. Then as now, King Street was downtown Charleston's chief shopping district. It had many Jewish-owned stores which were closed on the Sabbath but open on Sunday.

68. MMP, Charleston, to MPM, New Haven, April 4, 1871 [APF].

69. MMP, Charleston, to MPM, New Haven, April 4, 1871 [APF].

70. MMP, King Street, to RPF, n.p., July 3, 1871 [APF].

71. MMP, Charleston, to MPM, October 29, 1871 [APF].

72. "William B. Pringle in account with James R. Pringle," January 1 - December 31, 1870 [APF].

73. William B. Pringle to James B. Morrison and Samuel J. Lofton, Georgetown County Deeds, book D, page 236. For plats and a detailed analysis of the Richfield and Pleasant Meadows tracts, see Agnes Leland Baldwin, "Origins of Richfield Plantation, Prince George Winyah Parish, Georgetown District, South Carolina," May 22, 1995. Miles Brewton House Collection.

74. MMP, King Street, to RBF, South Island, November 30, 1871 [APF].

75. *Chronicles,* 99.

76. MMP, Charleston, to MPM, Edgewood, July 8, 1872 [APF].

77. Draft of the will of WBP, May 14, 1873 [APF].

78. Physician's Record, 1860-1874, also Admissions Book, 1828-1876. Records of the South Carolina Lunatic Asylum, S.C.D.A.H.

79. RBF, Charleston, to SP, n.p., November 7, 1868 [APF].

80. MMP, Charleston, to SP, December 15, 1868 [APF].

81. Admissions and Discharges Book, 1860-1875. Records of the South Carolina Lunatic Asylum, SCDAH.

82. RBF, South Island, to MMP, Charleston, August 12, 1874 [APF].

83. Charleston County Death Records card file, Charleston County Library.

84. MMP, Charleston, to a daughter, December 11, 1874 [APF].

85. MMP, Charleston, to MPM, December 18, 1874 [APF].

Chapter 12: The Ghost Planters

1. Heyward, *Madagascar*, 211.

2. Lachicotte, *Georgetown*, 191.

3. Author, playwright, and rice planter Gabriel Manigault (1809-1888) of Awendaw, Romney and White Oak plantations, served as aide de camp to General P.G.T. Beauregard. He, his wife, Anne Mazÿck, and family emigrated to London, Ontario, Canada in 1869.

4. Elizabeth W. Alston Pringle, *Chronicles of Chicora Wood* (New York: Charles Scribners' Sons, 1922), 269.

5. Agnes Baldwin, *Marsh Granting Practices in South Carolina* (Summerville, S.C.: The Committee for Preservation of Privately-Owned Marshlands, 1976), 26.

6. Stephen Duncan Jr., Duncansby, to My Dear Papa, January 11, 1863 [SDC].

7. Stephen Duncan Jr., Duncansby, to My Dear Papa, December 23, 1863 [SDC, 1843-1866, LSU].

8. Rogers, *Georgetown County*, 436.

9. EJP, San Francisco, to RBP, King St., August 9, 1866 [APF].

10. Doar, *Rice Planting*, 46.

11. William Miles Hazzard married a daughter of blockade-runner George Alfred Trenholm. After the war, Hazzard was a Santee rice planter and a director of the Georgetown Rice Milling Company. Rogers, *Georgetown County*, 465, 471.

12. FLF, Camp Main, to RBF, Charleston, November 22, 1867 [APF].

13. William Hazzard, Annandale Plantation, to Francis L. Frost, March 10, 1878 [APF].

14. Doar, *Rice Planting*, 46.

15. Edward Frost, Charleston, to FLF, North Santee, December 2, 1867 [APF].

16. Aleck Raphael (also noted as Aleck Lewis), a freedman working for Frank, was a skilled cook, handyman and house servant on the Santee in the late 1860s and early 1870s. *Chronicles*, 94, 97.

17. Charleston *News & Courier*, July 1, 1878.

18. FLF, Camp Huger, Suffolk, Va., to Richard Frost, January 6, 1862 [APF].

19. FLF, Hospital at Camp Huger, Suffolk, Va., to Mrs. Edward Frost, January 10, 1862 [APF].

20. In the yard: this indicates that Robinson's mother was a house servant rather than a field hand.

21. FLF, Hospital at Camp Huger, Suffolk, Va., to Mrs. Edward Frost, January 10, 1862 [APF].

22. James Armstrong, "Funeral of Dr. F. L. Frost," Charleston *News & Courier*, Sept. 7, 1912.

23. The 1870 federal census listed a William S. Miller, age 55, farmer, living with his daughter in the village of Sampit, in Black River Township, Georgetown County. A Frank Miller, 35, Inspector of Naval Stores, lived in the town of Georgetown at the same time.

24. Wando: a servant.

25. Several Hume families resided in Georgetown District at that time.

26. Brigadier General George Lafayette Beale, a Maine book-binder, commanded the Military District of Eastern South Carolina, headquartered at Darlington.

27. Mr. Miller was his overser.

28. Uncle Thomas: Thomas Lynch Horrÿ (1806-1871), brother to Frank's mother.

29. FLF, at Mr. Miller's House, Georgetown District, to Edward Frost, July 31, 1865 [APF].

30. William Rivers Maxwell (1794-1873), who was known to the family as "Mr. Max," married Anna Maria Johnston in 1819. In 1850 he owned 137 slaves and produced 600,000 pounds of rice at White Marsh, North Santee. Rogers, *Georgetown County*, 293.

31. In 1856 a summer chapel of the Church of the Messiah, North Santee and a parsonage were built on South Island. Rogers, *Georgetown County*, 300.

32. FLF, on Santee, to Mrs. Edward Frost, Pendleton, S.C., December 28, 1865 [APF].

33. *Reminiscences*, 94.

34. EJP, San Francisco, to RBP, King St., August 9, 1866 [APF].

35. Maxwell Lucas: a planter on the North Santee.

36. Dishabile [dishabille]: the state of being partially dressed or dressed in night clothes.

37. FLF, N. Santee, to RBP, Charleston, October 10, 1866 [APF].

38. FLF, N. Santee, to RBP, Charleston, October 14, 1866 [APF].

39. Arthur Middleton Manigault (1824-1886) was the son of Joseph and Charlotte Manigault. He inherited White Oak from his father in 1843, and in 1850, produced 390,000 lbs. of rice with 151 slaves. Rogers, *Georgetown County*, 296.

40. The 1870 federal census listed Andrew J. McCants, age 59, laborer, as residing in Black River Township, Georgetown County.

41. George Ford: a planter on the North Santee.

42. Francis W. Johnstone: a planter on the North Santee.

43. FLF, Annandale plantation, to RBF, Charleston, January 26, 1868 [APF].

44. FLF, n.p. [probably Camp Main], to RBF, Charleston, n.d., 1867 [APF #991]. The first and last pages have been lost.

45. Benjamin F. Dunkin, Midway Plantation, to Cleland K. Huger, November 9, 1865. Cleland Kinloch Huger Papers, South Caroliniana Library, Columbia, S.C.

46. *Chronicles*, 94-95.

47. *Reminiscences*, 95.

48. FLF, Camp Main, to RBF, Charleston, November 10, 1867 [APF].

49. FLF, Camp Main, to RBF, Charleston, November 20, 1867 [APF].

50. Piqué: a firmly-woven cotton fabric with vertical cords.

51. RBF, Charleston, to FLF, South Island, October 2, 1867 [APF].

52. Flats were small, flat, shallow-draft barges used to transport rice sheaths from field to mill.

53. FLF, Camp Main, to RBF, Charleston, December 18, 1867 [APF].

54. FLF, Camp Main, to RBP, c/o James R. Pringle, Charleston, January 2, 1868 [APF].

55. RBF, Charleston, to FLF, January 15, 1868 [APF].

56. RBF, South Island, to SP, San Francisco, June 14, 1868 [APF].

57. RBF, South Island, to SP, June, 1869 in *Chronicles*, 136-137.

58. FLF, n.p. [Santee] to [Mary P. Mitchell], n.d., 1871 [Inventory # 2046, APF].

59. RBF, Camp Main, to MMP, Charleston, April 4, 1869 [APF].

60. RBF, South Island, to SP, June, 1869, in *Chronicles*, 136-137.

61. FLF, South Island, to Henry W. Frost, July 11, 1867 [APF].

62. FLF, South Island, to RBF, August 13, 1867 [APF].

63. The *Emilie* and the *St. Helena* were coastal steamers which linked Charleston and Georgetown District approximately once a week.

64. Mt. Pleasant: a coastal village from whence travelers took the ferry across the Cooper River to Charleston.

65. The fishing village of McClellanville is located just off the Georgetown Road, 35 miles north of Charleston and 25 miles south of Georgetown.

66. Rebecca was five months pregnant with their first child at this time.

67. FLF, South Island, to RBF, Charleston, August 14, 1867 [APF].

68. By stain: red grain or muddy water stains which had to be hand-culled, thereby raising the cost.

69. FLF, South Island, to RBF, September 15, 1867 [APF].

70. FLF, South Island, to RBF, Charleston, September 18, 1867 [APF].

71. MMP, Charleston, to a daughter, September 24, 1867 [APF].

72. FLF, South Island, to RBF, Charleston, September 26, 1867 [APF].

73. FLF, South Island, to RBF, Charleston, October 5, 1867 [APF].

74. FLF, Camp Main, to RBF, Charleston, November 21, 1867 [APF].

75. Mr. Trenholm: George Alfred Trenholm, who had purchased Runimede.

76. Fiddles, tambourines and "knocking sticks" were popular musical instruments among the slaves and freedmen. Doar, *Rice Planting*, 33.

77. FLF, N. Santee to RBF, Charleston, January 15, 1871 [APF].

78. FLF, North Santee, to Edward Frost, April 16, 1868 [APF].

79. Located in the delta between the North and South Santee rivers, Middle Island was subdivided into over a dozen different plantations.

80. Weather house: an elevated storm shelter built to protect the planters from hurricanes.

81. FLF, North Santee, to Edward Frost, April 26, 1868 [APF].

82. A slip is a stem, root or twig cut or broken off a larger plant which is used for planting or grafting.

83. Richfield's production for 1868 was as follows: 250 acres in production, including 175 acres of rice (4,400 bushels), 70 acres of corn (400 bushels), ? acres of peas & beans (70 bushels) 5 acres of sweet potatoes (320 bushels), 160 lbs. honey and 25 lbs. beeswax. Also listed were 1 horse, 3 mules, 10 oxen and 30 swine. The farm implements were valued at $150, and the value of all "market garden" production was $120. South Carolina Department of Agriculture. 1868 State Census, Georgetown County, 11a & 11b.

84. FLF, South Island, to Edward Frost, Charleston, June 18, 1868 [APF].

85. "Return of Crops, And Other Statistics of Georgetown County, State of South Carolina, For The Year 1868," p. 11. Richfield also produced 320 bushels of sweet potatoes, 160 lbs. of honey and 25 lbs. of beeswax that year.

86. MMP, King Street, to SP, care of EJP, San Francisco, October 30, 1868 [APF].

87. RBF, Camp Main to MMP, Charleston, February 18, 1869 [APF].

88. RBF, South Island, to MMP, Wednesday [no date, 186_] [APF].

89. RBF, North Santee, to SP, n.p., February 19, 1869 [APF].

90. RBF, Camp Main, to MMP, Charleston, April 4, 1869 [APF].

91. FLF, South Island, to RBF, Charleston, April 1, 1871 [APF].

92. RBF, New York, to SP, Charleston, August 6, 1871 [APF].

93. MMP, Charleston, to FLF and RBF, South Island, November 27, 1871 [APF].

94. Dr. Francis Parker could not be identified.

95. MMP, Charleston, to a friend, October 25, 1871 [APF].

96. RBF, South Island, to SP, Charleston, November, 1871 [APF].

97. RBF, Charleston, to FLF, December 5, 1873 [APF].

98. RBF, South Island, to MMP, Charleston, October 6, 1876 [APF].

99. William M. Hazzard, Annandale plantation, to FLF, Camp Main, November 29, 1876 [APF].

Chapter 13: A Seven-Bottle Man

1. A book purchased for Stephen Duncan Pringle, then age 11, was inscribed, "Newport, 1865." MBH collection.
2. Mrs. John M. Huger, New Orleans to ?, January 1866 [SDSDJ].
3. 1870 Federal census. Agricultural schedules. Pointe Coupeé Parish, Louisiana.
4. "Two Americans Called 'Angels of Biarritz," *BAU Banner*, February 7, 1946 [APF].
5. MMP, Charleston, to MPM, December 18, 1874 [APF].
6. MMP, King Street, to JJP, n.p., September 2, 1866 [JJP].
7. WBP, Charleston, to JJP, n.p., July 20, 1869 [APF].
8. MMP, Dukeville, to JJP, July 12, 1865 [JJP].
9. JJP, Paris, to SP, Charleston, August 13, 1870, in *Chronicles*, 85.
10. Oaklawn, Camperdown, Dumesnil and Cypremort, the tracts which comprised The Snipery, are marked on an 1897 map pasted into volume 5 of Julius's shooting logs [APF].
11. JJP, Torwood, to a daughter, Paris, March 18, 1873 [JJP].
12. *Chronicles*, 78.
13. John Julius Pringle, *Twenty Years' Snipe-Shooting. Extracts from the Daily Journal of the Game-Books of the Snipery* (New York: Knickerbocker Press, 1899), 21.
14. *Snipe-Shooting*, 183, 202.
15. *Snipe-Shooting*, 303.
16. *Snipe-Shooting*, 12.
17. Heyward, 119-120.
18. *Snipe-Shooting*, 14.
19. *Snipe-Shooting*, 56.
20. *Snipe-Shooting*, 58.
21. *Snipe-Shooting*, 164.
22. *Snipe-Shoting*, 267.
23. "Cholly Knickerbocker" (Maury Henry Biddle Paul, d. 1942) was the well-known society editor of the New York Journal American. From an undated newspaper clipping [JJP].
24. L. Margaret Barnett, "Horace Fletcher," in The Historic New Orleans Collection Quarterly, vol. XVII, No. 1 (Winter 2000), 8-9.
25. *Snipe-Shooting*, 261.
26. Interview by the author with Peter Manigault, November 25, 1995.
27. "Miss Mary Pringle, Chevalier de la Legion d'Honneur," 1928 newspaper clipping in MBH Scrapbook, vol. 1, 116 [APF].
28. "Decorated By French Govt.," Charleston *News & Courier*, February, 1928, in MBH Scrapbook, vol. 1, 122 [APF].

29. Interview by the author with Peter Manigault, November 25, 1995.

Chapter 14: The Pringles in the Golden West

1. MMP, Dukeville, to EJP [Newport?], June 26, 1865 [JJP].
2. RBF, Charleston, to SP, San Francisco, November 7, 1868 [APF].
3. MMP, Charleston, to RBF, South Island, May 8, 1871 [APF].
4. William and Mary were 71 and 68 at the time. Frank refers to the journey from Charleston to New York. FLF, South Island, to Mrs. Edward Frost, Charleston, June 8, 1871 [APF].
5. Lt. Charles Pringle, who died of typhoid fever in 1862.
6. SP, Edgewood, to RBF, Charleston, June 12, 1871 [APF].
7. SP, Edgewood, to RBF, Charleston, June 12, 1871 [APF].
8. MMP, Charleston, to MPM, August 10, 1871 [APF].
9. William Alston Hayne (1821-1901), was the fourth child of Robert Y. Hayne (1791-1839) and the first child of his second wife, Rebecca ("Fanny") Alston. He and Edward (born 1826) were contemporaries.
10. Theodore D. Jervey, "The Hayne Family," in *SCHM* 5: 174-175.
11. Quicksilver: mercury.
12. Sou: a small French coin equal to 1/20th of a franc.
13. EJP, San Fransicso, to MMP, May 29, 1867 [EJP].
14. EJP, San Francisco, to MMP, Charleston, August 29, 1867 [EJP].
15. EJP, San Francisco, to WBP, Charleston, September 17, 1867 [EJP].
16. MMP, Charleston, to SP, Edgewood, September 17, 1867 [APF].
17. MMP, Charleston, to a daughter [Susan], September 24, 1867 [APF].
18. EJP, San Francisco, to MMP, March 9, 1868 [EJP].
19. EJP, San Francisco, to WBP, Charleston, March 18, 1868 [EJP].
20. EJP, San Francisco, to MMP, Charleston, July 5, 1869 [JJP].
21. John Brooks Felton was born in Saugus, Massachusetts in 1828. He graduated from Harvard in 1847 and died in Oakland, California in 1877. Harvard University Archives.
22. Adolphus Carter Whitcomb (1827-1888) was born in Hancock, New Hampshire in 1827. He graduated from Harvard in 1847 and died in Aix la-Chapelle, France in 1888. Harvard University Archives.
23. *Chronicles*, 69.

Chapter 15: Of Rice and Ruin

1. *Chronicles*, 58.
2. Charleston County Death records card file, Charleston County Library.
3. Certificate of Death #1716, Health Department, City of Charleston, at the Charleston County Library, Charleston.
4. JJP, Paris, to SP, Charleston, October 17, 1884. *Chronicles*, 60-61.

5. MPM, Edgewood, to SP, Charleston, no date. *Chronicles,* 60.

6. Will of MMP, from *Chronicles,* 59-60.

7. *Chronicles,* 13.

8. *Chronicles,* 13.

9. *Chronicles,* 13.

10. Pringle Family Bible.

11. JMAP, Columbia, to an aunt, August 28, 1865 [APF].

12. MMP, Dukesville to EJP [Newport?], June 26, 1865 [JJP].

13. MMP, n.p., to SP, New Port, December 7, 1869, in *Chronicles,* 86.

14. 1884 Charleston city directory.

15. SP, 27 King Street, to My Dear Cousins, September 8, 1886 [APF].

16. Notes by Mary Pringle Frost to accompany the Pringle Family Bible [MBH].

17. "'Ik Marvel' and Carlyle,' undated newspaper clipping [DGM]

18. *Chronicles,* 86.

19. Bubble-and-Squeak: an old English dish made from sausage, onions, cabbage and white sauce, prepared and then baked until bubbling hot. *Fannie Farmer Cookbook,* 208.

20. Harvey B. Gaul, "Southern City Combines Attractions of Others, Post Music Critic Says," in an unnamed Pittsburgh newspaper, April 24, 1921; MBH Scrapbook, vol. 1, 99 [APF].

21. *Highlights,* 64.

22. *Highlights,* 4.

23. Carpenter, "Rice Plantation," 40.

24. Waddell, *Charleston in 1883,* xiv.

25. Doar, *A Sketch,* 5.

26. Pennington, *A Woman Rice Planter,* 446.

27. E. M. Burton, in Doar, *A Sketch,* 5.

Epilog

1. MMP, 13 King Street, to Miss Mary R. Pringle, Legaré Street, December 16, 1882 [APF].

BIBLIOGRAPHY

This bibliography lists all sources used which provide significant information about the Pringles, their culture and the Miles Brewton House. General reference works such as the *Dictionary of American Biography* have been cited in the notes but are not repeated here.

MANUSCRIPT SOURCES

Aaron Burr and Burriana Autographs and Documents, C.P.G. Fuller Collection, Princeton University Library.

Alston, Jacob Motte. Jacob Motte Alston Papers. Library of Congress.

Alston, Jacob Motte. "Random Recollections of an Inconspicuous Life," 1890. Cited as "Random Recollections." I used the 355-page typescript in the Miles Brewton House collection. An abridged version edited by Arney R. Childs was published as *Rice Planter and Sportsman. The Recollections of J. Motte Alston, 1821-1909* (Columbia, S. C.: University of South Carolina Press, 1953).

Alston-Pringle-Frost Collection, South Carolina Historical Society. Guide: see Richard N. Côté, *Guide to the Alston-Pringle-Frost Manuscript Collection in the South Carolina Historical Society* (Charleston, S. C.: South Carolina Historical Society, 1990). SCHS Ms. 28/630-642. Cited as [APF].

Alston, William. Stud Book. SCHS Ms. 34-181.

Barnes, Fletcher Lathrop. "The Pugh Plantations, 1860-1865. A Study of Life in Lower Louisiana." Ph.D. dissertation, University of Texas, 1945.

Bell, Daniel J. "The Natural Legacy of the South Carolina Rice Culture." Lecture given at the Gibbes Museum of Art, April 10, 1992.

Bland, Sidney R. "Visions of a New Day: Susan Pringle Frost and her Charleston." Unpublished manuscript, 1993.

Board of Examiners Records. Naval Academy Archives, Special Collections Division, Nimitz Library, U.S. Naval Academy, Annapolis, Md.

Brookgreen Gardens [Tombstone incriptions from] "The Oaks Cemetery." N.p., n.d. An annotated transcription of the tombstone inscriptions. South Carolina Historical Society.

Burr Family Papers, 1750-1853, Yale University Library, New Haven, Conn.

Burr-Purkitt Family Papers, Washington University Libraries, St. Louis, Mo.

Carpenter, James G. "The Rice Plantation Lands of Georgetown County, South Carolina: A Historical Geographic Study." M.A. thesis, University of South Carolina, 1973.

Charleston County Death Records card file, Charleston County Library.

Chaplin, Joyce E. "Nature, Improvement and Degeneration: The Rural Lowcountry Landscape, 1720-1815." Paper delivered at the Gibbes Museum of Art, March 5, 1994.

Cleland Kinloch Huger Papers, Caroliniana Library, University of South Carolina, Columbia, S. C.

Coclanis, Peter A. "Economy and Society in the Early Modern South: Charleston and the Evolution of the South Carolina Low Country." Ph.D. dissertation, Columbia University, 1984.

Côté, Richard N. Interview with Mr. Peter Manigault, June 1, 1992.

Donald G. Mitchell Collection, Yale Collection of American Literature, Beinecke Rare Book and Manuscript Library, Yale University. Cited as [DGM].

Edward Jenkins Pringle Family Collection, Bancroft Library, University of California-Berkeley. Cited as [EJP].

Fickling, Susan Markey. "The Christianization of the Negro in South Carolina, 1830-1860. " M.A. thesis, University of South Carolina, 1923.

Frost, Pringle and Rhett family papers and photographs. Private collection of Dr. Rhett Pringle Walker, Montrose, Ala. Cited as [RPW].

Frost, Susan Pringle. "Jottings: Memories of My Father: A Tribute." May 26, 1948. Alston-Pringle-Frost Collection, S.C.H.S.

John Julius Pringle Collection, South Carolina Historical Society. Guide: see Richard N. Côté, *Guide to the John Julius Pringle Manuscript Collection* (Charleston, S. C.: South Carolina Historical Society, 1991). Cited as [JJP].

John Pierpont Collection, Beinecke Rare Book and Manuscript Library, Yale University. Cited as [JP].

Library of Congress, Washington, D.C. Geography and Map Division. Map files, Civil War collection and South Carolina.

Michie, James L. *The Excavation of Joseph and Theodosia Burr Alston's House Site, The Oaks Plantation, Brookgreen Gardens, Georgetown County, South Carolina.* Research Manuscript 5. Conway, S. C.: Waccamaw Center for Historical and Cultural Studies, Coastal Carolina University, 1994.

Michie, James L. *The Oaks Plantation Revealed: An Archaeological Survey of the Home of Joseph and Theodosia Burr Alston, Brookgreen Gardens, Georgetown County, South Carolina.* Research Manuscript 4. Conway, S. C.: Waccamaw Center for Historical and Cultural Studies, Coastal Carolina University, 1993.

Middleton Place Foundation Archives, Charleston, S. C. Cited as [MPF].

Miles Brewton House Collection, Charleston, S. C. Cited as [MBH]

Mitchell-Pringle Papers, South Carolina Historical Society, Charleston, S. C. SCHS Ms. 11-325. Cited as [M-P].

National Archives, Washington, D.C:

Microfilm Publication M789: Internal Revenue Assessment Lists for South Carolina, 1864-1866. Roll 1.

Record Group 105. Records of the Bureau of Refugees, Freedmen and Abandoned Lands. Entry 3207, Register of Complaints, November, 1865 - April, 1866. 1 vol. No. 195 (inside title: "Ration-Lists of dest[itute] White & Col'd Persons. Sub Dist. of Georgetown, South Carolina."). Also Entry 3209 & 3210. Register of [Labor] Contracts, Georgetown, S. C., December. 1865 - April 1866.

Record Group 109. War Department Collection of Confederate Records. Miscellaneous Files. Intercepted Rebel Letters. Baltimore, Md. Papers. Entry 109, Box 11. Cited as [Intercepted Letters].

Pierpont, John (1785-1866). Journal, 1805-1810, and letters. Collection of the Pierpont Morgan Library, New York, N. Y.

Ravitz, Abe C. "John Pierpont: Portrait of a Nineteenth Century Reformer." Ph.D. dissertation, New York University, 1955.

Samuel J. Hitchcock Papers, Yale University Library, Division of Manuscripts and Archives. Cited as [SJH].

Shields, David. "The Place of the Arts in the Culture of Colonial Carolina." A lecture delivered at the Gibbes Museum of Art, Charleston, January 11, 1992.

South Carolina. Department of Agriculture. 1868 Agricultural Census, Georgetown County. South Carolina Department of Archives and History, Columbia.

South Carolina. Department of Health. State Hospital. Physician's Record of the South Carolina Lunatic Asylum, 1860-1874, and Admission Book, 1828-1876. South Carolina Department of Archives and History, Columbia.

Stephen Duncan Correspondence, 1843-1866; also Stephen Duncan and Stephen Duncan, Jr., Papers, Louisiana and Lower Mississippi Valley Collections, Hill Memorial Library, Louisiana State University, Baton Rouge, La. Cited as [SDC].

Trapier Family Papers, Southern Historical Collection, University of North Carolina, Chapel Hill, N. C.

U. S. Census. Population, Slave, Agricultural and Manufacturing Schedules, 1840-1870.

Zierden, Martha. "Investigations of Elite Townhouse Sites in Charleston, South Carolina: A Preliminary Model." Paper presented at the 45th annual Southeastern Archaeological Conference, New Orleans, October 19, 1988.

Zierden, Martha. "The Urban Landscape: An Example From the Miles Brewton House." Paper presented at the 15th Annual Conference on South Carolina Archaeology, April 22, 1989, Columbia, S. C.

PUBLISHED SOURCES

"A Lady of S. Carolina" [Maria Middleton]. "Rebecca Motte," in Wister, Sarah (Butler), "Mrs. O.J. Wister" and Agnes Irwin, *Worthy Women of Our First Century.* 1877; reprinted 1975 by Books for Libraries Press, Plainview, N.Y.

Abbott, Martin. "The Freedmen's Bureau and its Carolina Critics", in *Proceedings of the South Carolina Historical Association,* 1962, 15-23.

Allston, Elizabeth Deas. *The Allstons and Alstons of Waccamaw.* Published by the author, 1936.

Alston, J. Motte. *Rice Planter and Sportsman. The Recollections of J. Motte Alston, 1821-1909.* Columbia, S. C.: University of South Carolina Press, 1953. The manuscript from which this book was abridged is known as "Random Recollections of an Inconspicuous Life."

Alston, J. Motte. "Theodosia Burr. The True Story of Her Death At Sea." *The New York Times Saturday Review of Books,* May 24, 1902.

Baldwin, Agnes Leland. *Marsh Granting Practices in South Carolina.* Summerville, S. C.: The Committee for the Preservation of Privately-Owned Marshlands, 1976.

Barnett, L. Margaret, "Horace Flectcher," in *The Historic New Orleans Collection Quarterly,* 18, No. 1 (Winter): 8-9.

Barr, Lockwood. *Ancient Town of Pelham, Westchester County, New York.* (N.p., Dietz Press, 1946).

Bell, Malcolm. *Major Butler's Legacy. Five Generations of a Slaveholding Family.* Athens, Ga.: University of Georgia Press, 1987.

Bellows, Barbara L. *Benevolence Among Slaveholders. Assisting the Poor in Charleston, 1670-1860.* Baton Rouge: Louisiana State University Press, 1993.

Biddle, Edward and Mantle Fielding. *The Life and Works of Thomas Sully.* Philadelphia, Wichersham Press, 1921; reprinted New York: Kennedy Graphics and DaCapo Press, 1970.

Bilodeau, Francis W., ed. *Art in South Carolina.* Charleston, S.C.: S.C. Tricentennial Commission, 1970.

Bivens, John and J. Thomas Savage, "The Miles Brewton House, Charleston, South Carolina," in *Antiques,* February, 1993, 294-307.

Bland, Sidney R. *Preserving Charleston's Past, Shaping Its Future: The Life and Times of Susan Pringle Frost.* Westport, Conn.: Greenwood Press, 1994.

Blassingame, John W. *The Slave Community. Plantation Life in the Antebellum South.* Revised and enlarged edition. New York and Oxford: Oxford University Press, 1979.

Bolick, Julian S. *Waccamaw Plantations.* Clinton, S.C.: Jacobs, 1946.

Bolton, Reginald Pelham. "Nanette Bolton, Principal of the Priory School for Girls," *Quarterly Bulletin of the Westchester County Historical Society,* vol. 9, no. 4 (October 1933), 84-85.

Booth, Sally Smith. *Hung, Strung and Potted. A History of Eating in Colonial America.* New York: Clarkson N. Potter, 1971.

Brewster, Lawrence Fay. "Ante-Bellum Planters and their Means of Transportation," in *Proceedings of the South Carolina Historical Association,* 1948, 15-25.

Brewster, Lawrence Fay. "Planters from the Low-Country and their Summer Travels," in *Proceedings of the South Carolina Historical Association,* 1943, 35-47.

Brewster, Lawrence Fay. *Summer Migrations and Resorts of South Carolina Low-Country Planters.* Durham, N. C.: Duke University Press, 1947.

Bull, Henry deSaussure. *All Saints' Church, Waccamaw.* N.p.: Historical Activities Committee of the South Carolina Society of Colonial Dames of America, 1948.

Burton, E. Milby. *The Siege of Charleston, 1861-1865.* Columbia, S. C.: University of South Carolina Press, 1970.

Cash, W. J. *The Mind of the South.* New York: Alfred A. Knopf, 1943.

Champomier, P. A. *Statement of the Sugar Crop of Louisiana, 1859-1860, with an Appendix.* New Orleans: Cook, Young & Co., 1860.

Chesnut, Mary Boykin. *A Diary from Dixie.* New York: Peter Smith, 1929.

Childs, Arney R, ed. *Rice Planter & Sportsman: The Recollections of J. Motte Alston, 1821-1909.* Columbia, S. C.: University of South Carolina Press, 1953.

Clifton, James M., ed. *Life and Labor on Argyle Island: Letters and Documents of a Savannah River Rice Plantation, 1833-1867.* Savannah, Ga.: Beehive Press, 1978.

Clinton, Sir Henry. *Narratives of the Campaign in 1781 in North America.* Philadelphia: John Campbell, 1865.

Coclanis, Peter A. *The Shadow of a Dream: Economic Life & Death in the South Carolina Low Country, 1670-1920.* New York: Oxford University Press, 1989.

Coclanis, Peter A. and John Komlos. "Time in the Paddies: A Comparison of Rice Production in the Southeastern United States and Lower Burma in the Nineteenth Century", in *Social Science History,* 36:343-354.

Copeland, J. Isaac. "The Tutor in the Ante-Bellum South," in *Proceedings of the South Carolina Historical Association,* 1965, 36-47.

Côté, Richard N. *Miles Brewton's Land: A History, 1694-1990.* Charleston, S.C.: South Carolina Historical Society, 1990.

Crouse, Maurice A., ed. "The Letterbook of Peter Manigault, 1763-1773," in *South Carolina Historical Magazine*, 70: 79-96, 177-195.

Davidson, Chalmers G. *The Last Foray. The South Carolina Planters of 1860: A Sociological Study*. Columbia, S.C.: University of South Carolina Press, 1971.

Dethloff, Henry C. *A History of the American Rice Industry, 1685-1985*. College Station, Tex.: Texas A & M University Press, 1988.

Devereaux, Anthony Q. *The Life and Times of Robert F. W. Alston*. Georgetown, S.C.: Waccamaw Press, 1976.

Devereaux, Anthony Q. *The Rice Princes: A Rice Epoch Revisited*. Columbia: The State Co., 1973.

"Diary of John Berkley Grimball," in *South Carolina Historical Magazine*, 56: 92-114.

Doar, David. *A Sketch of the Agricultural Society of St. James, Santee, South Carolina. . . .* Charleston, S. C.: Calder-Fladger Co., 1908.

Doar, David. *Rice and Rice Planting in the South Carolina Low Country*. Charleston, S. C.: Charleston Museum, 1936.

Dunn, Waldo H. *The Life of Donald G. Mitchell. Ik Marvel*. New York: Charles Scribner's Sons, 1922.

Easterby, J. H. "Charles Cotesworth Pinckney's Plantation Diary ," in *South Carolina Historical Magazine*, vol 41, 135-150.

Easterby, J. H. *The South Carolina Rice Plantation as Revealed in the Papers of Robert F. W. Allston*. Chicago: University of Chicago Press, 1945.

Edgar, Walter B. "Robert Pringle and His World," in *South Carolina Historical Magazine*, 76: 1-11.

Fabian, Monroe H. *Mr. Sully, Portrait Painter. The Works of Thomas Sully (1783-1872)*. Washington, D. C.: Smithsonian Institution Press, 1983.

Fenhagen, Mary Pringle. "Descendants of Judge Robert Pringle," in *South Carolina Historical Magazine*, 62: 151-164, 221-236.

Ford, Abbie A. *John Pierpont. A Biographical Sketch*. Boston: published by the author, 1909.

French, Justus Clement. *The Trip of the Steamer Oceanus to Fort Sumter and Charleston, S.C., comprising the Incidents of the Excursion, the Appearance At That Time, of the City, and the Entire*

Programme of the Exercises of re-raising the Flag Over the Ruins of Fort Sumter, April 14, 1865. Brooklyn, N. Y.: The Union Steam Printing House, 1865.

Frost, Mary Pringle. *The Miles Brewton House: Chronicles and Reminiscences.* Charleston, S. C.: privately printed, 1939.

Frost, Susan Pringle. *Highlights of the Miles Brewton House.* Charleston, S. C.: privately printed, 1944.

Gavaghan, Sister M. Ignatia. *The Biography of Nathalie deLage Sumter.* Sumter, S. C.: Sumter County Historical Commission, 1984.

"George Washington Tours The South: His Journey Through South Carolina." Columbia, S. C.: South Carolina Department of Archives and History, 1991.

Gilchrist, Robert G. "The Confederate Defence of Morris Island," City of Charleston *Yearbook,* 1884, 350-402.

Gray, Lewis Cecil. *History of Agriculture in the Southern United States to 1860.* Washington: Carnegie Institution of Washington, 1933. 2 vol.

Groves, Joseph A. *The Alstons and Allstons of North and South Carolina.* Atlanta, Ga.: Franklin Printing & Publishing Co., 1901.

Hardy, Norfleet. *Farm, Mill, and Classroom. A History of Tax-Supported Adult Education in South Carolina to 1960.* Columbia, S. C.: University of South Carolina, 1967.

Harrison, Margaret Hayne. *A Charleston Album.* Rindge, N. H.: Richard R. Smith, 1953.

Henderson, Archibald, ed. *Washington's Southern Tour.* Boston and New York: Houghton Mifflin Co., 1923.

Heyward, Duncan Clinch. *Seed from Madagascar.* Chapel Hill, N.C.: University of North Carolina Press, 1937.

Hilliard, Sam Bowers. *Atlas of Antebellum Southern Agriculture.* Baton Rouge, La.: Louisiana State University Press, 1984.

Hotten, John Camden. *The Original Lists of Persons of Quality, Emigrants, Religious Exiles, Political Rebels, Etc., Who Went from Great Britain to the American Plantations, 1600-1700.* London, 1874.

Irving, John B. *The South Carolina Jockey Club.* Charleston: Russell & Jones, 1857; reprinted 1975.

James, D. Clayton. *Antebellum Natchez.* Baton Rouge: Louisiana State University Press, 1968.

James, Hunter. "Carving His Niche," in *Historic Preservation,* November / December, 1989, 28-33.

Jervey, Clare. *Inscriptions on the Tablets and Gravestones in St. Michael's Church and Churchyard, Charleston, S.C.* Columbia, S. C.: The State Co., 1906.

Jervey, Theodore D. "The Hayne Family," in *South Carolina Historical & Genealogical Magazine,* 5: 168-188.

Jones, E. Alfred. *American Members of the Inns of Court.* London: St. Catherine Press, 1924.

"Journal of Josiah Quincy, Jr., 1773", in *Journal of the Massachusetts Historical Society,* June, 1916, 446-447.

Joyner, Charles. *Down by the Riverside. A South Carolina Slave Community.* Urbana, Ill.: University of Illinois Press, 1984.

King, Edward. *The Great South.* 1873; edited by W. Magruder Drake & Robert R. Jones. Baton Rouge, La.: Louisiana State University Press, 1972.

King, Susan L. *History & Records of the Charleston Orphan House.* Easley, S. C.: Southern Historical Press, 1984.

Lachicotte, Alberta Morel. *Georgetown Rice Plantations.* Columbia, S. C.: The State Co., 1955.

Lawson, Dennis T. *No Heir to Take Its Place. The Story of Rice in Georgetown County, South Carolina.* Georgetown, S. C.: The Rice Museum, 1972.

Leigh, Oliver H., ed. *Letters to His Son. On the Fine Art of Becoming a Man of the World and a Gentleman. By the Earl of Chesterfield.* New York: Tudor Publishing Co., 1911.

"The Limantour Claims. The Story of the Man Who Claimed to Own San Francisco. . . ." San Francisco: no publisher, 1983.

List of Taxpayers of the City of Charleston for 1859. Charleston, S. C.: Walker, Evans & Co., 1860.

Littlefield, Daniel C. *Rice & Slaves. Ethnicity and the Slave Trade in Colonial South Carolina.* Baton Rouge: Louisiana State University Press, 1981.

Manigault, Edward. *Siege Train. The Journal of a Confederate Artilleryman in the Defense of Charleston.* Ed. by Warren Ripley. Columbia, S. C.: University of South Carolina Press, 1986.

Mariana, John. *America Eats Out: An Illustrated History of Restaurants, Taverns, Coffee Shops, Speakeasies and Other Establishments Which Have Fed Us for 350 Years.* New York: William Morrow & Co., 1991.

McCrady, Edward. *The History of South Carolina,* 4 volumes. 1887; reprinted New York: Russell & Russell, 1969.

McGrew, Roderick E., ed. *Encyclopedia of Medical History.* New York: McGraw Hill, 1985.

Menn, Joseph Karl. *The Large Slaveholders of Louisiana – 1860.* New Orleans: Pelican Publishing Co., 1964.

Meriwether, Colyer. *History of Higher Education in South Carolina.* Washington, D. C.: Government Printing Office, 1889; reprinted 1972.

Michie, James L. *Richmond Hill Plantation, 1810-1868. The Discovery of Antebellum Life on a Waccamaw Rice Plantation.* Spartanburg, S. C.: The Reprint Company, 1990.

Middleton, Alicia Hopton. *Life in Carolina and New England During the Twentieth Century.* Bristol, R.I.: privately printed, 1929.

Middleton, Margaret Simons. *Jeremiah Theus. Colonial Artist of Charles Town.* 1953; rev. ed. (published privately), 1991.

Mills, W. H. "The Thoroughbred in South Carolina," in *Proceedings of the South Carolina Historical Association,* (1936), 13-24.

Minnigerode, Meade. "Theodosia Burr, Prodigy, An Informal Biography," in *Saturday Evening Post,* Sept. 6, 1924.

Mitchell, Harry W. *Mary Pringle Mitchell.* N.p. [New Haven?]: The Tuttle, Moorehouse & Taylor Press, n.d. [c. 1902-1909].

Moltke-Hansen, David, ed. *Art in the Lives of South Carolinians. Nineteenth-Century Chapters.* Charleston: Carolina Art Association, 1979.

Morgan, Philip D. "Work and Culture: The Task System and the World of Lowcountry Blacks, 1700-1880," in Robert Blair St. George, ed., *Material Life in America, 1600-1860.* Boston: Northeastern University Press, 1988, 203-232.

Norton, Charles Eliot. *Letters of Charles Eliot Norton, with Biographical Comment by His Daughter, Sara Norton and M. A. deWolf Howe.* Boston and New York: Houghton Mifflin, 1913. 2 vol.

Olmsted, Frederick Law. *A Journey in the Seaboard Slave States, With Remarks on their Economy.* New York: Dix & Edwards, 1856.

Parton, James S. *Life & Times of Aaron Burr.* Enlarged 1885 edition. New York: Mason Bros., 1858

"Pennington, Patience" (Elizabeth Waties Allston Pringle). *A Woman Rice Planter.* Edited by Cornelius O. Cathey. Cambridge, Mass.: Harvard University Press, 1961.

Pharo, Elizabeth B., ed. *Reminiscences of William Hasell Wilson (1811-1902).* Philadelphia: Patterson & White, 1937.

Phillips, Ulrich Bonnell. *Life and Labor in the Old South*. Boston: Little, Brown & Co., 1929.

Pidgin, Charles Felton. *Theodosia*. Boston: C. M. Clark Publishing Co., 1907.

Pillsbury, David B. and Emily A. Getchell, *The Pillsbury Family* .... Everett, Mass.: Massachusetts Publishing Co., 1898.

Pringle, Alexander. *The Records of the Pringles or Hoppringills of the Scottish Border*. Edinburgh, Scotland: Oliver and Boyd, 1933.

Pringle, Edward Jenkins. *Slavery in the Southern States*. Cambridge, Mass.: John Bartlett, 1853. Third edition.

Pringle, Elizabeth W. Alston. *Chronicles of Chicora Wood*. New York: Charles Scribner's Sons, 1922.

Pringle, John Julius. *Twenty Years' Snipe-Shooting. Extracts from the Daily Journal of the Game-Books of the Snipery*. New York: Knickerbocker Press, 1899.

Puleston, W.D. *Annapolis. Gangway to the Quarterdeck*. New York: D. Appleton-Century Co., 1943.

Ramsay, David. *Ramsay's History of South Carolina....* Newberry, S. C.: W. J. Duffie, 1858.

Ravenel, Mrs. St. Julien. *Charleston. The Place and the People*. New York: Macmillan, 1929.

Ravitz, Abe C. "John Pierpont and the Slaves' Christmas," in *Phylon, the Atlanta University Review of Race & Culture*, 21, No. 4 (Winter, 1960): 383-386.

Rawick, George P., ed. *The American Slave: A Composite Autobiography*. Volumes 2 & 3: South Carolina Narratives, Parts 1-4. Westport, Conn.: Greenwood Publishing Co., 1972.

"Report of the Committee on the Destruction of Churches in the Diocese of South Carolina, During the Late War. Presented to the Protestant Episcopal Convention, May, 1868." Charleston, S. C.: Walker, Evans & Co., 1868.

Riffell, Judy, ed. *A History of Pointe Coupee Parish and its Families*. Baton Rouge, La.: La Comité des Archives de la Louisianne, 1983. Vol. 1.

Ripley, R. S. "Charleston and its Defences in the Late War," Charleston *Yearbook*, 1885, 347-358.

Rogers, George C., Jr. *Charleston in the Age of the Pinckneys*. Columbia, S. C.: University of South Carolina Press, 1980.

Rogers, George C., Jr. "The Georgetown Rice Planters on the Eve of the Civil War," in *South Carolina History Illustrated*, 1 (1970).

Rogers, George C., Jr. *History of Georgetown County*. Columbia, S. C.: University of South Carolina Press, 1970.

Roll of Students of South Carolina College, 1805-1905. Columbia, S. C.: South Carolina College, 1905.

Russell, Andrew J. *Russell's Civil War Photographs*. New York: Dover Publications, 1985.

Salley, Alexander S. "Col. Miles Brewton and Some of his Descendants," in *South Carolina Historical and Genealogical Magazine*, 2: 128-152, 241-244.

Sanders, Betty Jean. "A Brief History of the Battery," in Middleton Place Foundation *Notebook*, vol. 17, No. 3 (Fall 1995), 2.

Savage, Henry, Jr. *River of the Carolinas: The Santee*. Chapel Hill, N. C.: University of North Carolina Press, 1956.

Schurz, Carl. "The South After the War," in *McClure's Magazine*, vol. XXX, No. 6 (April, 1908), 661.

Sellers, Leila. *Charleston Business on the Eve of the American Revolution*. Chapel Hill, N. C., 1934; reprinted New York: Library Editions, Ltd., 1970.

Severens, Martha R. & Charles L. Wyrick. *Charles Fraser of Charleston*. Charleston, S. C.: Carolina Art Association, 1983.

Simkins, Frances Butler and Robert Hilliard Woody, *South Carolina During Reconstruction*. Chapel Hill, N.C.: University of North Carolina Press, 1932.

Smith, Daniel E. Huger Smith. *A Charlestonian's Recollections, 1846-1913*. Charleston, S. C.: Carolina Art Association, 1950.

Smith, Daniel E. Huger; Alice R. Huger Smith and Arney R. Childs, eds. *Mason Smith Family Letters, 1860-1868*. Columbia, S. C.: University of South Carolina Press, 1950.

Sonn, Albert H. *Early American Wrought Iron*. New York: Charles Scribner's Sons, 1928. Vol. 3.

Statutes Relating to and By-Laws of the Parish of St. Michael, Charleston, S. C. Charleston, S. C.: Walker, Evans & Cogswell, 1938.

Stone, Edwin H. "The Unsolved Mystery of the Lady of The Oaks." *Sandlapper*, July & August, 1972, 45-48.

Swick, Ronald. "Theodosia Burr Alston", in *The South Atlantic Quarterly*, vol. 74, 4 (Autumn, 1975), 495-506.

Sydnor, Charles Sackett. *Slavery in Mississippi*. American Historical Association, 1933; reprinted Gloucester, Mass., by Peter Smith, 1965.

Tablet to Rebecca Motte. Erected by Rebecca Motte Chapter appof the Daughters of the American Revolution. Ceremony of Unveiling at

St. Philip's Church, Charleston, S.C., May 9th, 1903. Charleston: Daggett Printing Co., 1903.

Taylor, Rosser H. *Ante-Bellum South Carolina: A Social and Cultural History*. Chapel Hill, N. C.: University of North Carolina Press, 1942.

"The Culture of Rice." Charleston *Yearbook*, 1883, pp. 395-399.

Thomas, Albert Sidney. *A Historical Account of the Protestant Episcopal Church in South Carolina, 1820-1957*. Columbia, S. C.: printed by the R. L. Bryan Co., 1957.

Todorich, Charles. *The Spirited Years*. Annapolis, Md.: Naval Institute Press, 1984.

Trowbridge, John T. *The Desolate South, 1865-1866; a Picture of the Battlefields and of the Devastated Confederacy*. 1866. Edited and abridged by Gordon Carroll; republished New York: Duell, Sloan and Pearce, 1956.

U.S. Coast Survey. Map of part of the Santee Rivers and vicinity. South Carolina. 1875. Surveyed by W. H. Dennis. Scale 1:20,000.

Van Doren, Mark, ed. *Correspondence of Aaron Burr and his daughter Theodosia*. New York: Stratford Press, 1929.

Van Rensselaer, Mrs. John King. *Newport, Our Social Capitol* Philadelphia: J. B. Lippincott, 1905, p. 29.

Waddell, Gene. *Charleston in 1883*. Easley, S. C.: Southern Historical Press, 1983.

Wallace, David Duncan. *A History of South Carolina*. New York: American Historical Society, 1934. 4 vol.

Wallace, David Duncan. *South Carolina: A Short History*. Co lumbia, S. C.: University of South Carolina Press, 1951.

Wandell, Maude. "Nag's Head Portrait of Theodosia Burr is Exhibited For First Time in North Carolina." *Georgetown* [South Carolina] *Times*, December 25, 1936.

Wandell, Samuel Henry & Meade Minnigerode. *Aaron Burr*. New York: G. P. Putnam's Sons, 1925. 2 vol.

The War of the Rebellion: A Compilation of the Official Records of the Union and Confederate Armies. Series I, vols. XIV and XXVIII. Washington, D. C.: Government Printing Office, 1885 & 1890.

Waring, Joseph Ioor. *History of Medicine in South Carolina*. 1964-1967; reprinted Spartanburg, S. C.: The Reprint Co., 1977. 3 vol.

Way, William. *History of the New England Society of Charleston, South Carolina for One Hundred Years, 1819-1919*. Charleston, S. C.: Published by the Society, 1920.

Wayne, Michael. *The Reshaping of Plantation Society: The Natchez District, 1860-1880.* Baton Rouge: Louisiana State University Press, 1983.

Weatherby, Edward & James. *The Racing Calendar: Containing an Account of the Plates, Matches & Sweepstakes Run For in Great Britain & Ireland.* London, 1796 *et. seq.*

Wells, Edward L. *A Sketch of the Charleston Light Dragoons, From the Earliest Formation of the Corps.* Charleston, S. C.: Lucas, Richardson & Co., 1888.

Willcox, William B. *Portrait of a General. Sir Henry Clinton in the War of Independence.* New York: Alfred A. Knopf, 1962.

Williams, George W., ed. *Incidents in My Life. The Autobiography of the Rev. Paul Trapier, S.T.D., With Some of His Letters.* Charleston, S. C.: Dalcho Historical Society, 1954.

Winkler, John K. *Morgan the Magnificent. The Life of J. Pierpont Morgan.* New York: Vanguard Press, 1930.

Wise, Stephen R. *Gate of Hell. Campaign for Charleston Harbor, 1863.* Columbia, S. C.: University of South Carolina Press, 1994.

Wister, Owen. *Lady Baltimore.* New York: Macmillan Co., 1906.

Wood, Peter. *Black Majority. Negroes in Colonial South Carolina from 1670 to the Stono Rebellion.* New York: W.W. Norton, 1974.

ACKNOWLEDGMENTS

The five years of research and writing which went into *Mary's World* were made possible by grants from the Post-Courier Foundation of Charleston, administered by the South Carolina Historical Society. To me, *Mary's World* was the writing opportunity of a lifetime. I will always be indebted to the Foundation and the Society for their unflagging support.

History is an enormous jigsaw puzzle consisting of an infinite number of interlocking parts. The more parts one locate and connects, the clearer the picture. During the five years it took to research and write *Mary's World* I was blessed with help, encouragement, and support from a wide variety of scholars, volunteers, and Pringle descendants. I would like to express my thanks to all of them who believed that this story of the Pringles, the Frosts, the Stewarts, and their roles in nineteenth-century South Carolina deserved to be shared with a wider audience.

First among my respected advisors was Peter Manigault, publisher of the Charleston *Post & Courier,* ninth-generation descendant of Miles Brewton, and owner/restorer of the Miles Brewton House. For five years he patiently and enthusiastically shared with me his encyclopedic knowledge of South Carolina rice culture, the architecture, construction, and use of house, and the lives of its residents. A meticulous student of history and a demanding editor, his passion for accurate, unvarnished history pushed my research and writing skills to the limits. It was an immense pleasure and powerful learning experience to spend hour after hour with him in the third-floor boardroom of the *Post and Courier* building, exploring and debating the thousands of minute details which make up a book like this.

I was also extremely fortunate in that my two top choices for manuscript readers accepted the challenge. The late Dr. George C. Rogers, Jr., Distinguished Professor Emeritus, University of South Carolina, brought his vast knowledge of antebellum Georgetown District and its rice planters to bear on my efforts. Dr. Theodore Rosengarten, author of *All God's Dangers: The Life of Nate Shaw* and *Tombee: Portrait of a Cotton Planter,* held my feet to the fire every time I generalized or threatened to wax romantic about the Pringles or their culture. The book is stronger because of his rigor.

In addition, I had the benefit of many specialized manuscript readers and technical advisors, each of whom brought a specific discipline to bear. These included Vice Admiral David F. Emerson, Charleston (naval history); Mary Giles, Assistant Archivist, Charleston Museum, and Archivist, Catholic Diocese of Charleston (archives); Lynn Todd, College of Charleston (architecture); Jack Thomson, Charleston (photographic history), Thomas G. Graham, McClellanville, S.C. (colonial building construction); Joseph T. Holleman, South Carolina Historical Society (Confederate postal history); Priestly C. Coker, III, Charleston (South Carolina watercraft) and Bob Raynor, Awendaw, S.C. (British warships).

Colleagues who shared information and sources included Dr. Sidney R. Bland, James Madison University; Dr. Peter McCandless, College of Charleston; Dr. James L. Michie, Coastal Carolina College; Agnes Leland Baldwin, McClellanville, S.C.; Martha Severens, Charleston Museum; Robert Leath, Historic Charleston Foundation; Mrs. William John Doyle, Middleton

Place Foundation; Francis Kinloch Bull, Jr., Arlington, Va.; Daniel J. Bell, South Carolina Department of Parks, Recreation and Tourism and Willis J. ("Skipper") Keith.

Numerous Pringle, Frost, and Alston descendants were generous in sharing their collections of family letters and photographs. They included Mrs. Hervey Parke Clark, San Francisco; Mrs. Anne Evans Pegues, Spanish Fort, Alabama; Dr. and Mrs. Rhett Pringle Walker, Montrose, Ala.; Mr. and Mrs. McColl Pringle and Dr. Margaretta Childs, Charleston; Mrs. Jack L. Scott, Hallandale, Fla. and Mrs. Anthony H. Harrigan, Washington, D.C.

In my research I had the assistance of Marjory French in Charleston; Risher H. Fairey in Columbia, S.C., Zelda Long in Baton Rouge, La., and George H. Kirkland, III, in Atlanta, Ga. In addition, the reference staffs of the Charleston County Library (main branch) and Mt. Pleasant Regional Library cheerfully provided research services far above and beyond the call of duty, finding answers to hundreds of obscure questions and obtaining rare and scarce books for me. Two hard-working and perceptive Charleston volunteers, Rose Tomlin and Peggy Addison, helped abstract Mary Pringle's journals and inventory the Pringle library.

In the Holy City, I received help from every quarter. At the South Carolina Historical Society, Assistant Director Daisy Bigda cheerfully administered my grant. At the *Post & Courier* office, Ann Smyre, assistant to Mr. Manigault, and Mary Manning, Chief Librarian, both accelerated my work. I am also indebted to Ernestine Fellers and Susan L. King at the City of Charleston Department of Archives and Records; Paul C. Figueroa, Director, and Joyce N. Baker of the Gibbes Museum of Art; Dr. W. Curtis Worthington, Jr., M.D., Curator, and Jane Brown, Assistant Curator, Waring Medical Library, Medical University of South Carolina; Anne Allen, Library Director, Charleston Navy Base; Sally Murphy of the South Carolina Wildlife and Marine Resources Department, Charleston and W. E. "Beau" Booker, IV.

Thanks also to Dwain Skinner, for his fine maps, and to Sue McKeithan, Terry Bergdorf, and Dorian Gleason of Ritz Camera Center, Mt. Pleasant, for helping me prepare numerous photographs for reproduction. Appreciation, too, goes to my hard-working editor, Betty Burnett, Ph.D., and the extraordinary staff of Corinthian Books, especially Sarah Williams, Sandra White, and Kester Cockrell.

Other people and institutions "from away" were also extremely helpful. These included Doris Gandy and Jill K. Lyles of the Darlington County Historical Commission; Ronald W. Miller, Executive Director, Natchez Historic Foundation; Alice S. Creighton, Head, Special Collections, and Mr. Brian Fors, Nimitz Library, United States Naval Academy, Annapolis; Laura K. O'Keefe, Manuscripts Specialist, New York Public Library; Judy Bolton, Louisiana State University Libraries, Baton Rouge; Patricia Willis and William R. Massa, Jr., Beinecke Rare Book and Manuscript Library, Yale University; James McCarthy, Harvard University Archives; Bertram Lippincott, III, Librarian, Newport Historical Society and David W. Wright, Chief Archivist, Morgan Library, New York.

The following individuals and institutions have graciously granted permission to publish material from their collections:

Peter Manigault, for documents and photographs from the Miles Brewton House Collection;

The Bancroft Library, University of California-Berkeley, for the Pringle Family Papers (72/203);

The South Carolina Historical Society, for the Alston-Pringle-Frost and Mitchell-Pringle Papers;

The Charleston Museum, for the illustration "A typical rice field in the South Carolina Lowcountry," from David Doar, *Rice and Rice Planting in the South Carolina* (Charleston: Charleston Museum, 1936):

David Shields, for his lecture, "The Place of the Arts in the Culture of Colonial South Carolina," an address delivered at the Gibbes Museum of Art, January 11, 1992;

The Pierpont Morgan Library, New York, for the journal

(1805-1810) and letters of John Pierpont;

The Graduate School of Arts & Sciences, New York University, for Abe C. Ravitz's Ph.D. dissertation, "John Pierpont: Portrait of a Nineteenth Century Pioneer";

The Beinecke Rare Book and Manuscript Library and the Division of Manuscripts and Archives, Yale University, for letters from the Donald G. Mitchell Collection, the John Pierpont Collection and the Samuel J. Hitchcock Papers;

Hill Memorial Library, Louisiana State University, Baton Rouge, La., for the Stephen Duncan Correspondence, 1843-1866; also Stephen Duncan and Stephen Duncan, Jr., Papers;

Dr. and Mrs. Rhett P. Walker, Montrose, Ala., for Frost, Pringle, and Rhett family papers and photographs; and

Middleton Place Foundation, for correspondence from their archives.

The views and conclusions presented here are solely my own and do not necessarily represent the opinions of my many respected advisors.

Many people and institutions graciously granted permission to reproduce the illustrations used here. Every reasonable effort has been made to trace the owners of copyrighted materials in this book, but in some cases this has proven impossible. The author and publisher will be glad to receive information leading to more complete acknowledgments in subsequent printings of the book and in the meantime extend their apologies for any omissions.

The following abbreviations have been used: MBH: The Miles Brewton House Collection, courtesy of Peter Manigault; RPW: collection of Dr. & Mrs. Rhett Pringle Walker; CAA: courtesy of the Carolina Art Association and/or the Gibbes Museum of Art; CM: courtesy of the Charleston Museum; SCHS: the South Carolina Historical Society; RNC: photograph by or collection of the author, Richard N. Côté.

Frontispiece: carved woodwork from the drawing room entrance: RNC

Mary's Family: Mary Motte Alston Pringle, dust jacket front cover and 6: MBH; William Bull Pringle, 6: MBH; William Alston Pringle, 7: MBH; John Julius Pringle, 7: RPW; Pringle family, 7: MBH; Jacob Motte Alston Pringle, 8: MBH; Susan Pringle, 8: MBH; Mary Frances Pringle Mitchell, 8: MBH; Robert Pringle, 9: MBH; Rebecca Motte Pringle Frost, 9: MBH; James Reid Pringle, 10: RPW; Francis LeJau Frost, 10: MBH; Jacob Motte Alston, 11: MBH; "Alston and Pringle plantations in Georgetown District," 12, based on Mills Atlas, 1820, and "Runimede, the Pringle Family's Country Seat on the Ashley River," based on H.A.M. Smith, "The Ashley River: Its Seats and Settlements," in *SCHM*, vol. 20.

Chapter One: Mary's Charleston: Miles Brewton, 16: MBH postcard by Lanneau's Art Store, Charleston, 17: RNC; cheval-de-frise, 19: north parlor, 20: RNC.

Chapter Two: King Billy's Daughter: Col. Alston's rice mill at Fairfield plantation, 27: Elizabeth Deas Allston, *The Allstons and Alstons of Waccamaw*; "Nag's Head" portrait, alleged to be of Theodosia Burr, 29: MBH; William Alston's name on the door of the MBH garret wine room, 31: RNC; Col. William Alston, 32: MBH; Mary Brewton Motte Alston, 33: MBH; "The Castle," Debordieu Beach, 34: Elizabeth Deas Allston, *The Allstons and Alstons of Waccamaw;* the arms of Col. William Alston of Clifton, 35: MBH; the louvered main wine room in the MBH garrett, 38: RNC.

Chapter Three: Judge Pringle's Son: Judge John Julius Pringle, 49: MBH; trunk gate at White Oak Plantation, 54: RNC; "A typical South Carolina rice field," 57, from David Doar, *Rice and Rice Planting in the South Carolina Low Country*: CM.

Chapter Four: Children of the Pluff Mud: "The seat of John Julius Pringle, Esq., on Ashley River, 1800," by Charles Fraser, 63: CAA; Beneventum Plantation House, 64: RNC; Richfield and Pleasant Meadow plantations, 65: U.S. Coast Survey map, 1875, adapted by Dwain Skinner; joggling board at St. Stephen's Episcopal Church, Charleston, 67: RNC; the present MBH lot, 76: CM; the MBH kitchen, 77: MBH; MBH south parlor, 78: RNC; MBH graffiti of Sir Henry Clinton, 79: RNC; MBH drawing room, 80: RNC; the drawing room chandelier, 81: RNC; Susan Pringle Frost and servant pulls in the MBH drawing room, 82: MBH; Mary Pringle, 86: MBH; Robert Pringle, 86: MBH; Pringle family at Newport, 87: MBH.

Chapter Five: A Family of Substance: William Bull Pringle, 97: MBH; Mary Pringle, 98: MBH; Mary's handwriting, 101: Alston-Pringle-Frost Collection, SCHS; William's handwriting, 102: Alston-Pringle-Frost Collection, SCHS; "Meeting Street and St. Michael's

Church, Charleston, S.C.," 116: "Phostint" card #70250, Detroit Publishing Co.: RNC.

Chapter Six: Anything But Planting: Maria Linton Duncan Pringle, 136: MBH; *Slavery in the Southern States*, 145: MBH; Rebecca Motte Pringle, 163: MBH; Donald G. Mitchell, 165: MBH.

Chapter Eight: The Peculiar Institution: a slave gagging iron or muzzle, 185: Albert H. Sonn, *Early American Wrought Iron*, vol. 3; birth pages from Cretia's Bible, 188: MBH; "Slave Quarters, Santee River," 190: David Doar, *Rice and Rice Planting in the South Carolina Low Country*: CM.

Chapter Nine: Soldiers, Slaves, and Refugees: William Alston Pringle, 201: MBH; John Julius Pringle, 203: MBH; Jackob Motte Alston, 208; Mary Frances Pringle Mitchell, 213: MBH; Robert Pringle, 216: RPW; envelope dated August 24, 1863: RNC (gift from from Peter Manigault); James Reid Pringle, 225: MBH.

Chapter Ten: A Bitter Homecoming: damage to the pediment, 233: RNC.

Chapter Eleven: The Rice Paupers: Frank Frost, 266: MBH; Rebecca Motte Pringle Frost, 266: MBH; MBH exterior, 274: MBH; MBH drawing room, 275: MBH.

Chapter Thirteen: A Seven-Bottle Man: Sue, a servant of John Julius Pringle, 325: MBH; John Julius Pringle, 327: MBH; Maria and John Julius Pringle, 328: MBH; Julius and Maria Pringle's daughters, 329: MBH; Julius and servants at The Snipery: John Julius Pringle, *Twenty Years' Snipe-Shooting. Extracts from the Daily Journal of the GameBooks of the Snipery;* Julius shooting snipe, 332: MBH; "A Seven Bottle Man," from *New York Journal-American*: Alston-Pringle-Frost Collection, MBH.

Chapter Fourteen: The Pringles in the Golden West: James Reid Pringle, 338: RPW.

Chapter Fifteen: Of Rice and Ruin: William Bull Pringle, 349: MBH; Mary Motte Alston Pringle, 350: Mary Pringle Frost, *The Miles Brewton House: Chronicles and Reminiscences;* Mary and her son Joseph, 351: MBH; Robert Chisolm, 352: MBH; The Misses Frost, 356: MBH; The Frost family, 357: MBH.

INDEX